Vocabulary

How do we teach and learn vocabulary?

How do words work in literary texts?

'A timely state-of-the-art overview of the whole subject . . . the author's stance is broad . . . the work is eminently readable and coheres as a whole extremely well . . . an extremely wide range of research and literature is covered. This is certainly recommended for anyone who has occasion to wonder about words and their meanings.'

EFL Gazette

In this second edition, Ronald Carter draws on recent research in the field with particular reference to momentous changes in the computational analysis of vocabulary.

This book provides the necessary basis for the further study of modern English vocabulary with particular reference to linguistic descriptive frameworks and to educational contexts. It begins with an introductory account of linguistic approaches to the analysis of the modern lexicon in English. This fully revised and updated edition offers extended coverage on:

- vocabulary and language teaching
- dictionaries and lexicography
- literary stylistic study of vocabulary
- the relationship between vocabulary, grammar and discourse

Vocabulary: Applied Linguistic Perspectives has been widely praised since first publication for the breadth, depth and clarity of its approach. This new edition builds upon these foundations and develops further understanding of a key area of applied linguistics.

Ronald Carter is Professor of Modern English Language at the University of Nottingham. He has published extensively in the fields of applied, educational and literary linguistics. He is the editor of the Interface series and co-editor of the Intertext series, both published by Routledge.

Ronald Carter is the general editor of the Interface series and co-editor of the Intertext series, both published by Routledge. His previous publications with Routledge include:

Language and Literature: An Introductory Reader in Stylistics (ed.) (1982)
Linguistics and the Teacher (ed.) (1982)
Language, Discourse and Literature: An Introductory Reader in Discourse Stylistics (ed. with Paul Simpson) (1989)
Keywords in Language and Literacy (1995)
Working with Texts: A Core Book in Language Analysis (with Angela Goddard, Danuta Reah, Keith Sanger and Maggie Bowring) (1997)
The Routledge History of Literature in English: Britain and Ireland (with John McRae) (1997)
Investigating English Discourse: Language, Literacy and Literature (1997)

Vocabulary
Applied Linguistic Perspectives

Second edition

Ronald Carter

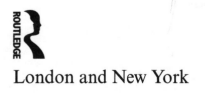

London and New York

First published 1998
by Routledge
11 New Fetter Lane, London EC4P 4EE

Simultaneously published in the USA and Canada
by Routledge
29 West 35th Street, New York, NY 10001

Typeset in Times by RefineCatch Limited, Bungay, Suffolk
Printed and bound in Great Britain by
Creative Print and Design (Wales), Ebbw Vale

British Library Cataloguing in Publication Data
A catalogue record for this book is available from the British Library

Library of Congress Cataloguing in Publication Data
A catalogue record for this book has been requested

ISBN 0–415–16864–3 (Pbk)
ISBN 0–415–16863–5 (Hbk)

Contents

List of figures and tables   x
Acknowledgements   xii
Preface to the first edition   xiii
Preface to the second edition   xvi

PART I
Foundations   1

1   What's in a word   3

1.0   Introduction: A form of words   3
1.1   Some definitions   4
1.2   Lexemes and words   7
1.3   Grammatical and lexical words   8
1.4   Morphemes and morphology   9
1.5   Word formation   10
1.6   Multiple meanings   12
1.7   In a word: A summary   13
1.8   Referential meaning   15
1.9   Componential analysis   17
1.10   Structural semantics: Words and other words   19
1.11   Basic English: A review   23
1.11.1 Styles and associations   28
1.12   Conclusion   29

2   The notion of core vocabulary   34

2.0   Core vocabularies: Some initial questions   34
2.1   Some tests for core vocabulary   36

2.1.1	*Syntactic substitution*	36
2.1.2	*Antonymy*	38
2.1.3	*Collocability*	38
2.1.4	*Extension*	39
2.1.5	*Superordinateness*	40
2.1.6	*Culture-free*	41
2.1.7	*Summary*	42
2.1.8	*Associationism*	42
2.1.9	*Neutral field of discourse*	43
2.1.10	*Neutral tenor of discourse*	43
2.2	*Applications and further research*	44
2.3	*Conclusion*	46
3	**Words and patterns**	**50**
3.0	*Introduction: Ways with words*	50
3.1	*Collocation: Lexis as a level*	51
3.2	*Sets and fields*	53
3.3	*Patterns, ranges and restrictions*	56
3.4	*Collocation and style*	57
3.5	*Collocation and grammar*	58
3.6	*Semantic prosodies: Lexis into grammar into meaning*	62
3.7	*Idioms galore: Fixed expressions and language structure*	65
3.8	*Fixing fixed expressions*	68
3.9	*Lexical patterns: A summary*	70
3.10	*Lexis and the language learner: What is lexical error?*	72
3.11	*Conclusion*	76
4	**Lexis and discourse**	**79**
4.0	*Introduction*	79
4.1	*Lexical cohesion*	80
4.2	*Lexical signalling*	83
4.3	*Evaluation and discourse*	85
4.4	*Anaphoric nouns*	88
4.5	*Densities and viewpoints: Spoken and written continua*	91

4.6	*Lexical patterning in spoken discourse*	94
4.7	*Corpus-based spoken language analysis*	98
4.8	*Lexis, coherence and writing development*	103
4.9	*Lexis and genre*	107
4.10	*Lexicalization, discourse and ideology*	108
4.11	*Conclusion*	114

PART II
Reviews   117

5   Lexis and literary stylistics   119

5.0	*Introduction*	119
5.1	*Sets, patterns and meaning*	120
5.2	*Lexis and register-mixing*	122
5.3	*Interpreting lexis in poetry*	124
5.4	*Measuring lexical associations in literary texts*	127
5.5	*Using informants*	128
5.5.1	*Who is the reader?*	129
5.5.2	*Competence: linguistic and literary*	130
5.5.3	*Analysis*	131
5.6	*Lexis and literariness*	132
5.7	*Metaphor*	138
5.8	*Lexis, poetics and mind*	142
5.9	*Arbitrariness, words, ideology: A note*	146
5.10	*Conclusion*	148

6   Lexis and lexicography   150

6.0	*Introduction*	150
6.1	*The image of the dictionary: User and use*	150
6.2	*Dictionary definitions*	152
6.3	*Grammar and the dictionary*	154
6.4	*Fixed expressions and the dictionary*	158
6.5	*Monosemy, polysemy and dictionary entries*	163
6.6	*Corpora, computers and lexicography*	167
6.6.1	*The COBUILD Project*	167
6.7	*Further major innovations (1990 onwards)*	174
6.7.1	*Lexicography and English-language learning: Contrasts and comparisons*	177

6.8   *A dictionary for production*   179
6.9   *Conclusions and prospects*   180

7   Learning and teaching vocabulary   184

7.0   *Introduction: Some historical perspectives*   184
7.1   *Early words: Mother-tongue English*   186
7.2   *The growth of word-meaning: Children into
        adults*   189
7.2.1 *The syntagmatic–paradigmatic*   190
7.2.2 *Concrete–abstract progression*   190
7.2.3 *Generalizations*   191
7.3   *L1 and L2*   191
7.4   *Memorization*   193
7.5   *What is a difficult word?*   195
7.6   *The Birkbeck Vocabulary Project*   197
7.7   *Recent developments: The explicit–implicit
        continuum*   202
7.8   *Transitions*   205
7.9   *Vocabulary and language teaching:
        Introduction*   205
7.10   *Word lists: Vocabulary for beginners*   206
7.11   *Words in context*   209
7.12   *Word sets and grids: Vocabulary for advanced
        learners*   213
7.13   *Vocabulary in discourse: Fixed expressions and
        lexis in use*   220
7.13.1 *Fixed expressions and learnability*   223
7.14   *Lexical foundations for language teaching*   224
7.15   *Cloze and its uses*   226
7.15.1 *Procedures*   226
7.15.2 *Discourse cloze*   229
7.16   *Computer corpora and word lists once more*   231
7.17   *Words and limits: Which words, and how many
        words?*   235
7.18   *Core vocabulary and language study: Back to
        the core*   236
7.19   *Conclusions: Knowing and teaching
        vocabulary*   238

PART III
Case studies 245

8 Case study: Lexis, tones and ironies 247

8.0   *Introduction* 247
8.1   *General framework* 248
8.2   *Gricean analysis of irony: Lexical perspectives* 249
8.3   *Irony, lexis and genre* 252
8.4   *Conclusions* 256
8.5   *Appendices: Informant tests* 257

9 Case study: Style, lexis and the dictionary 263

9.0   *Introduction* 263
9.1   *Semantics, associations and definitions* 263
9.2   *Semantic space* 267
9.3   *Informants and the measurement of 'meanings'* 270
9.4   *Core vocabulary and the dictionary: A sample
        entry* 275
9.5   *Conclusion* 279
9.5.1 *Further conclusion (1997)* 281
9.6   *Coda* 282

Bibliography 284
Bibliography of dictionaries 307
Bibliography of language corpora 309
Index 311

List of figures and tables

Figures

1.1	Lexicality cline	14
1.2	Basic English word list	26
2.1	Superordinate relations: *Furniture*	41
4.1	Canute Kinnock: The lexis of reporting	112
6.1	A dictionary entry for *mug*	169
6.2	Example from BCOET corpus: Extract from concordance for *declined*	170
6.3	A dictionary entry for *now*	172
6.4	A dictionary entry for *now*	173
6.5	Frequencies of the verb *mean* in spoken and written English	176
6.6	A dictionary entry for *freak*	176
6.7	A sample dictionary page	178
6.8	A dictionary entry for *borrow*	181
7.1	Illustration of 'keyword' technique	194
7.2	General service list: Entry for *head*	208
7.3a	A semantic grid for components of words meaning 'being surprised'	215
7.3b	A scale marking degrees of intensity for words meaning 'being surprised'	215
7.3c	A semantic grid of typical collocational patterns of words meaning 'attractive'	215
7.3d	Semantic grids for words meaning 'attractive'	216
7.4	A game-like task for vocabulary learning	217
7.5	A game-like task for vocabulary learning	218
7.6	Suggestions for ways of teaching words such as *just*	227
8.1	Knowing the meaning of words	256

9.1a   Representing semantic space: Using scales for words with
       the meaning 'rude'   269
9.1b   Representing semantic space: Diagrammatic
       presentation of the meaning of *cheeky*   269
9.1c   Representing semantic space: An informal–formal scale
       for words with the meaning 'rude'   270
9.2   Two scales, to measure formality and evaluation, for
       words with the meaning 'thin'   276
9.3   A dictionary entry for *thin*   277
9.4   Diagrammatic representation of semantic space for two
       words   279

Tables

3.1   Lexis as a linguistic level   52
3.2   Types of fixed expression   67
4.1   Fifty most frequent words in written and spoken corpora   99
4.2   Occurrences of *start*, *begin*, *too* and *also* in written and
       spoken corpora   100
4.3   Percentage coverage of words in rank 501–550 and
       1001–1050 in written and spoken corpora   101
6.1   Data about four learner's dictionaries of English   179
7.1   Examples of new terms and overextensions in L1
       acquisition   188
7.2   Associations made by native English speakers to French
       stimulus words   200

Acknowledgements

Very few adjustments are required to the acknowledgements made for the first edition of *Vocabulary*, and thanks to Tony Cowie for his support and advice remain. My debt to Michael McCarthy remains as strong as ever and I have continued greatly to value our close personal, writing and research relationship. I am also grateful to him for allowing me to use material co-written by us, especially Section 4.7. Particular thanks also go to Paul Meara and Paul Nation who gave generously of their time to offer their views on developments in the field of vocabulary studies; to Gwynneth Fox and Della Summers who provided very helpful comments on necessary revisions and updates to Chapter 6; to Norbert Schmitt for writing an excellent doctoral thesis which served to keep me in touch with many developments, especially with reference to vocabulary acquisition, and also for his generous help with parts of Chapter 7; to John Sinclair for remaining a singular inspiration in the field of lexical studies; to Louisa Semlyen at Routledge for being one of the most supportive editors ever.

My debt to Jane, Matthew, Jennifer and Claire, and their healthy scepticism about academic books, remains undiminished.

Preface to the first edition

This book is a guide to some ways in which linguistic insights into the structure of the modern English lexicon might be applied. Applied linguistics is generally associated with second- and foreign-language teaching and this book contains an extensive review of developments in vocabulary teaching. The book will, however, demonstrate that the possibilities for application can be broader in scope. In addition to brief discussions of mother-tongue early language development and a number of social issues in vocabulary use, such as the relationship between lexis and ideology, the book examines some applications of lexicological description in three main areas: language learning and teaching, lexicography, and literary-text study.

Although there are (in the third part of the book) two detailed case studies in which particular arguments are presented relevant to work in what might be termed 'lexical stylistics', the orientation of this book is mainly descriptive. It seeks to *report* on research, *review* developments in lexical description and *comment* on specific points of intersection between linguistic insight and areas of application. No description is entirely neutral, however, not least because, in a relatively wide-ranging book such as this, selection is inevitable and selection is itself a form of evaluation. For example, the importance of studying lexis in discourse and of using informants to assist description of lexical associations is stated regularly, both explicitly and implicitly, throughout the book. But, wherever possible, a descriptive overview constitutes the main design.

This is not an apology. There are very few books or studies of lexis in relation to applied linguistics and it is hoped that to an extent this book helps to clear some ground from a number of different perspectives at the same time as indicating areas in which work needs to be done. However, I should have liked to have devoted more space to the social, cultural and political issues which the study of vocabulary necessitates, in particular in the following areas: the vocabularies of world Englishes, and the implications of this for lexicographic practice and for stylistic analysis of international literatures in English; sociolinguistic and historical accounts of lexical change, particularly with reference to dialect; the lexicology of sexism, ageism and racism – areas which are beginning to attract the attention of language researchers. I also recognize that more space could have been given to psycholinguistic accounts of the lexicon, especially in relation to language learning. Such omissions have to be seen in relation to the biases which any 'perspective' entails but also to the need to describe the chosen areas of application in as much detail as possible.

Applied linguistics is a growth area in linguistics. There is an ever increasing number of books, journals, courses, conferences and professional associations which appropriate the term. However, although discussions in Kaplan (1980), Brumfit (1981), Crystal (1981) and Widdowson (1981; 1985) are notable exceptions, debate about the aims, goals and procedures for applying linguistics is not especially prominent. This book does not seek explicitly to address such issues; the domain of applied linguistics is not made any less undertheorized as a result of its appearance. And readers expecting to find a course book in lexical semantics may also be disappointed. The field is a wide and complex one, and work is reviewed here in which aspects of lexis are selected for what is judged to be their relevance to the above mentioned specific contexts of applications. The book is a practical guide to what has been done, what is being done and, where feasible, to *how* it is done. In this respect the book is not programmatic but this is not to say that programmatic as well as procedural issues are not of considerable importance to applied linguistics as a discipline.

The book is divided into three main parts. The first part, which consists of four chapters, outlines some basic issues and undertakes analysis of lexis in increasingly larger units of language – moving from the forms of words to the roles of words in discourse contexts. The second part consists of three chapters and is devoted to discussion of applied linguistic issues raised by vocabulary being 'used' in language learning and teaching contexts, in lexicography (especially with regard to learner dictionaries) and as a component in the stylistic analysis of literature. In all three domains vocabulary is of particular relevance and has not received as much attention as it merits. The third part of the book consists of two studies in lexical stylistics in which particular analytical procedures – based mainly on informant analysis – are shown to be applicable to fuller and more precise description of the role of lexis in the style of literary texts and in the way style levels can be marked in lexicographic entries.

It is hoped that these applied linguistic perspectives will provide some basis for further study and 'application' to be made. Vocabulary and vocabulary use are now beginning to attract the attention of applied linguists after a period of relative neglect. It is hoped that this book may contribute to this renewal of attention. And finally it is hoped that a frequently used word in the English lexicon – *he* – will be read to mean he/she wherever it occurs in the book.

Ronald Carter
Nottingham
1987

Preface to the second edition

This second edition of *Vocabulary* updates recent progress in the last ten years with particular reference to the momentous changes in the computational analysis of vocabulary. There are updated and re-worked sections on vocabulary and language teaching; dictionaries and lexicography; and the literary stylistic study of vocabulary. And there are newly written parts of chapters on the relationship between vocabulary, grammar and discourse. The emphasis remains squarely on the description of vocabulary and on the basis that the more we know about how vocabulary works the better our applications are likely to be. The second edition does not, any more than the first edition, pretend to extensive coverage of all aspects of vocabulary but rather offers *perspectives*. But they are perspectives, of course, which inevitably entail the limitations which accompany the viewing point. In a field as dynamic as vocabulary studies has been since the publication of the first edition of this book in 1987 it is always difficult to know where to begin, and where and when to end. In taking these decisions, it is inevitable that where you stop might be where others would start.

Ronald Carter
Nottingham
January 1998

Part I
Foundations

1 What's in a word

1.0 Introduction: A form of words

> Not only every language but every lexeme of a language is an entire
> world in itself.
>
> (Mel'čuk, 1981, p. 570)

A main aim in this chapter is to introduce some basic terms and concepts in the analysis of vocabulary. The emphasis is on an exploration
of what constitutes a word. There is an extensive literature on this topic
stretching back over at least twenty years. The area of linguistics which
covers the topic is generally known as lexical semantics and is most
clearly represented in John Lyons's two-volume study (Lyons, 1977). In
the next three chapters an introduction is given to work which is itself at
an introductory stage; but an introduction to this highly developed field
is bound to involve some degree of oversimplification. Word-level
semantic analysis features in almost all elementary courses in linguistics
and it is probable that some readers will be already acquainted with the
field.

However, this is not a book in theoretical linguistics; it is not even an
introduction to theoretical linguistics. Instead, a selection is made of
those features of lexical semantics which seem most relevant to an
understanding of some selected contexts of language use. For example,
one focus in this first chapter is on some applications of aspects of
lexical semantics to dictionary use, and to an evaluation of pedagogical
word lists. These and other features are also selected for their further
usefulness to us in subsequent chapters on vocabulary teaching, stylistics and English as a Foreign Language lexicography. This kind of
selection runs a further risk that the field of lexical semantics is mis-
represented or at best oversimplified. An applied linguistic perspective

cannot always avoid such risks. However, its strengths lie, I hope, in the ways in which some *practical* problems of language use are addressed and discussed (note that bold italics are used when a technical term is introduced or discussed).

1.1 Some definitions

Everyone knows what a **word** is. And it may therefore appear unnecessary to devote several pages of discussion to its definition, even in a book on vocabulary. Indeed, closer examination reveals the usefulness of everyday common-sense notions of a word; it also reveals, however, some limitations which have a bearing on the ways in which words are used and understood in some specialized applied linguistic contexts.

An **orthographic** definition of a word is a practical common-sense definition. It says, quite simply, that a word is any sequence of letters (and a limited number of other characteristics such as hyphen and apostrophe) bounded on either side by a space or punctuation mark. It can be seen that this definition is at the basis of such activities as counting the number of words needed for an essay, a competition, or telegram, to play 'Scrabble' and to write a shopping list. There are, of course, irregularities. For example, we write *will not* as two words but *cannot* as one word; *instead of* is two words, but *in place of* is three; *postbox* can also appear as *post box* or *post-box*.[1] But, generally, the notion of an orthographic word has considerable practical validity.

Orthography refers, of course, to a medium of written language. And although this issue is not explicitly dealt with at this stage (see Section 4.5), we should note that spoken discourse does not generally allow of such a clear perception of a word. The issue of word stress is significant and is explored in this section, but where stress, 'spaces' or pauses occur in speech, it may be for reasons other than to differentiate one single word unit from another. It can be for purposes of emphasis, seeking the right expression, checking on an interlocutor's understanding, or even as a result of forgetting or rephrasing what you were going to say. In such circumstances, the divisibility of a word is less clear-cut; in fact, spaces here can occur in the middle of the orthographically defined word unit. And we should, in any case, remember that not all languages mark word boundaries, the most prominent of these being Chinese.

However, even in written contexts, there are potential theoretical and practical problems with an orthographic definition. For example, if *bring*, *brings*, *brought* and *bringing*, or *long*, *length* and *lengthen*, or, less obviously, *good*, *better* and *best* are separate words, would we expect to find each word from the set listed separately in a dictionary?[2] If so, why and if not, why not? And what about words which have the same form but different meanings; for example, *line* in the sense of railway *line,* fishing *line* or straight *line*? Are these one word or several? Others have more extended meanings and even embrace different grammatical categories; examples of such polysemic words are: *fair, pick, air, flight, mouth.* Knowing a word involves, presumably, knowing the different meanings carried by a single form. An orthographic definition is one which is formalistic in the sense of being bound to the form of a word in a particular medium. It is not sensitive to distinctions of meaning or grammatical function. To this extent it is not complete.

It may be more accurate to define a word as the **minimum meaningful unit** of language. This allows us to differentiate the separate meanings contained in the word *fair* in so far as they can be said to be different semantic units. However, this definition presupposes clear relations between single words and the notion of 'meaning'. For example, there are single units of meaning which are conveyed by more than one word: *bus conductor, train driver, school teacher, model railway.* And if they are compound words do they count as one word or two? There are also different boundaries of meaning generated by 'words' which can be read in more than one way. For example, *police investigation* is read more normally as an investigation *by* the police but its appearance in a recent headline fronting a police bribery case enables us to read it as an investigation *of* the police. More problematically still, to what extent can 'meaning' be said to be transmitted by the following words: *if, by, but, my, could, because, indeed, them.* Such items can serve to structure or otherwise organize how information is received, but on their own they are not semantic units in the sense intended above. The presence of such words in the lexicon also undermines another possible definition of a word, namely, that a word is a 'minimal free form'.

This definition, which derives from Bloomfield (1933, pp. 178 ff), is a useful working definition and, like that of the orthographic word, has a certain intuitive validity. The idea here is to stress the basic stability of a word. This comes from the fact that a 'word' is a word if it can stand on its own as a reply to a question or as a statement or exclamation. It is not too difficult to imagine contexts in which each of the following words could exist independently:

Shoot! Goal! Yes. There. Up. Taxi!

And it is only by stretching the imagination that the word *shoot* could be reduced further to, say, *Sh. . . Goal!*, where it would, anyway, be dependent on the other word for its sense. By this definition, then, a word has the kind of stability which does not allow of further reduction in form. It is stable and free enough to stand on its own. It cannot be subdivided. We should note here, though, that a number of words do not pass this minimal free form test. Although we can imagine grammar lessons in which words like *my* or *because* appeared independently, it is unlikely that such items could occur on their own without being contextually attached to other words.[3] And we should also recognize that there are idioms such as *to rain cats and dogs* (to rain heavily) or *to kick the bucket* (to die) which involve three orthographic words which cannot be further reduced without loss of meaning, which can be substituted by a single word and yet which can stand on their own. For example:

Q: Is it raining hard?
A: Cats and dogs.

Where the reply serves more or less as a substitute form for the single item *hard*.

Another possible definition of a word is that it will **not** have **more than one stressed syllable**. Thus, *cats, shoot, veterinary, immobilize*, are unambiguously 'words'. Again, however, we should note that some of the forms designated above as not transmitting meaning (e.g. *if, but, by, them*) do not normally receive stress, except when a particular expressive effect is required. Also, some of our two-word orthographic units such as *bus conductor* would be defined as single words according to this test.[4]

It is clear that there are problems in trying to define a word. Common-sense definitions do not get us very far; but neither do a series of more technical tests. The discussion in this section has served, however, to highlight problems and in the following sections these problems will be discussed further with the aim of at least trying to identify what are the basic, prototypical properties of a word. Let us first summarize the main problems we have already encountered:

1   Intuitively, orthographic, free-form or stress-based definitions of a word make sense. But there are many words which do not fit these categories.
2   Intuitively, words are *units of meaning* but the definition of a word having a clear-cut 'meaning' creates numerous exceptions and emerges as vague and asymmetrical.
3   Words have different *forms*. But the different forms do not necessarily count as different words.

4 Words can have the *same* forms but also *different* and, in some cases, completely unrelated meanings.
5 The existence of *idioms* seems to upset attempts to define words in any neat formal way.

1.2 Lexemes and words

One theoretical notion which may help us to resolve some of the above problems is that of the *lexeme*. A lexeme is the abstract unit which underlies some of the variants we have observed in connection with 'words'. Thus BRING is the lexeme which underlies different grammatical variants: 'bring', 'brought', 'brings', 'bringing' which we can refer to as *word-forms* (note a lexeme is conventionally represented by upper-case letters and that quotation marks are used for its word-forms). Lexemes are the basic, contrasting units of vocabulary in a language. When we look up words in a dictionary we are looking up lexemes rather than words. That is, 'brought' and 'bringing' will be found under an entry for BRING. The lexeme BRING is an abstraction. It does not actually occur itself in texts. Instead, it realizes different word-forms. Thus, the word-form 'bring' is realized by the lexeme BRING; the lexeme GO realizes the word-form 'went'. In a dictionary each lexeme merits a separate entry or sub-entry.

The term lexeme also embraces items which consist of more than one word-form. Into the category come *lexical items* such as multi-word verbs (*to catch up on*), phrasal verbs (*to drop in*) and idioms (*kick the bucket*). Here, KICK THE BUCKET is a lexeme and would appear as such as a single dictionary entry even though it is a three-word form.[5] The question of idiomaticity is treated more extensively in Chapter 3 (Section 3.7).

We can also see that the notion of *lexeme* helps us to represent the *polysemy* – or the existence of several meanings – in individual words: thus, *fair* (n.), *fair* (adj.[1] as in good, acceptable) and *fair* (adj.[2] as in light in colour, especially of hair), would have three different lexeme meanings for the same word-form. The same applies to the different meanings of *lap* which include: *lap*[1] (n. and v. as in a race); *lap*[2] (v. as in 'the cat laps the milk'); *lap*[3] (n. as in 'sit on my lap'). But there are numerous less clear-cut categories. For example, in the case of *line* (draw a line; railway line; clothes line) is the same surface form realized by one, two or three separate underlying lexemes? And are the meanings of *chair* (professional appointment; seat) or *paper* (newspaper; academic lecture) or *dressing* (sauce; manure; bandages) specializations of the same basic lexeme or not?

An important question which also arises here concerns our own metalanguage in this book. Should we talk of *words* or *word-forms* or *lexemes* or *lexical items*? It is clear that the uses of the words *word* or *vocabulary* have a general common-sense validity and are serviceable when there is no real need to be precise. They will continue to be used for general reference. The terms *lexeme* and the *word-forms* of a lexeme are valuable theoretical concepts and will be used when theoretical distinctions are necessary. *Lexical item(s)* (or sometimes *vocabulary items* or simply *items*) is a useful and fairly neutral hold-all term which captures and, to some extent, helps to overcome instabilities in the term *word*, especially when it becomes limited by orthography. More precise differentiation and some further subdivision of *lexical item* is made in Chapter 3, but the term will be used in places where common-sense might have its limitations. Also, as we will see in the sections devoted to lexical cohesion in Chapter 4, writers of any kind of text produce particular effects on readers if they keep repeating the same words without any kind of variation. In some contexts, it will be useful to have *word*, *lexical item* and *vocabulary* as variants.

1.3 Grammatical and lexical words

One distinction which the above discussion clearly necessitates is that between grammatical words and lexical words. The former comprises a small and finite class of words which includes pronouns (*I*, *you*, *me*), articles (*the*, *a*), auxiliary verbs (*must*, *could*, *shall*), prepositions (*in*, *on*, *with*, *by*) and conjunctions (*and*, *but*). *Grammatical words* like this are also variously known as 'functional words', 'functors', 'empty words'. *Lexical words*, on the other hand – which are also variously known as 'full words' or 'content words' – include nouns (*man*, *cat*), adjectives (*large*, *beautiful*), verbs (*find*, *wish*) and adverbs (*brightly*, *luckily*). They carry a higher information content and, as we have seen, are syntactically structured by the grammatical words. Also, while there are a finite number of grammatical words, there is a potentially unlimited number of lexical words. It is lexical words, too, which are most subject to what linguists term diachronic change, that is, changes in form or meaning over a period of time. There are numerous examples of regular changes in meaning of lexical words in the course of the historical development of any language. But grammatical words remain generally more immutable.[6] This gives some obvious ground, therefore, for linguists to be able to refer to lexical words as an *open class* of words while grammatical words constitute a *closed class*.

Finally, we should note that the term *word* has occurred again. Here it is used informally but also because lexical 'word' and grammatical 'word' are key terms and are extensively employed in the literature. But they are reproduced here with an awareness of the theoretical importance of the notion of lexeme. In fact, the distinction drawn above between lexemes and word-forms enables an important theoretical point to be made concerning grammatical and lexical 'words': there is a regular co-occurrence between a grammatical word and its lexeme; but lexical words take on many different forms. For example, different lexical word-forms 'sing', 'sang', 'sings', 'singing', 'sung', are realized by a single lexeme SING. But a grammatical word will normally have a single word-form realized by a lexeme. Thus, the lexemes BY and OF have 'by' and 'of' as their word-forms. This observation is extended in the next section which introduces the notion of *morpheme*.

1.4 Morphemes and morphology

A *morpheme* is the smallest unit of meaning in a word. The word 'inexpensive' comprises two morphemes *in* and *expensive*. Each morpheme has its own meaning. The addition of *in* to *expensive*, for example, gives the sense of *not*. Morphemes can be a single orthographic letter and yet still change meaning. For example, the *s* in cat*s* is a morpheme and changes the first morpheme *cat* from singular into plural. Other examples would be *laughed* which is made up of two morphemes *laugh* and *ed*; with the addition of *ed* altering the tense of the first morpheme and thus the time of occurrence of the process it denotes. Or *indistinguishable*, which has three morphemes; and *antidisestablishmentarianism*, which consists of six separate morphemes.

Two observations can be made immediately. First, morphemes convey semantico-syntactic information. Secondly, there are two classes of morphemes: morphemes which occur independently as words and are co-terminous with specific word-forms, and morphemes which occur only as part of a word and which could not stand on their own. The first class, which are called *free morphemes*, would include *cat*, *distinguish*, *laugh*. The second class, which are called *bound morphemes*, would include *un*, *s*, *ed*, *able*, *anti* and *ism*. We should note, however, that some morphemes can have the same form but still be different morphemes, for example, the 's' in cat*s*, cat'*s* and laugh*s* or the 'er' in small*er*, win-n*er*, eras*er*.[7] These variants are usually termed *allomorphs*.[8] We should also recognize that like the term *lexeme*, *morpheme* is an abstraction. To be strict, morphemes do not actually occur in words. Morphemes are realized by forms which are called *morphs*. But the term *morph* will be used only when the more specialized sense is required. Like the word 'word', morpheme is widely used and has a usefully *general*, if not strictly accurate, reference.

1.5 Word formation

If we consider once again the design of entries in a conventional dictionary, then it will be clear that there are still a number of outstanding problems. When we look up a word in a dictionary, we have learned already: (1) that we are looking up a lexeme rather than a word, (2) that this may comprise more than one orthographic word, (3) that it may have a paramount lexical or grammatical function, (4) that we would expect to encounter free but not bound morphemes. The discussion so far does not, however, explain why we would expect to find the following two lists of words in separate entries:

(1) adapt, adapts, adapting, adapted
(2) adaptor, adaptable, adaptability, adaptation

The answer can in part be given by pointing out that the word-forms entered under (1) involve **inflections** while those under (2) involve **derivations**. A general distinction between the two categories is: inflection produces from the root or roots of a given lexeme all the word-forms of that lexeme which are syntactically determined; derivation is a process which results in the formation of different lexemes. Thus, it is a characteristic of inflections that they signal grammatical variants of a given root. They do not form new lexemes or change the grammatical class of a given item (i.e. all the word-forms in (1) are verbs); the inflections of the adjective *small* would produce the adjectives *smaller* and *smallest*. Derivations signal lexical variants of a given root; they change nouns into verbs, verbs into nouns, and so on; for example: *adapt/ adaptable/adaptation*; *sensitive/sensitivity*; *rich/richness*. Derivational word-forms can be substituted by a single morpheme (e.g. *inexpensive– cheap*), but inflectional forms cannot be so substituted. Note, too, that derivation still operates even when there are no formal changes to the root: e.g. *dirty* (v.) and (adj.); *change* (n.) and (v.). Derivations from complex and compound lexemes (e.g. *country cottage*; *training ground*) are discussed in detail in Lyons (1977, Ch. 13).

In the above definitions, the term **root** has been employed. This is an important concept in word formation. Morphemes may be generally divided into the category **root** and **non-root**, depending on whether they are primarily lexical or grammatical in function. Non-roots have important grammatical functions but belong to a relatively closed class of items and do not have particularly specific meanings. Roots are more open categories; they are usually lexical words (as defined in Section 1.3) and have more easily specifiable meanings. Examples of non-roots are *by*, *of*, *to*, *this*, *s*, *er*, *ist*, and, of these, the last three items would be termed bound non-roots since they have to be attached to a free morpheme or free root if they are to make a word-form. A more generally known term for bound non-roots is *affix*. Affixes (prefixes and suffixes) are added to roots to produce inflections and derivations. In English most roots are free, but a word like *dentist* is made from an affix *ist* and a root *dent* which is bound. *Dent* does not occur independently and neither do related examples such as *feas* (feas-ible), *ed* (ed-ible) or *leg* (leg-ible).[9]

To return to our dictionary examples, it makes sense for lexicographers to list all the inflections of a basic root word-form of a lexeme under a single lexeme entry. Only grammatical variations will be involved. As might be expected, greater problems arise when lexical variations are involved. Derivations can produce items with quite different semantic identities (e.g. *true/untrue*; *expensive/inexpensive*); and these clearly necessitate different entries since a markedly different lexeme is generated. Other derivations result in close formal and semantic identities (e.g. *encourage/encouragement*) where a closely related lexeme obtains. But there are intermediate or less clear-cut categories where the derivations are not so easy to demarcate. For example, what is the derivational relationship between *solve* and *solution*, or *destroy* and *destruction*? What is the root in each case? Or are they totally separate lexemes? Take also the following group of words:

medicine, medicinal, medical, medicament

Here, derivations from a root *medic* produce striking differences in stress and in phonological realization. And are all the obviously surface-related word-forms derived from the root of a single lexeme, or from more than one? Are *medical* and *medicament* more closely related than *medical* and *medicinal*? Issues of formal, semantic and derivational identity are involved here, and as with the assignment of polysemous meanings to underlying lexemes, the lexicographer and to an extent the dictionary user are faced with a complex question of interpretation. This also explains why dictionaries can differ in their entries. The solution adopted by the *Concise Oxford Dictionary* (*COD*) for the *medic* group is to list them all as separate entries (in contrast to this, *encourage* and *encouragement* have the same entry in the *COD*). But this may be a convenience afforded only by a proximity in the lay-out of the entries due to alphabetic listing. In any case, the examples illustrate the kinds of problems faced by students using a dictionary, or by teachers looking for a systematic way of developing reference skills.[10]

1.6 Multiple meanings

From the few examples of **polysemy** (the existence of several meanings in an individual word) already examined, it is clear that there are not always direct and unproblematic equivalences between words and meanings. Polysemy can produce meanings which are close or distant. Thus, *line* can be associated with drawing, fishing or railways, and share physical properties of material covering space between two points where the different senses are close; but *race* ('run in a race'; 'ethnic group') has meanings which are so distant as to be only arbitrarily related through the formal identity of the word. *Fat*, on the other hand (e.g. *'fat* stomach', *'fat* bank-account'), is both close and distant depending on the degree of figurative extension made.

Similarly, a bound morphemic non-root (an **affix**) such as *less*, can occasion different semantic (or meaning) values. For example, the *less* in *hopeless* is different from that in *faultless*; the *less* in *worthless* is different from that in *priceless*. Bolinger (1985) has pointed out that this **affix** produces derivations which are regularly adjectives or adverbs but which have five main semantic functions resulting in words which (1) 'lack something', or suggest deprivation and which have negative evaluation, e.g. *hopeless, tasteless*, (2) are 'free from' something and which have a positive evaluation, e.g. *faultless, spotless*, (3) are 'without something', e.g. *doubtless, sinless*, (4) are 'expressive of states beyond normal limits', e.g. *resistless*, (5) which 'suggest intensity' and 'poetic' hyperbole, e.g. *priceless, stormless, remorseless*. The difficulty of attaching precise meanings and the problem of semantic closeness but not semantic identity, is illustrated when opposites (**antonyms**) are sought. For example, *hopeful* is not an opposite of *hopeless*, and opposites for *priceless* such as *worthless* may involve the same affix but a completely different root-word. The general point to be made here is that the meanings contained and conferred by morphemes are not as easily specifiable as may at first appear. (For suggestions for teaching such relations to non-native students of English, see Rossner, 1985.)

Further anomalies and difficulties with multiple meanings occur not only with **homonyms** (a group of words pronounced or spelt in the same way but having different meanings) and polysemous items (e.g. *lap, line* above) but with homophones. **Homophones** are the category of words in which there is an identity between items and their phonological form (i.e. they are pronounced the same way). Often different parts of speech are involved, for example, the book was *red/read*, or the combination *by/buy*, or *for/four/fore*. And there are also lexical items which can be *both* grammatical *and* lexical words, as well as being homophones, homonyms *and* **homographs** (same spelling), for example, *round, off*.

The discussion here illustrates another aspect of the lexicographer's recurring dilemma. Faced with *line* or *bank* or *race* or with a lexical item such as *round* or *fat*, how many separate entries are needed? Where should the line be drawn between meanings which are related and thus conflatable under a single entry, and those which are unrelated and, therefore, need to be segmented in a dictionary? Given the distributional and semantic complexities of *off*, how might even some of its uses be best defined or explained to, for example, a foreign learner of English?

> Turn the light *off*.
> He's a bit *off* today.
> The milk's *off*.
> Run *off* some copies, please.
> They're *off*.
> The match is *off*.
> *Off* the boil.
> He jumped *off* the bridge.
> Come *off* it.
> The village is miles *off*.

For further discussion and analysis of word formation, see Adams (1973) and Bauer (1983), and for discussion of such issues, as well as further analysis of polysemous items, with particular reference to pedagogical lexicography, see Section 6.5.

1.7 In a word: A summary

Discussion so far has brought us a little closer to a definition of a word. The issue of dictionary use and of our expectations concerning the organization of lexical entries in a dictionary has helped to provide a focus. It is a relatively narrow focus and it raises only certain questions. But the questions are ones which are relatively widely and directly encountered in everyday use of the language. Here is a brief summary of some of the main points:

1   The variable orthographic phonological, grammatical and seman-
    tic properties of words are best captured, in a strict sense, by the use
    of the term lexical item(s). The underlying theoretic concept of a
    lexeme is especially valuable.
2   The category of polysemy is an important one, and potentially
    problematic for the analysis of word meaning. Lexical words can be
    polysemous; grammatical words can only be homophones in rela-
    tion to lexical words, e.g. *in/inn*; *by/buy*. The notion of lexeme is
    again useful when distinguishing the multiple surface forms and
    functions some words can have.
3   Some lexical items have greater 'lexicality' than others. Here the
    distinction between grammatical and lexical words (see Section 1.3)
    is an important one. The more grammatically functioning the item,
    the less saliently will it emerge as prototypically lexical. (It is
    grammatical words which can normally be omitted from tele-
    grams.) Roots or free morphemes have the greatest degree of
    lexicality and are not restricted or bound in predictable forms,
    meanings or distributions. Their relative mobility is measured by an
    inherent derivational creativity in forming new lexeme(s), combin-
    ations, compounds, etc. A ***cline of lexicality*** which runs from lexical
    free roots (most lexical) to bound affixes (least lexical) might be
    loosely represented as in Figure 1.1. The categories along the cline
    are not, of course, completely watertight. Thus, in the noun 'the
    incorruptibles' *corrupt* as the free lexical root would have greater

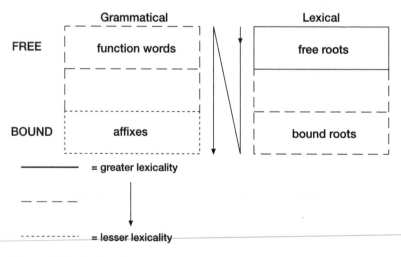

Figure 1.1 Lexicality cline.

lexicality than the bound affixes *s*, *ible* and *in*; but, by comparison, it is arguable whether the grammatical word *the* operates with an entirely 'freer' lexicality than each of the bound affixes.

Lexical words will be examined further in the next section where structural semantic relations will be shown to obtain between the more lexical words in the lexicon. However, a final word of warning is necessary. It is dangerous to suggest that lexicality is a primary *value*. The 'value' of grammatical words in discourse relations and in text formation is considerable, although this is not to be examined in detail until Chapter 4. We should also note that certain grammatical words (e.g. *because*) signal a greater lexicality (here of reason) than others (see in particular Section 4.2).

1.8 Referential meaning

Sections 1.1 to 1.6 have been concerned with word meaning but have focused primarily on more formalistic aspects of words. The next sections become progressively more concerned with semantic (or meaning) features beginning with a brief examination of the relationship between words as referring items and *referents* as the features of the world which words point to.

Just as the notion of a word has considerable intuitive validity, so too does the correlation between words and things, especially the notion that words point to or represent things. The notion is given further support, too, by the pre-theoretical supposition that children learn a language by virtue of having the objects of the world pointed out to them and named in an appropriate vocabulary. Such intuitions are powerful and they are clearly grounded in language experience to which many can testify. This section explores the referentiality of words and the nature of the fit between words and things; it is hoped that pre-theoretical or intuitive insights can be explored within the framework of some basic theories of language and meaning.

In varying degrees most 'content' or lexical words have a referent and it would be extremely difficult for communication in language to take place without reference. A referent is the object, entity, state of affairs, etc. in the external world to which a lexical item refers. Thus, the referent of the word *chair* is the object chair; the referent of the verb *run* is that process of locomotion which involves an action of lifting, at times, *both* feet from the ground and which, therefore, differentiates that process from the action denoted by *walk*. But it can be seen that the connection between a word and an object or process is not always as unambiguous as this. For example, there are, as we have seen, several words in the language which, when taken singly, have no obvious referents; for example, *the, because, might, which.* Also, ambiguities in the relationship between sound and meaning, or between graphology and meaning, can lead to confusion in the actual referent pointed to, or can simultaneously invoke more than one referent (see Section 1.1). Similarly, the same referent may be referred to by several different lexical items, some of which may, or may not, be synonymous. For example, a man pointing to his garden may say:

> This is my garden
>> a disgrace
>> a pride and joy
>> a consolation
>> the answer
>> a sun-trap

and thus produce a connection between word and 'object' which is alternately remote, arbitrary and, at certain points, abstract. It further leads to consideration of the extent to which 'a disgrace' or 'a consolation' can easily be equated with a referent in the narrow sense of its meaning as object or thing. Another problem is that 'garden' may have different meanings for different individuals according to the kind of society they live in, and, even more intricately, in the case of intercultural differences where stylistic and connotative or associative meanings are played upon. The meaning of 'garden' can thus be both narrow and broad, according to the particular context in which it is used. This can be contrasted with *cat* (domestic pet) and *cat* (big game) which have a different object of reference according to position of the referrer, but which would be different realizations of the same lexeme in most standard dictionaries. It might also be noted that there are times when we do not know the name of a place, or object or person, and yet can make an act of referral quite naturally and satisfactorily by means of a description, however periphrastic, or by means of a word such as 'thingummy' or 'whatsisname' which have no constant referent but which serve, none the less, to refer.[11] Also, reference is a property in language which extends beyond single words to lexical items in grammatical organization. We often need, for example, a defining relative clause in the phrase 'the man *who was here yesterday*' in order to make the referent definite and unambiguous.

There are also problems when we attempt to define a word's meaning on the basis of its 'properties', that is, in terms of the sensory attributes of the thing. A *cat* may be a 'cat' because of certain distinguishable generic peculiarities, but can still remain a cat when one of those features changes (i.e. size in the above example) even though the actual referent may be different and its societal role radically different. The name we give to a referent can also change spatially and temporally. *Pictures* is still the same object as *movies* or *cinema*, but is no longer in such widespread use. An object or set of objects can be initially referred to as *cargo*, yet within seconds of their transferral from a ship to a train they are referred to as *freight* even though the physical attributes of the objects remain constant.

Other objects or entities can only be defined with reference to the whole or to the 'system' of which they are a part, for example, *palm* (of a hand), *corner*, *page*, *orphan*, *cousin*, *employee*. This can create considerable difficulties, as can be imagined, in the compilation of entries in dictionaries for non-native language users from countries with different cultures, as the definition of the system will often have to be considerably in excess of the particular definition. The description of an action or process can also vary according to the intention of an agent. The definition of *wave* (moving one's hand to and fro), for example, may be no different in each case but the intention signalled by a person waving can often be quite different.

1.9 Componential analysis

Reference or denotation[12] is extralinguistic, that is, there is 'reference' to the entities, objects, states of affairs, etc. in the external world to which linguistic expressions refer. At the same time it should be recognized that words have sense relations: the system of linguistic relationships which a lexical item contracts with other lexical items.

A basis for an examination of this has been laid by a theory known as componential analysis. This refers to a technique for describing *relations of meaning* by breaking down each word into its irreducible *features*: those components which are absolutely minimal for its reference. The componential model of analysis is central to the conceptual area of semantics; its claims are to the fuller analysis of that finite set of components or semantic features in lexical items which are universal in that they underlie our basic cognitive processes for the ordering of meaning. Componential or semantic feature analysis thus presupposes a stable, universal word of concepts in which lexical items semanticize the structure of reality.

A main core of componential analysis is the concept of binarism. *Semantic features* are marked on the basis of semantic *opposition* or dimensions of **contrast**. For example *woman* can be defined as + HUMAN + ADULT – MALE, whereas *boy* can be defined as + HUMAN – ADULT + MALE. Such semantic notation thus enables us to differentiate *woman* and *boy* from *man, girl, house, cow*, etc.

This reduction of a word's meaning to its ultimate contrastive elements results in an atomization of meaning and is particularly useful for defining basic similarities and oppositions such as occur in kinship relations and in classifying, among many other contrasts, the animate and non-animate components of lexical items. Indeed, componential analysis first evolved in anthropological linguistics. It proves useful, as Leech (1981, p. 119) remarks, 'by allowing us to make generalizations covering a range of lexical items' and is similarly an essential component in the classification of the kind of semantico-grammatical relations into which certain words can enter: that is, certain verbs can only be associated with a noun with the feature + HUMAN (e.g. *confess, ask, deny cry*). Componential analysis can also assist in the disambiguation of homonyms as shown in the famous example of Katz and Fodor's semantic feature analysis of the four meanings of the word *bachelor* (Katz and Fodor, 1963; see also Chapin, 1971).

The problems of componential analysis are, however, numerous. The most prominent of these is that of appropriately delimiting the process of atomization. For example, there is no limitation to the subclassification of items. The word 'seal' could be designated + ANIMATE and – HUMAN but is also conceivable as – FEATHER – HAIR + AMPHIBIOUS + MAMMAL and so on. There is also the problem of defining the contrastive units since in the case of some words contrasts can occur simultaneously on more than one dimension. Is the minimal distinctive contrast of *woman* that of *man* or that of *girl*? Much depends on context, too. *Man*, for example, is on one level (i.e. in one sense) + MALE; on another level it is + HUMAN (with the MALE as + or – being irrelevant), that is, in the sense of mankind: 'man has conquered Everest'. Stylistic contrasts are not marked either. *Girl*, for example, can be – ADULT but, since a woman can be referred to as 'girl' and the term can carry certain evaluative or sexual overtones, in particular contexts the marker + ADULT is needed. In the case of some words, for example *horse*, the values of male/female are altogether irrelevant to the definition. There is also the further point that some binary or antonymous contrasts are not absolutes, but operate rather along a scale or cline. Examples here are *large–small, hot–cold*, which are matters both of degree and, more usually, of relative and gradable subjective assessment. (See also section 1.10.) Male and female are oppositions and – MALE implies the logical outcome + FEMALE but 'masculine' and 'feminine' are not self-cancelling to the same extent, since – MASCULINE would not automatically imply + FEMININE as we can see from the example *He looks rather feminine.* Certainly the notion of semantic contrast as a definitional procedure is very varied and complex, however neat the examples which can be produced. Certain sense components clearly lexicalize important semantic distinctions in the language; but as a taxonomic procedure componential analysis has certain limitations, although some semanticists argue that this is unavoidable (see Wierzbicka, 1984, for a discussion which uses the notorious difficulty of distinction between *cup* and *mug* as a main example). However, it does alert us to the need to account more precisely for the sense relations between lexical items covered by such traditional terms as antonymy and synonymy, etc – an area of investigation which has come to be described under the general heading of structural semantics.

1.10 Structural semantics: Words and other words

The basic principle of a structural semantic approach to word meaning is that words do not exist in isolation: their meanings are defined through the sense relations they have with other words. That such relations have psychological validity for individuals is indicated by the degree of uniformity unravelled by responses to word association tests.

In these tests, individuals[13] are given a word and asked to record the word with which, for them, it is most immediately associated. Typical responses are as follows (from Deese, 1965):

Stimulus	*Typical response*
accident	car
alive	dead
baby	mother
born	die
cabbage	vegetable
table	chair
careless	careful

Such associations are organized structurally in rather less incoherent a way than may at first appear. Some of the main networks between words can be classified. For example (from Slobin, 1971):

contrast or antonymy	wet–dry
similarity or synonym	blossom–flower

subordinate classification	animal–dog
coordinate classification	apple–peach
superordinate classification	spinach–vegetable

These relationships can be more fully classified along the following lines:

1   **Synonymy** – This is essentially a bilateral or symmetrical sense relation in which more than one linguistic form can be said to have the same conceptual or propositional meaning. This does not mean that the words should be totally interchangeable in all contexts; but where synonyms are substituted changes in the propositional meaning of the sentence as a whole do not occur. For example, sub-senses of *house, abode, domicile, home* are synonyms in some contexts; in the sentence *What an impressive _____ of books*, the words *range, selection, choice* are synonymous. However, stylistic differences limit substitutability. And in an absolute sense there can be no such thing as, nor any need for, totally substitutable synonyms.

2   **Antonymy** – As we have seen there are different kinds of contrasts in meaning, but basic to antonymy is a notion of semantic opposition or unrelatedness. Demarcations within antonymic sense relations can be made as follows:

(a)   **Complementarity** – This is where the presence of one sense component excludes another. For example, the relationship between *alive* and *dead* is such that to use one logically entails the denial of the other. An entity cannot be both simultaneously and there is no continuum or gradation between the terms. Other examples would be *single–married; male–female.* Thus, we can say he is 'rather tall' but not 'rather married' (see *antonymy* below).

(b)   **Converseness** – These are contrastive lexical relations where there is a measure of logical reciprocity, e.g. *husband–wife*; the sentence *he is her husband*, can be 'reversed' to produce the reciprocal correlate *she is his wife*. Converseness contrasts with 'complementarity' in that there is interdependence of meaning. Other examples would be *buy–sell*; *above–below*. But see Lyons (1977, p. 280ff).

(c)   **Incompatibility** – This refers to relational contrasts between items in a semantic field (words which co-occur with reference to a familiar topic). It occurs in such sets as seasons, days of the week, cycles, generic types, etc. For example, *rose*, *daffodil* and *chrysanthemum*; *red*, *blue* and *yellow* would be incompatibles. *The house is red* excludes that it is any other colour.

(d) *Antonymy* – This may now be used as an inclusive term for all the above contrastive sense relations but also, in relation to opposition, in the more restrictive sense of *gradable* opposites, e.g. *hot–cold*; *big–small*; *good–bad*, which are all gradable relative to each other with reference to a norm. We must note here, however, that the same word can be antonymous with more than one word depending on different semantic networks, e.g. *old* can be an antonym of *young* and of *new*.[14]

3 *Hyponymy* – Reference above to super- and subordinate relations leads to consideration of what have generally been termed 'inclusive' sense relations. Hyponymy is a relationship existing between specific and general lexical items in that the meaning of the specific item is included in, and by, the meaning of the more general item. In short, hyponymy is a kind of asymmetrical synonymy; its basic organization is hierarchical. *Tulips* and *roses* are co-hyponyms, for example, and are linked by their common inclusion under a **superordinate** (or **hypernym**) *flower* in whose class they belong. The following diagram may illustrate the nature of this relationship:

BUILDING
factory
hospital
House

museum	cottage
theatre	bungalow
school	villa
	mansion

Here *house* is a hyponym of *building* (which is its superordinate) but it also serves itself as a superordinate of another set of hyponyms. It is usual in dictionary definitions to define a subordinate item in terms of its superordinate, e.g. 'spinach is a kind of vegetable'. It should be noted, though, that there are certain inconsistencies in the relationship for certain verbs which denote actions or processes. It can be difficult to find a superordinate other than one which is somewhat vague and all-inclusive;[15] for example, *buy* and *steal* would be co-hyponyms subordinate to a verb such as *get*. See also Lyons (1981), for discussion of partial and quasi-hyponymy, as well as Lehrer (1974a). Hasan (1984) also coins the term **meronymy** to refer to a part–whole relation as in the case of *tree*, *branch* and *root* where *branch* and *root* are co-meronyms, named parts of the superordinate *tree*.

To conclude this section, the word *white* and its 'meaning' will be examined. The aim is to show how even a very ordinary and widely used word can have a complex relationship with its 'referents' and with the other words with which it exists in a structural semantic network. Although colour terms operate in a relatively clear pattern with each other (see Berlin and Kay, 1969), a certain indeterminacy and arbitrariness none the less characterizes the meaning of *white*, and such semantic features can create, for example, particular problems for language learners. (More extended discussion of the 'arbitrariness' of the sign and with particular reference to reading such signs in literary texts is found in Section 5.8.)

Although most languages have a translation equivalent for *white*, its meanings in English are not easily demonstrated. And to someone learning the word for the first time with no intralingual equivalents to work from, it is clear that merely pointing out objects in the world which possess the property of whiteness will not do. We can indicate visually that snow is white, that cotton-wool is white, or that sugar is white and leave the learner to infer the property in common (though they may come to the conclusion that white is a property of light powderiness). Alternatively, we can list the lexical sets or combinations of words into which *white* enters, for example, *white*, *grey*, *silver hair*; or the many collocations or idioms of which *white* forms a part can be listed. These can be learned but it will be apparent that the property denoted by the colour white is not specifically relevant in all of these cases (e.g. *white wine* is not white) and that culture-specific associations are an important feature of the meaning of several of them. For example, a *white wedding* does involve the bride in wearing white garments, but there are further *associations* or *connotations* of meaning produced, too, most notably those to do with purity and chastity. Thus we can have:

> white lie, white elephant, white nights, white coffee, white wine, white wedding, the white of an egg, white-collar worker, white space (technical term for the unused area of paper on a printed page), white man, white magic, white heat.

Most centrally, however, *white* is probably best learned in a general sense by being shown in relation to other colours along a colour spectrum as, for example, in a game of snooker and, in a very specific sense, in relation to other shades of white (e.g. *snow-white, petal-white, cream, off-white* and so on) in a paint colour chart.[16]

To know the meaning of *white* it is clear that it makes sense to start with this last dimension first. Meaning is thus primarily relational and the meaning of a word can, in most cases, be best illustrated by reference to the network of meanings which exist between senses and sub-senses of lexemes. Referential meaning on its own is insufficient and it would, in any case, exclude the other dimensions (associative, cultural, idiomatic) without the knowledge of which we cannot properly claim to know the meaning of the word *white*. The fit between *white* and its senses is an arbitrary one. It is almost as if we can say that 'white is white because it is not red'. As we have seen, however, the structural semantic definition, while important, is still not the whole story; issues of style, connotation, and association noted above receive more detailed discussion in subsequent chapters.

1.11 Basic English: A review

One of the aims of this book is to suggest that insights derived from descriptive accounts of the lexicon can be useful in contexts in which linguistic analysis is applied to the solution or clarification of specific problems of language use. It is naturally difficult to isolate any representative problem, especially one involving single 'words', for which some of the descriptive insights derived from this chapter might form a basis for discussion. But in this section the issue of *Basic English* is investigated. Basic English was a project designed to provide a basic minimum vocabulary for the learning of English. Since the project involves a word list of 850 words, it should be the case that aspects of the above discussion concerning the structure and function of words, the nature of the relationship between words, and the complexities of the word–meaning contract can illuminate some aspects of the possible linguistic applications of Basic English. It is interesting to note that the word 'white', together with others we have examined, is one of the 'basic' words in the project. One immediate question occurs: to what extent is it possible to present such a basic word to language learners without reference to the network of meanings it can enter?

Basic English was first proposed in the late 1920s and has been the subject of considerable discussion since then; indeed, the notion of a basic or nuclear English has been revived in the 1980s (see Stein, 1979; Quirk, 1982). The originators of the proposal were C.K. Ogden and I.A. Richards (Ogden, 1930; 1968), though the latter was responsible for numerous revisions, refinements and extensions to the scheme.

Throughout, the project had two main aims: 'the provision of a minimum secondary world language and the designing of an improved introductory course for foreign learners, leading into general English' (Richards, 1943, p.62). Its design has been outlined succinctly by Richards (who, in fact, uses Basic English for the outline) as follows:

> Basic English is English made simple by limiting the number of words to 850 and by cutting down the rules for using them to the smallest number necessary for the clear statement of ideas. And this is done without change in the normal order and behaviour of these words in everyday English. It is limited in its words and its rules but it keeps to the regular forms of English. And though it is designed to give the learner as little trouble as possible, it is no more strange to the eyes of my readers than these lines which are, in fact, in Basic English.
>
> (Richards, 1943, p. 20)

In other words, for Ogden and Richards it is a basic principle that, although their scheme will not embrace full English, it will at least not be un-English.

In Figure 1.2 is the list of words selected by Ogden and Richards as their basis. And the fact that they can be conveniently listed on a single side of paper is seen as one of the advantages of the proposal. A review of their proposal and its major advantages and disadvantages serves usefully as a summary of some of the main points made about the forms of words in this chapter. It also points to issues to do with style and meaning in later chapters and lays a clear foundation for exploration of the issue of a basic or 'core' vocabulary (for, *inter alia*, language learning purposes) in Chapter 2.

At the basis of Ogden and Richards's Basic English is the notion of a communicative adequacy whereby, even if periphrastically, an adult's fundamental linguistic needs can be communicated. Thus, even though more complex ideas may have to be paraphrased, it is claimed that the words supplied will both serve to express complex ideas and be in themselves easy and fast to learn. The learning burden is likewise kept to a minimum because, instead of introducing a wide range of verbs which, in English, necessitates the additional learning of numerous and often irregular inflections, Ogden and Richards confine their list to no more than eighteen main verbs, or 'operations' as they prefer to term them. The verbs are: *send, say, do, come, get, give, go, keep, let, make, put, seem, take* and *see*, plus the modal verbs *may* and *will* and the auxiliary verbs *be* and *have*. The only inflections to be learned (on verbs and nouns) are *-er*, *-ing* and *-ed* and Basic English does not even permit the bound morpheme inflection *s* for verbs so that *he make(s)* becomes 'ungrammatical'. An example of the kind of periphrasis made possible or, depending on your point of view, unnaturally enforced by the system, is the omission of the verbs *ask* and *want* from the list of operations for the simple reason that they can be paraphrased. That is:

$$\text{ask} \longrightarrow \text{put a question}$$
$$\text{want} \longrightarrow \text{have a desire for}$$

The idea that many notions can be re-expressed using more basic language is central to the Basic English project. Other examples might be *smoke* = have a smoke; *walk* = have a walk.[17]

The originators of Basic English claim that learning these 850 words will be a basis for 'leading into general English'. No rules for such extension are provided, however, and it is not altogether clear what kinds of unlearning may have to take place to facilitate this, nor how the extendability of the Basic English system can be effectively graded for learning purposes. For that matter, no clear operable principles have been made explicit for the processes of simplification which have lead to the construction of Basic English. It will also be clear that many of the words in the list bring with them the kinds of difficulties described in Section 1.1. That is, learning 850 word-forms is not the same thing as learning single senses. One calculation is that the 850 words of Basic English have 12,425 meanings (Nation, 1983, p. 11). The problem is particularly acute with what Ogden and Richards term 'picturable' words, thus revealing the inherent imbalances in the relationship between a word and a referent. It is difficult to know, particularly with the more polysemous items, such as *match, head, spring, horn, line,* which meanings are to be pre-eminently picturable. We might also note here the lexical and grammatical indeterminacies in a word like *round,* which appears as one of Ogden and Richards's 100 general qualities. Or take the example *off,* which is an 'example of word order' but which has distinct lexical meanings, too (see Section 1.6). This leads to the interesting question of whether it is better to learn all the senses and extensions of one word, or whether there are core meanings to polysemous words which should be learned first. (See discussion in Chapter 2 and also of the word *white* in Section 1.10.)

An issue of memorization is at stake here in that research has yet to establish clearly whether it is easier to retain the extended senses of a limited number of single word-forms, or to learn the different meanings of an almost equal number of lexical items (see Chapter 7). More

BASIC ENGLISH WORD LIST

OPERATIONS	THINGS		QUALITIES	
100	400 General	200 Picturable	100 General	50 Opposites
COME	ACCOUNT	ANGLE	ABLE	AWAKE
GET	ACT	ANT	ACID	BAD
GIVE	ADDITION	ARCH	ANGRY	BENT
GO	ADJUSTMENT	ARM	AUTOMATIC	BITTER
KEEP	ADVERTISEMENT	ARMY	BEAUTIFUL	BLUE
LET	AGREEMENT	BABY	BLACK	CERTAIN
MAKE	AIR	BAG	BOILING	COLD
PUT	AMOUNT	BALL	BRIGHT	COMPLETE
SEEM	AMUSEMENT	BAND	BROKEN	CRUEL
TAKE	ANIMAL	BASIN	BROWN	DARK
BE	ANSWER	BASKET	CHEAP	DEAD
DO	APPARATUS	BATH	CHEMICAL	DEAR
HAVE	APPROVAL	BED	CHIEF	DELICATE
SAY	ARGUMENT	BEE	CLEAN	DIFFERENT
SEE	ART	BELL	CLEAR	DIRTY
SEND	ATTACK	BERRY	COMMON	DRY
MAY	ATTEMPT	BIRD	COMPLEX	FALSE
WILL	ATTENTION	BLADE	CONSCIOUS	FEEBLE
ABOUT	ATTRACTION	BOARD	CUT	FEMALE
ACROSS	AUTHORITY	BOAT	DEEP	FOOLISH
AFTER	BACK	BONE	DEPENDENT	FUTURE
AGAINST	BALANCE	BOOK	EARLY	GREEN
AMONG	BASE	BOOT	ELASTIC	ILL
AT	BEHAVIOUR	BOTTLE	ELECTRIC	LAST
BEFORE	BELIEF	BOX	EQUAL	LATE
BETWEEN	BIRTH	BOY	FAT	LEFT
BY	BIT	BRAIN	FERTILE	LOOSE
DOWN	BITE	BRAKE	FIRST	LOUD
FROM	BLOOD	BRANCH	FIXED	LOW
IN	BLOW	BRICK	FLAT	MIXED
OFF	BODY	BRIDGE	FREE	NARROW
ON	BRASS	BRUSH	FREQUENT	OLD
OVER	BREAD	BUCKET	FULL	OPPOSITE
THROUGH	BREATH	BULB	GENERAL	PUBLIC
TO	BROTHER	BUTTON	GOOD	ROUGH
UNDER	BUILDING	CAKE	GREAT	SAD
UP	BURN	CAMERA	GREY	SAFE
WITH	BURST	CARD	HANGING	SECRET
AS	BUSINESS	CART	HAPPY	SHORT
FOR	BUTTER	CARRIAGE	HARD	SHUT
OF	CANVAS	CAT	HEALTHY	SIMPLE
TILL	CARE	CHAIN	HIGH	SLOW
THAN	CAUSE	CHEESE	HOLLOW	SMALL
A	CHALK	CHEST	IMPORTANT	SOFT
THE	CHANCE	CHIN	KIND	SOLID
ALL	CHANGE	CHURCH	LIKE	SPECIAL
ANY	CLOTH	CIRCLE	LIVING	STRANGE
EVERY	COAL		LONG	THIN
	EDUCATION	KNEE		
	EFFECT	KNIFE		
	END	KNOT		
	ERROR	LEAF		
	EVENT	LEG		
	EXAMPLE	LIBRARY		
	EXCHANGE	LINE		
	EXISTENCE	LIP		
	EXPANSION	LOCK		
	EXPERIENCE	MAP		
	EXPERT	MATCH		
	FACT	MONKEY		
	FALL	MOON		
	FAMILY	MOUTH		
	FATHER	MUSCLE		
	FEAR	NAIL		
	FEELING	NECK		
	FICTION	NEEDLE		
	FIELD	NERVE		
	FIGHT	NET		
	FIRE	NOSE		
	FLAME	NUT		
	FLIGHT	OFFICE		
	FLOWER	ORANGE		
	FOLD	OVEN		
	FOOD	PARCEL		
	FORCE	PEN		
	FORM	PENCIL		
	FRIEND	PICTURE		
	FRONT	PIG		
	FRUIT	PIN		
	GLASS	PIPE		
	GOLD	PLANE		
	GOVERNMENT	PLATE		
	GRAIN	PLOUGH		
	GRASS	POCKET		
	GRIP	POT		
	GROUP	POTATO		
	GROWTH	PRISON		
	GUIDE	PUMP		
	HARBOUR	RAIL		
	HARMONY	RAT		
	HATE	RECEIPT		
	HEARING	RING		
	HEAT	ROD		
	HELP	ROOF		
	HISTORY	ROOT		
	HOLE	SAIL		
	METAL			
	MIDDLE			
	MILK			
	MIND			
	MINE			
	MINUTE			
	MIST			
	MONEY			
	MONTH			
	MORNING			
	MOTHER			
	MOTION			
	MOUNTAIN			
	MOVE			
	MUSIC			
	NAME			
	NATION			
	NEED			
	NEWS			
	NIGHT			
	NOISE			
	NOTE			
	NUMBER			
	OBSERVATION			
	OFFER			
	OIL			
	OPERATION			
	OPINION			
	ORDER			
	ORGANIZATION			
	ORNAMENT			
	OWNER			
	PAGE			
	PAIN			
	PAINT			
	PAPER			
	PART			
	PASTE			
	PAYMENT			
	PEACE			
	PERSON			
	PLACE			
	PLANT			
	PLAY			
	PLEASURE			
	POINT			
	POISON			
	POLISH			
	SENSE			
	SERVANT			
	SEX			
	SHADE			
	SHAKE			
	SHAME			
	SHOCK			
	SIDE			
	SIGN			
	SILK			
	SILVER			
	SISTER			
	SIZE			
	SKY			
	SLEEP			
	SLIP			
	SLOPE			
	SMASH			
	SMELL			
	SMILE			
	SMOKE			
	SNEEZE			
	SNOW			
	SOAP			
	SOCIETY			
	SON			
	SONG			
	SORT			
	SOUND			
	SOUP			
	SPACE			
	STAGE			
	START			
	STATEMENT			
	STEAM			
	STEEL			
	STEP			
	STITCH			
	STONE			
	STOP			
	STORY			
	STRETCH			
	STRUCTURE			
	SUBSTANCE			
	SUGAR			
	SUGGESTION			
	SUMMER			
	SUPPORT			

NO OTHER SOME SUCH THAT THIS

I YOU WHO AND BECAUSE BUT OR IF

THOUGH WHILE HOW WHEN WHERE WHY AGAIN EVER FAR FORWARD HERE NEAR NOW OUT STILL THEN THERE TOGETHER WELL ALMOST ENOUGH EVEN LITTLE MUCH NOT ONLY QUITE SO VERY TOMORROW YESTERDAY NORTH SOUTH EAST WEST PLEASE YES

COLOR COMFORT COMMITTEE COMPANY COMPARISON COMPETITION CONDITION CONNECTION CONTROL COOK COPPER COPY CORK COTTON COUGH COVER CRACK CREDIT CRIME CRUSH CRY CURRENT CURVE DAMAGE DANGER DAUGHTER DAY DEATH DEBT DECISION DEGREE DESIGN DESIRE DESTRUCTION DETAIL DEVELOPMENT DIGESTION DIRECTION DISCOVERY DISCUSSION DISEASE DISGUST DISTANCE DISTRIBUTION DIVISION DOUBT DRINK DRIVING DUST EARTH EDGE

HOPE HOUR HUMOR ICE IDEA IMPULSE INCREASE INDUSTRY INK INSECT INSTRUMENT INSURANCE INTEREST INVENTION IRON JELLY JOIN JOURNEY JUDGE JUMP KICK KISS KNOWLEDGE LAND LANGUAGE LAUGH LAW LEAD LEARNING LEATHER LETTER LEVEL LIFT LIGHT LIMIT LINEN LIQUID LIST LOOK LOSS LOVE MACHINE MAN MANAGER MARK MARKET MASS MEAL MEASURE MEAT MEETING MEMORY

PORTER POSITION POWDER POWER PRICE PRINT PROCESS PRODUCE PROFIT PROPERTY PROSE PROTEST PULL PUNISHMENT PURPOSE PUSH QUALITY QUESTION RAIN RANGE RATE RAY REACTION READING REASON RECORD REGRET RELATION RELIGION REPRESENTATIVE REQUEST RESPECT REST REWARD RHYTHM RICE RIVER ROAD ROLL ROOM RUB RULE RUN SALT SAND SCALE SCIENCE SEA SEAT SECRETARY SELECTION SELF

SURPRISE SWIM SYSTEM TALK TASTE TAX TEACHING TENDENCY TEST THEORY THING THOUGHT THUNDER TIME TIN TOP TOUCH TRADE TRANSPORT TRICK TROUBLE TURN TWIST UNIT USE VALUE VERSE VESSEL VIEW VOICE WALK WAR WASH WASTE WATER WAVE WAX WAY WEATHER WEEK WEIGHT WIND WINE WINTER WOMAN WOOD WOOL WORD WORK WOUND WRITING YEAR

CLOCK CLOUD COAT COLLAR COMB CORD COW CUP CURTAIN CUSHION DOG DOOR DRAIN DRAWER DRESS DROP EAR EGG ENGINE EYE FACE FARM FEATHER FINGER FISH FLAG FLOOR FLY FOOT FORK FOWL FRAME GARDEN GIRL GLOVE GOAT GUN HAIR HAMMER HAND HAT HEAD HEART HOOK HORN HORSE HOSPITAL HOUSE ISLAND JEWEL KETTLE KEY

SCHOOL SCISSORS SCREW SEED SHEEP SHELF SHIP SHIRT SHOE SKIN SKIRT SNAKE SOCK SPADE SPONGE SPOON SPRING SQUARE STAMP STAR STATION STEM STICK STOCKING STOMACH STORE STREET SUN TABLE TAIL THREAD THROAT THUMB TICKET TOE TONGUE TOOTH TOWN TRAIN TRAY TREE TROUSERS UMBRELLA WALL WATCH WHEEL WHIP WHISTLE WINDOW WING WIRE WORM

MALE MARRIED MATERIAL MEDICAL MILITARY NATURAL NECESSARY NEW NORMAL OPEN PARALLEL PAST PHYSICAL POLITICAL POOR POSSIBLE PRESENT PRIVATE PROBABLE QUICK QUIET READY RED REGULAR RESPONSIBLE RIGHT ROUND SAME SECOND SEPARATE SERIOUS SHARP SMOOTH STICKY STIFF STRAIGHT STRONG SUDDEN SWEET TALL THICK TIGHT TIRED TRUE VIOLENT WAITING WARM WET WIDE WISE YELLOW YOUNG

WHITE
WRONG

SUMMARY
OF
RULES

PLURALS IN 'S'.

DERIVATIVES IN 'ER,' 'ING,' 'ED' FROM 300 NOUNS.

ADVERBS IN 'LY' FROM QUALIFIERS

DEGREE WITH 'MORE' AND 'MOST'.

QUESTIONS BY INVERSION AND 'DO'.

OPERATORS AND PRONOUNS CONJUGATE IN FULL.

MEASUREMENT, NUMERALS, CURRENCY, CALENDAR, AND INTERNATIONAL TERMS IN ENGLISH FORM.

Figure 1.2 Basic English word list.
Source: Richards, 1943.

specifically, though, there is the issue of the degree of naturalness produced by Basic English words and their potentially many derivations, combinations and senses. Basic English, after all, is something which has to be actively learned. Teachers of English have to learn it and learn how to operate it. This indicates a degree of inherent awkwardness in relation to natural English. Also, the system is one which is clearly not well-suited for purposes of social interaction in the spoken language, not only because items such as *good-bye* or *thank you* or *Mr* and *Mrs* do not appear in Basic English, or because communication would be inevitably rather neutral or slightly formal stylistically (e.g. *put a question, have a desire for*) but also because the extent of periphrasis required can make communication a relatively clumsy affair. Additionally, there is the problem already noted that in the process of transfer to Standard English, a relatively large number of constructions which will have been created in the course of learning Basic English will have to be unlearned. The relationship of Basic English to Standard English is not unlike the relationship of the Initial Teaching Alphabet (ITA) to Standard English orthography and spelling and it can be criticized for similar reasons (see Stubbs, 1980), not least for the fact that its basis, though intuitively sound and imaginative in concept, is not notably principled in linguistic terms. As Howatt (1983, p. 254) has put it, Basic English is not basic English.

This is not to say that Basic English is not eminently 'usable' as an auxiliary language for general purposes of simplified international communication and as a practical introduction to a more standardized form of English than can be found in many intranational contexts of English usage. It is also, as Ogden and Richards themselves have amply demonstrated, a useful system for producing clear and comprehensible *written* texts, particularly where high degrees of communicative expressivity are *not* required, such as in expository texts or material with high levels of information content. It illustrates, too, the point made in Section 1.3 that grammatical words are essential and ubiquitous in the basic communication uses of a language. In terms of lexicality, however, we might note that the specification of core lexis in the sense of a set of communicatively enabling semantic primitives is no easy task. In this respect, it would be helpful to have more information in order to try to retrieve Ogden and Richards's own decisions and choices.

1.11.1 *Styles and associations*

One more example must suffice to illustrate not only the strengths and weakness, but also the inherent potential of the Basic English scheme. It involves reference to the sections above on componential and structural semantic analysis. The main example is provided in a useful examination of the issues of basic, or 'nuclear', vocabulary in Stein (1979).

Stein examines a set of lexical items relevant to the semantic features of the kinship term FEMALE and discusses the kinds of 'dimension' to the semantic features which might enable the isolation of those lexical items from the set which are more basic or 'nuclear'. Stein comes to the conclusion that the most nuclear words are *female*, *woman*, *married*, and *mother*, and argues that one key factor is that these items are basic to the kinds of paraphrase necessary for definition or explanation of related items from the set. This means that a number of these related items can be excluded from a basic word list because they are, in theory at least, substitutable. For example, *aunt* = my mother's sister; *widow* = married woman with no husband; *wife* = married woman; *sister* = my mother's daughter.

However, the isolation of such items is not without problems. The kind of periphrasis necessitated can result in varying degrees of conceptual awkwardness, ambiguity and stylistic unevenness. For example, to refer to one's wife as 'This is my married woman' can have associations in excess of the 'object' of reference itself. To refer to a sister as 'my mother's daughter' is not only conceptually clumsy, but can suggest by virtue of the 'style' of paraphrase no necessary familial or emotional ties between the speaker and the referent. It is also interesting to speculate what the stylistic effects would be of paraphrases for *divorcee* or *spinster* or *girlfriend*. (We might note here that *sister*, *female*, *woman* and *married* and their opposites are included in Basic English but that *aunt* and *wife* are excluded.) The exercise illustrates that referential meaning and structural semantic sense relations are important aspects of the acquisition of meaning by language learners. Stylistic and associative meanings in specific contexts of use are of equal importance, but it is much more difficult to convey this kind of information in word lists. Word lists can be very valuable, but however ingeniously devised, they are no more than lists of words and should be treated with caution.

1.12 Conclusion

In this introductory chapter, the following main points have been established:

1   The vocabulary of a language is not just a list of words.
2   Words *are* listed in dictionaries and in inventories for learners beginning to learn a language. But the apparent simplicity of

alphabetic ordering, on the one hand, and of the notion of 'basic
vocabulary', on the other, conceal complexities in our definition of
a 'word', in the meanings carried by and between lexical items and
in the morphological, syntactic and phonological properties of
those items.

3   Polysemy is an especially problematic feature of words in dictionaries and pedagogical word lists.

4   The structural semantic and relational properties of lexical words
(which are often important for their 'meaning'), the notion of a
basic or core vocabulary and of some words having greater lexicality than others are of considerable potential relevance and interest
for studies with an applied linguistic perspective. (This issue is taken
up further in Chapter 2.)

5   It is dangerous to pursue the meaning of a word by exclusive reference to what it denotes; stylistic and associative meanings are often
as significant. But such features emerge distinctly only when words
are examined in contexts. (Issues here are examined in Chapter 3.)

6   An analysis of words which remains at the level of the word (as
generally understood) and does not consider the role and function
of words in larger linguistic and contextual units will be
inadequate. As C.E. Bazell (1954, p. 339) has put it:

> to seek a semantic unit within the boundaries of the word
> simply because these boundaries are clearer than others, is like
> looking for a lost ball on the lawn simply because the thicket
> provides poor ground for such a search.

(Issues here are further examined in Chapters 3 and 4.)

7   Readers should, however, be able to explain and discuss the
humour of the following story with some reference to the terms
outlined in the chapter (especially Section 1.10):

> Once upon a time a lady was sitting in a train with a small dog
> upon her lap. The conductor came along, looked at the dog
> and then said, 'Madam, do you have a ticket for the dog?' 'No,'
> she answered, 'but he's just a little dog, and he's not taking up
> a seat . . .' 'I'm sorry, madam,' said the conductor, 'but rules
> are rules, and you'll have to buy a ticket for the dog.' So the
> lady paid. Meanwhile, a clergyman sitting next to the lady is
> becoming visibly uneasy and, before the conductor passes on,
> he reaches up to the luggage rack and lifts down a small box.
> He opens it, revealing to the conductor that he is transporting
> a tortoise. 'Must I buy a ticket for my tortoise?' he asks. The

conductor scrutinises the animal, scratches his head, opens his little book of rules and searches through the pages. Finally, he snaps the book shut and makes his pronouncement. 'No,' he says, 'you don't have to pay. Insects are free.'

(From a story by Jon Udall)
(See also Catford, 1983)

However, the 'establishment' of certain key points concerning what's in a word should not obscure the existence of certain problems. Two main areas of 'applied' investigation which need to be taken further involve vocabulary in language teaching and the description of the contextual associations of vocabulary. Both areas bring with them a number of questions.

For example, and in relation to points (3) and (4) above in particular, should some words be learned before others? Are some words more useful (e.g. grammatical rather than lexical words)? Can we assume that all the word-forms of a lexeme are equally valuable? How many words should make up a pedagogical word list? Should polysemic items be avoided? If they cannot be avoided (and there are many of them in a list such as Ogden and Richards's Basic English), should certain meanings be seen as more basic than others? What are the best ways of treating polysemy in a dictionary? Is this likely to be different for native speakers than for non-native speakers? Without necessarily claiming to come to easy answers to such questions, these and others raised in this chapter are taken up in Chapter 6, which is devoted to lexis in lexicography, and in Chapter 7, which is devoted to issues in the teaching and learning of vocabulary.

In relation to point (5) above, one major question is that of how such associative properties of words are to be examined in context. For example, what kinds of context need to be accessed? How can we ensure that responses to such lexical associations are not merely subjective? Is it possible to move towards methods of description which reveal more 'agreed' intersubjective assessment? Or is there a danger that the underlying meaning to a word gets lost in a welter of extra, contextual connotations? Also lexical connotations are particularly dense in literary texts. Do such texts constitute a further context and, if so, how can we appropriately account for the lexical stylistic effects they produce? These and other questions are discussed in Chapter 5, which is devoted to literary text study, and in the case studies in lexical stylistics in Chapters 8 and 9. Before this we return, however, to the issue of a basic or core vocabulary which was discussed above and which is basic to our discussion in more ways than one.

Notes

1 Items such as *I'll* and *you're* are thus one orthographic word, though they are also two words for some purposes. Note that *'ll* has achieved what is almost independent word status in contexts where neither *will* nor *shall* could be happily substituted, e.g. 'There's a bakers; we'll buy some bread'.

2 Word counts using a computer would need to program recognition that the different forms of *go* and *went* are really both word-forms of the same lexeme. For some initial discussion of these issues see Nation (1990, Chs. 1 and 2). The term lexeme (see also note 4 below) is discussed in Section 1.2.

3 It is important to recognize a distinction here between examples in which words are used and those in which a word is mentioned, that is, where it appears in citation-form. A citation-form might be used, for example, to cite an instance of grammar: 'You can't use *if* in this way'. There are, however, marginal cases where grammatical words are lexicalized such as: 'That's a very big *if*'; 'No *buts*, it has to be butter'. Generally, grammatical words and morphemes can be mentioned but not used.

4 The monosyllabic words *cats* and *shoot* have stress here by virtue of being cited (see note 3). It is also necessary to note the supporting role of second-ary stress; otherwise *pro,nunci'ation* or *transub,stantia'tion* will not rate as a word on this test. Stress, vowel quality, etc do play an important part in distinguishing different forms of the same lexeme.

5 There are problems created by calling idioms lexemes. Chief among them is that inflections operate on only certain items within the unit: in the case of *kick the bucket* it is *kick* which is inflected. The other items cannot be modified in any way. For further discussion see Chapter 3 Section 3.6 as well as Weinreich (1980) and Makkai (1972).

6 There are, of course, the generally well-cited examples of shift in personal pronouns from 'thou' to 'thee' to 'you' and, more recently, attempts not to discriminate pronominally by gender by using 'he/she' or variations thereof as well as shifts in the system Mr/Mrs/Miss/Ms.

7 Recognizing the boundaries between morphemes is no easy task. The bound morphemic affix *ty*, for example, as Bolinger (1976) points out, can exhibit *degrees* of boundary in the case of two separate words, *anxiety* and *productivity*: in the first example, 'ty' is conditioned in a way in which 'ty' in the second example is not. The morpheme in *anxiety* is more bound to the root because the divergence between *anxious* and *anxiety* is of a different order from that which obtains between *sensitive* and *sensitivity* or *productive* and *productivity*.

8 Allomorphs can also be phonologically conditioned; for example, the dif-ferent realizations of 's' in cat*s*, dog*s* and house*s* are determined by the different preceding consonants.

9 A root is also referred to as a *stem* or *base*, although, to be precise, roots are forms which are not further analysable and might be better termed minimal stems. Stems are thus the elements to which inflections can be attached. For example, *ball* is a root, but *football* or *trainer* would be stems (to which affixes are linked, e.g. *trainers*). In this instance, the root *train* would be a minimal stem. Sometimes the more general term base, which subsumes root and stem, is used.

10 For a recent survey of some relevant issues see Ilson (1985b).

11 Names are, in any case, a peculiar form of referring. Expressions such as 'Have you seen my *Jane Austen*?' or 'The *Queen Elizabeth* was launched' or the different names in different languages for towns and countries (e.g. *Peking–Beijing*; *London–Londres*; *The Netherlands–Holland* (although this example, strictly speaking, refers to different geographic areas); *Liège–Lüttich*) illustrate the relative arbitrariness involved.

12 The denotative meaning of a word is defined in Crystal (1980b) as 'the relationship between a linguistic unit (especially a lexical item) and the non-linguistic entities to which it refers – it is thus equivalent to referential meaning'. For an argument that probabilistic statements and expression of beliefs about a word's meaning capture the essential vagueness of words, see Biggs (1982).

13 Deese's informants were adults. There are, it should be noted, differences in the kinds of responses produced by adults and by children; see particularly Anglin (1970) as well as relevant material in Chapter 7 (Section 7.2). Note, too, that the response *car → accident* is a syntagmatic response. Structural semantics aims to capture paradigmatic organization of the lexicon.

14 It is commonly understood that no two words are exactly synonymous. Precise synonymy implies a rivalry in usage leading to (1) the loss from the current language of one or other term or (2) the dialectalization of one or the other term, or (3) the development of some special aspect of meaning (including the degree of intensity or the level of formality) in one or the other term (see Section 9.2). Antonyms are determined in context; we need to know the synonymic value of an item, so to speak, before we can locate its antonym. Thus, the antonym of *love* may be *hate* or *fear* or *lust*, in accordance with the particular meaning of *love* suggested by the context.

15 Hudson (1980, pp. 93–6) points out, however, that in several cases the more superordinate item is not necessarily the more generalized substitutable item in a lexical set. The most unmarked items, at least, from a cognitive point of view, are at a middle degree of generality, e.g. *house* and *horse*, respectively, may be more basic than *building* or *mammal* in contradistinction to *bungalow* and *filly*. For further discussion see Section 2.1.4.

16 Some of the uses of *white* here can, of course, be distinguished with reference to their morphological and syntactic properties. For example, *white* in *white elephant* cannot normally be inflected but *white hair* can.

17 Stein (1979) points out the difficulties of deciding on an appropriate collocation in some paraphrases. For example, *to decide* can be substituted by *make a decision, give a decision, take a decision, have a decision* all of which have distinctly different meanings.

2   The notion of core vocabulary

2.0 Core vocabularies: Some initial questions

We spent a long time deciding on a title for this book. We wanted to find a word that made it clear that this brand new book of tantalising crosswords from the Daily Telegraph was the largest and most enjoyable ever and was crammed full of puzzles.

We tried the Amplitudinous Book of Crossword Puzzles, but that didn't sound right. So then we tried monumental, towering, elephantine, thumping, Brobdingnagian, Cyclopean, megalithic. But none of them produced quite the right effect. There's really only one word that works – and so we settled on the Daily Telegraph BIG Book of Crosswords.

(*Daily Telegraph Big Book of Crosswords*,
London, The Daily Telegraph, 1983)

In the first chapter some of the main general structural properties of single words were discussed; in this chapter and with reference to contemporary English some 'basic' structural properties of the lexicon are examined. The focus here is on the notion of *core vocabulary* and, in particular, on some further dimensions for its analysis. Although detailed discussion of relevant applications is postponed until later chapters in order for attention here to be given to specific definitions of and *tests* for coreness in vocabulary, it will be seen that issues can still be focused by reference to practical contexts of vocabulary use. The reference point in this chapter will be to vocabulary learning and teaching.

Exploration of tests for core vocabulary has to begin by recognizing that there are several core vocabularies rather than a completely unitary and discrete core vocabulary. In this respect much depends, of course, on particular circumstances of communication since competent users of a language have sets of core vocabularies. Underlying these sets is a recognition (advanced in several studies) that users of a language need to have recourse to processes of simplification in order to communicate in a basic and simple fashion in specific contexts, such as in relating to children, foreigners, etc.[1] In the domain of lexis, core items are generally seen to be the most basic or simple.

It will not be surprising that language teachers should have been among the first to attempt to define a basic core vocabulary for initial language learning purposes. Such attempts range from the generally not widely used Basic English (Ogden, 1930) which was discussed in Section 1.11 to Michael West's influential controlled vocabulary lists (West, 1953) (see Section 7.9) and to more recent proposals for an international 'nuclear English' (see Quirk, 1982; Stein, 1979). Of course, such word lists (and, where appropriate, including a reduced syntax) are very basic. Indeed they serve the needs only of the most general expression and will be, according to Quirk (1982, p. 43), inevitably 'as culture-free as calculus, with no literary, aesthetic or emotional aspirations'.[2]

The topic of core vocabulary has not been systematically discussed by descriptive linguists. It has been observed that, as with other levels of language organization, there are complementary distinctions between marked and unmarked features since otherwise degrees of expressivity in lexis cannot be adequately measured by either addressor or addressee. Lyons (1977, pp. 305–11) has pointed out that certain lexical items are more central than others in accounting for how particular cultures organize their perception of the universe. Thus in the case of the following:

How big was it?	(How little was it?)
Was it very long?	(Was it very short?)
Was it this wide?	(Was it this narrow?)

the former question will contain the unmarked, the latter the marked item. Similar observations embrace gender-related semantic organization where there is male unmarkedness in a number of key generic words in English (e.g. *dog–bitch*; *lion–lioness* etc.). But beyond such subsets attempts to describe the structure of lexical word organization have been confined only to narrow ranges of words, such as those for colours (Berlin and Kay, 1969), family relationships and the like (Lyons, 1977) and have, as in the above examples, not extended far beyond a decontextualized range of word pairs.

A main aim in this chapter is to discuss whether there *is* a core vocabulary which is internal to the structure of the English language. One result of this may be to isolate some of the structural and functional features which different core vocabularies share. As already mentioned, identification of a basic underlying structure to the lexicon should aid processes of language study and teaching, particularly since vocabulary has not generally been subject to much systematic inspection. This is not to suggest that a core word, thus isolated, will automatically be a core word for language learning purposes or that a culturally or perceptually salient item will be central to the language system as a system. In extreme cases, for example, in adult–child communication, 'core' words such as *bow-wow* or *gee-gee* will be non-core according to most criteria.

It is also necessary to note that any core word derived from a description of British English will be one of 'anglicity', although it is hoped that the following proposed tests will be sufficiently principled to be generalizable to lexical systems in other Englishes or languages other than English. And finally core words here are *lexical words* as defined in Section 1.3, although this is not to say that grammatical words are not also central to the language. We have already seen that they are.

2.1 Some tests for core vocabulary

These tests are divided into two main but interrelated categories: (1) the syntactic and semantic relations of core words, (2) the neutrality of core words. Tests for the first category aim to show the extent to which some words are more tightly integrated than others into the language system; that is, they occupy places in a highly organized network of mostly structural-semantic and syntactic interrelations. The second category results from a group of tests which aim to explore the extent to which some words are more discoursally neutral than others, that is, generally they function in pragmatic contexts of language use as unmarked and non-expressive. Some of these tests involve the use of informants. It is difficult at present to develop any more reliable measures of the intersubjectively perceived values and functions of words, but such tests do at least offer, where appropriate, a stage beyond purely personal intuition. (For further discussion of the use of informants, see Chapters 8 and 9.)

2.1.1 Syntactic substitution

The basis of the following is the widely employed notion of a defining vocabulary for language learning purposes. The most widely known example of 'syntactic substitution' in a context of language study is the 2,000 word restricted defining vocabulary used for the *Longman Dictionary of Contemporary English* (*LDOCE*, 1978) (see Section 6.2).

The test demonstrates that some words can substitute for others while some words are more indispensable. Thus in the lexical set *gobble, dine, devour, eat, stuff, gormandize* each of the words could be defined using 'eat' as a basic semantic feature but it would be inaccurate to define *eat* by reference to any other of the words in the set (i.e. *dine* entails *eat* but *eat* does not entail *dine*). In this sense, *eat* is the core word and core words cannot easily be defined by words which are non-core. More empirically based versions of the test are reported in Carter (1982c). There, as one of five separate syntactic substitution tests, informants were asked to define a limited range of words in lexical sets. One group was:

> *guffaw, chuckle, giggle, laugh, jeer, snigger*

The results were that approximately 80 per cent of the informants defined the non-core words with what was the most core word from the set. Thus, *chuckle* would tend to be defined as 'laugh quietly' and *guffaw* as 'laugh in a loud and rude manner'; that is, by core verb + adverb or adverbial phrase. In the case of different parts of speech the definition assumed the following form:

```
noun       = adjective + core noun
verb       = core verb + adverb/adverbial phrase
adjective  = core adjective + adverb
```

From the following lexical sets the core word (in italics) was defined:

> perambulate, stroll, saunter, *walk*, hike, march
> podgy, corpulent, stout, *fat*, overweight, plump, obese
> weedy, emaciated, skinny, lean, *thin*, slim, slender
> adode, *house*, domicile, residence, dwelling

The test for syntactic substitution is related to description of verbs in Dixon (1971), who argues that 'nuclear' verbs have all the syntactic and semantic properties of non-nuclear verbs but that the reverse does not apply. So, for example, we have in English:

I gave it to him	I donated it to him.
I gave it him	*I donated it him.
I gave him it	*I donated him it.

Here *give* is more substitutable than related items such as *donate* or *award.* The substitutability of words may be a measure of their coreness. It relates fairly obviously to the kinds of generic or subordinate qualities a word possesses.[3]

2.1.2 Antonymy

The less 'core' a word is, the more difficult it is to find an antonym for it. So, while *fat–thin* and *laugh–cry* are antonyms, it is problematic to locate precise antonyms for items occupying different points in the semantic space created by these words. Thus *emaciated, corpulent, obese, guffaw, sob* are by this definition less core items.

2.1.3 Collocability

Collocability describes the company a word keeps; that is, single words operate in a lexical environment of other words. We often know a word like *lean* because it collocates with *meat.* And some words can only be differentiated by citing their normal collocability range; for example, strong *tea–*powerful* tea. (See Sections 3.1 ff and Firth, 1957).

This test is based on a hypothesis that the more core a lexical item is, the more partnerships it will contract with other lexical items. That is, if the words *bright, radiant, shiny, gaudy* are hypothesized as operating along a continuum from core to non-core, then one measure of the relative coreness of *bright* is that we have:

bright	sun
	light
	sky
	idea
	colours
	red, green
	future
	prospects
	child

Radiant collocates less widely. Since there are few true synonyms, it contracts its own partnerships but it is not generally able to collocate within the same range as bright. For example:

radiant	light
	smile
	sun
	flame?
	*green
	*idea
	*prospects
	future?
	*child

Gaudy is more restricted and furthermore carries marked evaluative connotations (see Section 2.1.8). So:

gaudy	colours
	*green
	dress?
	*idea
	*flame
	light?
	*future

It is important to note here the problems of adequately measuring collocability relations. What is 'normal' and possible will always be a matter of stylistic choice and relative to a dynamic and negotiable interactive context; and more precise measurement will be dependent on studies of collocational frequency still to be undertaken on a large scale. There is also a possible counterargument to such a test that we are dealing here simply with different senses. So, *shiny*, for example, creates its own collocations (e.g. *shiny nose*, *shiny coin*, *shiny car*) because it has a particular meaning which is different from *bright*, *radiant* or *gaudy*. Core words are then, according to this argument, simply polysemous words dressed up by collocation theory. However, without collocation theory and associated tests, crucial factors in the determination of stylistic effects can be too easily overlooked and such information may be just as important as basic componential semantic information, particularly in language learning contexts.

2.1.4 Extension

Stubbs (1986a) has commented insightfully on the property of extension possessed by core or what he terms 'nuclear' words. Stubbs points out that simple tests can be made by checking the number of entries which a word has in a dictionary. He notes that the *Collins English Dictionary* (*CED*) lists about 150 combinations starting with *well* and notes that the coreness of a verb like *run* is, in part at least, signalled by the way in which it is 'extended' into compounds, idioms, multi-word verbs, phrasal verbs and so on; e.g. *run-of-the-mill, run about, run up* (debts), *run down* (criticize), *on the run, in the running, run in* (a car). The same observation can be made of the property of extension possessed by the core item *bright* (Section 2.1.3) which gives us: *a bright spark, bright and early, bright and breezy, brighten up* (a house, a mood, an appearance), (look) *on the bright side, the brighter moments* (in one's life, etc.).

The test is obviously quite closely connected with the previous test and illustrates a basic point that one test or one set of uses alone is not sufficient for determining a word's coreness.

2.1.5 *Superordinateness*

This test embraces, in the same way, to a greater or lesser extent, as all the preceding tests, the notion that core words have generic rather than specific properties. As we have seen in Section 1.10, a hyponym is a kind of asymmetrical synonym. *Tulip* and *rose* are hyponyms and are linked by common inclusion under a 'generic' superordinate *flower*. Similarly, *car, lorry, coach, van, motor-scooter* all belong to a class which is able to be described generically under the label of *vehicle*.

This is not to say, however, that all superordinates will be core words or that superordinateness itself is as easy to specify as is implied by the neat but limited examples cited above or in the literature on structural semantics (e.g. do *caravan, bulldozer, bicycle* all come under *vehicle*?) In fact, as Cruse (1977) points out, as soon as such groupings of words are explored in use in communicative discourse, it is the case that superordinates are sometimes distinctly marked rather than un-marked.[4] For example, particular affective connotations are conveyed by:

Q: What are you doing?
A: I'm putting my vehicle (*car, motorbike*) away.

Or:

Q: What did you buy?
A: A piece of furniture (*a chair, a sofa*) for the front room.

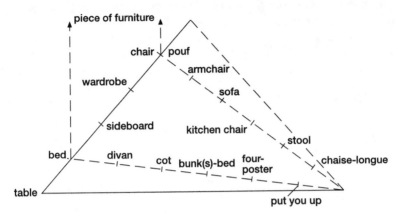

Figure 2.1 Superordinate relations: *Furniture*.

In fact, it may be more productive in certain cases to consider items which are, as it were, one stage lower in the hierarchy of generality as being more core or unmarked (see Hudson, 1980, pp. 93–6). A schema for *furniture* might be represented as in Figure 2.1 and in such a way as to suggest that items such as *bed* or *chair* may be more appropriately superordinate. However, the existence of a further word *seat* which is more widely usable in so far as it can be used in more contexts than either *chair* or *furniture* further problematizes the relations between coreness and superordinate terms. It is indisputable, however, that a close relationship exists and that a more refined version(s) of the test needs to be developed.

The remaining group of tests are more direct expressions of the discoursal or pragmatic neutrality which core words might be said to possess.

2.1.6 Culture-free

The test here is that the more core a word is the less likely it is to be restricted to culture-specific uses. Stubbs (1986a) discusses the extent to which it is rare for words in certain categories to be borrowed from one language into another. Thus, in English, while certain cooking terms or furniture terms (e.g. *pouf*, *chaise-longue*) are borrowed from French, words for basic bodily functions, natural physical phenomena, dimensions of size and shape, words for pronouns etc. will form core components in a language. Stubbs cites *sleep*, *eat*, *sun*, *earth*, *big*, *round* as culture-free in this particular sense. The notion itself must, however, be relative to particular geographical areas. For example, the dimensions of human shape conveyed by the word *thin* would be 'neutral' in most Western cultures but would be marked for certain African cultures; also, related words with positive and sex-specific associations in Western culture such as *slim* and *slender* may be reversed elsewhere. By this test *round* would be more core as a word than *thin*.

2.1.7 Summary

The test here is another informant-based one and derives from empirical literary stylistic investigation reported in Stubbs (1982). It is based on evidence that informants use a high proportion of core words when summarizing events, plots, etc. Thus, in summaries of Hemingway's short story *Cat in the Rain* informants unanimously preferred the term *cat* to alternatives available within and outside the story such as *kitty*, *pussy*, *feline*, *mog*, *il gatto* (the story is set in Italy). This seems to suggest that summaries are a genre in which it is perceived that the propositions conveyed should be represented without stylistic, rhetorical or evaluative overlay. It explains why for literary critics there will always be a 'heresy of paraphrase'. Further tests could be designed here by asking informants to summarize texts constructed from sets of lexically related items.

2.1.8 Associationism

The test here derives from work by C.E. Osgood and associates dating from the 1950s (Osgood *et al.*, 1957), and later updated (Osgood, 1976). Osgood's lexical analysis is basically scalar in orientation and allows the meanings of words to exist in semantic spaces which result from informant-based assessment along sets of semantic continua. The work can be criticized on a number of grounds but its usefulness for core lexical analysis and lexicographic work should be noted (see Carter, 1982c; 1983, and Chapter 9). In tests reported by Carter (1982c) informants were asked to rate words along scales. The scales were those revealed by Osgood as being most relevant to semantic space analysis – an *evaluation* scale and a *potency* scale and to these were added a *formality* scale. The results of the tests are interesting in themselves for word definition but for our purposes here it is not insignificant that certain words from each lexical set gravitated towards a central or neutral point in each scale. In the case of a lexical set involving *emaciated*, *skinny*, *lean*, *slender*, *slim*, *thin*, *weedy*, the word *thin* came out along formality, potency and evaluation scales around the mid-point of a 10-point cline:

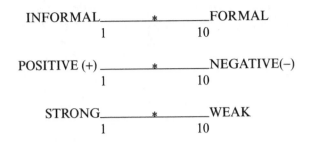

INFORMAL_____*_____FORMAL
　　　　　1　　　　　　　　10

POSITIVE (+) _____*_____NEGATIVE(−)
　　　　　1　　　　　　　　10

　　STRONG_____*_____WEAK
　　　　　1　　　　　　　　10

Other words from the set converged less consistently, thus carrying greater associations and being less neutral. *Skinny*, for example, rated low-number assessment for formality, high for evaluation and medium-number for potency. By contrast, *slim* rated medium-number for formality, low-number for evaluation and medium-number (lower than skinny) for potency. Further tests were carried out on lexical sets such as: *mean, thrifty, ungenerous, tight, stingy, parsimonious*. Other obvious candidates would be lexical sets for taboo subjects such as sex, madness or drunkenness, which possess formidably complex ranges of associative values but which also contain core items which allow relatively neutral, association-free transmission.

A neater but non-informant and thus less intersubjectively verifiable version of this test is implicit in discussion in Brown and Yule (1983, p. 125), where the same description *She's tall and thin and walks like a crane* is preceded by two contrasting evaluative comments: *I like Sally Binns* and *I can't stand Sally Binns*. Such sequencing is more permissible with core words such as *tall* and *thin* in the sentence which follows.

2.1.9 Neutral field of discourse

Core words do not normally allow us to identify from which field of discourse they have been taken. Thus the words *galley, port* and *starboard, fore* and *aft, knots* immediately recall nautical or aeronautical contexts while corresponding items like *kitchen, left* and *right, miles per hour* etc. do not. This is of course not to say that for specific purposes such nautical lexis is not core in a quite crucial sense. But for general purposes general items are such by virtue of their neutrality of field. (For comments on *mode* of discourse see Section 2.2.)

2.1.10 *Neutral tenor of discourse*

This relates quite centrally to clines of formal and informal use and is closely connected with a criterion of lexical associationism at Section 2.1.8. It comes fittingly as a final main test because, in terms of possible applications of an isolation of core vocabulary, it is an area of linguistic stylistic use where errors most frequently occur in both first- and second-language learning. Here core words will be those which emerge as neutral in formality tests. For example, of *podgy, corpulent* and *fat, fat* will in most tests emerge for most informants as the one word expressing greatest neutrality in respect of tenor of discourse. Certain sets, however, are more problematic in respect of tenor of discourse and reflect the difficulties of measuring meanings in set-related ways, the culture-inherent procedures or activities denoted as well as connoted and the obvious fact that formality in language is not a wholly lexical matter. A good illustration of these kinds of difficulties would be the words *whine, moan, grumble, complain, bellyache, whinge, lodge a complaint*. Certain items here carry associative values which one is usually happier to attribute to others rather than to oneself and no word from this particular set could be said to be culture- or value-free. This does not in itself invalidate the claim that some words are more core or neutral than others but it does clearly demonstrate that any communicative discourse in core vocabulary may also be initially restricted in terms of the semantic notions involved and would probably be a peculiarly 'detached' noncommittal activity and, for better or for worse, be as 'unliterary, unaesthetic and unemotional' as Quirk (1982) claims.

2.2 Applications and further research

Further research may allow the obvious overlap between certain tests to lead to a reduction in the number of tests; and, alternatively, new tests may be devised or improvements on the existing ones developed. Some of the problems of overlap which can occur between tests can be illustrated as follows: in tests on the set *odour, stench, aroma, smell, fragrance, stink, scent, bouquet*, items which occurred low on the association (formality) scale (test 2.1.8), for example, *stench, stink* were also non-neutral in the test for tenor of discourse 2.1.10; also *smell* and *scent* which occur regularly as **syntactic substitutions** (test 2.1.1) were the same items used by informants for summarizing discourse involving this lexical set (test 2.1.7). Tests on other groupings confirm degrees of overlap between low formality and non-neutral tenor and that syntactic substitution also works as a form of summary.[5] There are additional problems with this set in that *smell* and *scent* appear to have equal claims to being the core item but neither candidate has any marked property of extension or wide collocability relations. This leads to further key questions: are all the tests of equal *relevance* in determining coreness and should there be then a hierarchical ranking of the relative criteriality of the individual tests?

It is, however, important to underline at this point that no single test will on its own be a sufficiently systematic measure and that core vocabulary itself has no unambiguously clear boundaries. That is why it is more accurate to speak of clines and gradients and of *degrees of coreness* in words and why as a general rule it is claimed that, once the tests have been satisfactorily tested, the more tests a word passes the greater the degree of coreness it will have.

Stubbs (1986a) has pointed out a number of additional formal syntactic, phonological, graphological and morphological characteristics of core vocabulary. He suggests that core words will not normally include loan-words, words with unstable pronunciations and spellings or foreign plurals and spellings and will normally be mono- rather than polymorphemic (see also Stubbs, 1980). Stubbs also has some very detailed data based on the London–Lund corpus[6] on -*y* endings to words in relation to their expressivity and *non-coreness* (e.g. words like *podgy, tubby, snotty, stroppy, dodgy, tatty*, etc. Also noted are the wide range of -*y* endings in sets for madness: *barmy, loopy, nutty, dotty* etc., which again produce non-core items). To these observations it could be added that in British English Anglo-Saxon based words tend to be generally more core, that non-core words are less easily translatable (though the often polysemous nature of core words needs to be taken into account) and that, inflectionally, core words tend to be more irregular (perhaps reflecting that such words have sufficient centrality to resist regularization over a period of time).

Another major factor whose criteriality will always be central is that of frequency of occurrence. As Dixon (1971, p. 441) has put it:

> Nuclear words tend to have greater frequency than non-nuclear items. This is not to say that the least nuclear verb is more frequent than the most common non-nuclear-one; rather that in almost every case a certain nuclear word will have greater frequency than non-nuclear words that are related to it . . .

It is, however, a factor which requires that researchers use it only with clear qualifications and with an awareness of certain parameters to the notion of 'frequency' itself.

There is insufficient space to deal here with all the problems associated with frequency counts (for a very clear introductory account, see Nation, 1990, Chs 3 and 5) but these include some lexical features noted in foregoing discussion. Among the main problems are: the lemmatization problem (whether different meanings of the same word-form are listed), inflections and derivates of, especially, high frequency words and their place in a 'count' (e.g. *run/runner/running, critic/criticize*; do these count as one word?), and indeed the operational definition used for a 'word' (i.e. do we mean 'word' or 'lexical item'?). There are also questions to be raised about the optimum size of a corpus. These range from the half million words of the Lund corpus used as a basis for the *A Grammar of Contemporary English* (Quirk *et al.*, 1972) to the 320 million words (in 1997) of the COBUILD corpus (now called The Bank of English) held at Birmingham University (see Section 6.6.1). There are also important questions concerning the extent of the database for corpora, the range and type of sources used and the even more crucial issue of the relationship between spoken and written *modes* of discourse. These last issues lead directly into the need to obtain not simply frequency counts but accurate measures of range, distribution and coverage (see Mackey and Savard, 1967 for useful pedagogical insights in this area). Core words will have to be words of high frequency but they will also need to have an evenness of range and coverage of text in the broadest sense of the term: that is, they will have to be measured as being evenly distributed over a range of different spoken and written text. See also Carroll *et al.* (1971) for a number of useful points concerning the correlation between frequency and range and further discussion of computer corpora in Sections 6.6 and 7.16. And, finally, we should recognize that the above tests are linguistic tests with a focus on linguistic data even where informants' responses are utilized. The selective focus excludes the interesting potential for determining coreness with reference to more psycholinguistically oriented tests which measure, for example, the perceptual salience of some words over others (see Rosch, 1973) or user's own perceptions of the relative 'utility' of lexical items (see Richards, 1970).

2.3 Conclusion

It is clear from the above discussion that the notion of core vocabulary needs to be examined with some caution. The example of superordinate relations (Section 2.2.6) illustrates that what may be 'core' in the internal structure of the language is not automatically perceived as core by users of the language. A similar example may apply in language acquisition where learners, including young children learning their mother tongue, may acquire 'core' words which are of general utility to them or which are more perceptually available. It is also clear that frequency is no guarantee of coreness. And we should note further that if Basic English (see Section 1.11) is to be replaced by a list of words which has been more rigorously defined in linguistic terms then that will in turn not necessarily constitute a core list for pedagogical purposes. One final note of caution is that the more formal of the tests discussed in this chapter illustrate, notably in the case of polysemic words, that isolation of a core vocabulary does not lead to a definition of what are the core meanings.

However, the distinction between core and non-core vocabulary, though never a hard and fast one, is an important feature of the basic structure of the lexicon of a language. Although the notion still requires more extensive 'testing', it is important to recognize the significance of core vocabulary because it cuts across and to an extent incorporates other binary structuring categories such as spoken and written, grammatical and lexical or marked and unmarked. It is also a potentially useful framework for discussing stylistic and expressive effects in vocabulary use. And it creates a basis for discussion of what is 'basic' in vocabulary which makes it significant in a number of contexts of application. Inspection of the index to this book shows how extensively the notion is used in subsequent chapters.

Core vocabulary is discussed extensively in Chapter 7 in relation to the teaching of vocabulary and the construction of pedagogical word lists. In Chapter 4 its potential usefulness for illustrating the deployment of 'expressive' lexis in newspaper reports is highlighted; and in Chapter 9 reference to core vocabulary is central to an argument that style levels in dictionaries can be better described if some lexical entries are defined around core words.

Notes

1 Such sets include categories for 'child talk', 'motherese', 'foreigner talk' and processes of pidginization (see Blum and Levenston, 1978; 1979, for useful accounts of what can be derived from such studies for second-language teaching and learning). There is also a body of work on acquisition order in first language lexical development (see reviews in Elliot, 1981; Clark, 1993), psycholinguistic studies of memorization and association in relation to the ease or difficulty of lexical recall of core vocabulary (Anglin 1970; Craik and Lockhart, 1972; Lehrer, 1974a; and review by Meara, 1980) as well as attempts in some anthropological–linguistic studies to isolate core or 'nuclear' vocabulary which has cultural or cross-cultural salience (Dixon,

1971; Hale, 1971). Also of significance here is Kellerman's work on *transferability* in which native speaker's own perceptions of the structural core of their language are examined in terms of their ease of transfer to a given second language or L2 (Kellerman, 1977; 1983; Jordens and Kellerman, 1981). Kellerman (1983, p.117) has defined 'transferability' as follows:

> Transferability is to be seen as a theoretical notion, which derives from native speakers' own perception of the structure of their language. If a feature is perceived as infrequent, irregular, semantically or structurally opaque, or in any other way exceptional, what we could in other words call 'psycho-linguistically marked' then its transferability will be inversely proportional to its degree of markedness. Transferability is not itself a predictor of performance but is one of the determinants of whether an L1 structure will be treated as *language-specific* (not transferable to a given L2) or *language-neutral* (that is, transferable to a given L2).

Kellerman's use of terms such as markedness and language-neutrality compare interestingly with definitions in Section 2.1.8. Comparison also underscores the main point made in Section 2.2 concerning the relativity of a notion of coreness.

2 Within the domain of language study and teaching, observations concerning the degrees and types of simplification involved are common: these include descriptions of simplified language used for non-technical explanations in technical contexts (Hutchinson and Waters, 1981; Mountford, 1976; Widdowson's 'procedural vocabulary', Widdowson, 1983, pp. 92–5); the language used for written précis or summaries (Stubbs, 1982) and 'neutral', non-committal communication in interactive exchanges (Cruse, 1977, 1986; McCarthy, 1984a).

3 It is important to recognize that *syntactic* criteria cannot usually exist separately from *semantic* criteria. For example, on purely *syntactic* grounds *steal* may be more versatile or core than *rob*:

> He stole a book.
> He robbed a bank.
> He stole an apple from the garden.
> *He robbed £100 from a bank.
> Go on! Steal me an apple.
> *Go on! Rob me an old lady.

But we do have.

> He robbed an old lady.
> *He stole an old lady.

where *steal* cannot take an animate object and is thus, semantically at least, less core. See also discussion in Sections 3.2–3.5.

4 Space precludes here detailed exemplification of what McCarthy (1984a) terms 'the potential of lexical relations for the realization of important functions such as concurrence, divergence, topic-change, transaction-closing, etc ... the communicative effects of such relations as synonymy, antonymy and hyponymy across sentence, conversation and discourse boundaries'. As McCarthy points out, much depends here on interlocutors' perception of 'the

coreness of certain items, the marked nature of questions containing non-core items, the appreciation of relations of scale and intensity between items'. Several issues here are touched on in this paper but a separate paper would be needed to explore the role of core vocabulary in spoken discourse and conversation analysis and point to areas for further research relevant to vocabulary teaching. See Section 4.6 for further discussion of core lexis and spoken discourse, as well as McCarthy (1988).

5 There is a related problem, too, in that the more formal items on association tests (2.1.8) are sometimes the most restricted to a particular field of discourse (test 2.1.9); for example, *bouquet* (from the set at 2.2), or *inebriated* (from a set of words for drunkenness). Sometimes, though, field-restricted specialist items are not formal and occur widely (for example, *insane*), losing in the process the strict denotative sense of their core meaning (e.g. 'this weather is *insane*').

6 Corpora are collections of naturally occurring language data, usually in computer-readable form and often comprising millions of words, which are now used extensively for purposes of language description and teaching. See Section 6.6.

3 Words and Patterns

3.0 Introduction: Ways with words

A: Caught you! Eating cream cakes again.

B: Yes.

A: You'll be too fat to play in the game.

B: *Fat* is not the word I'd use. I'm just pleasantly plump.

A: Well, you've got a pleasantly plump chance of playing if you carry on eating like that.

(Adapted from 'Will of the Wisp' cartoon)

In the previous two chapters the emphasis has been for the most part on the character of lexical items as single words. The structure of words and the structural relations between words have been examined and, in the discussion of core vocabulary, the marked and unmarked nature of lexical items (again mostly orthographic 'words') has been recognized. But there has been so far only cursory inspection of levels of organization beyond that of single words and, although some stylistic and pragmatic functions of core vocabulary have been explored, little attention has been given to lexis in contexts of use. This chapter is devoted to lexical patterning and includes discussion of collocation, idiomaticity and the complex issue of fixed expressions.

The study of such patterning has not been widely undertaken by linguists, although some pioneering research exists in an East European tradition. The most innovative work by British linguists has been achieved in the construction of learner's dictionaries, especially dictionaries of idioms. Increased discussion of the topic of words and their patterns is important for applied linguistics and, to demonstrate its relevance, this section ends with a brief analysis of mistakes made by second- and foreign-language learners in the use of words in different kinds of lexical patterns. Discussion of lexis in use in the more extended contexts of naturally occurring texts and discourses occurs in Chapter 4. Together, this chapter and the next are progressively concerned with more expressive and communicative uses of vocabulary and involve as it were a gradual turn from locating a *form* of words to discovering a *way* with words.

3.1 Collocation: Lexis as a level

Collocation is a term used to describe a group of words which occur repeatedly in a language. These patterns of co-occurrence can be ***grammatical*** in that they result primarily from syntactic dependencies or they can be ***lexical*** in that, although syntactic relationships are involved, the patterns result from the fact that in a given linguistic environment certain lexical items will co-occur. Studies of collocation in English have tended to be within two distinct traditions: one oriented towards specifically grammatical and one towards specifically lexical patterning. The former has tended to result in studies which have been of distinct value to language learners and have to an extent emerged from the demands of particular pedagogic projects. Work in this tradition is examined in Section 3.5. We shall begin by examining notions of collocability which are lexical in that they also presuppose the operation of lexis as an independent linguistic level. Such work aims to describe the lexical patterning of texts and has considerable potential for future computerized lexical research. But separate discussion of these two traditions should not be taken to imply that collocation of lexical items can be neatly subdivided nor that there can or should not be any categorical overlap in the kinds of analysis produced.

Linguists working in the tradition of ***lexical collocation*** have produced seminal studies which have contributed substantially to our understanding of lexis. Such work has often been within a broad tradition of systemic linguistics (see Berry, 1977 on 'levels' and 'links'). For example, Halliday (1966), Sinclair (1966), Sinclair *et al.* (1970), Sinclair and Jones (1974) and, more recently, Hasan (1987) have been interested in describing 'lexis as most delicate grammar'. Their starting point is to seek to study lexis in the same way as grammar, that is, with reference to patterns of chain (syntagmatic axis) and choice (paradigmatic axis). But the relation to grammar is an analogical one; the aim is to examine lexis as a linguistic level in parallel with and overlapping grammar but as a level which is separate and independent. This can be schematized as in Table 3.1.

The independence of the lexical level is not total but the figure illustrates the simultaneous patterns realized by a stretch of language. The

Table 3.1 Lexis as a linguistic level

	chain	choice
grammar	structure	system
lexis	collocation	set

kinds of questions asked about collocations and 'sets' (see Section 3.2) by linguists working within the lexical-collocation tradition are important ones, especially for the study of lexis in larger stretches of text. They are interested in the company words keep and in the places where they keep such company.

Theoretically, it is possible for any lexical item of English to co-occur or 'keep company' with any other lexical item. However, for any particular lexical item X there are certain other items which have a high probability of being found near X. For instance, we might expect *snow* to have a high probability of co-occurrence with *block, road, fall, winter, cold*, etc. but a low probability of co-occurrence with *cider, apple, dog*, etc. The total list of words which are found to collocate with a particular lexical item X is called the **cluster** of X. Some members of the cluster will be more central than others, in that their probability of co-occurrence with X is high.

If we investigate the collocational behaviour of other lexical items, say Y and Z, within the cluster of an item X, then it is probable that the clusters of Y and Z will contain not only X, but also many of the items within the cluster of X. When two or more clusters have a high proportion of items in common, then, we can amalgamate the clusters to form a **lexical set**. For example, if we investigated the behaviour of the lexical item *fishing*, we should probably find that *line, rod, bait, reel, net* are important members of the cluster of *fishing*. If we also found that *fishing, net, rod, reel* were members of the cluster of *bait*, and so on, we should be justified in setting up a lexical set containing the items *fishing, net, rod, reel, line, bait*. However, compared with the analysis of grammatical relations or with what we shall see below of grammatical collocation, where patterns are more fixed and deterministic, it is clear that we are dealing here with patterns which are probabilistic.

The fact that the patterns are probabilistic raises some methodological problems. For example, a fundamental difficulty in 'measuring' collocational relations is that of deciding the maximum distance between items that can be said to be collocating. The solution generally adopted has been a relatively arbitrary and *ad hoc* one of restricting the collocating items to a *span* of a fixed number of words on either side of the specified focal word or *node* whose patterning is being investigated. It is also difficult, however, appropriately to demarcate what might be the upper limit of a lexical unit and to decide whether a larger unit could itself be the limit of the collocational relationship. In Sinclair (1966) and Sinclair *et al.* (1970) the aim was to study large quantities of text in order to focus in a statistically significant way on the company kept by particular words and for the 'strength' and 'weakness' of partnerships to be expressed in terms of percentile frequencies of co-occurrence. But not enough data could be processed for either a wide range of lexical collocational probabilities or interesting lexical sets to be described. In the intervening years the advent of micro-chip technology and advances in data-processing by computational linguists have brought the possibilities of such description considerably closer (see especially Section 6.6).

3.2 Sets and fields

Analysts in the tradition of systemic linguistics such as Halliday and Sinclair represent the general view of those interested specifically in what we have termed **lexical collocation**: that we choose lexical items from **lexical sets** rather as we choose types of grammatical items from grammatical systems to build up grammatical structures (see Table 3.1). Words are grouped into lexical sets as a series of semantically related options from which a coherent text can be constructed. Thus, *stag*, *geometry* and *innocence* would be unlikely to co-occur in a lexical set whereas *thirst*, *drink*, *beer* would be more likely to. The existence of lexical sets enables us to see the structure of the lexicon as consisting of clusterings into patterns of reference usually related to a single topic. Such patterns are obviously not of such an exclusive character that an item can belong to one set and one set only. Sets overlap and intersect with each other in such a way that one and the same item may occur in different axes of meaning. The notion of lexical set is best illustrated and examined with particular reference to a specific field.

By *field* (or *field of discourse*) is meant the particular activity, cultural feature, social institution or topic for which a particular set of ideationally related lexical items is often evolved or adapted. Air transport, for example, constitutes a field with special items such as *flight*, *take-off*, *runway*, *check in*, etc. Each field usually has a specialized, topic-related vocabulary (for preliminary discussion see Section 2.1.9) some items of which may turn up in other fields with different meanings (and often in different grammatical collocations – see Section 3.5): for example, *wings* in air transport and in theatrical parlance; *lock* in the field of river or canal transport and in the language of security. The lexicon of fields consists of:

1   nouns labelling technical features – artefacts, equipment, structures, etc.
2   verbs identifying and distinguishing between processes, types of event, methods, etc.
3   adjectives and adverbs indicating conventional properties of an artefact, process, structure, etc. (e.g. in cookery, good pastry is said to be *light*; a very full tablespoon is a *heaped* tablespoon; stock is left to simmer *gently*, etc.)
4   phrases and conventional collocations that may expand, modify or combine any of the above functions (e.g. *boil over, bring to the boil*)

It is common (and indeed in the nature of language) for figurative extensions and transfers of meaning to be made from familiar fields of discourse into the general stock of usage. This results partly in common metaphors (e.g. 'I sat and seethed', 'I was in a seething temper', 'My temper boiled over', 'I couldn't keep the lid on my temper') and partly in the development of clichés, idioms and proverbs (e.g. 'A watched pot never boils').

Here is one field of discourse – that of *cookery* – and a few items of its vocabulary. These items are grouped according to: (1) names of artefacts, etc., (2) names of processes, events, etc., (3) indications of characteristics, qualities or properties, (4) common phrases and collocations, (5) figurative extensions. Note, however, that these groupings are intuitive and await more statistically significant measurement in a computational study.

COOKERY
1   *Artefacts*, etc.
     pot, stock-pot, kettle, pan, frying pan, skillet, saucepan, dish, jug, bowl, ladle, (carving/bread) knife, (carving) fork, steel, spoon, fish-slice, rolling pin, bread board, cooker.
2   *Processes*, etc.
     boil, roast, bake, brew, stew, braise, simmer, poach, grill, seal, glaze, prick, brown.
     cut, dice, slice, chop, carve, shred, peel, skin, portion, mix, stir, beat, whip, fold, pour, strain.
3   *Properties*, etc.
     tender (meat)/tough, stringy; fresh (fish, bread, butter, cheese,

milk)/stale (fish, bread, cheese); rancid (butter); sour (milk, cream); curdled (milk); off (meat, fish, butter, cheese, milk); turned (milk); light (pastry, bread, cake)/heavy, soggy, doughy, leathery; crisp (toast, biscuits)/soggy, chewy; flaky (pastry); welldone, underdone, rare (steak); hard-boiled, soft-boiled (eggs).

4   *Phrases, Collocations*, etc.
boil over, on the boil, off the boil, come (bring) to the boil, brew tea (beer, cider, etc.), let the tea brew (draw), the tea is stewed, carve a joint (chicken, turkey, etc.), bake bread, bake a cake, fry fish, boil eggs, toast bread, dice carrots (and other 'solid' vegetables), chop onions (parsley, all vegetables or foodstuffs with suitably resistant texture), slice meat, bread, tomatoes (and other 'softish' substances), shred cabbage, skin onions, shell nuts (also peas), peel and portion fruit, ladle out, spoon out, strain off, leave to set, leave to simmer (liquids).

5   *Figurative Extensions*
   (a) *Proverbs, common sayings, idioms*: out of the frying pan into the fire, what's sauce for the goose is sauce for the gander, the pot calling the kettle black, to stew in one's own juice, take it with a pinch of salt, neither fish, flesh, nor fowl, too many cooks spoil the broth, hunger is the best sauce, in the soup, a pinch of salt, a taste of one's own gruel.
   (b) *Metaphor and slang:* 'I was boiling/seething', 'She told me to simmer down', 'He came off the boil after a while' (= relapse into a calmer temper), 'Jack likes to stir things up' (= make trouble), 'There's trouble brewing' (= in the process of being made), 'This place is an oven' (= very hot), 'They grilled him for several hours' (= interrogated very closely), 'My boss roasted me/gave me a roasting' (= reprimanded severely), 'C's speech was a large helping of rhetoric with a tiny pinch of common sense' ('helping' and 'pinch' = large and small quantities of anything), 'I went through a gruelling time in hospital' (= physically painful, taxing or exhausting). Gruel, a kind of thin porridge, was the traditional diet of prisoners. In present-day criminal slang, *porridge* = prison, a prison sentence, cf. *to do one's porridge, to serve prison* = to serve a prison sentence; earlier *to stir one's porridge*, whence *stir* (= prison), *in stir* (in prison).

A more detailed version of a *cookery* field is worked out in Lehrer (1974b).

3.3 Patterns, ranges and restrictions

Linguists studying grammatical relations in language are concerned primarily with the establishment and description of allowed patterns and with the rejection of whatever falls outside these patterns. In the case of lexis, however, as McIntosh (1966) points out, the underlying patterns which are relevant are of a quite different order from grammatical patterning. For this phenomenon McIntosh suggests that the term 'range' is more applicable. Certainly it is clear that some words have different ranges from others: for example, items to do with the inferior qualities of food have restrictive ranges. *Putrid, rotten, rancid* and *addled* are all virtually synonymous but *putrid* collocates with fish, *rancid* with butter, oil, lard, etc., *addled* is confined only to eggs, while *rotten* can collocate with fish and eggs but also specifically with fruit. *Friendly* and *amicable* are synonyms (though the latter is more formal) but only *amicable* is acceptable in the sentence *The divorce was an amicable one.* On the other hand, some evaluative adjectives have a much wider range and, compared with putrid, rotten, etc., are more generally interchangeable: for example, *gruesome food, party, weather*, etc.; *awful dress, weather, performance, film*, etc.; *exciting team, food, film*, etc. Lying between such groupings are words which can collocate widely but which are normally restricted to certain partners and thus in certain lexical contexts cannot be readily substituted: for example, *soft, mild* and *gentle* can all collocate with *voice, breeze, rebuke* or *soap* but each word has exclusive collocations: *soft water, soft ground, soft drink; mild beer, mild steel; gentle slope*, etc. (see also Mitchell, 1971, pp. 154–5).[1]

The description of restrictions on the range of collocability of particular items can provide a way of differentiating words from each other. The study of combinational or **selection restrictions** is not new. Within lexical semantics the theory of componential analysis (see Section 1.9) developed the analysis of word meanings into sets of semantic features or components such as ANIMATE, NON-HUMAN, FEMALE, QUADRUPED and provided a way of distinguishing semantic incompatibility. For example, *the stream danced* contains a combination of features which are not normally allowed: that is, a verb which normally takes an animate subject is assigned a non-animate one. But the limited number of semantic components made available by analysts and the arbitrary combination of items in some contexts make such an account of selection restrictions a not altogether satisfactory one. For example, there appears to be no semantic explanation for the collocation of *green* (as opposed to *yellow* or *blue*) with *envy*, or of *mild* (as opposed to *soft* or *gentle*) with *steel*. We should also note that not all semantically related lexical items have the same ranges. Consider the following generally synonymous words: *obese, fat, plump stout*. If we take the most familiar of these *fat* it will appear that it can enter into quite a wide range of collocations: for example, *fat man, fat woman, fat belly, fat baby, fat chicken, fat salary, fat wad of notes, fat book*. Moving to *plump*, we find the same range of collocations will admit *plump man, plump woman, plump belly, plump baby* and *plump chicken*, but not *plump salary, plump wad of notes* and *plump book*. *Stout* permits *stout man* and *stout woman*, but not *stout baby, stout chicken, stout wad of notes* or *stout book*; *stout belly* is doubtful. On the other hand, there are certain collocations, for example *stout construction, stout defence, stout fellow* (= 'reliable man' not 'fat man'), which will not admit *fat* or *plump*. Finally, *obese* is restricted to *man, woman* and *belly*, and will not admit *babies, chickens, salaries, books*, etc. On the showing of our example, therefore, *obese* appears to be rather restricted in range while the range of *fat* is much wider. As we have seen in Section 2.1.1 these properties of *fat* mean that by this criterion it is a core word and, by contrast, *plump, stout* and *obese* are less core. We should also note that synonymic relations between words can be usefully distinguished with reference to the different collocational ranges of the synonyms involved.

It is important, too, to note that collocational ranges are not fixed to the same degree as grammatical patterns; for example, there are what McIntosh terms 'range-extending tendencies' in which new collocates can be formed because one word lends itself to such formation (e.g. the lexical item *key* which has recently considerably extended its range: *key move, component, policy, book*, etc., or *fun* which follows the pattern of *key* in *fun size, fun book, fun relationship*, etc.).

The examination of collocational ranges of items begins where semantic analysis of selection restrictions leaves off. Although accurate description (especially indication of relative strengths and weaknesses of combination) depends on extensive text-processing, and although many such patterns are grammatically as well as lexically determined, this aspect of collocation is a valuable and revealing one and, as we shall see below in Sections 3.10 and 7.12, is one of particular relevance to vocabulary in language teaching.

3.4 Collocation and style

McIntosh (1966, p.193), in his article 'Patterns and ranges' referred to above, offers the following framework for the determination of style in language:

There is the possibility of four obviously distinct stylistic modes: normal collocations and normal grammar, unusual collocations and normal grammar, normal collocations and unusual grammar, unusual collocations and unusual grammar.

As McIntosh admits, such classification is rather crude but it does supply us with a useful framework. At either end of the scale it is self-evident that we run the risk of producing language which is too familiar and thus banal (normal collocations and normal grammar, e.g. *This is guaranteed to meet your special requirements*) or which is unfamiliar and thus indecipherable (unusual collocations and unusual grammar. e.g. *The ants with and swore the bald-headed carpet-sweeper*). Between these two extremes is a dimension in which more individual or creative effects can be produced. But no two people share the same experience or set of associations so there must be a continual appeal to a shared norm of one sort or another or communication becomes impossible. Hence lexical associations which are too private or too individual often fail to meet this code of generality. Although 'norms' will vary from one context to another and will allow the generation of in-group languages or 'anti-languages' (Halliday, 1978) (see also Section 4.10) we are talking here of standard language norms of the kind which might, for example, be described in a dictionary. Of course, in such cases of styles of collocation, questions of acceptability are much more difficult to determine than the decision over what is grammatical or ungrammatical. Collocational acceptability can be analysed using techniques of informant analysis in which the intersubjective intuitions of groups of native-language speakers are statistically measured and a line drawn between what can be generally allowed and what cannot. As demonstrated in Chapters 8 and 9, these techniques can be useful for the analysis and interpretation of collocational relations in a context such as that of poetry or that of describing the style values of lexical items for lexicographic purposes.

3.5 Collocation and grammar

Not all linguists believe that the study of collocation can be made largely without reference to syntactic function.[2] The second main tradition in the study of collocation is that which views lexical and syntactic patterning as distinct but *interrelated* levels of structure. The study of lexical collocations, based on an attempt to establish lexis as an independent and separate linguistic level, has tended to concentrate on linear, syntagmatic co-occurrence of items and has not included the syntactic and semantic statements that are often essential in a treatment of collocations. A number of examples can be cited in support of this position. One of them is given by Greenbaum (1970, p.11):

A serious disadvantage of a purely item-oriented approach to the study of collocations is that it obscures syntactic restrictions on collocations. For example, *much* collocates with a preceding verb *like* in negative sentences but not in affirmative sentences. We can therefore say:

I don't *like* him *much*

but not

* I like him much

However, this last sentence becomes perfectly acceptable if *much* is premodified, e.g.:

$$\text{I like him} \begin{cases} \text{very} \\ \text{too much} \\ \text{so} \end{cases}$$

Positional restrictions also apply. We can say:

Some people *much prefer* wine

even though the sentence is in the affirmative. Yet *much* and *prefer* do not collocate if the intensifier is transposed to the end of the sentence:

* Some people prefer wine much

As Mitchell (1971) also puts it: 'Lexical particularities are considered to derive their formal meaning not only from contextual extension of a lexical kind but also from the generalised grammatical patterns within which they appear.'

The term given to the specifically grammatical relations along the syntagm is **colligation.** Take the example of the word *consent*. In explaining the way this word is used in English we would need to supply not only information concerning its lexical collocates (e.g. *mutual, common*), lexico-grammatical information (e.g. that it occurs in adverbial phrases headed by the preposition *by: by mutual consent*; that it collocates with and is a direct object for certain verbs: *give consent, offer consent*), but also that it is a member of a class of verbs which is followed by the preposition *to* and another verbal or nominal group (e.g. 'they gave their consent *to* their daughter's marriage'; 'he finally consented *to* go'). Similarly, in its syntactic role as a noun then the same preposition and string follows. The verb *consent* can thus be said to be in colligation with a complement construction *to* + infinitive and thus cannot co-occur with the construction + *-ing* form of a verb (e.g. **He consented going*). Clearly, these different syntagmatic relations are interdependent but the meaning of a 'word' cannot really be adequately given without the fullest possible information concerning the place the word occupies and the contrasts it develops within a network of differential relations which includes patterns and ranges and the syntactic patterns which operate within particular ranges.

Of course, grammatical collocations can involve a range of different syntactic patterns. Benson (1985) defines grammatical collocation as a recurrent combination of a dominant word (verb, noun, adjective) followed by a 'grammatical' word, typically a preposition: e.g. *abide by* (verb and preposition); *abstain from* (verb and preposition); *admiration for* (noun and preposition); *adjacent to* (adjective and preposition); *aghast at* (adjective and preposition). Benson also uses the term 'lexical collocation' in a different sense to its use above; that is, to refer to a partnership of 'two "equal" lexical components': for example, adjective and noun combinations; noun and verb combinations. At the same time he argues for more extensive representation in dictionaries of such collocations and points to pioneering lexicographic work in this area by East European linguists and lexicographers such as Apresyan *et al.* (1969).

It is important, too, that lexical sets be differentiated with reference to the different syntactic behaviour of their constituent items. For example, if we take the item *needle* and examine its collocational relationships in terms of other lexical items we might find that the cluster of *needle* includes items such as *cotton, thread, cloth, material, eye, sew* and *pin*; also *dentist, injection* and *anaesthetic*. Further work would probably show that *needle, cotton, thread, cloth, material, eye, sew, pin* and certain others form a lexical set, and that *needle, dentist, injection, anaesthetic*, etc. form another set. We could then postulate the existence of two lexical items, *needle*[1] and *needle*[2]. We might also find, however, that *needle* collocates with *pin, pain, arm, leg* and *rub*, and that in such collocations there is a regular association of *needle* and *pin* in the form of *pins and needles*. We should then be justified in suggesting that *pins and needles* is one single lexical item, whose cluster is different from the cluster of the separate lexical items *pin* and *needle*. But we must also note the danger in bringing items together in a set without due recognition of their syntactic patterning. For example, *needle and thread* are syntagmatically related in a fixed pattern in a way that *cloth* and *material* are not. And *pins and needles* would be a striking item in any corpus by virtue of its grammatical oddness (non-reversible; always plural) and its constant collocability with the verbs *get* and *have.*

This last example also illustrates the important point that a lexical item need not show a one-to-one correspondence with any particular grammatical unit, although we can say that the most usual situation is for the lexical item to be co-extensive with the orthographic word. In the following utterances, each of the italicized parts could be considered a single lexical item, on the basis of its distinctive collocational properties:

(1) This *horse* has won the Derby three times.
(2) Mr Benn is *a dark horse.*
(3) They are *putting the cart before the horse* in trying to control wages rather than prices.

In (1) the lexical item *horse* is co-extensive with a grammatical word, in (2) *a dark horse* is co-extensive with a group, and in (3) *putting the cart before the horse* is not co-extensive with any grammatical unit, being more than a group but less than a clause but allowing inflectional marking of the verb *put.*

Finally, pedagogical treatments of collocations, at least, would be seriously lacking if grammatical patterning were not included alongside lexical patterning and if such elementary distinctions were not made between them. A main difficulty in this interaction between lexis and grammar is, as we have seen, one of precisely and systematically accounting for the different degrees of fixity in the patterning. Some items enter into tight grammatical patterns and into relatively narrow collocational ranges; others into looser configurations. It is the aim of the next three sections to try to account for such relations. It is an area of some complexity for the language learner and for the mediating role occupied by the applied linguist between linguistic analysis and pedagogical presentation.

3.6 Semantic prosodies: Lexis into grammar into meaning

> ... words enter into meaningful relations with other words around them, and yet all our current descriptions marginalise this massive contribution to meaning. The main reason for this marginalisation is that grammars are always given priority and grammars barricade themselves against individual patterns of words.
>
> (Sinclair, 1996, pp. 76–7)

In the above section it was commented that words enter into grammatical patterns as well into patterns which are primarily lexical. What studies of such patterns have lacked is a sufficiently systematic description both of the patterns and of the meanings created by the choice of one pattern rather than another. In recent years computational analyses of language corpora have begun to point to new methods and techniques of description.

In the history of linguistics in this century linguists have experienced difficulties in linking form and meaning, with many in the transformational generative tradition disavowing any connection between formal accounts of syntactic structure and theories of meaning. Throughout the history of language study there has also been an unchallenged acceptance of the individual, independent word as the repository of meaning.

As we have seen in Sections 3.1–3.4 linguists such as Firth, Halliday and Sinclair have taken a consistently different line and argued that collocational and colligational patterns are meaning-creating, that there are crucial interdependencies between grammar, lexis and semantics and that the preoccupation of many linguists with the formal properties of grammar runs constant risks of ignoring lexis and lexico-grammar as the doorway to the creation of meanings. More fundamentally, though, it is only through access to large-scale corpora that such descriptions of meaning can be made possible:

> ... in all cases examined so far, each meaning can be associated with a distinct formal patterning ... There is ultimately no distinction between form and meaning ... [The] meaning affects the structure and this is ... the principal observation of corpus linguistics in the last decade.
>
> (Sinclair, 1991, pp. 6–7)

An apparently straightforward example of Sinclair's point is the word *eye*, which behaves differently if it is in singular or plural form. The plural patterns with adjectives such as *blue, attractive, beady* and *dishonest*; in singular form, however, the word *eye* is only rarely used to refer to the visual organ (except when there is an injury, or during an optical test). More commonly, both singular and plural forms are used metaphorically and in different fixed phrases such as *rolling his eyes, all eyes will be on the match, keep an eye on sth* or *turn a blind eye.* Thus, not only different words but different grammatical forms of the same word have different distributions and meanings.

Corpus data can also identify the co-occurence of particular words with particular grammatical patterns. For example, Francis (1994) points out that two verbs *find* and *make* occur in 98 per cent of cases in the extraposed structure with *it* in clauses such as: *I find it amusing that he never replies to my faxes, Can you make it more exciting?* and *I owed it to you that I passed the final exam.*

Grammars, which until recently have not made extensive reference to corpus data or have not had access to the kind of distributional analysis afforded by computer-assisted techniques, have not tended to give such information. And, conversely, dictionaries, which have tended to concentrate on the unit of the single word, have ignored the kinds of patterns which result when a word forms different syntactic partnerships. For example, Sinclair (1991, pp. 67ff) notes with reference to a multi-million-word corpus that the verb *set* occurs much more commonly in the form *set* than in other morphologies such as *sets* or *setting* and that in phrasal-verb form *set in* has a negative semantic prosody (Louw, 1993) in so far as the meaning created by the phrasal verb is almost exclusively negative, and the noun which accompanies it is frequently an abstract noun: for example, *Disillusionment with the government's policies has set in; Now the rot's set in* and *A state of moral decay set in without anyone really noticing it.*

In a paper on patterns of grammar and vocabulary Hunston, Francis and Manning (1997) basing their evidence on a 320 million word corpus at the University of Birmingham (the COBUILD Bank of English; see Section 6.6.1) assert:

> There are two main points about patterns to be made: firstly, that all words can be described in terms of patterns; secondly, that words which share patterns, share meanings.
>
> (Hunston, Francis and Manning, 1997, p. 209)

In a volume entitled *Grammar Patterns: 1. Verbs* (COBUILD, 1996) (a work involving Francis and Hunston) a grammar of verbs is presented (mainly for learners of English) in groups which share the same pattern and therefore frequently the same or a closely related meaning. For example, about 20 verbs in English have the pattern '*V + by + -ing*', where the verb is followed by the preposition *by* and an *-ing* clause. Most of the verbs in this group fall into two main groups, one group meaning 'start' or 'finish', the other group meaning 'to respond to' or 'compensate for something': for example, *They started off by collecting money for unfortunate children, She ended by singing three songs in Italian* (group 1); *They reacted to the news by cutting off all communication with the outside world, He compensated for the bend by breaking sharply* (group 2).

The volume *Grammar Patterns: 1. Verbs* aims to eradicate what is argued here to be an artificial divide between grammar and vocabulary by strengthening rather than impoverishing the interdependence and interconnection between the two. Such connections are not, of course, absolute but corpus-based analysis does demonstrate there to be clear tendencies and probabilities in the relationship which can benefit learners of English. These observations can have profound possibilities for reforming our understanding of syntagmatic and paradigmatic choices, traditional word class units, syntactic structures, and, in a very basic sense, linguistic form and meaning.

It is important, nonetheless, to register some caution concerning the descriptions made in corpus-based grammars. For example, Owen (1993) argues that much depends on the size, range and comprehensiveness of the corpus (even with a corpus of 300-million-plus words, particular grammatical forms may not occur) and that the absence of a lexico-grammatical pattern in a corpus does not preclude the possibility of such a pattern. Owen also argues that a corpus-based pedagogical grammar is still only as good as the descriptions it offers and as good as the pedagogical adequacy of its explanations and examples. It is important that dictionaries which contain grammatical information and grammars which contain lexical information should be corpus-based and not corpus-driven. As Owen puts it: 'The grammarian and the language teacher need the corpus as servant, not as master' (1993, p. 185).

It is also important to underline the implications for language users in the views expressed above concerning the symbiotic relationship between form and meaning. It should not be taken to imply that all language patterns are fixed patterns. Indeed, Sinclair (1987b, 1991) proposes two governing principles of language organization: the 'open-choice principle' and the 'idiom principle'. The former principle refers to the natural variational tendency of language; the latter refers to the tendency of language towards a formation of phrases and idioms. The main characteristics of language lie, however, between these two principles along clines of varying degrees of fixity and pattern because not all 'open choices' are open and not all 'idioms' are are immutably fixed. (See also Sinclair's papers collected in Foley (ed.), 1996.)

3.7 Idioms galore: Fixed expressions and language structure

In the previous sections of this chapter we have examined words in varying degrees of free and fixed combination. In this section attention will be given to those fixed expressions which can most obviously cause difficulties for non-native learners of a language. We shall begin with idioms. These present particular difficulties because they are restricted collocations which cannot normally be understood from the literal meaning of the words which make them up. Thus, *to have/get/give cold feet* (= to be/to make afraid) cannot be modified to 'frozen feet' or 'chilly feet' without changing the meaning. And in its idiomatic meaning *cold feet* is 'semantically opaque' in so far as the meaning of the whole is not obvious from the individual meaning of the constituent parts. Similarly, *to let the cat out of the bag* (= to reveal a secret) cannot be decoded if only the meanings of *let, cat, bag* and *out* are known as separate items. However, not all idioms are quite as fixed as this; in the case of an item such as *to drop a brick* (= to make a mistake) transformations are possible and insertions allowed in certain positions. For example:

He's dropped a really enormous brick this time.
A brick has been dropped.

where the paraphrase relations (*he made a really serious mistake this time; a mistake has been made*) form a basis for possible structural changes to the form of the idiom. Even more structurally flexible are items such as *she broke my heart*, which undergoes a particularly wide range of morphological, and other, transformations, producing, for example, *heart-breaking, heart-broken, heart-breaker*, etc. By contrast, however, an idiom such as *it's raining cats and dogs* is more immutable. It cannot be passivized, does not normally allow of insertions, is in a fixed syntactic and morphological order (**it's raining cat and dog/*dogs and cats*) and is a whole unit (*it's *thundering/*pouring cats and dogs*). In a related way we can *take/have/manage forty winks* (= have a short sleep) but not **sleep forty winks, *take thirty winks* or **have fifty winks*.

However, in both these examples the phrases are not so petrified as to prevent substitution by past and future tenses. Idioms might thus be tentatively defined as (1) non-substitutable or fixed collocations, (2) usually more than single word units,[3] (3) semantically opaque. But the different *degrees* of possible fixity or 'frozenness', both syntactic and semantic, should be noted. The hold-all term which will be used in this book to describe such a phenomenon is *fixed expressions*.

There are other fixed expressions which are not idioms but in some of their features behave almost as if they were. With reference to the above recognition criteria some are more fixed than idioms though most exhibit generally lesser degrees of structural fixity. Such units have been widely discussed within lexicological theory and have obtained various designations. These include: 'prefabricated routines' or 'prefabrication' (prefabs) (Bolinger, 1976); 'patterned lexical phrases' and 'frozen forms' (Nattinger, 1980; Nattinger and DeCarrico, 1992); 'routine formulae' (Coulmas, 1979); 'conventionalized language forms' (Yorio, 1980); 'lexicalized sentence stems' (Pawley and Syder, 1983); more generally, they are known as 'stable collocations, routinized or patterned speech, fixed expressions, lexical stereotypes, gambits' (Keller and Warner, 1977) and so on. (For helpful overviews see Alexander, 1978, 1984a; Fernando and Flavell, 1981; Fernando, 1996; Moon, 1998.) The recognition of fixed expressions owes much to psycholinguistic work on the phrasal lexicon (Becker, 1975) which suggests that language production consists of piecing together such ready-made 'prefabricated' units appropriate to a situation, and that lexical acquisition may involve the learning of complete collocational chunks of language. In any case, the designations refer to units which come in various shapes and sizes with varying degrees of fixity and opacity. They facilitate essentially non-creative, stereotyped formulaic expression which (1) serves a maintaining, stabilizing role within communication[4] but which (2) allows both for larger grammatical units to be built from their base, and for internal and external modification as more creative and cognitively richer speech is generated.

Some examples of fixed expressions are: as *a matter of fact, to smell a rat, as old as the hills, honesty is the best policy, further to my letter of the ___th inst., spick and span, for good, if I were you, bottoms up, a watched pot never boils, a good time was had by all, light years ago, how do you do?, as far as I know, no way, you can say that again, in no uncertain terms, down with the Liberal Democrats, a stitch in time saves nine, I thought you'd never ask, by and large, like it or lump it.* Such expressions as these are syntactically, semantically and discoursally varied, and classification necessarily involves some structural overlap. The tentative classification in Table 3.2 might, however, give an idea of the range of fixed

Table 3.2 Types of fixed expression

	Types of fixed expression	Examples
I	*Idioms*	
	(i) irreversible binomials/ compound idioms	spick and span; dead drunk; red tape.
	(ii) full idioms	run up (a bill); tear off (rush away); to smell a rat; to rain cats and dogs; to be in the doghouse.
	(iii) semi-idioms	beefy-looking; dead drunk; a fat salary; the meeting kicks off at nine.
II	*Proverbs*	A watched pot never boils.
III	*Stock phrases*	When all is said and done; a recipe for disaster; unaccustomed as I am to . . .; a vicious circle.
IV	*Catchphrases*	That's another fine mess you got me into; What do you think of it so far?; Are you sitting comfortably? Then I'll begin.
V	*Allusions/Quotations*	You've never had it so good; We are not amused; The lady's not for turning.
VI	*Idiomatic Similes*	as sober as a judge; as old as the hills; as daft as a brush.
VII	*Discoursal Expressions*	
	(i) social formulae/clichés	How do you do? Long time, no see; bottoms up!
	(ii) connectives; structuring devices	Mark my words; Once upon a time; Finally; to conclude.
	(iii) conversational gambits	We'll now take questions from the floor; Guess what!; I wondered if I could have a word.
	(iv) stylistic formulae	Further to my letter of 11th inst.; My lords, ladies and gentlemen.
	(v) stereotypes	We're just good friends; I thought you'd never ask; It's not what you think!

After: Alexander, 1984a.

expressions in the modern English lexicon as well as prepare some ground for the more formal recognition criteria suggested in the next section.

The list contains fixed expressions which are generally known as *clichés* and **proverbs**. Proverbs have formal and semantic characteristics in common. For example they convey some kind of aphoristic truth, are usually in the simple present tense and are normally neither syntactically divisible nor substitutable (though this is not to say that creative mutations or distortions are not possible; see particularly Mackin, 1978 for a range of examples). On the other hand, the proverbs (1) *honesty is the best policy*, (2) *a watched pot never boils* and (3) *a stitch in time saves nine* display different degrees of semantic opacity. (1) can be derived from a knowledge of the individual constituent items, (2) is less transparent and requires a metaphoric-analogical interpretive process and (3) is semantically opaque, the meaning not being as openly recoverable. Clichés are like idioms in that they are fixed expressions but are unlike idioms in two important respects. They are more fixed than idioms in terms of syntactic, morphological and semantic commutability. Their meaning is usually derivable from the semantic sum of the individual constituent parts. When it is not derivable then features of the linguistic or social context will aid interpretation. For example, it is probable that 'social' clichés (social formulae/clichés at VII (i) in Table 3.2) like *how do you do?* (transparent) and *bottoms up* (opaque) will only occur in specific situations and will be accompanied by clarifying gestural and paralinguistic expression. Examples such as this illustrate the important point that fixed expressions cut across spoken- and written-language use and that they can vary in relation to contexts of discourse.

3.8 Fixing fixed expressions

As far as the relative fixedness of fixed expressions is concerned, it will be seen then that all the above expressions are in some way fixed but that some are more fixed than others. This section brings together discussion of such units in the preceding sections by positing the usefulness of clines of lexical relations. A cline is able to capture essential features of this kind of lexical phenomena by seeing lexical items as distributed along continua of relative fixity.

Fixed expressions such as *in no uncertain terms* or *further to my letter of* . . . are quite transparent semantically, are not normally commutable in structure, and are collocationally restricted in terms of component parts. *A good time was had by all*, however, does allow of greater creative transmutation (e.g. *a good time was had by none* or *a bad time was had by all*) and it is again transparent in meaning. Alternatively, as Nattinger (1980) points out, some expressions are fixed by virtue of a closed syntactic structure into which a variety of lexical insertions are possible. Nattinger gives the example of ADV + *with* + NP which can produce a range of structures such as: *down with the Tories/politicians/war/petrol taxes/the king*, etc. On the other hand, the lexical item *for good* (e.g. *He's going away for good*, meaning 'for ever') would be 'fixed' according to all criteria. That is, it is semantically opaque (its meaning cannot be derived from a knowledge of *for* or *good*), syntactic-structural insertions or substitutions are not permitted (e.g. **for very good, *for goods, *for good and good*), and it is a restricted collocation with both elements restricted in relation to each other.

However, no fixed expression is able to collocate with *any* other item; and nothing is completely closed and cut off from anything else. For example, *further to my letter* is domain-restricted; that is, it is likely to occur largely within a field of discourse of business correspondence. Similarly, *in no uncertain terms* is likely to occur only with performative verbs of saying or telling (e.g. *I told/warned him in no uncertain terms*). And the unit *for good* enters into clausal environments in which it is usually dependent on verbs with a meaning of 'removal or detachment from':

> He's leaving for good.
> She's giving up smoking for good.
> *I'll love you for good.

And, as we have already observed, some seemingly opaque units such as *bottoms up, here's to . . .* (accompanied by raising of drinks) and *see you* (good-bye) are largely socially formulaic and can normally be so deciphered in most spoken and written contexts. This does leave some proverbs, however, such as *a stitch in time saves nine* or *he knows which side his bread's buttered on* as more intractably closed than other units along the cline(s). They are collocationally restricted, noncommutable, semantically opaque and unlikely to be immediately decipherable by reference to contextual factors. Lastly, it is necessary to draw attention to a set of units which may need to be separately categorized. These are fixed expressions which can be understood figuratively but the process of analogizing is direct rather than oblique because such expressions do not have the semantic opacity characteristic of idioms. Examples would be *kick off* in *The meeting kicks off at 9 o'clock* or *dead drunk* where the figurative specialization occurs in one part of the expression and not in the whole. These are related to 'semi-idioms' but it is possible for them also to be linked to 'idiomatic similes', which are separately categorized in Table 3.2 on account of their fixed structural patterning.

3.9 Lexical patterns: A summary

We have seen from the preceding two sections that the following criteria are relevant in determining how fixed particular lexical patterns are:[5] *collocational restriction; syntactic structure; semantic opacity*. This section focuses on more strictly formal matters and discusses the lexical units of fixed expressions with reference to formal linguistic recognition criteria. It will be argued that the notion of the *cline* can continue to help us to range these units in terms of sets of continua with fixed points but several intermediate categories.

This section is also designed to serve as a summary of discussion so far concerning the lexicality of fixed expressions.

1   *Collocational restriction*

   (a) *Unrestricted collocation:* This describes the capacity of particular lexical items to be open to partnership with a wide range of items. Most core words fall into such a category (e.g. *fat, bright, head*) as do structures with core verbs such as *have* or *take* in the structures: *take a look/a holiday/a rest/a letter/ time/notice/a walk*. Another example would be the verb *run*, which in its sense of 'manage' or 'operate' collocates relatively unrestrictedly with a range of animate and inanimate, concrete and abstract entities: e.g. *run a business/football team/car/shop/ scheme* and so on.

   (b) *Semi-restricted collocation:* This category embraces lexical patterns in which the number of items which can be substituted in different syntactic slots is more determined. Examples here would be *harbour doubt/grudges/uncertainty/suspicion* or *fan* (in the sense of 'incite', 'encourage'), e.g. *fan a riot/discontent/ disturbance/hooliganism* (see also Aisenstadt, 1979).

   (c) *Familiar collocation:* Combinations here are between words which keep regular company with each other. There are obvious overlaps here with types of fixed expression categorized above as stock phrase and metaphoric usage (e.g. *vicious circle*): *innocent bystander/unrequited love/unmitigated disaster/ readily admit/lukewarm reception/pregnant with possibilities/ amicable divorce.*

   (d) *Restricted collocation:* Partnerships in this category are generally more fixed and closed: e.g. *stark naked/pitch black*. A range of syntactic patterns are involved, however: e.g. *consider seriously/lean meat/soft water/gin and tonic/accept defeat*. Also included here are irreversible binomials such as *cash and carry/ ups and downs/hit and miss/assault and battery/swings and roundabouts*.

The cline in collocational restriction runs from: (a) less fixed to (d) more fixed.

2 **Syntactic structure**

(a) Flexible	e.g. *break somebody's heart* (see above p. 65); *nice to see you.*
(b) Regular with certain constraints	e.g. *to drop a brick; to smell a rat; we'll now take questions from the floor.*
(c) Irregular	e.g. *to go one better; to be good friends with somebody; to hold true; to go it alone; the more the merrier.*

The cline in syntactic structure runs from: (a) less fixed to (c) more fixed.

3 **Semantic Opacity**

(a) Transparent	e.g. *long time, no see; when all is said and done; honesty is the best policy; we're just good friends.*
(b) 'Semi-idioms'/ metaphor/idiomatic similes	e.g. *we are all in the same boat; an open-door policy; a fat salary; as sober as a judge.*
(c) Semi-transparent	e.g. *the business really took off; to get round somebody; a watched pot never boils; a skyscraper; there's more here than meets the eye; bumper to bumper traffic.*
(d) Opaque: (i) overt (uninterpretable without contextual/cultural knowledge)	e.g. *O.K.; right on; yuk; bottoms up.*

(ii) covert   e.g. *to be on the wagon; to be on the ball; to carry the can; to kick the bucket.*

The cline in semantic opacity runs from: (a) less fixed to (d) more fixed.

We can conclude that there are no unequivocally clear clines of fixity whatever the main categories involved. It is necessary to separate the clines but it is also clear that there are points of intersection and overlap between the clines which allow us to define the most fixed expression as those which are 'closed' in more than one category. Thus, an expression such as:

Fat chance you've got.

which is relatively closed syntactically, semantically and collocationally, might be defined as one of the more intractable of fixed expressions (though an additional difficulty for foreign learners of the language would be the otherwise relatively unrestricted collocability of the adjective *fat*). Alternatively, *take a chance*, which is likewise a fixed expression, is less fixed semantically, syntactically and as a collocation and would thus be more readily comprehensible.[6]

A focus on the intelligibility of lexical patterns can be closely linked with assessing the degrees of difficulty involved in learning and encoding fixed expressions. In the next section this focus is intensified by a consideration of the kinds of potential and actual lexical errors made by learners of English as a foreign language. As can sometimes be the case with a focus on the learner's production this section will enable some main strands of the discussion in this chapter so far to be summarized.

3.10 Lexis and the language learner: What is lexical error?

Isolating what might be specifically lexical in errors of language production is no easy task. Much depends on exactly what is understood by knowing a word (see Richards, 1976, and Section 7.19 for a list of more specific categories). Particularly in the early stages of learning a language, errors may result from a mismatch in morphophonemic correspondence (the fit between sound and written form), from inserting the word in the wrong grammatical slot or failing to locate grammatical dependencies, from inaccurate first-language transfer (often leading to specific semantic errors), and from intralingual confusion, that is, as a result of failing to distinguish appropriately between and among lexical items in the target language. Related errors occur in first-language as well as second-language learning but they are likely to be more acute in the second language. Martin (1984) argues that in the case of advanced second-language learners, who do not have the luxury of exposure to words over a long period of time and in a rich variety of contexts, the errors are most likely to be interlingual. Examining the nature of such lexical errors can be instructive for description of lexical structure and organization; as far as applied linguistic work is concerned, it can help to clarify and suggest teaching procedures which relate to what knowing a word involves.

Martin's research leads her to conclude that advanced students regularly set up false equivalences between items and that the practice of glossing new words in terms of synonyms can be a primary factor in establishing errors in second-language production. Martin isolates four main types of dissonance between a lexical item and its appropriate use: **stylistic, syntactic, collocational** and **semantic**.

Stylistic dissonances occur when lexical items at one level of formality are selected and used in a context demanding another level of formality; for example, '*dunk* the pieces of chicken in the beaten egg mixture'; 'a committee was appointed by the government to examine specific *grouses*'; 'where is her *abode*?' In such instances more information is needed about the usage of such words than that they are synonyms of *place, complaint* and *home*.

Syntactic errors can occur, according to Martin, if no warnings are supplied in textbooks against using the synonym in the syntactic patterns which belong to the item being glossed or defined. Thus, if *persist* were to be presented as a synonym of *continue* then there would be no check on learners producing errors such as **He persisted to shout.* Unaware that, in the case of the 'synonyms' *yield/concede*, only *concede* is able to take a *that*-clause, there would be no constraint on a student producing **She yielded that I was right.* Particularly elusive too are the transitivity relations contracted by synonymic change verbs. Glossing *elapse*, for example, by reference to *pass* without reference to the fact that *elapsed* is used intransitively (while *pass* can be both transitive and intransitive) would not prevent the generation of **We elapsed a nice couple of hours in the park.* These errors are essentially colligational (see Martin, 1984 for a host of further examples, as well as Section 3.5).

Collocational mismatches are frequent in the language production of second-language learners since learners never encounter a word or combinations of words with sufficient frequency to demarcate its range or narrow the item down to its more fixed partnerships. Particular difficulties result from collocations which are relatively opaque semantically (e.g. a *heavy drinker*) or which are restricted to particular fields of discourse (e.g. '*light* pastry'; '*slick* gear-change'). Thus, explaining *amicable* as a synonym of *friendly* does not explain why *amicable divorce* is collocationally acceptable but **friendly divorce* is not, nor why *fat paycheque* cannot be substituted by **obese paycheque* without producing comic results. Adjective–noun collocations are notoriously slippery[7] but the extension of collocational partnerships over other syntactic chunks can produce similarly infelicitous combinations. Martin does not, however, discuss mistakes with idioms.

Martin's final category is **semantic**, and she admits this to be the most complex of all the four main types. There are several subtle and delicate distinctions among words of similar meaning and semantic analysis can help with some necessary demarcations; for example, work on **selection restrictions** using fundamental binary oppositions such as state–event, animate–inanimate, abstract–concrete (see Section 3.3). Thus, **I injured my car in the accident* can be explained quite straightforwardly by pointing out that *injure* requires a direct object which is animate unlike *damage* which only takes an inanimate object and would be the correct selection here. Martin also cites the instructive example of a list of items from what could be a thesaurus entry under a general superordinate *correct*. The items include *rectify, reform, remedy, emend, redress* and she points to the lexical error in: **I must rectify my younger brother all the time.* Here the more general superordinate verb would have sufficed but the word *rectify* applies to abstract properties (such as abuses, errors, etc.) which are deemed inherently bad. Similar errors can be generated using all the hyponyms in this list as if they were interchangeable (e.g. you can *remedy* but not *redress* a situation). And, above all, the example illustrates some problems inherent in directing foreign-language learners to thesaurus entries (see also Section 9.5 and, for criticism of lexicographic glossing procedures using synonyms, see Jain 1979; 1981). It also illustrates once again the difficulties in deciding where selection restrictions end and collocational probabilities begin.

We should note, finally, that errors of more than one type can converge. For example:

*We alighted off the bus.

is a syntactic error derived from matching the phrasal verb with a synonym such as *get off* but it is also inappropriate stylistically as *alight* is a particularly formal register. An interesting study of an overlap of 'syntactic, semantic and pragmatic' factors is given in McKay (1980b) in a study of synonyms listed under a superordinate *inform*. These include: *announce, communicate, declare, disclose, discuss, expose, express, mention, refer, report* and *state*. Examples given by McKay include discussion of semantic and collocational differences between *express* (which takes objects involving emotion or opinions, together with a human subject), *announce* (which is more likely to have as its object a significant event) and *mention* (which is pragmatically a verb with both less strength and formality than its semantic partners).

This section has concentrated on a limited range of examples of lexical errors in language production. The extent to which the same factors affect language comprehension has not been examined but we cannot assume that they will be the same. Another interesting factor to investigate would be the storage in memory of such items, especially the collocational and stylistic/pragmatic dimensions to word meaning, and particularly whether items are stored singly or as whole composite units. It is clear, however, that knowing a word involves a complex of factors and that learning words should, as far as possible, take account of syntactic, semantic, stylistic and collocational dimensions if the types of dissonance catalogued here are to be avoided.

We have not, however, so far accounted for the nature of the 'lexical' errors in the following examples:

(1) *He tried to swim across the lake. *Consequently*, it was very cold and he had to give up.
(2) *He ran very fast *and* failed to win the race.
(3) *She passed the exam. *This move* pleased her parents.
(4) *He broke a cup, plate and saucer. *By these means* people thought he was clumsy.

The main point here is that once again grammatical as well as lexical units are involved but that beyond-the-sentence relations are generated by the italicized errors. It is interesting that errors of this type do not figure in Martin's categories though it can be argued that both syntactic and semantic criteria are relevant. In fact, the area of the part played by lexical items in the cohesion and coherence of a text is one which has been receiving increased attention from linguists interested in lexicology and discourse analysis. The basic assumption is that, however important it is to account for and understand lexical patterning at the level of the clause, ways with words depend just as crucially on the patterns created by lexical items in the wider context of naturally occurring discourses. The next chapter is devoted to this area.

3.11 Conclusion

In this chapter we have looked at words in varying degrees of combination and this has once again raised the theoretical problem of adequately defining a word. The patterns into which words enter are, in fact, of both theoretical and applied interest. Although idioms have been relatively widely analysed by linguists, the importance of a wide range of fixed expressions and, in particular, their potential relevance for language teaching is now beginning to be examined in greater detail. It has also been noted in this chapter that errors in vocabulary use by non-native speakers of English can also be more systematically accounted for if we are aware of the kinds of patterns and interrelations which words contract with one another. We should note, however, that it is once again the patterns created by the more frequent, core words in the lexicon – words such as *round, have, take, run* – which are the most problematic to describe as well as to teach and to codify lexicographically.

One main conclusion can be drawn from this chapter: it is commonly assumed that using words entails a creative deployment of the resources of the language, particularly in the *selection* of items from our lexical store; but many lexical items are either themselves patterns or form part of patterns which are quite fixed and stable and which are used routinely in relatively predictable situations. Meanings can, of course, be uniquely generated but stability is a pervasive feature of normal vocabulary use and it is clear that there are numerous communicative contexts in which language can be used formulaically. As is the case with core and non-core words, however, it is no easy task to draw a dividing line between expressions which are fixed and those which are open to more 'creative' formulation. As a result, it is necessary to talk in terms of *clines* of fixity.

This chapter has tried to suggest classifications and categories for different lexical patterns which may provide a basis for further exploration. Although it is corpus-based computational analysis of such patterns, particularly in the important area of collocation, which holds out most promise for future categorization, Chapters 6 and 7 in this book discuss the role of fixed expressions in lexicographic work and language teaching. In those chapters much of the discussion assumes the general conclusions about lexical patterning reached here.

Notes

1 The example of *soft water* which also collocates in such relationships as 'the *soft*ness of the refreshing spring-*water*'/'*water-soft*ener'/'the ministry have *soft*ened the *water*' demonstrates that within collocational ranges we are dealing with **roots** rather than **words** (see Sections 1.4 and 1.5). A collocation is a composite structural element in its own right: roots are zero collocations and we should study the contract between a root and its other lexico-grammatical relations. Collocations cut not only across word class boundaries such as noun and verb, but also across such sentence parts as 'subject' and 'predicate', as well as across sentence boundaries. For example, *Use the water from the stream beyond the main farm buildings. Its softness will be particularly beneficial*. It is clear that, to capture collocational relationships in a text, decisions concerning the **span** will be crucial.

2 Subsequently, both Halliday and Sinclair have modified their position regarding lexis as a linguistic level. Halliday (1978) refers to lexico-grammar as a 'stratum' where lexical and grammatical structures which realize the output from the semantic component of a text are mapped onto one another. Halliday's three strata which make up the linguistic system are: lexico-grammar, semantics and phonology. See also Section 4.8 for a review of work by Hasan on the interaction of lexis and grammar in the formation of textual cohesion and Section 6.6.1 for Sinclair's collocational and colligational descriptions for word entries in the COBUILD dictionary.

3 Cowie and Mackin (1975, p. viii) define an idiom as 'a combination of two or more words which function as a unit of meaning'. Exceptions to the rule here would be 'units' such as 'He's a *livewire*' or 'It's *blackmail*' though it could be argued that formally more than one 'word' is involved in each case. We should also note here that certain single lexical items do not have meaning in contemporary English except in some fixed combination; for example, *kith* in *kith and kin*; *spick* in *spick and span*; *aback* in *to be taken aback* and *jiffy* in *in a jiffy*. Cowie and Mackin (1975) and Cowie *et al.* (1983) would also want to describe idiomaticity as a feature cutting across all fixed expressions rather than have *idioms* as a separate category included within and subsumed by an overall framework of fixed expressions. And this is the policy adopted in *ODCIE* (1975). In this study the term 'idiom' is reserved for lexical patterns which are specifically characterized by semantic opacity.

4 'Conventionalized forms make communication more orderly because they are regulatory in nature. They organize reactions and facilitate choices, thus reducing the complexity of communicative exchanges. They are group identifying . . . serving as instruments for establishing rapport, reinforcing awareness of group membership . . . and defining social relations and the relative status of the different communicators' (Yorio, 1930, p. 438). We should also note that these categories and classifications emerge from distinct linguistic traditions and for different explanatory needs; for example, those listed here include the domains of language acquisition, conversational discourse analysis, ethnomethodology as well as lexicology. But these different traditions have also learned from each other.

5 For a useful survey of relevant issues and with acknowledgement of East European work in the field see Weinreich (1980).

6 For example, *chance* collocates quite fixedly with *take* but *take* allows

synonymic substitutions which do not greatly alter an overall meaning. Thus, *take a risk/gamble/chance.*

7 Benson (1985, p.63) argues that such combinations are of considerable importance to compilers of general use dictionaries and follows Apresyan *et al.* (1969) in marking 'expression of the highest degree' in this combination as especially important for the learner, for example, *reckless abandon;* chronic *alcoholic; rank amateur; burning ambition.*

4 Lexis and discourse

Polonious: What do you read, my lord?
Hamlet: Words, words, words.

(Shakespeare, *Hamlet*, Act II, scene ii)

4.0 Introduction

In this chapter there is a distinct shift from examining lexical items at the level of the orthographic 'word' or in the patterns which occur in fixed expressions towards a consideration of lexis in larger units of language organization. It is also here that greater differentiation than in previous chapters is made between *spoken* and *written discourse*. Thus, the operations of lexis will be explored in written discourse across the boundaries of the sentence and in spoken discourse across such boundaries as *conversational turns*. The terms *text* and *discourse* will be used interchangeably in this chapter to refer to these larger organizational units of language, although distinctions between the terms can and have been made (see Stubbs, 1983, pp. 9–11, who also discusses issues in the appropriate collection and analysis of naturally occurring data). We should also note that 'discourse' is used with systematic ambiguity to refer to (1) a complete stretch of naturally occurring language – *discourses*, and (2) the theoretical level at which stretches of spoken and written language are analysed – *discourse*. In the first of these uses, note that 'discourse' takes a plural.

The 1980s and 1990s have witnessed considerable progress in the analysis of naturally occurring texts and several books devoted to discourse analysis, pragmatics and text linguistics have been published (e.g. Stubbs, 1983; Brown and Yule, 1983; Leech, 1983b, Levinson, 1983; Cook, 1990; Nunan, 1994; McCarthy and Carter, 1994). It is nevertheless the case that the role of lexis in discourse has been relatively neglected. This chapter reports on the developments that have taken place with particular reference to written text where more work is available. A main argument throughout is that lexical items in discourse require to be constantly interpreted and re-interpreted by the language user and that, when analysts move beyond constructed examples to a consideration of real texts, the 'values' of lexis become of considerable significance. This point is further underlined in the final section of this chapter (Section 4.10) which is devoted to the ideological implications of particular lexicalizations.

4.1 Lexical cohesion

The analysis of *cohesion* is a key topic in the study of discourse and considerable advances have been made, especially in the last twenty years. The term *cohesion* embraces the means by which texts are linguistically connected. There has been an emphasis on the role of grammatical words in performing this function, for example:

> Wash and core six cooking apples. Put them into an oven-proof dish.

In this example, the pronoun *them* connects with cooking apples and is the main surface linguistic means by which the two sentences are connected.

In this section the main focus is on *lexical* cohesion in written text. This is a problematic type of cohesion mainly because we are dealing with *open* rather than *closed* class items. Work on lexis in discourse tries to account for more obvious features of cohesion such as repetition of items as well as more complex relations of collocation and of structural-semantic sense-connections across sentence boundaries (e.g. Dressler, 1970). Lexical items create a set of expectations which readers (and hearers) of a text seek to fulfil; but accounting for such associations and mutual expectancies in any replicable way is no easy task.

Gutwinski (1976, p. 57) suggests the following features of lexical cohesion:

1   Repetition of item.
2   Occurrence of synonym or item formed on same root (e.g. *run/ sprint* or *run/ran/running*).
3   Occurrence of item from same lexical set (e.g. *train, track, station, platform*).

These features will be seen to involve both formal (forms of words) and semantic (word meaning) criteria. Halliday and Hasan (1976), in their major study *Cohesion in English*, offer a similar blend of criteria, although there is only one chapter devoted to lexical cohesion, the remainder being primarily concerned with the role of closed-class items in establishing connectivity in texts. Halliday and Hasan propose the following components of lexical cohesion:

1   same item
2   synonym or near synonym (including hyponymy)
3   superordinate
4   general word
5   collocation

For example, the following sentences link by means of lexical cohesion with a target sentence *There's a boy climbing that tree*:

1 The boy's going to fall	(same item)
2 The lad's going to fall	(synonym)
3 The child's going to fall	(superordinate)
4 The idiot's going to fall	(general word)

Halliday and Hasan classify the components 1–4 as *reiteration*, by which they mean 'not only the repetition of the same lexical item but also the occurrence of a related item'. Halliday and Hasan's fifth component, that of collocation or collocational cohesion, embraces all lexical relations that do not depend on referential identity, that is, all relations not covered by reiteration. Collocation (see also Section 3.1) is defined as a recognizable lexico-semantic word–meaning relation, but it is extremely difficult to define in any systematic way the nature of such collocational relations because, as we have already seen (Sections 3.1–3.5), some patterns are distinctly semantico-syntactic and others are more generally probabilistic. For collocational patterns to be predictable, the analyst would need to have access to the kinds of description of semantic sets which would be made available by an extensive computer-based collocational thesaurus. In the past, relevant lexical research projects (e.g. Sinclair *et al.*, 1970) have not been able to process sufficient text for the strength of probability of co-occurrence of related items to be shown (but, see discussion of the COBUILD project in Section 6.6.1).

Another problem is defined by Martin (1992) who differentiates **taxonomic** and **collocational** relations. For Martin, taxonomic relations are subdivided into (1) superordination (e.g. synonymy, hyponymy, antonymy) and (2) composition (e.g. part–whole relations: *hour/*

minute; part–part relations: *hand/foot, door/window*). He suggests further that collocations can be divided into different types, for example:

componential	tall, high
modificational	bright, sun
resultative	explosion, fire
utilitarian	hammer, pound

Martin agrees that collocational relations present the greatest problems of replicable identification and that a crucial difficulty remains one of interpreting how loosely or tightly collocating items are strung together.[1] But this is not to say that analysis of reiteration (or **taxonomic**) relations is not without problems when the analysis takes place in naturally occurring texts. Such problems, we should note, will not generally arise in the case of the more static, decontextualized semantic analysis of Lyons and others (see Sections 1.9–1.11), which is usually undertaken with reference to sentences made up by the analyst.

Examples of the kind of descriptive problems encountered by analysts of lexical cohesion beyond the boundaries of a single decontextualized, constructed sentence include the following:

1   How far away do items have to be in a text before we can say that a meaning relation does not obtain? In the case of collocational links, Sinclair *et al.* (1970) (see Section 3.1) posited a span of four words either side of a key (or **node**) word; but while appropriate for the purposes of that research, such a procedure would not in this sentence net *chips* and *computer* as belonging to the same collocational environment: *Computers are more useful now that silicon chips have been invented.*

Over how many clauses, sentences or paragraphs do such lexical connections stretch? Is there an upper word-limit to the distance apart these items (which Halliday and Hasan describe as forming 'lexical chains') have to be?

2   Are some relations stronger and more binding than others? Does repetition of the same item produce a more cohesive patterning than derivationally and inflectionally repeated items or than synonyms? And do certain kinds of text give prominence to certain relations?

3   In terms of taxonomically or macro-set related items which can be more hierarchically ordered, how far does the hierarchy stretch? For example, *mosquito* relates to *insect* and *insect* to *animal*, but is

mosquito in any semantic relation to *animal*? Can it be made to have such a relation in a *text*?

4   The last two problems indicate that the problem of interpretation may be most central of all. And interpreting the connectivity of items can depend on individual responses to the presence of lexical associations and evaluative elements in a text as well as on the kinds of knowledge of a field of discourse or topic needed for lexical set construction (see Sections 4.3 and 4.10).

4.2 Lexical signalling

In this book so far, words have been divided into *open* and *closed* classes with the latter class containing a finite number of what have been termed grammatical words. In a seminal article for the analysis of lexis in discourse, Winter (1977) abolishes any easy division between open and closed items, segmenting a finite set of lexical *and* grammatical words into three main groups which he calls Vocabulary 1, Vocabulary 2, and Vocabulary 3. Each group is distinguished by its clause-relating functions. The first group includes 'subordinators' (e.g. *by, after, unless, whereas, except that, although, as far as*); the second group includes what are termed the 'sentence connectors', that is, lexical items which 'make explicit the clause relation between the matrix clause and the preceding clause or sentence' (Winter, 1977, p. 15) (e.g. *alternatively, in any case, anyway, therefore, generally, hence, for example, thus, yet*, etc.). The difference between both groups can be illustrated in the following examples:

   (1) *By* appealing to scientists and technologists to support his party, Mr Wilson won many middle-class votes in the election. (Vocabulary 1)
   (2) Mr Wilson appealed to scientists and technologists to support his party. He *thus* won many middle-class votes in the election. (Vocabulary 2)

In the case of clause relation through Vocabulary 1, one of the clauses is subordinated to the other; in the case of Vocabulary 2, the connection allows the two sentences to remain independent. The most interesting of these sets of words is Vocabulary 3 – a group of words which serve to establish certain semantic functions in the connection of clauses or sentences in discourse. Here are examples of lexical items from Vocabulary 3 in operation:

(1) I *chose* wood rather than aluminium or steel for the structure.
(2) There is a *difference* between George and David's respective characters.
(3) One *condition* for the success of the team is obvious.

Each of the italicized words here fulfils what might be termed an anticipatory function. They project the reader forward by creating expectations of what is to ensue in the next part of the discourse. The words have their own intrinsic meanings but they also function in the formation of intersentential relations. In (1), for example, the word *chose* points to a following clause in which an explanation will be given. The sentence sets up a question 'why' to which an answer should normally be provided. In (3) we are forced into expecting a further clause or sentence in which a fulfilment of the condition will be logically formulated. Winter's examples and analysis cannot be summarized simply but it is important to note that there are a limited number of Vocabulary 3 items (Winter postulates 108) and that although these may be 'open' or 'content' words in one context, in the discoursal context they represent a closed system and can perform a 'semantic' and grammatical function simultaneously. Though closed in one sense, Vocabulary 3 words are unlike Vocabulary 1 and 2 in that they can be modified and qualified, for example, 'One *obvious* condition. . .' or 'I *wisely* chose. . .'. (See also Winter (1982) for further consideration of the linguistic context in which grammatical and discourse relations are lexically realized.) Here is a short selection of Winter's Vocabulary 3 items:

action	event	reason
cause	expect	result
compare	fact	situation
conclude	kind	solution
condition	manner	specify
contrast	point	thing
differ	problem	way

Winter's work has been lucidly developed by Hoey (1983) and Crombie (1985), the latter of whom argues for the construction of second-language-teaching pedagogies and syllabuses based on explicit attention (1) to the signals of what is coming, what is present or what has gone in relation to other parts of a discourse, and (2) to the lexicalizations of intersentential semantic relationships in texts.

Valuable though Winter's work has been in showing some ways in which readers process texts as dynamically related semantic constructs, there are still some important questions to be raised for the analysis of lexis in discourse. These range from relatively minor observations that certain items overlap categorically (e.g. *because* simultaneously signals a reason relation, operates as a subordinator and thus functions as Vocabulary 1 and Vocabulary 2) to more substantial questions concerning the relationships between propositions. For example: how is it that readers read relationships between different parts of a text when there are *no* explicit lexical signals of those relations?; how do we know, in the absence of signals, what relationships are intended in a particular text?; do certain kinds of text signal more explicitly than others?; how is it that texts both containing the same lexical items and including explicit lexical signals, can be interpreted differently?

Analysis of the kinds of textual relations and patterns realized by vocabulary remains a major lexical research goal, and there have been several notable recent attempts to explore the questions raised by and about Winter's work. They all, in their different ways, challenge the notion that vocabulary might be best described in a dictionary or lexicon. For example, Hoey (1991) shows that much of the coherence, as well as the cohesion, of text is created by the lexical ties of individual words with one another. Hoey is less interested in itemizing cohesive features than in describing how they combine to organize text, and proposes a methodology for the summarization of texts that is capable of some degree of automation. Stainton (1997) develops the notion of *metadiscourse* (discourse about discourse) and proposes frameworks for establishing relative degrees of success in a wide range of types of writing or 'genres' (see Section 4.9) in relation to the uses of metadiscourse by writers. Metadiscourse involves use by a writer of words and phrases such as *to summarize, as we have seen, as a result, however, therefore, the main point is* and *in the next section* which establish a relationship with the reader by previewing, highlighting, evaluating and summarizing the rhetorical and organizational planes of the text. Crismore (1990) gives a particularly useful account of metadiscourse in relation to discourse and text organization.

4.3 Evaluation and discourse

There is not space here to discuss all the above questions in detail, although research into problems raised by such questions is growing rapidly. The discussion, however, can illustrate some key issues in lexico-semantic discourse analysis of written text. One such issue is that of what can be generally termed *evaluation*.

In a wide-ranging paper, McCarthy (1984b) challenges Winter's assumption that there is a one-for-one relation between a particular lexical item and a particular set of relations in discourse. He points to Winter's example:

I chose wood rather than aluminium or steel.

Winter argues that the verb *choose* signals a close association with the reason relation and that somewhere in the immediately preceding or closely subsequent portion of the text a reason or justification for the act of choosing will be given. McCarthy points to a number of weaknesses in this view of lexical signalling and in the assumption of a closed set of Vocabulary 3 items. The first point is that *chose* could be substituted by items not connected with the reason relation but a reason relation can still be signalled. For example, 'I *used* wood rather than aluminium or steel' or *ordered/bought/sat on/decided on*. Even *rather than*, a specific grammatical feature, is not exclusive to this relation since *instead of/in contrast to/in place of/to the exclusion of* can be substituted without fundamental alteration to the underlying semantic relations. The same applies to sentence connectors such as *because* or *if*, which do not automatically signal reason/justification (*because*) or a condition (*if*):

(1) The table is ready. *If* you'd like to come this way.
(2) Wait until you have children. *Because* you'll find you have no time for yourself.

McCarthy argues that readers of texts seek *motivation* in a text. They want to know why the message is being sent and what is in it for them; they will consequently evaluate or interpret it in the same pragmatic way as any other piece of discourse, spoken or written, and try to make sense of it by assuming that it is coherent and by finding what is, for them, significant and relevant in that text. Thus, the absence of a Vocabulary 3 item *example* will not prevent most readers, quite reasonably, from interpreting the second paragraph of the following text as an *example* to support the point made in the preceding paragraph, even though there is no overtly marked lexicalization of this relationship.

Second, to avoid those heavy shadows under the eyes with bounce flash, try keeping your distance with a medium telephoto for portraits.

I took the portrait of the little girl on the left with a 100mm lens on my Minolta from about 3m, with a Sunpak 4205G hammer gun aimed at a wall on the left and only slightly upward.

Here the relevance of the two paragraphs is understood pragmatically and lexically, so to speak. The second paragraph links plausibly to the first as an example, but this is, of course, dependent on a recognition of lexical items belonging to the same lexical set (e.g. *bounce flash, hammer gun*) and realizing a topic about which both writer and reader have to have shared knowledge.

A further point made by McCarthy concerns the analysis of *collocation* which is, for him, another instance of lexicalization in text being a pragmatic process and not one constrained either by a fixed set of lexical items realizing only certain specific functions or by lexical items which have their meanings fixed once and for all and which cannot, therefore, be analysed independently of their place in a system of meanings. In real texts, McCarthy argues, the abstract phenomenon of collocation has to be replaced by the notion of *significant collocation*. Significant collocates are italicized in this passage:

It is one of the most *atmospheric* railways in the Sub-continent.

I decided to trace a line from Peshawar to Chittagong in Bangladesh, and take all the trains that lay in between. It was neither an ordeal nor a vacation but rather a kind of *sedentary* adventuring – an *imperial* progress along the railways of the old Raj.

The train was *fascinating* but *filthy*. It is often the case in India. The sleeping compartment had not been swept; it was *small, badly painted* and *dirty*. But the air conditioning, in its *grumbling* way, actually worked.

Although *train, railways, compartment* and *line* could be agreed on as belonging to a collocationally linked lexical set, the words *atmospheric, sedentary, imperial, fascinating, filthy, small* and *badly painted* would not be associated in an abstract version of the lexicon (one would not expect that they would be used to define each other in a dictionary, for example). But, in this instance, they are significantly collocated in the writer's argument, and are coherently related to his evaluation of the railway journey as one which had attractive *and* unattractive features (i.e. features which were not automatic polarities). The key word here is evaluation. In naturally occurring text, words which have fixed values in an abstract lexicon can be subjected to a process of negotiation. It is a process which can change their meaning or, at least, the values which normally attach to them. Take, for example:

(1) He is a politician to his fingertips. He can sort out people's problems with the minimum of fuss and disruption.

(2) He is a politician to his fingertips. He is devious and syco-
phantic and manipulates people to his own ends.

Here, the lexical item *politician* can be negotiated into different evaluations and, as a result, will significantly collocate with quite different
lexical items. The same applies to words such as *diligent* or *efficient*. A
'*diligent* student' or an '*efficient* tutor' may be either more positively or
negatively evaluated according to context. Words may also change their
values according to cultural relativity. *Hot* and *cool* carry different
evaluations which depend on where the writer or speaker is situated.

Biber and Finegan (1989) explore how lexis and lexico-grammatical
structures encode what they term 'stance': expressions of affect, judgement and varying degrees of commitment to a proposition. Hunston
and Thompson (eds) (1998) is an extensive study of evaluation in text,
underlining, through papers which cover a wide variety of text-types,
that evaluation is not something 'added on' to the information structure
of a text but is often essential to that text's coherence. For example,
words like *unfortunately* or *surprisingly* can assist in organizing the
information structure of a message as well as the reader's attitudinal
response to it.

Work on lexical signalling and collocational patterning in naturally
occurring text is of considerable importance. There is little doubt that
the discourse-sensitive features revealed by the studies of Winter and
his associates can form a systematic basis for vocabulary teaching and
for development of reading and writing. But this cannot take place in
isolation from an equally significant development of interpretive skills:
understanding the semantic relations between parts of a text should
also involve the ability to interact with the text so that different points
of view can be evaluated and varied inferences negotiated. The relations
between lexical items are *not* fixed once and for all.

4.4 Anaphoric nouns

In this section we will continue to consider the role of evaluative words
in discourse. We begin, however, by returning to a category of lexical
cohesion which was proposed by Halliday and Hasan, but which has
been relatively neglected. This is their category of 'general words'.
According to the example given above (in Section 4.2), a general word
idiot provides an intersentential link between the following statements:

There's a *boy* climbing that tree.
The *idiot*'s going to fall.

The general word here belongs to a class of nouns with potentially wide-ranging reference to human beings. It is also attitudinally marked; that is, it constitutes an evaluation of its referent in the preceding discourse and operates as an expression of interpersonal meaning. But, Halliday and Hasan (1976, p. 276) confine their review of general nouns to those referring to human beings (e.g. *idiot*), their view of attitudinal meaning to contemptuous or sympathetic expression (e.g. 'I've been to see my great aunt. The *poor old girl's* getting very forgetful these days') and their consideration of particular lexical items to a limited set.

In an extensive study, Francis (1985) examines a range of items which she collectively terms **anaphoric nouns** (A-nouns):

> A-nouns are a group of nouns which, first and foremost, fall into a certain semantic class: by virtue of their meaning they can be used metadiscursively; they are nouns which can be used to *talk about* the ongoing discourse. If it meets this requirement, any noun is potentially an A-noun, but in order for it to be identified as such within a discourse it must meet two further criteria. First, it must be functioning as a proform and as such be an anaphorically cohesive device, referring metadiscursively to a stretch of discourse preceding it. . . . Second, it must also face forwards: it must be presented as the *given* information in terms of which the *new* propositional content of the clause or sentence in which it occurs is formulated.
>
> (Francis, 1985, p. 3)

A-nouns operate as organizational signals, as it were. They serve to label a preceding stretch of discourse, integrate and align it with the ongoing argument and thus represent a position which the writer hopes to have established with the reader. The word *position* would be an anaphoric noun in this example:

> J.R. Lucas, in a famous article published in *Philosophy* in 1961, argued that the most important consequence of Gödel's work was that the human brain cannot, in principle, be modelled by a computer program – that minds cannot be explained as machines. For although computers can be programmed to generate formal systems, they can never be programmed to spot the Gödelian traps inherent in them. This latter ability, Lucas argued, remains the sole prerogative of the human brain.
>
> Surprisingly, perhaps, Hofstadter disagrees with this anthropocentric *position*, . . .

Position is, of course, neutral here but distinct attitudinal marking can be conveyed by substituting items such as *distortion, gobbledygook, confusion, nonsense* or *guff.*

In data drawn mostly from argumentative discourse in *Encounter* magazine, Francis found the following items (among many others) operated as anaphoric nouns:

accusation	consideration	interpretation	report
admission	criticism	judgement	repudiation
allegation	declaration	observation	retort
answer	definition	point	revelation
argument	denial	prediction	statement
assumption	description	proposal	stipulation
belief	diagnosis	proposition	suggestion
challenge	estimate	reading	threat
complaint	evidence	reasoning	theory
conclusion	examination	reference	viewpoint
confession	hypothesis	refusal	

Francis offers subclassification into 'illocutionary', 'verbal activity', 'text' and 'ownerless' nouns[2] but recognizes that boundaries between subclasses are fuzzy, that some items can operate across classes and that as a group A-nouns *are* open-ended. Also included might be nominal groups which include fixed expressions such as *point of view, line of reasoning* or *way of putting it*, which are more than an orthographic word; and we should note that verbs can also operate metadiscursively:

> Comparison of the strategic nuclear forces gives rise to controversies which I believe it is possible to *sum up* as follows.

An interesting category of A-nouns are those which generally signal attitudes. Such items do more than merely label the preceding discourse. They mark it in an interpersonally sensitive way, revealing the writer's positive or negative evaluation of the antecedent proposition. So, as McCarthy (1984b) points out, a more neutral item such as *characteristic* could be replaced by *fault* or *snag; means* could be replaced by *deception, trick* or *subterfuge* or by the more positively marked *advantage* or *benefit.*

This also raises an issue of coreness relative to A-nouns; that is, whether certain lexical items are more core than others. Intuition suggests that items such as *means, move, issue, problem, question, fact* and *truth* are both more frequent across a range of discourse types and more discoursally neutral (unless modified or qualified) than other items which can be more intrinsically evaluative. But, this leads to a further question: whether these items may belong more centrally anyway in contexts such as news-reporting where discoursally-neutral metadiscursive items are required and expected (see note 2 and also Sections 4.9 and 4.10).

> Britain is to carry its fight against drugs to the world's narcotic nerve centres. The *move* signals the Government's increasing awareness of the drugs *problem* and its worldwide ramifications.

A-nouns are an important group of lexical items and their identification, even if only in relation to one type of discourse (argumentation, in the case of Francis's study), is a considerable descriptive step forward in the analysis of lexical cohesion. (See Francis, 1994 for extensions to this argument.) The description of anaphoric nouns and their functions underlines the importance of lexical signals in discourse and demonstrates that signals can be multifunctional. It also demonstrates that the category of lexical signal can have multiple-occupancy. Above all, the presence of evaluative elements in discourse shows how important it is that meanings in naturally occurring texts are discourse-specific and have to be negotiated relative to what may be unique and specific purposes. Word meaning in discourse is regularly instantial. It depends on relations contracted as part of its place as a single item in an abstract lexicon; but that same item can have different values every time it is used in real texts.

The next sections look more closely at the relations, not between words and referents or words and other words, or even words and their collocates in any idealized sense, but at words in a range of discourses. These discourses range from spoken to written but also from one *discourse type* or *genre* to another.

4.5 Densities and viewpoints: Spoken and written continua

> The lexicographer still has a tendency to consider the occurrence of a word in print the chief or sole criterion for its inclusion in the dictionary; the grammarian rarely ventures beyond the safe confines of the sentence, a unit that is of doubtful value in the description of casual speech.
>
> (Svartvik, 1980, p. 167)

This is not the place to rehearse the distinctions made in many sources between spoken and written language (for accounts, see Stubbs, 1980, Ch. 2; McCarthy and Carter, 1994, Ch. 1). The main aim is to draw attention to the fact that it is written discourse with which we are mostly concerned in this section, and in the book as a whole (although Sections 4.6 and 4.7 also report briefly on research into lexis in spoken discourse). In this section we examine with reference to lexis some general differences between speech and writing.

In one of few studies in this area, Ure (1971) undertook research into lexical density in spoken and written texts. An important reason for studying lexical density is that spoken and written texts differ in their relative degrees of lexical density. Put very generally, it is the case that there are more lexical words relative to grammatical words in written text compared with spoken texts. Ure studied 34 spoken texts and 30 written texts with a total length of 21,000 words in each medium. She found that the spoken texts had, on average, a lexical density of under 40 per cent; the written texts had, on average, a lexical density of over 40 per cent (ranging, in fact, from 36 to 57 per cent). One main reason for this difference is that written texts can carry a higher information load than spoken texts. Written texts are permanent and can be re-read, if necessary. Spoken texts are more ephemeral, are less planned, and rely more on an immediate physical context for their interpretation. Spoken texts must also be more predictable. Since lexical words are generally less predictable than grammatical words it is reasonable to expect that written texts have a higher proportion of lexical words. The lexical density of a text is normally calculated in percentage terms by the following formula:

$$\text{Lexical Density} = \frac{\text{number of separate words}}{\text{total number of words in the text}} \times 100$$

For example, in a text of a total of 60 words with the presence of 33 separate lexical words, the lexical density would be 55 per cent.

Other studies of lexis along the continua between spoken and written texts include research reported in Crystal (1980a) into the relative distribution of adverbial phrases. These are very common in spoken discourse, especially in casual conversation. It is widely recognized that adverbials are an indeterminate, or at least mixed, class in standard grammar. They can have extralinguistic reference and describe occurrences in the real world (e.g. *He walked home quickly*); they can convey attitudes (e.g. *Fortunately, they lost the match*); and they can also act as connectors between one part of a discourse and another (e.g. *Anyway, I am sure he will come*).

Crystal discusses spoken texts in which adverbials occur in 59 per cent of clauses. Ochs (1979), who distinguishes between 'planned discourse' and 'unplanned discourse' (roughly, written and spoken), points out the higher density of nouns in spoken discourse. Brown (1982), though she cites no data, supports the general conclusions of Ochs and Crystal. Halliday (1989), however, argues that nominalization is a feature of written discourse.

Other studies have examined the discourse functions of certain items which are more common in spoken than in written discourse. These include items such as *well, OK, right, anyway, now* and *so*, which have been given the suitably vague term 'particle' largely because such items have an uncertain status within the categories of standard grammar. Such items complicate matters further in that they do not have propositional content and, when occurring in utterance-initial position in spoken discourse, for example, do not have ready counterparts in conventional written text. Their function is often to indicate a boundary between what has gone before and a new stage in the discourse (see Sinclair and Coulthard, 1975, for their function in marking boundaries in classroom discourse). A useful collective term for these items is ***discourse markers***. Some detailed studies of particular discourse markers have been made (see Schiffrin, 1988). For example, *well* has been quite extensively studied (see Svartvik, 1980; Owen, 1981; Stubbs, 1983, pp. 68–70) for its role in interaction where it has a variable function: it can indicate a break in the discourse; it can preface a modification of assumptions made in the immediately preceding discourse; it can serve to begin to close down a topic or conversation; or it can signal a change from one topic to another. Lexical items such as this need to be studied in ways that do not rely on traditional grammatical categories which are, in any case, based on written discourse. (See Owen, 1985 for an analysis of *anyway*.)

Another feature of lexis which is again more endemic in spoken rather than written discourse, that of ***vague language***. Vague language is an inherent property of language; indeed, arguably, all lexical items have a vague denotational range. We are interested here in lexical markers of such vagueness, although we must again recognize that interpretation of degrees of vagueness depends on contextual factors such as whether the discourse is a formal or informal one. Informal spoken contexts usually produce the highest degrees of vagueness.

Examples of vagueness include 'number approximations' such as *about, approximately, or so, (a)round* and *or* (occurring between two numbers), and what Channell (1993) terms 'vague category identifiers' such as *and things, anything/something like that,* and *or something.* Examples are:

(1) I've bought some oranges *and things.*
(2) There are *about* twenty *or so* people in the room.
(3) Let's examine two *or* three examples.
(4) It's called a piston valve or *something like that.*

Vague language produces specific effects, and primary among them is a *detachment* on the part of the producer from the absolute truth of the propositions asserted. But lexical vagueness can also signal a lack of knowledge or a failure to find the required words; and it can convey simply a judgement that, in a certain context, too great a degree of precision would be out of place, or would not be understood by an interlocutor. In (3), for example, specification of a precise number would indicate a markedly systematic and rigorous approach. The presence of number approximation suggests a more informal and relaxed procedure.

Stubbs (1986b) examines further categories of lexical vagueness which he points to as obvious surface markers of detachment. The existence of items such as *so-called, so to speak* and *quote unquote* enable language users to distance themselves, often ironically and satirically, from what they are saying. For example:

This Government's *so-called* education policy militates against innovation.

In this example, the presence of *so-called* suspends any commitment to what the words refer to and marks the utterance attitudinally. By contrast, Stubbs points out, items exist which allow a commitment to what is said or which signal to an interlocutor that what follows is to be taken 'seriously'. Examples would be: *strictly speaking, to be accurate* and *technically.* The existence of all such lexical markers indicates the extent to which point of view can be encoded, lexically. Reference to 'what is said', 'interlocutor' and 'utterance' also indicates a view that examples of vague language occur more frequently and extensively in spoken discourses, although, 'technically', this claim would need to be more extensively attested by reference to corpora of spoken and written data.

4.6 Lexical patterning in spoken discourse

This section examines the role of lexical items (and, to be precise, lexical words) in spoken discourse. The aim is not simply to draw attention to some differences between speech and writing, but also to explore a relatively neglected dimension in the structural analysis of two-party conversations: the rule-governed structural links which can operate between lexical words across speaking turns. In contexts such as this the meanings of words also become more negotiable. They can register distinct attitudinal shifts and can acquire evaluative force. The research reported here is, thus, parallel to that into lexical signals and lexico-structural relations across sentences in written discourse, in that examination of lexis in use in communicative settings reveals that abstract, decontextualized accounts of the lexicon and of lexical relations may offer an impoverished view of lexical meaning.

In seminal work, Cruse (1977; 1986) explores the pragmatic dimensions of what he terms 'lexical specificity'. His data is drawn from sets of lexical items which are hierarchically related, and he concentrates particularly on the communicative effects which can result from using such items in discourse. In order to begin to capture these effects, Cruse posits the notion of INS or 'inherently neutral specificity'. He argues that taxonomies of structurally related lexical items will have some items which are more neutral and unmarked than others, and that it is by such 'norms' that the more markedly affective items can be measured. Thus, in a set *alsatian*, *dog* and *animal* the item *dog* emerges in an INS category. Cruse cites the following utterances:

> *Context*: Said by someone who is the owner of only one domestic animal – an alsatian. Hearer knows this.
>
> 1 I think I shall take the alsatian for a walk.
> 2 I think I shall take the dog for a walk.
> 3 I think I shall take the animal for a walk.

and argues that (2) is the unmarked neutral utterance because it is 'least motivated', that is, in most contexts it has the highest degree of generality (neutral specificity). (In the specialized context of a dog show, however, the use of the term dog would normally be *too* general and *alsatian* preferred.) *Alsatian* in the above examples would be overspecified; *animal* would be underspecified. However, Cruse cites the following example of a customs officer speaking to someone entering the country with a dog as an unusually marked use of lexis:

> I'm sorry, sir, but all dogs coming from abroad must be put in quarantine for six weeks.

and argues that the use of *animal* here would have maximum generality and be the less marked item. The example illustrates the fact that there is no such thing as an *inherently* neutral item, but that in most contexts, and in a taxonomy such as this, *dog* is the more usually neutral specification. This allows us to observe in a relatively systematic way that the more under- or overspecific an item, the more immediate the communication and the more marked the evaluative overtones produced by use of the item. Thus, 'Take that *animal* away' is less positive than the 'Take that *dog* away' which has a more unmarked level of specificity. And in the utterances:

> 1 I was chased down the road by a huge alsatian.
> 2 I was chased down the road by a huge dog.

1 is less positive than 2.

In question/answer sequences, further lexical values accrue to deliberate underspecifications. For example, we can note that:

> (1) *A*: What have they got in that cage?
>   *B*: An animal.

or:

> (2) *A*: What did you buy in the pet shop?
>   *B*: An animal.

or, in a parallel set with the option of *roses*, *petunias*, etc. in the reply slot:

> (3) *A*: What did you buy for mother from the florists?
>   *B*: Some flowers.

may involve either expressions of forgetfulness, reluctance to give information, sarcasm, etc. But the lexical item will be attitudinally marked and communicatively expressive.

Examination of lexical semantic relations across conversational boundaries produces a range of distinct communicative effects which, since they mark in a discourse a speaker's individual involvement and point of view, cannot always be precisely specified. And this applies to lexical relations of antonymy, synonymy, etc. as well as, as we have just seen, to hyponymy. For example, in the exchange:

> (1) *A*: It's cold today.
>   *B*: Yes, freezing.

speaker *B* uses a lexical item which marks clear agreement with speaker *A*. McCarthy (1983; 1984b) argues that such lexical marking is as normal a feature of conversational exchanges as the use of proforms (e.g. *yes it is, isn't it?*) and points out how very different effects can be produced if the relational sequence is reversed; for example:

(2) *A*: It's freezing today.
     B: Well, it's cold.

Here speaker *B* produces a response which indicates, by a combination of contrastive use of intonation, utterance-initial *well* (see above p. 93) and set-related lexical items *cold–freezing*, some measure of detachment from speaker *A*'s proposition.[3] McCarthy argues that consideration of the functions of such lexical items can provide a framework for explaining processes of negotiation between speakers and especially expressions of convergence and divergence. *Lexical* norms can be proposed for particular sequences. For example, McCarthy would argue that (1) above was a less marked sequence than (3) below:

(3) *A*: Were you furious?
     B: I was cross (I was livid/I was furious).

Here the use of core and non-core items (see Chapter 2), particularly in relation to a scale of intensity (e.g. *furious*–strong; *livid*–stronger; *cross*–weaker) indicate different degrees of acceptance, contrast or even challenge to the proposition of speaker *A*. We can also note the marked nature of questions containing non-core items ('were you *livid?*') and the potential for transaction closing made available by lexical repetition across the boundaries of conversational turns (e.g. 'Were you *furious?*/I was *furious*'), though the role of intonation cannot be ignored.

Lexical research has generally ignored the discourse functions of lexical items and, although greater predictability and fuller specification will only be possible on scrutiny of large amounts of conversational data, the kinds of negotiation conducted by speakers can be studied in terms of lexis when the structural relations of words are examined in actual use and not confined to the limits of the sentence or the decontextualized example. McCarthy (1984a) (see Section 7.13) discusses how vocabulary teaching might take account of these aspects of language performance. The discussion of marked/unmarked items might also be usefully read in conjunction with the proposal for a series of tests in Chapter 2 to help us determine coreness in vocabulary.

4.7 Corpus-based spoken language analysis

As we have seen, much of the existing literature on vocabulary has grown out of the study of written texts and the study of relatively minimal conversational exchanges. Most researchers seem to have concentrated on lexical *repetition* in spoken language (for example, Persson, 1994, who uses spoken and written data; Tannen, 1989; and, most notably, Bublitz, 1989 who looks at various functions of repetition in spoken data). There has also been a limited amount of discussion of formality in vocabulary choice in spoken language (Powell, 1992).

There are obvious historical reasons why spoken vocabulary has been under-researched: lack of good spoken corpora, the frustrating inability of analytical computer software to cope well with the 'messiness' of spoken transcripts, and, above all, the immense effort and resources required to collect spoken data compared with the ease (nowadays) of optically scanning large amounts of written text into databases, which offer access to hundreds of millions of running words (see Section 6.6). Thus it is the written word which has dominated our view not only of which words are the most important ones, but also of how words are used in acts of communication.

One of the most obviously useful types of output from computerized corpora is the frequency list. Frequency lists for everyday spoken language differ significantly from those dependent only on written databases. The two lists in Table 4.1 are each based on samples of approximately 330,000 words of data, and reveal interesting differences. The data is from the *Cambridge International Corpus* (*CIC*).

Immediately noticeable in these lists are both the similarity of occurrence of basic function words and some interesting differences which give the spoken language some of its characteristic qualities. The written list is made up of function words (function words here include all non-lexical, that is, non-contentful items, such as pronouns, determiners, prepositions, modal verbs, auxiliary verbs, conjunctions, etc.), but the spoken list seems, at first glance, to include a number of lexical words such as *know*, *well*, *got*, *think* and *right*. Quite as expected, the function words dominate the top frequencies of both lists, and, indeed, one of the defining criteria of function words is their high frequency. Nonetheless, as we go down the frequency list, there is no absolute cut-off between function words and lexical words of high frequency (such as *thing*). Using frequency alone, without other criteria (e.g. whether the word in question belongs to an open or closed set), results in a blurred borderline between 'grammar' (function) and

Table 4.1 The fifty most frequent written (left-hand column) and spoken (right-hand column) words from 330,000 words in the *Cambridge International Corpus* (*CIC*, 1996).

No.	Written	Spoken	No.	Written	Spoken
1	the	the	26	by	we
2	to	I	27	me	he
3	of	you	28	her	do
4	a	and	29	they	got
5	and	to	30	not	that's
6	in	it	31	are	for
7	I	a	32	an	this
8	was	yeah	33	this	just
9	for	that	34	has	all
10	that	of	35	been	there
11	it	in	36	up	like
12	on	was	37	were	one
13	he	is	38	out	be
14	is	it's	39	when	right
15	with	know	40	one	not
16	you	no	41	their	don't
17	but	oh	42	she	she
18	at	so	43	who	think
19	his	but	44	if	if
20	as	on	45	him	with
21	be	they	46	we	then
22	my	well	47	about	at
23	have	what	48	will	about
24	from	yes	49	all	are
25	had	have	50	would	as

'vocabulary' (lexical) words. This is something which becomes apparent in spoken data of the kind exemplified in Table 4.2.

On closer examination, some of the lexical words which intrude into the high-frequency function-word list prove to be elements of inter-personal markers (e.g. *you know* and *I think*) or single-word organiza-tional markers (e.g. *well* and *right*). Stenström (1990) discusses such words that seem to belong quintessentially to the spoken mode, and offers a useful set of headings for what she generally refers to as 'dis-course items', which include apologies, smooth-overs (e.g. *never mind*), hedges (e.g. *kind of* and *sort of*), and a variety of other types unlikely to occur in the written mode. *Well* occurs approximately nine times more frequently in spoken than in written texts. The hedging-word *just* ranks as 33 in the spoken; in the written it ranks at 61 and is two and a half times less frequent. Other items in Table 4.1 call for closer scrutiny too.

Table 4.2 Total occurrences of verb-inflections of *start* and *begin*, and total occurrences of *too* and *also* in the written and spoken parts of the *CIC*, 1996.

Items	Written	Spoken
start (verb-inflections)	232	260
begin (verb-inflections)	119	27
too (excluding *too* + ADJ)	119	132
also	289	107

What are the commonest functions of the extremely frequent spoken uses of *got*? Is *got* used differently in the spoken and the written? Let us consider some statistics. *Got* occurs approximately five and a half times more frequently in our spoken sample than in the written. By far the most frequent use of *got* in spoken is in the construction *have got* as the basic verb of possession or personal association with something. But frequency statistics alone do not tell us everything: McCarthy and Carter (1997) comment on the colligational properties of *got*, observing that structures such as *I've got so many birthdays in July* and *I've got you* are typical spoken uses. In the first case the speaker is referring to the responsibility of sending birthday cards to members of the family: *I've got* seems to mean something like 'I have to deal with'. In the second case the utterance means roughly 'I understand you'. Neither meaning might crop up in formal, written texts; spoken data is likely to be the best source for such uses.

It is not only that *got* shows such interesting differences in distribution and usage between written and spoken; other words display significant differences too, especially apparently synonymous everyday words such as *start* and *begin* (see Rundell, 1995), and *too* and *also*. The occurrences in the samples of written and spoken texts from *CIC* and CANCODE respectively, are shown in Table 4.2.

What can be noticed here is that *start* seems equally at home in spoken and written discourse, but that *begin* is relatively rare in informal spoken discourse of the kind recorded in CANCODE (part of *CIC*). A very similar picture obtains with *too*, which occurs more or less equally in spoken and written discourse; *also* occurs less than half the number of times in spoken than it does in written discourse. In the case of *begin*, it is perhaps also worth noting that, in the written data, the form *beginning* used as a noun occurs 41 times, but in the spoken only 15 times, reflecting the tendency towards nominalization in the written

Table 4.3 Percentage coverage of words in rank 501–550 and 1001–1050 in the written and spoken parts of *CIC*, 1996.

Rank in word list	Coverage (%)	
	Written	*Spoken*
501–550	1.00	0.80
1001–1050	0.52	0.36

mode. For further illustrations of the different distributions of a wide selection of words in spoken and written texts, see Engels (1988).

One final point that needs to be considered with regard to the 'top 50' spoken and written word-forms is that of how much of the total text in the corpus samples they cover. The top 50 written word-forms cover 38.8 per cent of all the text; the top 50 spoken cover 48.3 per cent, almost 10 per cent more of the total. Schonell *et al.* (1956, pp. 73–4) report a similar percentage difference in coverage for their first thousand words of spoken data, as compared with coverage figures for the first thousand words of written. This would suggest that, on the face of it, the top 50 spoken words were more useful for learners wanting an emphasis on speaking skills in their learning programme and that the view, often anecdotally expressed, that the written language is the best basis for learning both spoken and written codes, may be difficult to defend. However, another way of looking at the problem is that the figures suggest that almost half of spoken discourse has virtually no content (i.e. many of the items are function words), which would seem to make the teaching of such words as 'vocabulary' extremely difficult without accompanying contentful words to provide the necessary context. One position here would be to advocate situation-bound teaching of spoken language, where 'content' is provided by context. But it is also worth noting that the consequences of the heavy burden carried by the top 50 words in the spoken data means that, as we go down the frequency list, the spoken words in lower frequency bands will cover slightly less text than the written word. Table 4.3 shows what percentage of the total text words in the ranks 501–550 and 1001–1050 cover in the written and spoken parts respectively.

Two basic positive points may be made about the use of corpora:

1   It is worth separating spoken and written corpora for the examination of the distribution and usage patterns of individual words.

2   It is worth separating spoken and written corpora for the

examination of the distribution and usage patterns of pairs or groups of words that are apparently synonymous.

However, some problems also arise with such comparisons:

1   There is a problem with the status of the term **word** or **word-form** in the spoken corpus. Not included in the top 50 above are vocalizations transcribed in the corpus such as *mm*, *er*, *erm* and so on, some of which would merit being in the top 20 in terms of frequency of occurrence. They are not commonly thought of as relevant items for vocabulary teaching; yet they may be quite significant discoursally, and of interest in cross-cultural comparisons with languages that have phonetically different equivalent vocalizations (see McCarthy, 1990, p. 127 for a further brief discussion). On the other hand, we have included *oh* in our list, since it seems to express great affective and interpersonal meaning. But the cut-off line is by no means easy to justify.

2   Equally problematic in the spoken data is the very high incidence of contracted forms such as *it's*, *that's*, *don't*, etc. They are included as single items here, since they are often in the same general bands of frequency as their non-expanded forms (e.g. *it* and *it's* both occur in the top 20 spoken forms; *do* and *don't* are also within 20 places of each other). However, major problems present themselves to transcribers. Are *cos* and *because* to be recorded and counted as two different word-forms? If *going to* is transcribed as *gonna* when it is uttered as such, should *got to* become *godda* and *have to* become *hafta* when they are uttered informally? Such decisions can greatly affect the count for these basic, everyday spoken word-forms and there is no simple criterion that can always be followed.

3   Word-lists consisting of single word-forms (as we saw with the case of *know*) may hide the fact that the respective form regularly occurs as an element of a multi-word expression. For example, how many of the 500 plus occurrences of *thing* in the CIC spoken sample are embedded within the extremely common expression *the thing is . . .* (meaning 'the problem/point is . . .')? How many are in vague expressions such as *things like that*? Only a concordance can properly reveal whether *thing* is occurring in this way or not. (A **concordance** is a computer-assisted program for studying patterns of words as they occur in corpora of natural language.)

4   The discussion of coverage suggested that spoken words covered much more text than written. This is so, but it is also true that

spoken-word meanings are often elusive and more cryptic than their written-word equivalents (note again the meaning of *have got* discussed above). It is equally true that, in texts where there is a very high proportion of common function words, occasional, low frequency content words may provide the crucial and only convincing clues as to what the text is 'about'. This is particularly so in case of 'language-in-action' texts, that is, situations where the language is directly generated by the actions speakers are performing, such as cooking, loading luggage into a car and arranging furniture (see Carter and McCarthy, 1997, for examples).

Computational analysis of language corpora can reveal many interesting and pedagogically useful differences between spoken and written vocabulary use, and even relatively small samples (by today's standards) can yield original insight, or can raise awareness for future observation and verification in the field. However, computers are less useful when it comes to understanding the way vocabulary is used as a communicative resource by individual speakers in individual situations. A discourse- or conversation-analysis approach may be the best way of getting at how vocabulary is used in everyday spoken interaction. For example, the most common occurrence of *see* in the spoken corpus is in the unit *you see* (meaning 'understand'). Does this necessarily mean that the prototypical meaning of 'perceive with the eyes' should be relegated to second place? However, conversation analysis of itself (especially of just one textual fragment) may yield no more than an account of that particular piece of data, with little generalizability. The subsequent checking in a large corpus would always be advisable to see if insights from the individual text hold good across a wide range of samples. Corpus- and conversation-analysis are complementary for linguistic analysis.

4.8 Lexis, coherence and writing development

The discussion so far has been about the surface linguistic features which mark the organization of individual sentences or utterances into larger units of discourse. We have looked chiefly at lexical words although a range of such cohesive functions can also be performed by a large number of grammatical words. *Cohesion* concerns the ways in which the components of the surface text are mutually connected within a sequence. *Coherence*, on the other hand, concerns the ways in which the components of the *textual* world, that is, the configuration of concepts and relations which underlie the surface text, are made mutually accessible and relevant. Coherence is not merely a feature of texts, but rather the outcome of cognitive processes among text users; it is a conceptual network which has to be recognized and interpreted by the sender and the reader of a text. Not only has lexis been neglected, until recently, in the study of cohesion, but it has also been neglected in the study of coherence. Sections 4.9 and 4.10 do no more than ask some questions about the relationship between lexis and coherence, although this section does introduce a specific descriptive framework. It returns us first to the question raised by McCarthy (1984b) (Section 4.3): how is it that readers recognize texts as coherent or incoherent, and can do so independently of the presence or absence of specific lexical signals or other surface markers of cohesion? In other words, the importance of *interpretation* of lexical patterning in discourse is stressed once again. And we return once again to *written* discourse. The next section also raises a further question concerning readers' expectations concerning particular kinds of lexical items relative to type, or **genre**, of discourse. Examples are taken mostly from writing by children since a number of 'applied' studies have taken such discourse as a starting point for investigation.

Carter (1986) is devoted to the relations between vocabulary, style and coherence in children's writing, in which the following three sentences from a piece of descriptive prose by an 11-year-old boy are examined in respect of their lack of cohesion:

(1) The giant ant is enormous.
(2) All the children run away and the dogs grumble.
(3) And we stare at t.v.

(Passage A)

Here it is not clear whether the *we* in sentence (3) refers to *the children* in sentence (2); nor is there any preceding referent for '*the* children' and '*the* dogs'. There is thus no explicitly signalled relation between the sentences. Devices of simple repetition and the use of grammatical words could be deployed to secure greater cohesion. For example: *The giant ant is enormous. Our children run away from it and our dogs grumble. We are afraid of the ant and stare at t.v.*

But the presence of cohesion devices alone cannot ensure the organization of a text. Take the following example (again from a piece of children's writing discussed in greater detail in Carter, 1986):[4]

(1) Then we found our way outside from the cloakroom.
(2) Next we went outside into the pleasents and we practest the fire drill makeing sure we were quick to line up in the pleasent.

(3) Then we went back through the cloakroom.
(4) Then we had break and Jill dropped the crisps.
(5) We could go into the dining room or go outside and eat our food.

(Passage B)

This piece of writing is cohesive in so far as several devices (e.g. *we, then, next,* etc.) underline a connectedness between the sentences; but it is not consistently coherent. Part of the problem is the lack of variation in the devices used, but even if changes were made or more cohesive items added, it is unlikely that they would contribute significantly to the underlying organization of the text or remedy the general 'flatness' of the vocabulary used. When teachers write 'good word' and put a tick in the margin it is likely that they are responding not merely to a word in isolation, but signalling their perception that it contributes to the coherence and impact of the text as a whole.

It is important to locate more precisely what in vocabulary might underlie the use of terms such as 'impact' or 'flatness'. It has to be recognized that judgement here may be more variable from one individual to another, but it is certainly an impression among teachers who have been shown the two passages above that Passage A contains unusual but expressive lexical choices not to be found in Passage B. Examples pointed to are *dogs grumble* and *stare at t.v.* Further exploration of 'expressivity' is offered below, but we should note here (1) that expressive words alone – however many and varied they might be – do not make for a well-organized coherent text, (2) that relations *between* words are as important as what is *in* the word, and (3) that our judgements of effectiveness may also be relative to the genre of writing undertaken. Here, for example, more expressive words might be expected in *descriptive* writing about a giant ant than in a *report* on a sequence of actions performed in a day at school.

To summarize, then, we may say that the number and range of 'grammatical' words which contribute to the cohesion of a text are of significance in effective writing. But counting cohesive devices will not explain why some pieces of writing can be perceived to be better organized than others. (For further discussion, see Morgan and Sellner, 1980; Hasan, 1980.) Similarly, density and variability of open-class 'lexical' words should be encouraged in children's writing, but a relation of types to token – that is, the number of different words in a text (types) expressed as a relation of the total number of words (tokens) – is not of itself an effective measure of expressivity and cannot of itself either ensure that a text is coherent or account for why one text might be marked higher or lower than another for its use of vocabulary. (See Harpin, 1976 for discussion of type–token ratios. For an analysis of the role of open- and closed-class words in the development of reading comprehension see Lam, 1984 – though she uses the terms 'content' and 'function' words respectively.)

Few appropriate analytical models exist which enable vocabulary to be examined for its role in the *coherence* of a text. Daneš's work on thematic progression has considerable potential for development and has been successfully applied to the analysis of coherence in writing (see Dillon, 1981; Morgan and Sellner, 1980; Harris and Wilkinson, 1986). It is, however, focused largely on syntactic relations and does not, as developed so far, allow for particularly rich description of lexical patterning.

A potentially productive model is one outlined by Hasan (1980; 1984). Hasan's model is based on analysis of semantic relations in a text and does not accept any easy division or formal distinction between grammatical and lexical relations. Hasan proposes a 'lexical rendering' of texts which focuses not simply on those lexical items which can be cohesively interpreted, but on those which interrelate and 'interact' recurrently *across* a text. Take the following example cited by Hasan:

(1) Once upon a time there was a little girl
(2) and she went out for a walk
(3) and she saw a lovely little teddybear
(4) and so she took it home
(5) and she got home she washed it
(6) and when she took it to bed she cuddled it.

(Passage C)

Here there is 'interaction' between clauses (2) and (5) because *she* is engaged as a 'doer' in a related process of doing in both clauses. Similarly, the transitive process in (3), *she saw a teddybear*, which is related to (6), *she took it to bed* and *she cuddled it*, embraces the same doer–doing relations across the text. More importantly, the relation between words and the actions denoted is multiple not singular. It is not a case of just a single connection between lexical items. In the following examples (also from Hasan), items can be cohesively interpreted but no deeper textual relation established:

(1) The sailor goes on the ship
(2) and he's coming home with the dog

(3) and the dog wants the boy and the girl
(4) and they don't know the bear's in the chair
(5) and the bear's coming to go to sleep in it.

(Passage D)

Here there is cohesion between particular items and there is lexical repetition, but there is no deeper semantic relation between the 'coming' in (5) and the 'coming' in (2) because a different 'actor' is involved in each case. The relation is thus singular and no interaction takes place. Hasan divides the items involved in each of the relations in the following terms:

1 *Relevant token*: those lexical items in a text which exist in some singular semantic relation to each other.
2 *Central token*: that subset of relevant tokens which enter into direct and multiple interaction with each other.
3 *Peripheral token*: the difference between the total number of tokens in a text and the relevant ones. Peripheral tokens would thus not need to be used in any summary or paraphrase of content and in a normally coherent text could be expected to be in a low ratio to the *total* number of tokens.

Of these 'tokens' Hasan argues that it is the number of central tokens, expressed as a proportion of the relevant tokens, which contribute most to the *coherence* of the text. As she puts it, in simple terms, this enables us to account for our intuition that in Passage C the writer is discoursing on much the same kind of thing and stays with the topic long enough for some coherent progression/development to take place. This is not the case with Passage D, even though there are a number of grammatical and lexical words which contribute to cohesion. In other words: Passage C is cohesive and coherent; Passage D is cohesive but not particularly coherent. In both cases, lexico-grammatical relations play a notable part in the respective textual organization. The model suggested by Hasan forms the basis of analyses of writing by children which are conducted by Carter (1986) and valuably develop the work of Halliday and Hasan discussed above.

4.9 Lexis and genre

In the previous section it was observed that lexical choices can vary relative to text-type or *genre* of writing. In Carter (1988) this hypothesis is developed with reference to tests for core vocabulary as outlined in

Chapter 2 and in relation to samples of children's writing from different subject lessons across the curriculum. The following samples were selected from the writing of a 14-year-old pupil to illustrate what teachers confirmed to be appropriate to the particular genres of writing of *report*, *description* and *explanation*.

Report (subject-core: physics/science):
A bimetal bar is taken. The bar is *composed* of two layers of metal. There is brass on the outer layer and iron on the inner. When heat is *applied*, the brass layer bends the iron *over*. This *demonstrates* that brass expands *at a faster rate* than iron.

Description (non-core):
I once saw two metals have a fight. They fought in *sweltering* heat. The metals were iron and brass and they were on either side of a piece of metal. As they got hotter and hotter the brass began to win. It grew larger and the iron became *feeble*. Finally, the brass *wrestled* the iron. The iron *surrendered.*

Explanation (core):
You *take* a strip of metal. Half the strip is brass and half the strip is iron. Then you *heat* it. The bar gets longer and then *bends*. The curve *outside*, which is brass, is longer. This *shows* that brass expands more quickly than iron.

The basic point here is that the different genres normally exhibit different degrees of lexical coreness. For example, *heat* is more core than *apply heat*; *bimetal bar* is more subject-core (i.e. core to a particular field of discourse) than *strip of metal*; *sweltering* is non-core, and so on. Clearly non-core, expressive or attitudinal elements are expected to be more foregrounded in the genre of description, but would be inappropriate in others. As with the role of lexis in the creation of discourse coherence, this is another domain of discourse analysis which requires further investigation by teachers and researchers (see also Cassells, 1980; Perera, 1982; Corson, 1985).

4.10 Lexicalization, discourse and ideology

In this final section, we return to some issues raised at several points (notably Sections 4.3–4.5) concerning the ways in which lexis serves to mark evaluative elements in discourse and to encode the viewpoint and attitude a speaker or writer adopts towards a topic. The observation that language is a 'loaded weapon' and can be used for persuasive and exploitative purposes is a not uncommon one (see especially Bolinger, 1980); but there have been a number of studies recently which have sought a more systematic account of the relationship between language and ideology (e.g. Fowler *et al.*, 1979; 1991; Kress and Hodge, 1993) arguing that ideological systems exist in and are articulated through language and can, therefore, be retrieved by language analysis. The main advances in such analysis have been in the area of syntax, and these have shown the ways in which syntactic processes are employed to mediate the world from a specific point of view.

The term ***ideology*** is often used to mean 'false or distorted consciousness' but it is used for the discussion here to refer to a theory or system of beliefs which has come to be constructed as a way of comprehending the world. Ideology impregnates a society's ways of thinking, speaking, experiencing and behaving. It cannot be removed, only replaced by an alternative ideology. Thus, a choice of words or of one syntactic construction instead of another will function not just in a vacuum but to articulate ideology. Fowler *et al.* (1979) and Fowler (1991) study the particular roles of nominalization, passivization (especially agent-deletion) and transitivity in newspaper reports, and attempt to demonstrate how a consistent linguistic structuring of events is likely to encode the power structure and political position represented or favoured by the newspaper.

In the case of vocabulary, discussion of such issues has been more impressionistic, restricted in particular by the less advanced nature of lexicological analysis. It is relatively easy, however, to demonstrate how vocabulary choices are crucial to the expression of a viewpoint which extends beyond personal attitudinal marking (the focus of Sections 4.3–4.5) towards a more sociopolitical position. For example, the well-known example of *freedom-fighter* versus *terrorist* illustrates how lexical items can articulate opposing viewpoints but retain the same referential identity. A not dissimilar representation occurs in the reference in different newspapers to the prime minister of Great Britain in 1998 (Mr Tony Blair) as *Tony, Mr Blair, Blair, The Prime Minister*; and the alternative modes of address used by and about women (*Mrs, Ms, Miss*) encode different ideological viewpoints concerning the social and sexual 'position' of women. Sometimes expression of social and political attitudes can be more or less overt as in:

the £*375,000-a-year* water-company boss
the *self-styled* liberator of the coal miners

'Self-styled' here is an explicit evaluative marking, while the reference to the large salary requires interpretation on the part of the decoder. Sometimes ideological presuppositions require unravelling with reference to the semantics of particular verb-types; for example:

> The Prime Minister *explained* that the disclosure was necessary.
> The Leader of the Opposition *claimed* that the disclosure was unnecessary.

In this example, the factivity of *explain* allows reference to the presupposed truth of the subsequent statement; this is not the case with *claim* which does not encode access to truth. Newspaper reports regularly allow ideological positions to be signalled in this way, although they would doubtless not wish them to be unmasked. It is precisely such a task of unmasking ideologies and pointing up alternatives that Fowler *et al.* (1979) envisage for what they term 'linguistic criticism'. In fact, Fowler (1982a) argues that 'linguistic criticism' should replace literary criticism, abolishing distinctions between literary texts and other kinds of texts and allowing a pedagogical focus on the uses of style for expressing or concealing sociopolitical viewpoints. Fowler (1982b) has also been instrumental in developing analysis of the relationship between lexis and ideology, drawing in particular on work by Michael Halliday on 'anti-languages' (Halliday, 1978).

The term 'anti-language' is used by Halliday to refer to the development of extreme social dialects by language users such as criminals or political terrorists who exist in an oppositional relationship to the norms and ideology of the dominant culture. The ***anti-language*** created by such groups takes many forms, although Halliday points out that lexical transformations are the most visibly and obviously open to study. The lexical features of anti-language result from two main processes: ***relexicalization*** and ***overlexicalization***. The former refers to the provision of new lexical items for the new concepts developed by each oppositional group. The latter refers to the development of alternative lexical items for those domains of the counter-culture which are of especial ideological significance. Fowler (1982a) examines the use of invented anti-languages and their attendant lexicalizations in the world of criminal anti-heroes in Anthony Burgess's novel *A Clockwork Orange*, noting in relation to a range of texts that relexicalization can involve the creation of a dialectical semantics, a reversal of the normal meanings of words so that in criminal slang *upright man* might mean 'leader of a gang of criminals' and *law* might mean 'crime'.

Overlexicalization also refers to the development of a specialized technological lexicon and to the jargons developed by subgroups within a society and need not automatically exist in opposition to socially dominant norms. In fact, overlexicalization is a process which works to semanticize areas deemed by society to be of taboo status and which are, therefore, often of obsessive concern. There is a corresponding and widely known overlexicalization of items which refer to sexual inter-course or to death; and there is specialization of lexical items for homo-sexuals and old people. In this connection, standardized reference itself sometimes develops overlexicalized avoidance strategies where what are also commonly known as euphemisms cloak direct use even of the more generally sanctioned terms; for example, a homosexual lover is referred to as a *friend, associate* or *companion*, and old people are referred to as *the aged, elders, OAPs, geriatrics, seniors, senior citizens, over 60s, pen-sioners, Darby and Joan*, etc. This kind of lexicalization is not an 'anti-language' as such but it operates to identify ideologically sensitive areas of societal discourse. We should also note in this connection the many and widely codified ways in which 'man-made' language structures a male-dominated world (e.g. '*man*kind', 'odd-*man*-out', '*man* hours', '*man*handle', etc.), or the ways in which direct reference to a nuclear *bomb* is avoided by selection from an overlexicalized and suitably anaesthetized range of items (e.g. *missile, device, vehicle, arsenal, weap-onry*). (See Montgomery, 1986, Ch. 10 for fuller discussion of social representation through lexis.)

An illustration of the role of lexis in the construction of ideology in newspaper reports can be provided by the extract from *The Daily Mail* (8 October 1983) in Figure 4.1. The report, describing the then leader of the Labour Party, Neil Kinnock, is not neutral, and the lexis used is perceptibly non-core in many places. It is also often attitudinally marked in such a way as to encode the ideological position of the political editor and, presumably, the newspaper for which he is writing. We are clearly not at a stage where a systematic analysis of lexicaliza-tion and ideology in discourse can be offered. Instead, a number of observations and questions offer 'linguistic-critical' insights into the passage and may also provide a basis for subsequent methodological development.

Attitudinal marking of lexis in this passage is pervasive. This ranges from non-core items such as *swamp*, (argument) *boiling, nightmare* question, *posing, ducking, novice* leader, *frantically buttonholing, nail* and *razzmataz* to more text-specific evaluation in which lexical items which are generally neutral in the abstract lexicon are negotiated into assum-ing negative connotations: for example, *youngest* leader at 41, *young* Mr Kinnock, *trendy new* leader, *new* beginning, *novice* leader. Structural

A soaking on the beach ... a snub by the Left

CANUTE KINNOCK

By GORDON GREIG, Political Editor

NEIL KINNOCK, just elected Labour's youngest leader at 41, saw an old party tide threaten to swamp his new beginning last night.

Once again, the nightmare question came up. How far are you going to dismantle Britain's nuclear defence shield?

The answer helped Michael Foot lose the last election and from the way the argument was boiling at Brighton, it clearly threatened to help Mr Kinnock lose the next one.

His induction to the mantle of leadership began with a soaking on Brighton beach as he stumbled and fell at the sea's edge while posing for photographers. But the embarrassment of that Canute-like ducking was nothing to the problem of a backroom row between Labour's Left and Right over the rising tide of pacificism and one-sided nuclear disarmament in the party.

Toe the line 'or we'll have you'.

Suicide

An angry session of the National Executive provided a curtain-raiser to a debate on Wednesday which may nail young Mr Kinnock more firmly than ever to getting rid of all nuclear weapons.

It saw the novice leader frantically buttonholing colleagues in an attempt to avert what he sees as political suicide. It also saw Denis Healey angrily pounding the table and warnings from Anthony Wedgwood Benn and Ken Livingstone that Mr Kinnock could blow it in the next year if he does not stick to Left-Wing policies.

And there was a blunt message to Mr Kinnock from veteran Left Winger Joan Maynard at a fringe meeting: 'If you don't walk your shoes straight we'll have you next year.'

But for a few moments the trendy new leader enjoyed the razzmatazz of an election night with an overwhelming victory for the 'dream ticket'—Mr Kinnock plus Roy Hattersley as his deputy.

The result of the leadership ballot, with Mr Kinnock streets ahead of his nearest rival Mr Hattersley and Peter Shore and Eric Heffer nowhere, produced an explosion of cheers.

Mr Kinnock clenched his hands above his head boxer-style and gave his wife—and inspiration—Glenys a hearty kiss.

Figure 4.1 Canute Kinnock: The lexis of reporting.
Source: Daily Mail, 8 October 1983.

semantic patterning also assists such a process: for example, *novice* leader/*veteran* Left Winger; *youngest* leader/*old* party/*new* beginning (with *old* doing here a double semantic duty by contrasting with *young* and *new*). An ideological position is also signalled by devices such as switches in formality, for example:

> His induction to the mantle of leadership began with a soaking on ˙Brighton beach.

Here the transition from formal to informal lexis parallels, in an almost comic burlesque, the action of Kinnock's momentary loss of dignity, but it also deliberately undercuts any pretension to serious leadership on the part of Kinnock. Repetition also plays its part in reinforcing key content: for example, *lose* the *last* election/*lose* the *next* one (where a structural semantic pattern again reinforces and foregrounds the message). And the morphological root repetition – *mantle* of leadership/ dis*mantle* – may be an even more subtle underlining of irresponsibility, especially when framed by the question:

> How far are you going to dismantle Britain's nuclear defence shield?

which cleverly presupposes that a decision to dismantle has already been taken by the Labour leader. Other comparably subtle (as it were, poetic) parallelisms are provided by phonological associations; for example, 'a *s*oaking on the beach . . . a *s*nub by the Left' and the juxtaposition (reinforced by typography) of '*C*anute' and '*K*innock'. There is also a sustained metaphor in the idea of Canute being unable to resist a 'rising tide'/'party tide' which threatens not only a 'ducking' but also to 'swamp' him. And discussion would not be complete without reference to the ideological distancing brought about by the use of disassociating quotation marks in 'dream ticket'.

Fuller analysis would also need to take account of the selection of certain syntactic processes which encode an ideological position of opposition to Mr Kinnock and to the events of his election as Labour Party leader. One example, but probably chief among them, would be the attribution of insight to an abstract non-human entity in: 'An angry session of the National Executive . . . It saw . . .' which subtly removes the need for attribution to, or attestation by, anyone who might have been there to corroborate these 'facts'. And fuller semantic analysis of the passage would also need to take account of the way lexically cohesive items cluster in a semantic set associated with *problems* and *questions* to which answers are either not forthcoming or are inadequate. However, what this discussion does demonstrate, is that lexis can be both overt and instrumental in signalling ideology and that some of its more interesting functions can be located in the discourse of news reports. There is further discussion of lexicalization and ideology in Section 5.9 with particular reference to the study of literary texts and in Section 9.1 where the importance of a stylistic overlay to the meaning of words and of ideological representation is examined in relation to lexicographic practice. Carter and Nash (1990) and Fairclough (1995) also contain much relevant material.

4.11 Conclusion

This chapter demonstrates the extent of research still needed to provide adequate and replicable analyses of the part played by lexis in spoken and written discourse. As a level of language analysis, discourse analysis is itself at relatively formative stages; but I have discussed some features of lexical behaviour which show how important lexical patterns are in discourse organization. The underdevelopment of analysis and application in this domain is reflected by the way in which the subsequent chapters in this book discuss pedagogic and other applications which relate more directly to the bases provided in the previous three chapters than to any foundations laid here. However, applications of insights in this chapter to vocabulary teaching, in particular, are discussed in Chapter 7; and reports of lexicographic work for the COBUILD project at 6.6.1 indicate that some foreign learners' dictionaries aim to draw more extensively and systematically on insights into the role of lexis in discourse.

Notes

1 Stubbs (1983, pp. 77–82) refers to such items as 'pragmatic connectors' and offers a wide-ranging discussion of their discourse functions. See also Schiffrin (1988).
2 'Ownerless' nouns are an interesting class. They include items such as *fact* or *issue*, which are not associated with a particular writer or source. Their meanings do not normally carry evaluative or attitudinal marking.
3 We should note in this connection that syntax and intonation also signal marked acceptance of the proposition; but that in a three-part exchange the *third* slot open to speaker A allows for agreement by synonym, normally one involving a process of intensification; for example:

    A: It's cold
    B: Yes, it *is* cold, isn't it?
    A: Mm. Freezing

4 The examples here are similar to that cited by Van Dijk (1985a):

> This morning I had a toothache.
> I went to the dentist.
> The dentist has a big car.
> The car was bought in New York.
> New York has serious financial troubles.

Here there is cohesion by lexical repetition and by membership of lexical set (*toothache/dentist*) but the text lacks a coherent global organization. See also Petöfi (1985).

Part II

Reviews

5 Lexis and literary stylistics

5.0 Introduction

The next three chapters are all devoted to applications of lexicological studies. Three main domains are considered: *literary stylistics*, *lexicography* and *vocabulary learning and teaching*. In all three domains applications are inevitably restricted, as we have seen in the preceding sections, by the limited nature of the advances made in the linguistic description of the lexicon.

In the case of literary stylistics, lexis is rightly recognized as a significant component in any multi-levelled stylistic description but studies undertaking description at a lexical level have been generally unsystematic and, in comparison with syntactic or phonological analyses, have lacked depth and delicacy. This overview of descriptive work in what might be loosely termed *lexical stylistics* covers some key theoretical areas in contemporary literary stylistics. Chief among these are the issues of literariness, the existence of 'literary' tropes and the question of interpretation.

Sections 5.1–5.4 examine the kind of lexical analyses of literary text which have been undertaken in the past 30 years or so and pay particular attention to some theoretical issues underlying the nature of readers' responses to literary vocabulary. Here some basic questions in the use of informants for literary text analysis are examined, and one section in particular (Section 5.4) should serve as a basis for empirical informant-based studies of lexis undertaken in relation to a range of literary texts in Chapter 8. It is in Sections 5.5–5.7, however, where the more fundamental theoretical questions are reviewed and some introduction to these questions may be useful here.

Literary stylistic analysis during the 1960s and 1970s adopted a critical framework which was in several respects parallel to that of practical criticism. The main aim was to undertake a close reading of the language of canonical literary texts and to use this as a basis for their fuller interpretation. This is still an approach shared by many literary stylisticians and it reveals much that is understood to be characteristically 'literary' about language in general and vocabulary in particular: for example, associations, subtle connotations, lexical ambiguity, striking metaphor, etc. This approach is illustrated in Section 5.3. In the 1980s and 1990s, however, questions have been asked about the nature of literary texts which have been influential in the field of stylistics: what exactly *is* literary about canonical literature?; to what extent is the definition of literature an ideological one?; is it only in 'literary' texts that metaphors and lexical ambiguities are found?; and, what is literary language anyway? This focus inevitably means that less attention is given to an interpretation of the meanings for the texts concerned and this in turn has led to fuller consideration of the nature and theory of interpretation itself. An account of these issues, with particular reference to lexical matters, is thus given in the last half of this chapter. Readers interested in a much fuller and more general survey of work in stylistics should consult Carter (1985b; 1997).

5.1 Sets, patterns and meaning

Recent textbooks in literary stylistics have attempted to remedy the situation of neglect of specifically *lexical* studies. Leech and Short (1981, pp. 75–80) include useful points of reference for lexical analysis in their checklist of stylistic categories; Traugott and Pratt (1980, pp. 110–14) offer insightful discussion of lexical cohesion in a poem by Robert Bridges; and Cummins and Simmons (1983) devote a whole section to lexis, seeing it, within a framework of systemic linguistics, as a distinct level, and discussing the metaphorical and other effects brought about by collocation, cohesion and other kinds of lexical patterning. A significant proportion of Cummins and Simmons's section on lexis is devoted to lexical-set analysis, and their discussion of a number of texts, notably Dylan Thomas's 'Fern Hill', in terms of differently organized patterns of lexis, suggests a useful starting point for examination of relative degrees of thematic prominence. The discussion of 'Fern Hill' (Cummins and Simmons, 1983, pp. 183–5) isolates sets of words in the poem which are grouped predominantly around the 'themes' of *the farm* and *nature* with subsets and thus subsidiary themes of *nobility*, *religion*, *happiness*, *colour* and *water*. Stanza 3 from the poem reads as follows:

All the sun long it was running, it was lovely, the hay
Fields high as the house, the tunes from the chimneys, it was air
  And playing, lovely and watery
    And fire green as grass.
  And nightly under the simple stars
As I rode to sleep the owls were bearing the farm away,
All the moon long I heard, blessed among stables, the nightjars
  Flying with the ricks, and the horses
    Flashing into the dark.

The stanza could be analysed, using the 'themes', as follows:

The Farm	*Nature*	*Religion*
stables	sun	blessed
ricks	moon	
fields	stars	
farm	air	
hay	nightly	

and so on.

It is clear how the analysis proceeds and along what lines it would be extended, and it must be stressed that Cummins and Simmons do not propose that such lexical analysis is anything more than preliminary. However, even limited demonstration illustrates that lexical-set analysis, particularly of literary texts, where fine gradations of meaning, associations, ambiguities, metaphors and semantic overlaps between words are often densely exploited, does carry some inherent limitations. For example, in the case of this stanza from 'Fern Hill' it is difficult appropriately to demarcate a number of items. Are 'owls' and 'horses' to be grouped under the category *farm* or *nature* or some further subset such as *animals*? Is 'blessed' to be allocated to *religion* or to *happiness*? Does 'lovely' belong to *happiness* or, because of its co-reference to 'air', does it more appropriately belong to the *nature* set. If, as seems likely, it is the case that some words can be assigned to more than one category, then by what means can relative degrees of 'belonging' be assessed? And what about constellations such as 'All the sun long' or 'All the moon long' where 'sun' and 'moon' belong on one level to *nature* but metaphorically displace items such as 'day' and 'night', which might more reasonably require a further *time* subset? There is also the problem that repetition of items contributes to the semantic loading of a particular category, but repetition as a rhetorical or stylistic feature signifies much more than mere thematic prominence.

Although there are initial advantages to such a procedure, lexical-set analysis is inevitably dependent on the intuitions of the analyst and thus not markedly systematic in a linguistically principled sense. In fact, it is probably more dependent on such intuitive operations than is usual in literary stylistic analysis. One problem in isolating lexis and lexical-set formation from meanings and effects at other linguistic levels may be a corresponding analytical narrowing and a failure to perceive the semantic densities which result from an inter-penetration of levels (a criticism which could be levelled at Roger Pearce's work on 'assimilation' and 'dissimilation' in lexico-literary analysis; Pearce, 1977). Thus, the way a lexical item is stressed, or the particular syntactic environment in which it operates, may provide more 'evidence' for interpretive-thematic assignment. In any case, it is reasonable to say that in the absence of more rigorous methods the subjective, personal and even idiolectal nature of our use of and response to words will continue, for better or for worse, to determine the nature of analysis and interpretation of many literary stylistic studies of lexis.[1]

5.2 Lexis and register-mixing

Lexical-set analysis is a primarily language-internal, lexical semantic procedure. Its operation exposes the need for examination of those more indeterminate areas of word-meaning which appear to resist easy classification because they rely on connotation and association. It is often particularly the case in poems that such connotative meanings and associations are exploited. Discussion and analysis of such associations requires close attention to the registers of use in which certain lexical items belong.

One of the first questions this raises is whether there is an identifiable 'register' of poetry. As Levenston (1976) points out, the issue has been widely discussed by literary critics but not systematically by stylisticians. Levenston cites an extensive treatment of the topic by Davie (1967) in a book entitled *The Purity of Diction in English Verse*; Davie points out that at particular periods in the history of English literature certain lexical items and locutions have existed which were markedly literary. Such usages were particularly prevalent in eighteenth-century poetry where they would often serve to mark a certain stylistic integrity or purity in treatment and an elevation in the seriousness accorded to the topic. A good illustration of such diction is Thomas Gray's 'Ode on a Prospect of Eton College' discussed in terms of its lexical poeticality by Leech (1969, pp. 14–16):

> Say, Father Thames, for thou hast seen
> > Full many a sprightly race
> Disporting on thy margent green,
> > The paths of pleasure trace.

It would be untrue to suggest that such diction involves a finite set of items but it is possible to mark recurrent features such as syntactic inversions, subjunctives, archaic pronouns and a range of regularly deployed lexical items; for example, *disporting, margent, verdure, nymph, slumber, swain.* It should be noted, too, that when used outside poetic contexts the poeticality of such items carries over as it were and invokes associations of use in poems situated in history and thus of archaism, temporal distance, and even, for some purposes, what might be termed irony (see Chapter 8). In terms of accounting for responses to such diction, Levenston asks how analysis and criticism cope with periods 'in which there were few or no restraints placed on the language of poetry' with the result that the poet can exploit items that deviate from expected norms for poetic diction or can even utilize a juxtaposition of several registers in the same poem. (For further discussion in this area, see Bronzwaer, 1970, p. 30; Crystal, 1972; Lipski, 1976; Cluysenaar, 1976, p. 106; and for specific studies: Zumthor, 1971, on medieval poetry; Milroy, 1977, Ch. 4, on G.M. Hopkins; and Carter, 1978; 1979, Ch. 4, on W.H. Auden.)

Essentially, the distinction being drawn here is one between literary language and literary diction, and between poetical and unpoetical words. This lexical mixing or 'logopoeia', as it has been termed by Ezra Pound (see Pound, 1927, and also Section 5.3), is a particular feature of much twentieth-century poetry and it is this characteristic which presents especial descriptive problems for stylistic analysis. Also significant in this respect is the way in which a literary text is often innovative in the kind of associations it draws on so that in the process new associations can be created. Bronzwaer has noted this to be a feature of the logopoeia he discerns in Eliot's *The Waste Land*:

> The 'situation' of *The Waste Land* is so difficult to grasp because it is described in a register that is 'new' and consists of a deliberately startling mixture of elements from different registers that were traditionally kept very clearly apart, the pastoral and the urban, the 'poetic' and the 'prosaic', the ancient and the contemporary, the metrical and the non-metrical, the aristocratic and the vulgar.
>
> (Bronzwaer, 1970, p. 30)

The practical implications for precise description of such lexical patterns are thrown into focus by a number of factors. First, use of such terms as 'colloquial', 'poetical' and 'circumlocutory' together with such general notions of language as 'bureaucratic', or in the case of Bronzwaer, the even more imprecise 'aristocratic' and 'vulgar', leads directly into the question of how such impressions or intuitions can be verified. Secondly, even more problematic in such contexts might be the kind of presuppositions underlying any use of the word 'normal'. Thirdly, as Bronzwaer suggests, when a literary genre is employed factors such as 'tradition', 'archaism' and 'the contemporary' inevitably point towards a diachronic perspective for analysis. Within the perspective of particular traditions and their associated literary-historical dimensions, the difficulties of measuring the degree of poeticality attaching to particular locutions are considerable. Shifting tastes, too, allow different 'acceptances' of poetic vocabulary, different kinds of syntax and different views of the function of archaism in poetry. Pearce (1977) has usefully posed the question of appropriate norms:

> Unfortunately, since the concept of register is variable in delicacy, it is difficult to use it to maintain a consistent norm: should the relevant register be poetry, Augustan poetry, Pope's poetry or *The Rape of the Lock*?
>
> (Pearce, 1977, p. 33)

5.3 Interpreting lexis in poetry

Interpreting lexis in poetry involves close scrutiny of the lexical choices made in relation to the overall meaning of the poem. The process can involve consideration of alternative choices and an evaluation of the significance of particular selections. The specifically semantic considerations can be supplemented by interpretation of lexical patterns. Lexical patterns can embrace repetition, grouping into semantic sets, synonymic variation and so on. Particular significance is also attached to unusual collocations and to the effects brought about by these and by striking metaphors or similes. The literary critical aim is often one of making a correlation between the discerned patterns and the effects or meanings produced by those patterns. This correlation between formal and semantic features is in the hands of the individual interpreter who then seeks to convince readers of the validity of his/her critical statement.

An example of this interpretive procedure which is a very common and conventional practice in discussions of literary language use can be provided by examining a stanza from a poem. Here is the first stanza from 'Janet Waking' by the modern American poet John Crowe Ransom:

> Beautifully Janet slept
> Till it was deeply morning. She woke then
> And thought about her dainty-feathered hen
> To see how it had kept.

Readers regularly remark that some lexical choices and patterns in this stanza sound unusual. The 'unusual' words are agreed to be:

> 'Beautifully', 'deeply', 'kept', '*dainty*-feathered'

Extracting the words from their context in the poem and jumbling them up with other words from the stanza leads to a recognition that some words collocate more easily than others. There is, in fact, a kind of magnetic field at work which forcefully draws some of the words together. For example:

> beautiful and morning
> deeply and sleep

seem to attract each other more closely than is the case in this text where 'beautifully' is closer to 'sleep' and 'deeply' closer to 'morning'. Most native speakers would tend to agree on the usualness of:

> I slept *deeply* (rather than *beautifully*) or
> I had a nice deep sleep.

or

> It was *a beautiful morning* (rather than *a deep morning*)

although, if we convert 'morning' into 'mourning' then it attracts the word 'deep' much more strongly, for example:

> They were in deep mourning.
> His death was deeply mourned.

But the two other words most often singled out, 'dainty' and 'kept', do not seem to have any ready-made partners internal to this stanza. In such cases, jumbling up and rearranging does not lead to anything. Instead, a procedure of substitution needs to be adopted. That is, we do not readily find 'kept' fits 'hen' so we try to substitute 'hen' with other words:

```
*The hen kept
*The house kept
                    ⎧ the key    (kept here would be a
The man kept       ⎨             transitive verb)
                    ⎩ hens
The milk kept
The meat kept
The cheese kept
*The car kept
```

'Kept', then, when used in this way (i.e. intransitively) seems only to go with what can be loosely called perishable items (things, that is, which, to put it colloquially, 'go off').

We can thus discern links between perishable, deeply mourning (and, if necessary, 'sleep', 'waking') and conclude a common association with death. The death of the hen is thus, in part, subtly foretold in the first stanza of the poem. There may even be from one viewpoint a rather cruel 'overtone' in the word 'kept' in that the hen is already putrefying as Janet runs across her world to see it. The way the words in the first sentence change their natural places seems on one level to parallel the way in which the world of Janet is turned inside out, reversed and otherwise dislocated from normal expectations. We can thus make direct equations between language observation and literary meaning.

'Janet Waking' is an example of a logopoeic poem. Logopoeia is defined by Pound (1927) as:

> the 'dance of the intellect among words', that is to say, it employs words not only for their direct meaning, but it takes count in a special way of *habits of usage*, of the *context we expect to find with the words*, its *usual concomitants*, of its known acceptances and of ironical play.
>
> (Pound, 1927, p. 25)

Logopoeia produces lexical relations which are difficult to measure and to interpret except in somewhat impressionistic terms. The above interpretation of a stanza from 'Janet Waking' shows it can be done, but only informally. Such informal interpretations of lexical usage are common in literary-text study, particularly when practical criticism is undertaken. The next sections are not so explicitly concerned with interpretation, however; they address questions to do with both the nature and operation of lexis in literary texts and with attempts to define and measure specific lexical effects and associations in a more precise and retrievable manner. In turn, they lead to further questions concerning the nature and operation of interpretation of lexis in literature (see Section 5.7).

5.4 Measuring lexical associations in literary texts

A limited and small-scale attempt to invoke an *intersubjective* basis for measuring responses to words as a preliminary step to fuller lexical analysis is reported in Carter (1982a). The study made use of a group of informants (undergraduate students of English language and literature) and sought to explore both the validity of the notion that 'poetical' words *are* recognizable both in and out of the inner context of a poem and that 'logopoeic' transitions and switches in lexical association in much modern poetry can be to some degree attested. The study is based on responses to a modern poem – W.H. Auden's 'Oxford' – and one aim is to try to introduce a more empirical dimension to the discussion outlined in the previous section. In addition to 'poeticality' the main variable tested for is that of formality in lexis. There are many norms to work with in such a text but a norm of 'casual conversation' was selected to guide informants in recording their responses and to provide a basis for less impressionistic analysis of those terms, such as 'colloquial', 'stilted' or 'formal', judged to be needed for description of what the analyst felt were foregrounded lexical effects in the poems. An extended example of this kind of informant-based analysis of lexis in literary text, together with sample informant test questionnaires, is provided in the case study in Chapter 8. However, the following example from the poem (stanza 3), together with a sample analysis from the informant tests, gives some indication of what is involved:

> Outside, some factories, then a whole green country
> Where a cigarette comforts the evil, a hymn the weak,
> Where thousands fidget and poke and spend their money:
> > Eros Paidagogos
> > Weeps on his virginal bed.

Informants' responses to the lexis indicate a number of areas of potential interest in Auden's style at this point in the poem. First, informants marked the existence of 'virginal' as 'poetic diction' and the same item, perhaps not surprisingly, scores high (i.e. formal) on a formality cline.

'Eros Paidagogos' is similarly marked as formal. Secondly, 80 per cent of informants assessed 'fidget and poke' to be (1) 'not usable by a poet from the previous century' and (2) a markedly informal deviation from a norm of casual conversation. Thirdly, 'a cigarette comforts' scored low as poetic diction (48 per cent of informants) and low (i.e. informal) on the formality cline. Fourthly, there were also tests for expected and unexpected collocations. Only 'fidget and poke' were tested for but, on the evidence gathered, it is a reasonable prediction that, as with 'fidget and poke', other items from this stanza would be assessed as unusual collocations.

Quantitative analysis of informants' responses to these preselected features in the poem's lexical organization was then taken as a starting point for further discussion and interpretation of lexical effects in the text. And in this respect the marked 'impurity' and instability of the associations in stanza 3 of the poem were taken to be of particular significance. Indeed, the language encodes a sense of insecurity about incursions from 'outside' on the settled world of Oxford and the uneven, unsettled lexical associations help to draw attention to this. The informant testing allows a degree of intersubjective attestation of such effects to be claimed though any *interpretation* remains the responsibility of the analyst. As with most stylistic analysis, interpretive equations between formal linguistic features and meanings are necessarily personal, provisional and partial (see Section 5.7).

The study described here also needs to be located within a context of some proposed strategies for teaching poetry (involving close procedures, formality clines, etc.) and the article does have avowed additional pedagogic aims. (For further examples of vocabulary study in literature see Carter, 1981; Carter and Long, 1987; 1991.) However, such an orientation should not preclude the need for discussion of how the analytical and procedural strategies adopted in the study can be improved and refined or of how generalizations might be made about informant analysis and the measurement of lexical associations and patterning in literary and non-literary texts.

5.5 Using informants

This section is designed to be read in conjunction with the case study in Chapter 8. There is space here to do no more than briefly list some of the theoretical and practical issues encountered in using informants for purposes of stylistic analysis, and to point to one or two areas for possible development. More extensive review of issues can be found in Carter (1979, Ch. 4) and Van Peer (1986).

5.5.1 *Who is the reader?*

There is a relatively long history of using informants for literary text studies and recently this has to some extent run in parallel with developments in what has been variously termed 'affective stylistics', 'reader response criticism', 'the aesthetics of reception' (see Holub, 1984). A presupposition basic to such analysis and one implicit in the above discussion is that the literary text is not an autotelic, intransitive event, a container from which a reader extracts a message, but a dynamic, linear and temporal process. That is, it is something which happens to a reader in interaction with the words of a text as he reads and experiences them. Meanings are thus not text-immanent but contextual. Most analysts would follow Guiraud (1971) in attempting, by appeal to actual readers, to recover the 'image of the reader' which all texts could be said to create, but most studies have also had to contend with the questions of 'who reads' and what kind of 'reading competence' readers might be assumed to possess.

Fish (1970) outlines a possible profile for 'an informed reader' in the following terms:

The informed reader is someone who
1 is a competent speaker of the language out of which the text is built up
2 is in full possession of the 'semantic knowledge that a mature . . . listener brings to his task of comprehension'. This includes the knowledge (that is, the experience both as producer and comprehender) of lexical sets, collocation probabilities, professional and other dialects, etc.
3 has literary competence.

Fish's definition begs a number of important questions. For example, how is literary competence to be defined? For his 'affective stylistics' Fish defines it as follows:

He is sufficiently experienced as a reader to have internalised the properties of literary discourses, including everything from the most local of devices (figures of speech etc.) to whole genres.

Perhaps an indication of the difficulties involved in locating such informants and in both defining and attesting such competence is that Fish relies ultimately on his own competence as an 'informed reader' and becomes his own informant.[2] Others have sought to postulate a 'superreader' – an aggregate of many readers' responses – or have worked with a combination of such responses supplemented by the reading of the analyst himself.

5.5.2   Competence: Linguistic and literary

Related questions under this heading would be whether linguistic literary competence is primary, which in turn poses further questions about their separability. Also, to what extent can 'lay language users' without this 'literary competence' be usefully employed, and would this inevitably mean that responses to, say, lexical patterns might only get explained as linguistic peculiarities?[3] Again, this raises the issue of how far such problems might be subsumed within the competence of the controlling analyst (a differentiation, that is, between what Eaton, 1972; 1978 terms 'introspective semics' and 'semic accompaniment'; see also Van Peer, 1986). Such questions are related, too, to the extent to which it is possible to exclude or even control the personal and evaluative reading preferences of individuals or groups of informants (particularly if informants are from a single age group as in Carter's 1982a study). Furthermore, any familiarity informants may have with certain texts or authors, what Kuhns (1972) terms 'learning the language of author X', which may condition responses, would need to be checked and, where possible and appropriate, controlled. More difficult to control, however, is the problem raised by Pearce (1977) about norms and acknowledged by Riffaterre (1959, p. 162): 'The AR's ('average reader') validity is limited to the state of the language he knows: his linguistic consciousness, which conditions his reaction, does not reach beyond a short span of time in the evolution of his language.' Thus, in reading, say, poems by Auden, it is difficult to measure contemporaneous response. What was innovative in 1930 may have become conventionalized by 1995 and vice versa.

It is in the light of problems such as these that more practical problems in the design of instructions to informants have to be located. Analysts have to exercise considerable caution that informants do not simply indicate responses which have been unconsciously predicted and thus signalled in the selection of items for marking or 'topics' for attention. For example, it must be asked whether or not the instruction in Carter (1982a) for informants to underline 'words not usable by a poet in the previous century' actually suggests distinctions in poeticality or draws attention to features which might not otherwise be 'read'. The institutionalization of such tests in educational settings involving teacher and taught may also generate pressures to conform to expectations, whether covertly or overtly transmitted, which may, whatever the claims for greater empiricism and 'intersubjectivity' affect the validity and authenticity of results.

Finally, most definitions of competence will probably be expressed in educational terms. For example, undergraduate students of English language and literature will have a certain institutionally defined competence. But such competence will be that which exists in a relatively restricted community of readers. In turn, such readers are being asked to respond to institutionally defined canonical literary texts (see also Section 5.9). The potentially dangerous circularity in such definition needs to be acknowledged. (For elaboration of these and further social and ideological factors in the 'institution' of reading see Chilton, 1983; Toolan, 1984, and on the dangers of 'empiricism' in informant-based work see Holub, 1984, pp. 134–46.)

5.5.3 *Analysis*

The responsibilities of the analyst in this area then are considerable. He must remain alert to problems of theoretical importance and of procedural practicality. Decisions must be taken in the selection of informants, the design of tests (particularly crucial in the area of lexical associations), the uses made of the results and the claims advanced for them. There is also the issue raised in Section 5.1 of the extent of overlap between lexis and other levels, particularly lexical semantics and syntax. Design of tests needs to anticipate that responses to lexical patterns are matters of sequential processing which involve interpenetration of language effects. Connected with this is a seemingly minor but, in fact, major question of whether responses should be conditioned by more than one reading of the text. It should be noted too, that quantitative analysis of lexis or language generally is only one dimension. As Kintgen (1984) has demonstrated, in a study involving tape recording of responses to poems by only four graduate students, qualitative analyses are also possible and might be used to supplement the more quantitative work (see also Van Peer, 1986 for examples of much more detailed and refined statistical analysis than in Carter, 1982a). Finally, the analyst must remain supplementarily alert to the kinds of problems of ideology and interpretation raised in much recent literary theoretical work (see Eagleton, 1983; Butler, 1984) and particularly, to his own 'position' as a reader (see also Section 5.9).

5.6 Lexis and literariness

One important theoretical question which underlies discussion of lexis in literature and which is almost taken as given in applied stylistic studies of the kind reported above is the nature of the literary lexicon itself and the role of what is specifically lexical in such an operation. More precise determination of the literary uses of vocabulary is dependent on what is generally understood by literary language and this is in turn dependent on what 'literature' is. There is insufficient space here to enter such debate in depth but the relevant broad parameters need to be outlined. Indeed, even the provision of very preliminary and tentative answers to such theoretical questions constitutes a process of investigation which may be as valuable to the study of language and literature as more conventional stylistic analyses (lexical or otherwise) of texts by authors established in a 'canon' of literature. This section and the next will thus review and explore briefly issues connected with the existence or otherwise of a literary lexicon and, among other related questions, explore the role of lexical features in the organization of those tropes such as metaphor which are generally considered to belong to markedly literary domains. In particular, it is argued that it is more accurate to speak of literariness in language use (see Carter and Nash, 1983; 1990) than of literary language. Illustrative examples are taken from three passages from three different contexts of use which are connected by the theme of the motor car:

> Commence by replacing the hub-bearing outer race (33), Fig. 88, which is a press fit and then drop the larger bearing (32) into its outer member followed by oil seal (31), also a press fit, with lip towards bearing. Pack lightly with grease.
>
> If the hub is to be fitted to a vehicle equipped with disc brakes, a concentric ring of Prestic 5686 must be applied between the shield and axle face. On hubs with drum brakes, apply sealing compounds between shield and back-plate.
>
> Fit hub (28) to sub axle (1) and fit the inner member of the outer race, also greased. Replace the inner nut (34) and tighten to remove all end-float. If discs are fitted check run-out. Slacken inner nut two holes and check end-float (0.004–0.006 in.) using a dial gauge.
>
> (Passage A)

The most prominent feature of this passage is that the lexical items are only effective in conjunction with another medium, that is, the technical drawing referred to as Fig. 88. It is generally apparent that the text has to do with the fitting of a hub assembly to the axle of a car; but its details cannot be properly understood without the accompanying diagram. Such 'medium dependence' is not a characteristic of literary language, though there are certainly special cases (e.g. the dramatic text and the film commentary) in which a verbal process is linked with another channel of communication. One of the ways in which such cases differ from the present example is that in them words function descriptively and inferentially rather than directively. This text implies the relationship of the instructor and the instructed. It specifies performances and, in that way, is markedly non-literary. Literary language is sometimes axiomatic, carrying directives in the form of moral injunctions, but it never directs us to perform particular actions in current response to the text.

In these two respects, then, Passage A lacks the property of literariness: it depends on a parallel, non-verbal, form of communication, and it treats the reader as an agent responding to a directive process. It is also unliterary in its restrictive *monosemy*, that is, its use of precise technical terms which are valid only in special application by a special type of audience. Some of these terms, like *end-float* and *run-out*, must be obscure to all but the motor mechanic; others (for example, *hub-bearing outer race*, *oil seal* and *stub axle*) are difficult in the absence of the diagram with which they have an ostensive (= 'What's this called?') relationship. This brings us back to the question of 'medium dependence'. The uninformed reader of a workshop manual can struggle to come to grips with it by studying the text in relation to the diagram and the diagram in relation to the text. In literary discourse, by contrast, there are vital and increasingly complex relationships between words; as we read, we try to follow these semantic networks and create in our own minds the experiential pattern they imply. This is a difficulty of a different order from that of discovering the meaning of a set of technical terms.

The Company will indemnify the Insured against damage to or loss of the Insured Vehicle (and its accessories and spare parts while thereon while in the Insured's private garage).

Provided always that in the event of damage to or the total destruction or total loss of the Insured Vehicle the liability of the Company under this Clause shall be limited to the market value of the Insured Vehicle immediately before such damage, destruction or loss or the Insured's estimate of the value of the Insured Vehicle (as last advised to the Company), whichever is the less.

If to the knowledge of the Company the Insured Vehicle is the subject of a hire purchase agreement any payment for damage to or loss of the Insured Vehicle (which damage or loss is not made to the vehicle by repair, reinstatement, or replacement) shall be made to the owner described therein whose receipt shall be a full and final discharge to the Company in respect of such damage or loss.

(Passage B)

Here is another piece of utilitarian prose. It is, like Passage A, as devoid of literary resonances. Yet by examining its presuppositions and its management of language, we may take a step towards the definition of literariness. This text supports itself, through its own verbal elaborations, and although it presupposes knowledge of a certain type of social convention (the exchanging of contracts) it at least does not rely on another medium or on the co-presence of some extra textual object. It is syntactically elaborate; every sentence is stacked with co-ordinate and dependent constructions. It is also lexically elaborate, with abstractions designed to cover all lines of meaning and obviate most possibilities of misunderstanding.

Here, as in Passage A, we have 'working language' appropriate to a special register. One significant point of contrast presents itself. In Passage A, vocabulary items are concrete, specific, and semantically disjunct, that is, each makes its own meaning without entering into complementary relationship with others. In Passage B, by comparison, the items of vocabulary are companions or complementary elements in a semantic pattern. The Company, the Insured and the Vehicle, are characters in the document's unfolding 'plot'; while items such as *damage*, *loss* and *destruction* establish, through their communities and diversities of meaning, a broad central theme. Such 'plotting' of the vocabulary suggests analogies with literary process, though there are reasons (discussed below) why in Passage B this elaborate cohesion does not achieve the character of 'literariness'.

In one particular sense Passage B is the least literary of all the passages presented in this section. The feeling of speech is suppressed; and hence we lose all sense of the text as a 'live' interaction. It does not say 'listen, let me tell you'; it records a transaction – The Company promises to pay the Insured. One symptom of this transactional character is that the lexicon is designedly monosemic. Important terms like Company, Insured, and Insured Vehicle are accorded proper-noun status (markedly by the initial capitals), having been defined elsewhere in the document. Where the vocabulary is elaborated (as in *repair, reinstatment* or *replacement*), this is done in order to specify the semantic components of a broad concept (i.e. made good), rather than to institute some dynamic, text-informing process of branching associations and psychological connections. The elaboration of the vocabulary, noted above as a mark of 'literariness', is therefore literary here in semblance only. It has the 'analytic' elaboration of the thesaurus, which lists synonyms and equivalents, not the 'organic' elaboration of a poem or a piece of prose fiction, in which items of language progressively gather meaning in relationship to each other.

For these reasons (among others) Passage B lacks the property of 'literariness'. This need not mean, however, that its language could never be available for literary purposes. In our search for emphasis and variation in style, we make continual borrowings from familiar registers (e.g. the language of sport, the language of the theatre or the language of commerce). One consequence of this is a traffic in idioms and figurative expressions that gradually lose the colouring of their derivation and become standard turns of phrase; we may speak of 'being covered' or 'securing something at a premium' without being more than vaguely conscious that these phrases belong to the language of the broker. A second, perhaps more interesting, consequence of this 'register borrowing' is the restructuring of technical terms so that they enter into new relationships and acquire a special symbolic value in the context of the literary work. James M. Cain's crime novel *Double Indemnity* (1936) (made into a film in 1944 with the same name) had for its plot a variation on the well-worn theme of murder for the insurance money. Accordingly, its title might be read simply as a technical term denoting a certain type of policy agreement. Yet for the audience it is bound to mean much more than this; the significance of 'indemnity' and 'double' is conditioned by the particular circumstances of the plot. The technical terms acquire a new relevance; it is, so to speak, re-registered as an element in the language of fiction.

Such re-registrations are by no means uncommon. It would be possible, for example, to re-register the vocabulary of Passage B, by placing it in a somewhat different syntactic environment. For example:

> The Insured found himself trembling uncontrollably. Where was the Vehicle? Lost? Damaged? Destroyed? What would the Company do when they heard? Would he be indemnified this time? Or would the liability fall on him?

This may illustrate how precise, functional monosemy might be transmuted into vaguely symbolic literary polysemy. It is possible in this case because the vocabulary of Passage B, precise and monosemic though it certainly is, consists nonetheless of abstractions and superordinates, that is, of generalized terms that can be related, if we so wish, to an altered set of implications and subordinates. Thus Company, which implies 'board', 'Chairman', 'management', 'sales staff', 'shareholders', etc. can be semantically reconstructed so as to imply 'government', 'hierarchy', 'junta', 'party', 'overseas', and so forth; and Insured may be analogously reconstructed, to entail the meanings 'citizen', 'servant', 'slave', 'worker', etc. The imposition of a new thesaurus entry, by blending or realigning registers, is a typical literary act.

> A minute later Dixon was sitting listening to a sound like the ringing of a cracked door-bell as Welch pulled at the starter. That died away into a treble humming that seemed to involve every component of the car. Welch tried again; this time the effect was of beer-bottles jerkily belaboured. Before Dixon could do more than close his eyes he was pressed firmly back against the seat, and his cigarette, still burning, was cuffed out of his hand into some interstice of the floor. With a tearing of gravel under the wheels the car burst from a standstill towards the grass verge, which Welch ran over briefly before turning down the drive. They moved towards the road at walking pace, the engine maintaining a loud lowing sound which caused a late group of students, most of them wearing the yellow and green College scarf, to stare after them from the small covered-in space beside the lodge where sports' notices were posted.
>
> (Passage C)

Passage C does not need to be analysed in great detail since the basic terms of discussion have been established and readers can extend them to this extract for themselves. The basic point to underline is that attention to the fine detail of linguistic organization here guarantees a place for this text further along the *cline of literariness*. It involves recognition that the lexical items deployed are more *polysemic* in that they are selected as much for the resonance they create, the associations they produce and the interaction they generate semantically (in conjunction with syntactic and phonetic contouring) within, across and beyond the text itself. Examples might be 'beer bottles jerkily belaboured' which depends crucially on complementary phonetic syntactic patterning and in the case of 'belaboured' produces a shifting set of transitions between what are, for this reader at least, colloquial items (*jerkily, cuff, lowing*) and more formal (appropriate in context) literary/academic vocabulary such as *involve, component, belaboured* and *maintaining*. The resulting semantic density and constellation of *satiric/ironic effects* (see Chapter 8) allows much more to be conveyed than a description of a car being started and driven from a college courtyard. There is little restrictive monosemy, the text acquires a degree of sovereignty (or 'medium independence') and words are not being held, however creatively and skilfully, within any one domain or register nor within any direct author–reader channel of communication.

Some aspects of the analysis here need to be qualified. First, it is clear that semantic density is not attributable merely to operations at the level of lexis, however significant such features may be. Secondly, interpretations of literariness are to an extent dependent on a predisposition and competence to see things that way. This means that, if the context is judged to be an appropriate one, most pieces of language *can* be read in a literary way. This point has been well illustrated by Fish (1980) who gave students a 'poem' consisting of no more than a random selection of names of well-known stylisticians. Out of context, the language was not particularly meaningful but in the classroom context much interpretive effort was expended on assigning meaning to the words (see also discussion by Culler, in Schiff, 1977, pp. 63–72; Eagleton, 1983, Ch. 1). A similar example is that cited in Herrnstein-Smith (1978, p. 67), of the extended readings made possible if the first line of a newspaper report on Hell's Angels were laid out in a particular form and lineation:

> Only one in
> Ten
> Angels has regul-
> ar
> employment

Such activities also demonstrate that literary competence involves modes of interpretation taught in educational institutions and strategies of reading which may not normally be extended beyond such contexts and, certainly only rarely, to language uses not institutionally authorized as literary. Analysis of lexis in literature should not therefore take place independently either of other levels of language organization or of the ways in which we are taught to read and appreciate language in literature. Thirdly, such study also requires fuller consideration of the relationship between words and the changing historical, social and cultural conditions in which reading takes place, and writing is defined to be literary. One strong educational implication would be to argue for studying texts as continua of language and for avoiding an artificially imposed division into literature and language study. However, the main point to stress here is that it may be more instructive to see literary uses of language and of lexis in language as existing along a cline or continuum rather than as discrete sets of features or as a language-intrinsic or unique 'poetical' register.

5.7 Metaphor

Recent work on the literariness of texts has focused on continuities rather than differences in language use for 'literary' purposes. A number of studies have also emphasized the existence of what are commonly understood as literary tropes in contexts which are not conventionally considered to be literary. A major contribution to this area is that of Lakoff and Johnson (1980) who in a study, *Metaphors We Live By*, demonstrate that metaphor – supposedly a primary poetic device – is abundant in the language generally. Lakoff and Johnson provide a whole range of examples illustrating how our conceptual system (i.e. a standard Western cultural system) is as a whole structured by metaphors which are capable of generating related metaphors and images across whole areas of discourse. One representative example might be that of the metaphorical analogy ARGUMENT IS WAR, which, as Lakoff and Johnson show, produces the following standard usages:

> Your claims are *indefensible*.
> He *attacked every weak point* in my argument.
> His criticisms were *right on target*.
> I *demolished* his argument.
> I've never *won* an argument with him.
> If you use that *strategy*, he'll wipe you out.
> They *shot down* all of my arguments in *flames*.

Similar examples demonstrate how time is treated as a valuable commodity (i.e. it is expended, bought or wasted as if it were money), love as a journey, or theories as buildings and so on. The systematic and pervasive nature of such metaphorical 'models' shows the extent to which, in a 'literary' way, one area of experience is regularly structured and analogized in terms of another. Such modelling determines to a considerable extent how we see the world or how our perceptions of reality can be culturally and socially conditioned. The metaphors we habitually live by play a not insignificant part in the shaping process.

However, the fact that such metaphors are often so deeply impregnated in language and culture that they are not noticed as such indicates the automatized and conventionalized role they occupy. This raises two further questions. One concerns the appropriate modes of analysis of deautomatized metaphors, that is, those that are immediately perceived as striking and original. The other concerns the linguistic nature of the processes underlying such perception. Both these questions are necessarily connected with the issues of lexis and literariness raised in the previous section (see also, Lodge, 1977 for discussion of metaphor and metonymy as predominant tropes in relation to modes of writing in different historical periods).

A useful starting point for such discussion is work on the lexico-semantic constituents and relations involved in metaphor (e.g. Leech, 1969), the basis of which is a distinction between **tenor** and **vehicle** in metaphor (also referred to as the metaphoric 'frame' and 'focus'). The basic assumption here is that metaphor involves a deviant use of language (the vehicle) which is in some way semantically foregrounded against literal norms of language (the tenor). In such instances 'literal' usually has the sense of a reasonable claim on truth as generally perceived and understood so that metaphoric uses involve non-literal or non-true statements, which it is the task of a reader or hearer to interpret in such a way as to rescue their falsity.

Linguists have suggested that such 'falsity' is brought about by a violation of selection restrictions and that there may be linguistic rules by means of which sense is made of such violation. Leech (1969, pp. 154 ff), taking a metaphoric line from Chaucer:

But ye loveres that bathen in gladnesse.

argues that it can be divided into a tenor 'loveres that (are/do something) in gladness' and a vehicle '. . .bathen in. . .'. The vehicle involves lexical items not normally semantically compatible with 'gladnesse', and thus the reader must look for what Leech terms a 'ground of likeness' between tenor and vehicle. And this, he argues, involves selecting certain common features and rejecting others. Thus, 'bathe' might connote 'feeling pleasure' which links with 'love' and 'gladnesse' but does not involve semantic features such as 'remove dirt'. This example is an interesting one, however, in that further semantic density can be generated by positing that 'lovers bathe in' could, with only a little less probability, serve as the tenor. Thus 'gladnesse' can be analogized to water in that, for example, immersion in deep water is semantically equivalent to immersion in feelings of happiness or 'gladnesse'. In this way, tenor and vehicle are potentially reversible.[4]

A not unrelated process occurs with metaphors such as that contained in a widely cited example (for further analysis see Levinson, 1983, pp. 147–62; Butler, 1984, pp. 9–10):

Encyclopaedias are gold mines.

Such a process involves discovering grounds of likeness by aggregating some semantic features and deleting others; the result is an interpretation which would prevent the normal rules of lexical selection rendering encyclopaedias and gold mines semantically incompatible. The normal infringements of sense are thus suspended and the statement rescued from falsity. Thus, possible connections between encyclopaedias, working underground, panning, prospecting or locations in South Africa would be deleted and possible meanings in the vehicle of value, wealth, investment, etc. are activated and thus retained in preference.

It can be pointed out that the example here, unlike the line from Chaucer, does not promote any reversibility of tenor and vehicle and may be said to be less dense semantically and thus carry a reduced degree of literariness. The 'conventionalized' nature of analogy with gold mine can also be demonstrated by pointing to its frequency in the lexicon and to the cultural shaping inherent in the measurement or comparison of things (here the possession of knowledge) in terms of wealth and money.

A third and final example illustrates a further necessary dimension in the analysis of metaphoricity. This is the way in which interpretations of 'grounds of likeness' do not depend exclusively on language-internal semantic criteria but also on the 'knowledge of the world' possessed by the interpreter. Take, for example, the metaphoric line:

Americans are petrol alcoholics.

How we might interpret this is crucially dependent on how much we know and this is, in turn, culturally relative. The fact that we know a world in which Americans enjoy driving long distances in large energy-consuming cars aids interpretation more than a semantic classification that petrol cannot be drunk by humans in the way that alcoholic beverages can or that 'alcoholic' carries a semantic feature + addiction. Christopher Butler has put it in the following terms:

> The grounds of likeness in metaphors thus involve all sorts of conventions of reference to the real world; and these could never be specified in advance by a linguistic or any other theory. . . . Metaphor consists in the implication by likeness of a certain description of the world . . . and the acceptability of these implications depends ultimately upon the nature of the world, or if one prefers, upon the nature of our beliefs about it.

(Butler, 1984, p. 16)

This statement is also not without its own implications for the way in which metaphors can be interpreted in conventional literary contexts. It could be that grounds of likeness are sought with greater persistence in such contexts because metaphor is generally believed and taught to be central to effects there. By contrast, in contexts not conventionally signalled to be 'literary', our interpretations of metaphor may stop after seeking for two or three dominant grounds since extending analogies could impede the processing of the text for other more contextually dominant purposes such as, for example, obtaining information. Literariness in metaphor may be as much a matter of the beliefs of the reader about the world or the conventions of what readers should or can do in reading than it is a matter of linguistic organization. It is anyway possible to propose that semantic density is activated by pragmatic *as well as* lexico-semantic means and, tentatively, to conclude with Cohen (1979, p. 75) that:

> Lexical entries of a natural language can draw no clear distinction between features that are supposed to be 'purely linguistic' and features that are supposed to represent common knowledge or commonly accepted beliefs.

Butler's statement does seem one-sided. The examples cited in this section would seem to demonstrate that pragmatic *and* semantic modes of analysis are prerequisites for fuller definition of metaphor. However, the limited nature and extent of these examples do beg a number of important questions and show how much further investigation in this area is required. Among such unanswered problems are: the appropriate modes of analysis for how, in unravelling grounds of likeness, certain semantic–pragmatic features are cancelled and others activated, and whether they can be systematically accounted for (see again Cohen, 1979); the appropriate analyses of metaphors which do *not* directly assert grounds of likeness; the relationship of all metaphors to the culture-relative and culture-shaped analogical processes by means of which we habitually perceive and live in the world; the relationship of such metaphoric models to the kinds of defamiliarization of or deviation from the routine common-sense perception of the world brought about by those metaphors generally assumed to possess greater degrees of literariness (e.g. those involving a rose or the moon); the precise nature of the overlap between pragmatic and lexico-semantic features in the construction and reception of metaphor (Searle, 1979). Ortony ed. (1979; 1993), Goatly (1997) and Steen (1994) review and extend material covered in this section.

5.8 Lexis, poetics and mind

Increasingly, empirically-based, investigative studies of language continue to reveal the pervasiveness of literariness in everyday discourse. However, whereas the data collected are often treated in an essentially descriptive vein, and within a broadly sociolinguistic and functional view of language, several of the more recent parallel studies adopt a more distinctively cognitive orientation. One of the most seminal of these studies is Gibbs (1994).

The basic assumption of much work in literary linguistics has been that figurative language acquires literary force by being deviant, and a main emphasis has therefore been on accounts of the ways in which such language departs from or 'deviates' from the norms of language use. However, a continuing influence on much ongoing study of figurative language is seminal work by Lakoff and Johnson (1980) and Lakoff and Turner (1989). Although the continuing emphasis of this and related research is that human language and the human mind are not *inherently* literal, the orientation of this work can be seen to be principally social and cultural.

In writings by cognitive linguists such as Gibbs there is less emphasis on the deviant nature of figurative language and, correspondingly, less attention to the ways in which such language examples deviate from the norms of language use. Instead, figurative language is seen neither as deviant nor ornamental but rather as ubiquitous in everyday speech. Such discussions of figurative language proceed on the assumption that the fundamental roots of language are figurative.

The research paradigms which follow from such an assumption present a radically different set of beliefs to the beliefs about human thought and language which have traditionally dominated the disciplines of the humanities and social sciences in the Western intellectual tradition. Gibbs has argued for a 'cognitive wager' which contrasts with the more standard 'generative wager'. The generative wager hypothesizes that explanations of language and of language universals in particular are structure dependent and that linguistic constructs are autonomous of general conceptual knowledge. The cognitive wager of Gibbs and other cognitive linguists aims to show that there is no autonomous language faculty and to illustrate that language is not independent of the mind. Gibbs argues that *figurative* schemes of thought structure many fundamental aspects of our ordinary, conceptual understanding of experience.

An example of this position is provided by Gibbs with reference to the polysemous word *stand* which has a range of everyday meanings:

for example, *He couldn't stand the pressure, The law still stands, The barometer stands at 29.56* and *The house stands in a field.* Gibbs points out that the 'basic' meaning of *stand* is one of a physical movement or a physical act. Other meanings of *stand* extend this basic sense, often metaphorically, to convey meanings of verticality, resistance to attacks (as a result of 'standing firm' and remaining vertical in the face of attempts to unbalance you or knock you down'), and endurance ('to remain upright'): for example, *He stands over six feet tall, He stood up to all the attacks against his theory* and *The law still stands.*

One interesting conclusion from these examples is that there is a link by metaphoric extension between physical action and mental representation. The figurative often has an origin in physical, bodily experience, and the figurative framework of everyday thought motivates a surprising number of meanings in this and other examples. It follows from this that phrases such as *to take a stand on something, to uphold* (principles/the law) and to remain an '*upright*' person derive from the same underlying, conceptually coherent domain. Traditional studies in lexical semantics attempt to uncover the componential set of features underlying each separate word *stand* and begin from an assumption of literalness. Cognitive linguists put 'the body back into the mind', arguing that 'metaphor, and to a lesser extent metonymy, is the main mechanism through which we comprehend abstract concepts and perform abstract reasoning. . . . (and that) metaphorical understanding is grounded in nonmetaphorical preconceptual structures that arise from everyday bodily experience' (Gibbs, 1994, p. 17). While traditional lexico-semantic studies search for literal meaning on the grounds that literal meaning best reflects the truth values of an objectively determined external world, cognitive linguists such as Gibbs recognize that so-called literal language is itself constituted by fundamental processes of figuration.

Gibbs summarizes this developing view of the poetics of mind and the new cognitive approaches to language as follows (Gibbs, 1994, pp. 16–17):

- The mind is not inherently literal.
- Language is not independent of the mind but reflects our perceptual and conceptual understanding of experience.
- Figuration is not merely a matter of language but provides much of the foundation for thought, reason and imagination.
- Figurative language is not deviant or ornamental but is ubiquitous in everyday speech.

- Figurative modes of thought motivate the meanings of many linguistic expressions that are commonly viewed as having literal interpretations.
- Metaphorical meaning is grounded in nonmetaphorical aspects of recurring bodily experiences or experiential gestalts.
- Scientific theories, legal reasoning, myths, art and a variety of cultural practices exemplify many of the same figurative schemes found in everyday thought and language.
- Many aspects of word meaning are motivated by figurative schemes of thought.
- Figurative language does not require special cognitive processes to be produced and understood.
- Children's figurative thought motivates their significant ability to use and understand many kinds of figurative speech. (See Winner, 1988.)

Gibbs raises fundamental questions for our understanding of the nature of literary language. Metaphor has always been seen as a fundamentally literary property as a result of the apparent propensity of its users to create new insights into human experience and values; and metaphorization has been conventionally regarded as a liberating process in which divergent and deautomatizing ways of thinking are made possible. Gibbs offers an alternative mapping of creative metaphoric processes by illustrating the extent to which 'poetry' can depend on basic underlying metaphors which structure our everyday experiences. (See also Sweetser, 1990.)

A not uncommon response to the above line of reasoning is, however, to point out that the metaphors we live and think by are often dead metaphors or at least metaphors which have been overused and that the creative artist is one who can transform our ways of seeing by displacing ordinary, stale and overstrained expressions with metaphoric choices which introduce new 'schema refreshing' perceptions. Gibbs's position in such now-standard debates is that supposedly dead metaphors often have roots which are alive and which actively work to provide a framework for us continually to make new understandings.

An example is the verb *see* which is one of the most common verbs in English. One of its most frequent metaphorical meanings, however, which is substantiated by major computational lexical studies of semantic patterns such as the COBUILD project, is that of *understanding*. *See* in the sense of 'understand' or 'know' is three times more frequent than the sense of *see* as 'visual perception by the eye'. Examples of such a metaphor would therefore be *I see what you mean*, or *They've seen the point at last!* The shift from physical action to metaphorical entailment has taken place over time and has indeed now become dead. But Gibbs would argue that metaphoric extensions of various kinds (which keep the relationship alive) remain possible, and that both poets and ordinary people make use of the same figurative schemes of thought. A poem such as Margaret Atwood's 'This is a photograph of me' contains, for example, a chain of words ('see', 'look', 'scan') to do with seeing the photograph of the poem's persona in terms of penetrating below the surface of personality to understand and develop 'insight' into the nature of a personality who is on the verge of suicide by drowning and the reader is made aware of the dangers inherent in 'closing their eyes' to such a situation.

Although metaphor is a major mode of conceptual organization in language, Gibbs and others also explore the role of other figurative expressions such as metonymy, irony and sarcasm, idioms and proverbs, indirect speech acts and oxymora as basic, endemic constituents of language, concluding that an easy facility with such expressions by speakers of a language is indicative of the *poeticality* of much everyday discourse and suggestive of universally poetic components of the human mind. And to make such a claim, Gibbs argues, is not inconsistent with saying that figurative thought functions for the most part unconsciously and automatically in people's daily processing of linguistic meaning. Cognitive linguists stress that figurative knowledge motivates people's use of and understanding of both ordinary and literary language and that the 'easy facility' with metaphorical modes is necessary because so much of ordinary language use is figuratively patterned.

Gibbs also attempts to explain the pleasure derived from patterning in poetry in terms of mental mechanisms which fulfil basic needs of the human species as a whole. Among the more basic of mental mechanisms are those which are renewed and refreshed as a result of the destabilizing effects of literary patterning. One suggestion is that playing with words may be genetically determined and that recasting or deviating from established patterns is a natural and normal 'biological' reflex of the human mind which cognitive linguists such as Gibbs in seminal studies such as *The Poetics of Mind* are in any case increasingly inclined to regard as figuratively predisposed. Literariness in language is normal and widespread. This is an insight reinforced in another recent major study of metaphor in relation to continua of literary and non-literary discourses (Goatly, 1997).

5.9 Arbitrariness, words, ideology: A note

It is necessary to point out that the ways in which words have been assumed to be used in the previous sections do have important theoretical implications and that such theories do affect the nature of any interpretation of lexical use.

A starting point should be the assumptions underpinning the uses of terms such as 'literal', 'normal' and 'common sense' in the assignment in Section 5.7 of features of a metaphor to a literal base of tenor. Another starting point should be the assumption in interpretations of texts of an unproblematic 'obvious' fit between words and the world.

An article relevant to such considerations is an analysis of the nature of language in poetry by the French Structuralist critic Michael Riffaterre (1973). Riffaterre's central point concerns what he terms the 'referential fallacy'. This is the view that the connection between a word and some object or referent is no more than arbitrary and that, in poetry in particular, it is the case that words point to each other as much as they do to 'things'. The basic tenet is that of de Saussure and his view of the arbitrary nature of the sign. (In fact, Riffaterre misunderstands Saussure as suggesting that words are non-referential.) Put crudely, a view of the arbitrariness of the sign questions whether there is any real symmetrical unity or harmonious one-for-one correlation between a word or 'signifier' and the objects, entities and states of affairs ('signifieds') to which they refer. The relationship between the sound *dog* and the concept *dog* is no more natural, intrinsic or necessary than that of the sounds *Hund* or *chien*. In fact, Saussure (1974, p. 118) argues, 'Signs function . . . not through their intrinsic value but through their relative position'. That is, the signifier *dog* gives us the concept *dog* because it divides itself from other signifiers such as *bog*, *dot*, *cog*, *doc*, and the less immediately related, *frog*, *dote*, *flog*, *done*, *dig*, *dagger*, etc. Meaning is achieved by the differential relation of words to other words. The signifier is then as much a product of differences between signifiers as it is anything else and these differences vary from one language to another. Saussure argues therefore that the 'meanings' of words inhere not in the material substance of words but in a larger and abstract system of signs of which these 'words' are the barest tip. We can conclude then that meanings become assigned more as a matter of convention and that different linguistic communities agree to abide by such 'arbitrary' conventions. The agreement produces a normal, common-sense and manageable traffic between words and things.

These socially agreed, convention-bound processes should not serve always to obscure, however, that meanings are absent as well as present.

The meanings of words are thus a matter of what the sign is *not* as well as what it *is*. Meanings are perpetually deferred and always bear the traces of other words and meanings. Analysis of what texts say or what the meanings of metaphor may be are, therefore, in a crucial sense, unstable and provisional. Indeed, the interpreter needs to recognize that selection of a tenor, recognition of lexical foregrounding or of relations between lexical sets, or interpretations of textual meanings may not have any intrinsically prior validity since they operate from a basis in a referential theory of language.[5] Such a referential theory involves degrees of relativity and arbitrariness as well as conventions which, however socially, psychologically or culturally powerful, allow only conventional access to reality.

It is this convention-bound nature of access to meaning and reality which ideology embraces. The term ideology denotes here 'the system of imaginary representations within a society so that ideology impregnates a society's ways of thinking, speaking, experiencing and behaving. Ideology is therefore a necessary condition for all action and belief within a social formation, and hence crucial in the construction of personal identity' (Giles, 1983). (See also Section 4.10.)

The main implication of this 'note' for a chapter which surveys and illustrates aspects of on-going work in the area of lexis and literature is strongly to underline that a text, whether conceived as a poem, a metaphor or whatever, offers no single position from which it is intelligible. This should not mean that this is a recipe for 'anything goes'; rather it should serve to remind us that meanings occur only by courtesy of the conditions or systems under which meanings can be conferred. It is clear that Saussure's system cannot be a pure linguistic system but must be contingent on competing social, cultural and historical systems. It is clear, too, that previous and subsequent chapters proceed by means of widely held and common-sense assumptions about the relations between words, meanings and the world. Because they are widely held or ideologically rooted does not mean that they cannot or should not be challenged, deconstructed or shown to be limited. For further theoretical investigations in this domain and with particular reference to literary and cultural studies see particularly Bennett (1979, pp. 61–75); Belsey (1980 Chs 1 and 2); Norris (1982, pp. 57–60, 129–35); Eagleton (1983, pp. 127–40); Bhaba (1994, Ch. 1). For a brief study of 'words' in concrete poetry from within such analytical perspectives and with particular reference to teaching poetic discourse see Carter and Long (1987; 1991). Further reference to the role of ideology in text analysis and in lexicographic work is made in Section 9.1.

5.10 Conclusion

The field of stylistics is a rapidly developing one, although stylistic analysis of lexis in 'literary' and 'non-literary' texts has not advanced much recently. Examination of vocabulary in literary texts cannot proceed, however, without some encounter with recent literary theoretical work within the domain of English Studies. Such an encounter problematizes both the category of 'literature' itself and the role of words within literature as a medium for conveying reality. One main conclusion in this chapter is that common-sense assumptions concerning the role of language in literature need to be challenged. In particular, the idea of a special language of literature has been questioned in the light of the existence in a wide range of texts of such pervasive 'literary' features as metaphor. However, it is important to underline that the kind of lexically-based interpretation illustrated in Section 5.3 is still a dominant approach within literary studies in schools both in mother-tongue teaching and in the teaching of English as a second or foreign language.

One particular argument to emerge from this chapter is that informant-based lexical studies can contribute both to theoretical and practical analytical concerns. In Chapters 8 and 9 it is further argued that lexical analyses which draw on informants can contribute to the creation of a 'lexical stylistics'. Topics for lexical stylistic investigation in these chapters include the definition of 'literary' tropes, interpretation of lexical associations in poetry, and fuller definition of stylistic levels in lexis for lexicographic purposes. Discussion of issues in this chapter is intended to form a basis for such 'case studies'.

Notes

1 One potentially systematic approach to analysis of lexis in literature is that suggested by Halliday (1962) in an essay 'Descriptive linguistics in literary studies'. In an analysis of Yeats's poem 'Leda and the swan' he makes an equation between the 'less verbish' verbs in the poem and the notion of 'lexical power'. Lexical power is defined as being in inverse proportion to the number of lexical items with which a given item is habitually associated. That is, the fewer the lexical items with which a particular word collocates the more 'powerful' Halliday would claim it to be. (A good example would be the verb 'staggering' from the poem.) Measurement of collocational partnerships has now been greatly facilitated by computer counts; there is now scope for considerable extension and application to literary texts of this suggestion.

2 Hasan (1971) expresses her doubts about the existence of such a reader: 'in practice, it is difficult if not impossible to find an actual reader who combines the maximally exhaustive knowledge of language and literature which would be required for an "ideally exhaustive" interpretation'.

3 This would seem to be a particular problem with the informant studies reported in Riffaterre (1959).
4 See essay by Reinhart 'On understanding poetic metaphor' in Ching *et al.* (1980). Also, for illuminating discussion of the way in which metaphors create 'new paradigms' see Kates (1980), Carter (1997: ch.7).
5 As Wittgenstein (1953) has put it:

> There is no need for a metaphysic of the proper to justify the difference between literal and figurative. It is use in discourse that specifies the difference between the literal and the metaphorical and not some sort of prestige attributed to the primitive or the original.

6 Lexis and lexicography

The value of a work must be estimated by its use: It is not enough that a dictionary delights the critic, unless at the same time it instructs the learner.

(Samuel Johnson)

6.0 Introduction

There has been considerable interest recently in the part played by dictionaries in language development, particularly in the learning of second and foreign languages. This chapter aims to review some of the main developments in EFL and ESL (English as a Foreign Language; English as a Second Language) *lexicography*. Lexicography is a good example of a domain in which linguistic insights can be directly applied and practical advantages quite readily recognized. But we should not forget that lexicographic practice can also, as Ilson (1985a) demonstrates, be of service to refinements in linguistic description. Most of the innovative work described in this chapter is in the presentation to second-language learners of lexical, lexico-syntactic and idiomatic information; paradoxically, this occurs at a time when greater interest is now centred in such areas as intersentential relations and discourse analysis but this should not diminish its importance. The case study in Chapter 9 is also devoted to lexicography and this chapter should be read in close conjunction with it as well as with Chapter 7 on vocabulary learning and teaching.

6.1 The image of the dictionary: User and use

Dictionaries have a good image. They have social prestige. Many families believe that every good home should have one. Almost every learner or user of English as a second or foreign language owns one;

and it is probably one of the few books which are retained after following a language course. A dictionary is normally a long-term investment and continues to give service long after it has been bought. Whether it is a monolingual or a bilingual dictionary, or whether it is used to aid translation or to check a spelling or to settle a dispute in a game of Scrabble, the dictionary is a trusted and respected repository of facts about a language. And an important part of its good image is that it has institutional authority. (For further discussion, see Quirk, 1973.)

The focus in this chapter is set more sharply on the dictionary as a tool of learning than on other aspects of its image. The last 25 years have seen rapid developments in lexicography directed at improving the image of dictionaries within the language teaching profession (see Section 6.7). Two dictionaries, in particular, *The Oxford Advanced Learner's Dictionary* (*OALD*, 1974) and the *Longman Dictionary of Contemporary English* (*LDOCE*, 1978) have contributed considerably to the development and design of dictionaries for non-native learners of English. Their appearance and widespread adoption have served to highlight the differences which exist between ***bilingual*** and ***monolingual dictionaries*** and between dictionaries for the native speaker and for the second- or foreign-language learner.

Bilingual dictionaries are more generally employed in the initial stages of learning a language. As proficiency develops, greater use is made of a monolingual dictionary; in fact, Baxter (1980) concludes that prolonged dependency on bilingual dictionaries probably tends to retard the development of second-language proficiency even though such dictionaries are usually retained for use when definitions given in a monolingual dictionary are insufficiently understood. Monolingual dictionaries come in many more varied shapes and sizes. These range from 'pocket' dictionaries, dictionaries for children, specific purpose dictionaries (for example, medical, aeronautical and legal) to the more global general purpose dictionaries which supply semantic, pronunciation, spelling, grammatical and etymological information. Extreme examples of the latter would include *The Oxford English Dictionary* (*OED*) (Murray, 1933) and Webster's *Third New International Dictionary* (Gove, 1961), each of which contain more than 450,000 separate entries. Monolingual dictionaries, even comprehensive general purpose ones, are not, however, automatically suitable for use by and with language learners. We need to examine the specific properties of those monolingual dictionaries which are designed for the EFL/ESL user and evaluate the part played by lexicographical theory and practice in the development of such dictionaries. It is in this area that work in applied linguistics has recently had much to contribute and it is in the writing of definitions of words that the most striking and innovating developments are recorded.

6.2 Dictionary definitions

Major distinctions between monolingual dictionaries for native and for non-native speakers lie in the kinds of information supplied. For the non-native user a main aim is to supply encoding information which will allow for productive *use* of the language. In particular guidance is given concerning the *syntactic behaviour* of individual items. For example, the monolingual *Concise Oxford Dictionary* (*COD*) gives one piece of grammatical information about the noun *work* (i.e. 'n.' for noun), whereas the *OALD* marks it as an uncountable noun (i.e. 'u.' for uncountable) thus preventing the production by learners of:

It was a hard work.

Such mistakes could be produced because the *COD* is not designed to provide encoding information. Learners' monolingual dictionaries also often provide more detailed guidance both on matters of syntax (see particularly the coding of verb patterns in the *OALD* originating in Hornby, 1948), on pronunciation, and on cultural and stylistic restrictions. The nature of the syntactic information provided will be explored in greater detail in Section 6.3 and issues of stylistic marking are considered in Chapter 9. (For a review of pronunciation data in learners' dictionaries see Gimson, 1981.)

Another marked distinction is in the different ***definitions*** of words which are supplied. Particularly notable here is the use of either restricted defining vocabularies or at least a concerted effort to write clear and unambiguous definitions. In the case of the first edition of *LDCE* the use of a defining vocabulary was explained by Procter as follows:

> All the definitions and examples in the dictionary are written in a controlled vocabulary of approximately 2000 words . . . particular reference having been made to *A General Service List of English Words* (1953) by Michael West . . . This very important feature marks this dictionary out from any but the smallest of its predecessors as a tool for the learner and student of language . . . the result of using the vocabulary is the fulfilment of one of the most basic lexicographic principles – that is that the definitions are always written using more simple terms than the words they describe,

something that cannot be achieved without a definite policy of this kind.

(*LDOCE*, 1978, pp. viii–ix)

Defining or restricted vocabularies are not without problems, however. First, even though the words used in the *LDOCE* are supplied in a list at the back of the dictionary, the learner may first have to learn a number of them; there is no guarantee that they will be known by the learner. And not all the words are particularly common. For example, the 1978 Longman defining vocabulary contains the following items: *account, bacteria, arch, bitter, conscience, determine, empire, grey, character.* Secondly, defining vocabularies can achieve simplicity at the expense of accuracy. When more words are needed the result can also sometimes be clumsy or unnaturally circumlocutory. Compare the *LDOCE* definition of *history* with that in the *OALD*, which seeks to avoid difficult words but is not restricted by any list of defining words:

(1) ... (the study of) events in the past, such as those of a nation, arranged in order from the earlier to the later esp. events concerning the rulers and government of a country, social and trade conditions etc.

(*LDOCE*, 1978)

(2) ... branch of knowledge dealing with past events, political, social, economic, of a country, continent, or the world.

(*OALD*, 1974)

Thirdly, as Michael West has himself acknowledged (West, 1935, p. 12), defining vocabularies work rather better in the explanation of concrete rather than abstract terms. Learners themselves, however, report that they *prefer* a restricted vocabulary (see research by MacFarquhar and Richards, 1983) although the relationship between the perceived intelligibility of a definition and the actual learning of lexical items has yet to be investigated. Searching examinations, too, of definitions in learner dictionaries reveal that advantages clearly outweigh disadvantages (see Jain, 1979; 1981; Bauer, 1980). For discussion of the use of synonyms in definitions and of the problematic distinction in learner dictionaries between whether entries should *define* or *explain*, see Hanks (1979) and Section 6.5.

In spite of many recent innovations and continuing development in foreign- and second-language lexicography it is important not to lose sight of what learners use dictionaries for. In this regard studies reveal that users are predominantly conservative in attitude and practice and that there can be potentially dangerous gaps between the sophistication of some features of dictionary design and the user's often rudimentary reference skills. Béjoint (1979; 1981; 1994) reports that students tend to use EFL dictionaries rather as they would general monolingual dictionaries, that is, for looking for meanings and synonyms (especially low-frequency specialist terms), for checking spellings and for decoding activities in the written medium such as translation and reading. The image of the dictionary as a source of encyclopaedic and factual information is one which dies hard (see also Quirk, 1972).

6.3 Grammar and the dictionary

In the design of a monolingual EFL dictionary it is clear that a balance must be preserved between a portrait of the vocabulary of the language and an adequate description of the use of words in the productive mode. Obviously, the expectations of learners that they will be supplied with explanations of the rarer senses of words has to be met; at the same time too much attention to the complex syntactic relations which 'core', high-frequency items often enter can be impractical. In this respect the nature of the syntactic information supplied by the lexicographer will be crucial. For example, Cowie (1983a) points out that in the case of a quite common verb such as *enter*, it is not adequate for the EFL learner to be told, as occurs in the general monolingual *Collins English Dictionary* (*CED*), that the verb is transitive and that among its more frequent collocates are [society, army, church] or [names, details, information etc. in a book, inventory etc.] or [as competitor for a race]. Such learners of English require more detailed and arguably more crucial information about the syntactic patterns formed by the verb and its different but inseparable prepositions:

> enter sb. *as* a member
> enter sb. *at* public school
> enter sth. *in* a diary

Additionally, learners would need to know that the passive form cannot be used with *enter* [room] but is permissible with other collocations (e.g. *the details were entered in the book*); also that *enter* [society, room] can take both indefinite and definite articles before the noun but that *enter* [army, church] is more usual with the definite article before the noun (except where the latter is a building as opposed to the institution). Another 'simple' verb such as *die* also lends itself to the production of errors with prepositions. Non-native learners should know, at least, that the verb has the following prepositional patterns: 'die *of* hunger; *by* violence, *by* one's own hand; *from* a wound; *through* neglect; *in* battle; *for* a cause; *at* the hands of the enemy; *on* the scaffold; *at* the stake'. In an interesting discussion of grammar in dictionaries, Sinclair (1981) cites the phrase *It's not in his nature to complain* and points out that the learner needs to know a lot of information about individual words in the phrase. For example, that *it* is invariable and obligatory; that *not* is optional and can be substituted by adverbs such as *hardly*, *quite*, *very much*; that *in* is invariable; that *his* and *to complain* can commute with, respectively, any possessive pronoun or proper name and with almost any infinitive clause. Additionally, *to complain* can front the phrase in place of *it;* and it is also necessary for this phrase to be distinguished from *It's in the nature of* (e.g. *It's in the nature of a celebration*). In the face of such facts (and assuming, Sinclair argues, that such usage can be attested in a database) it is clearly inadequate for a single example to be supplied without any indication of the morphological, syntactic and stylistic patterns the phrase can generate.

For the specification of syntactic patterns, especially those in the simple sentence and the noun phrase, learner dictionaries such as the *LDCE* and *OALD* have adopted coding systems. These enable learners to check, for example, object–complement relations, transitive/intransitive patterns, whether a noun is countable or uncountable or an adjective or attributive. The verb *determine* has the following entry in the 1974 *OALD:*

> determine . . . vt, vi 1 (VP6A, 10) decide; fix precisely: to ___ the meaning of a word; to ___ a date for a meeting. 2 (VP6A) calculate; find out precisely: to ___ the speed of light/the height of a mountain by trigonometry. 3 (VP6A, 7A, 9, 8, 10, 3A) ___ to do sth; on/upon sth, decide firmly, resolve, make up one's mind: He ___d to learn Greek. We ___d to start early/___d on an early start. He has ___d on proving/___d to prove his friend's innocence. Have they ___d where the new school will be built? He has ___d that nothing shall/will prevent him. His future has not yet been ___d, but he may study medicine. 4 (VP17, 14) sb to do sth/against sth, cause to decide: What ___d you to accept the offer? The news ___d him against further delay. 5 (VP6A) be the fact that ___s: The size of your feet ___s the size of your shoes. Do heredity and environment ___ a man's character? . . .

Coded grammatical information in the *OALD* explicitly tells the learner how the word in each of its senses, 1 to 5, takes a particular type or types of clause pattern. Thus, for example, with definition 3 are listed, among others, grammatical codes 7A and 10, which, supported by illustrative sentences, stand for the following construction types:

VP7A	Subject + vt	(not) + to infinitive, etc.
	He determined	to learn Greek.
VP10	Subject + vt	dependent clause/question
	Have they determined where the new school will be built?	

But with definition 5 the sentence pattern is YP6A, which denotes the following type:

VP6A	Subject + vt	noun/pronoun
	Do heredity and environment determine a man's character?	

The coding system here derives from research by Hornby in the 1940s which aimed to provide the learner with illustrations and information designed to eliminate errors in language production. One main problem with such codings is that learners have to invest a considerable amount of time and effort in mastering a system which is in itself very complex and requires constant reference to another part of the dictionary before any clear return is shown. Not all learners are prepared to invest in this, though such systems are not without considerable advantages in language-learning contexts (see also Cowie, 1981).[1]

More acute problems arise in the appropriate provision of entries for phrasal verbs and related idiomatic expressions. Such difficulties include the need to differentiate semantically between *get sth. over*, *get over sth./smb.*, *get smb. over sth.* (where *sth.* stands for *something* and *smb.* stands for *somebody*) as in:

She can't *get* her ideas *over* to her students.
She can *get over* the loss of her mother.
She tried to *get* her sister *over* the disappointment.
She was in love and couldn't *get over* him.
I am so surprised. I can't *get over it.*

Here examples need to be juxtaposed for the different meanings to be derived and for positional variation and restriction in the use of the preposition to be recorded. Comparison with other phrasal verbs illustrates the complexities here:

He *took* (off) his clothes *off*.   (remove)
He *took* (off) his voice *off* perfectly.   (imitate)

where in the case of *take off* there is greater mobility in the transposition of the adverbial particle. It should be noted though that such devices as bold type, abbreviations like *sth.* and *smb.*, semantically contrasting citations, and brackets and oblique strokes can assist overall clarity of presentation.

Capturing the syntactic behaviour of items necessarily involves more than positional variations and patterns. It also involves complex issues of compounds and derivatives. Problems here include matters of sequential arrangement. For example, should a compound like *time-wasting* be listed under the entry for *time* or for *waste*? Should *pen-pusher* be listed under *pen* or *push*? And if the admissibility of the construction in declarative clause form is taken as a criterion (**He pushes pen*; *He wastes time*) then can the learner be reasonably expected to know this in advance? It is clear that entering the item under the verb form emphasizes grammatical relationships but the inexperienced dictionary user, who will probably rely on alphabetic ordering, may be easily deterred by necessary inconsistencies. For example, in the case of nominal compounds such as *lock-keeper* or *strike-breaker* the frequency of the verbs *keep* and *break* and a correspondingly dense and detailed entry may mean that inclusion under the noun is preferable. Though, by the above criteria, an item such as *air-traffic controller* or *keep-fit fanatic* or *price-war-zones* would prove notably intractable. Hyphenization, stress and spelling (though, of these, hyphenization is most variable in usage) can also be determining factors (see Cowie, 1983b for detailed discussion of a range of relevant examples). In the case of derivatives, decisions over points of entry can involve sharper semantic differentiation as well as issues of spelling. It is reasonable that *encouragement* should be listed under the entry for its root *encourage* from which it derives in a simple way rather than as a separate entry. But such is not the case with an item such as *high* from which the following items may be said to derive: *high class*; *highly strung*; *height, heighten, heights.* Should there be one entry here or six separate ones? Or can the items be grouped semantically or inflectionally in any way: e.g. *high/high class*(?); *height/heights*(?)? Should differences in spelling in a derived form merit separate treatment or might this too readily assume that the learner knows the different spellings involved (e.g. *critic, critical, criticize*; *medicine, medical*; *satisfy, satisfaction*). There are also problems where the derivations reflect closely related but distinct differences of meaning. Cowie (1983a) cites the example of *adhere* in this connection.

The verb has derivatives such as *adhesion, adhesive, adherent, adherence* which relate to different senses of the verb. Cowie asks:

> What consequences can these contrastive relationships have for the design of a productive dictionary? One possible approach is to say that since the sentences:
>
> > He adheres to another political party
> > He is an adherent of another political party
> > His adherence is to another political party
>
> are all transformationally related (as alternative realisations of the same collocation adhere + political + party) they, and the derivatives they contain, should all appear in the same entry. Conversely, since *adhere* (in the sense of 'stick'), *adhesion* and *adhesive* represent a quite distinct line of derivation they should be treated in a separate entry.

The problem with such a decision, Cowie observes, is that, if carried to a logical conclusion, retrieval of individual items may become too taxing for the learner since the existence of too many separate entries entails the need for much cross-referencing. But the alternative strategy of grouping complex forms together because of spelling similarities and thus ease of learner access can be counter-productive and may not necessarily assist learner interpretation and production. Two observations can be reiterated here: it is difficult to draw a line between sufficiently detailed exemplificatory information and brevity and economy in the entry; it is often the simplest and most common words which contract the most complex syntactic and collocational partnerships. To these can be added the observation that the balance between accessing and interpreting related lexical items is an extremely delicate one within pedagogical lexicography.

6.4 Fixed expressions and the dictionary

The relationship between grammar and the dictionary is certainly a complex one and considerable care is needed in order to specify accurately and as unambiguously as possible the role of items in a syntactic framework. Syntactic patterns do, however, generally exhibit stability and have been codified extensively. Learners, too, are anxious to achieve grammatical acceptability in their use of language. In this section more complex questions of *lexical* acceptability are engaged; it is immediately noticeable here that the units we are dealing with are less stable, they have not been extensively codified and the particular problems they present for inclusion in learner dictionaries extend beyond economy of entry. The existence of these lexical relations and the attempts to represent them highlights the need for greater refinement in lexicological theory.

One strong conclusion from the discussion in Sections 3.6–3.9 was that *clines* exist between fixed and stable patterns and patterns which are more indeterminate, negotiable and subject to 'creative' transmutations. It is a line which runs from the relatively unrestricted relations into which a verb like *run* enters to the greater predictability and immutability of more restricted relations in units such as *on the spur of the moment, as old as the hills* or *give smb. the cold shoulder.* An appropriate sequence and set of points along continua from *fixed* to *less fixed* (see also Weinreich, 1980) was suggested with reference to clines of collocational restriction, syntactic structure and semantic opacity. For example:

1 *Collocational restriction*
   From unrestricted collocation, e.g. *keep*: 'keep house, a diary, a shop, a hotel, pets, a job, a boat', etc. to relatively restricted collocation, e.g. *stark naked, gin and tonic, cream tea*, etc.
2 *Syntactic structure*
   From flexible, e.g. *break somebody's heart, heart-breaking, heart-broken, heart-breaker* to irregular, e.g. *to go it alone, the more the merrier, to hold true, to be running scared.*
3 *Semantic opacity*
   From transparent, e.g. *long time, no see, honesty is the best policy* to opaque, e.g. *to kick the bucket, to be over the moon, to smell a rat.*

For fuller list of examples illustrated with further points along and across respective clines see Section 3.9.[2]

Such clines as this illustrate the importance of viewing the lexicon of a language as a repository of potential for open and creative exploitation but also as a source of non-transacted, given, or even stereotyped communication. Such processes are not without considerable significance for the teaching of vocabulary, and language teaching generally (see Seidl, 1978; Nattinger and DeCarrico, 1992; Fernando, 1996). Some of the implications for vocabulary teaching are considered in Section 7.13. In the final part of this section attempts to present such features of the lexicon lexicographically to second- or foreign-language learners are briefly reviewed.

One of the most significant of recent developments in lexicographic description of fixed expressions is the *Oxford Dictionary of Current Idiomatic English* (*ODCIE*, 1975/1983). The presentation of entries in the two volumes of this book represent some imaginative solutions to the complex problems of the *open* to *closed cline* and point the way to future developments.

The main aim of treatment of collocation in a learner's dictionary is to enable the learner to understand usage and put this understanding to productive use. In *ODCIE* the main strategy is to present information which is selected as representative of unrestricted collocability and thus suggestive of the total range of available choices. An example of this procedure is the entry for *break down* which in one of its non-metaphorical senses collocates quite 'openly' with a range of objects grouped semantically in a category of material barrier or obstacle:

> *break down . . . O*: wall, door, fence.

From this the learner might quite suitably derive *gate, barrier* or *partition* as appropriate collocates in the position of grammatical object (*O*). In the case of collocates which are 'semi-restricted', in that they are formed from different semantic sub-classes, the convention is to use semi-colons to separate off the different senses. For example:

> *Shoot up . . .* rise, increase sharply *. . . S*: price, cost, rent; temperature, pressure; applications, attendance.

Here (*S*) stands for grammatical subject. In the case of more restricted collocational boundaries, learners have to be warned about appropriate limits. *ODCIE* uses a warning sign '!' for this purpose. For example:

> *blow up . . .* make bigger, enlarge. *O*: ! negative, photograph, picture, snap.

Finally, in the case of idioms which allow of some slight modification, an oblique stroke can be employed to reinforce the nature of the restriction. Thus:

(1) to not have the slightest/least/faintest/foggiest idea
(2) to grease a person's hand/palm
(3) raise/lift yourself up by your own bootstraps.
(4) to be in someone's good graces/books

For a range of examples and for some preliminary informant testing concerning the predictability or otherwise of collocates in a range of composite units see Mackin (1978); and for further discussion of illustrative material in *ODCIE* see Cowie (1978). An argument for dictionaries of 'open' collocations restricted only according to subject matter or in overall coverage is given in Tomaszczyk (1981). And for an interesting attempt to systematize the kinds of collocability relations which can be represented lexicographically see Apresyan *et al.* (1969) and commentary by Benson (1985).

In its present form *ODCIE* has advanced the principled lexicographic treatment of fixed expressions and is particularly strong in its presentation of idiomaticity. In view of theoretical discussion earlier in this section and in Chapter 3 above there is no real advantage in drawing strict lines between idioms and non-idioms or in treating collocations separately from idioms; instead it makes more sense to try to illustrate the different degrees of variability of fixed expressions. In this Cowie *et al.* in *ODCIE* have made great strides, particularly in the specification of relevant formal properties. But considerable problems remain. First, students require information concerning the relative frequencies and currency of particular patterns. Secondly, style levels are notoriously variable, too, in the area of conventionalized language. The differences in formality level, for example, between *hit the road, hit the target, hit the nail on the head, hit the sack, hit the bottle* and *hit an all time low* need to be specified. Connected with this would also be fuller description of particular connotations or associations which attach to some of the expressions. Thirdly, it will be clear that the greatest problems arise at the points in the cline where patterns and collocations are not fixed but rather 'familiar' or 'semi-restricted'. Alexander (1984b) illustrates the problem with respect to the complex collocability relations contracted by ostensibly synonymic items such as *small* and *little*. And the freer the possible collocations of such synonyms, the more complex the learning becomes. Lexical errors of this type are frequently made by advanced learners but it is difficult to illustrate distinctions unless dictionary entries are synonymically rather than alphabetically arranged.[3] Fourthly, there are groups of idiom-prone items such as *go, give, break, hit, take, come* which have very extensive but not completely open collocations. The problem to be resolved by lexicographers here is whether the idiom-proneness and thus polysemy attributed to them is, as Ruhl (1979) argues, due more to contextualized and inferential meanings when, in fact, the single inherent general sense conveyed by the item remains constant. For example:

break the ice
break a rule
break the speed-limit
break a cup
break a promise
break a leg

Here it could be argued that the meaning of these phrases cannot be easily separated from their meaningfulness to individuals who bring different kinds of knowledge to the process of interpretation. The question is whether numerous separate sub-entries are required or whether the basic sense of *break* should be explained with some clear indication that users can generate a wide range of possible meanings according to context (see Section 6.5). Finally, lexicographers and compilers of separate dictionaries of fixed expressions need to resolve how far the *complete range* of fixed expressions is to be represented. The growth of interest in the implications to language teaching of conventionalized language, and the fact that pre-patterned chunks of language are extensively used as exponents of particular communicative functions, has led to proposals to include more fixed expressions in language coursebooks and related materials (see particularly Yorio, 1980; Nattinger, 1980; Nattinger and DeCarrico, 1992). Among the problems here might be the ephemeral nature of allusions and catch-phrases, the domain-restrictedness of certain stylistic formulae and the fact that explanations of 'stereotypes', conversational 'gambits' and 'social formulae' would need to be sufficiently detailed to allow appropriate use in the right context but not so detailed that they became descriptions of the contexts themselves. Consider, in the case of such 'discoursal expressions' (see Table 3.2) the complexities involved in explaining the appropriate use of stereotypes such as *That's more like it; You can say that again; I thought you'd never ask; We're just good friends; In for a penny, in for a pound.*

The emphasis on problems may in itself be dangerous since it concedes to idiomaticity and fixed expressions a problematic status and thus ignores arguments concerning the naturalness and pervasive normality of such 'universal' relations in language (see Makkai, 1978). Neither should an emphasis on problems conceal the developments already undertaken nor the possibilities revealed by increasing access to extensive computer-based corpora of naturally occurring written and spoken texts (see Section 4.7 and 6.6).

6.5 Monosemy, polysemy and dictionary entries

At the end of Section 6.3 it was observed that criteria for entry design can be especially problematic in the case of lexical items with complex patterning in their compounds and derivatives. In this section we examine a potentially more fundamental aspect of the ordering and interrelation of items in lexicographic entries: the problem of monosemous and polysemous words.

The main difficulty encountered by lexicographers is that of establishing appropriate divisions between the various senses of words. It is an area in which they are not necessarily helped by work in lexicological theory, although Nida (1975), Cowie (1982), Cruse (1982) and Catford (1983) are notable exceptions; in fact, this may be an area where lexicographic work can cross-fertilize refinements in linguistic theory of the kind outlined in Ilson (1985a). The fundamental questions raised are: whether all the words treated as polysemous in dictionaries are actually polysemous and whether in the case of genuine blurring between senses lexicographers have sufficiently developed techniques for the representation of such meanings. Not for the first time in this book, the notion of *clines* is a helpful one: the existence of clear-cut instances alongside indeterminate cases necessitates the construction of a cline of relatedness of meaning from monosemous to polysemous words.

In a paper, 'Monosemous words and the dictionary', Moon (1984) argues that the problematic instances are words which are *quasimonosemous* since strict monosemy can be reserved for items with a single meaning, referent and function such as technical vocabulary (for a fuller discussion of this area and its related terminology see Catford, 1983, p. 24). Taking the example of the adjective *light*, Moon cites ten possible contexts or collocate groups all of which arguably generate different senses of the word:

1	not very great in amount, degree or intensity	*a light rain was falling* *a light crop of tomatoes*
2	weak in colour, not dark	*a light blue shirt*
3	blowing gently	*in the light breeze*
4	easily woken or disturbed	*a light sleep* *a light sleeper*
5	not strong or deep in sound	*her light voice*
6	small in quantity and easily digested	*a light lunch*
7	containing only a small amount of alcohol	*a light white wine*

8	causing relatively little damage, suffering, hardship	*light injuries*
9	easy and not onerous	*light housework*
10	graceful and gentle	*her light graceful step*

Moon argues that these senses are heavily context-dependent and flexible, intertwining to produce meaning variations which have more to do with the context of the particular nominal group collocation in which *light* finds itself than with anything intrinsic to the meaning of the word itself. And the larger the dictionary the more likely it is that such a word may be allowed to take on as many meanings as the imagination of the lexicographer can produce or as there is space for in the dictionary. Light is clearly *not* monosemous but it could be said to have only *two main* strands of meaning: (1) not great in intensity, (2) to only a small degree (see also Moon, 1998). Similar examples include verbs such as *keep* or *take*, the latter of which has 134 senses in Johnson's *Dictionary of the English Language* of 1755 and 341 separate senses in Murray's *Oxford English Dictionary* of 1928. These are basic, core words but they may not be so complicated that narrower bands of meaning with radically fewer separate subsenses cannot be isolated. Ruhl (1979, p. 93) puts it rather more boldly:

> Common verbs such as *take*, *give*, *come*, *go*, *break* and *hit* are monosemic (but are) judged as polysemic by dictionaries and linguists because their essential general meanings are confused with contextual, inferential meanings.

The dilemma of the lexicographer in such cases is that words do not exist in isolation but in variable contexts and the dictionary user (especially the foreign learner) needs to have appropriate citation. At the same time we do not want to force polysemy onto words by overspecifying the context and undergeneralizing the word.

The nature of this dilemma is explored further in a paper by Stock (1984). Stock's aim is to explore whether existing lexicographic conventions adequately represent polysemous words, particularly the clines of meaning which exist in some words and which therefore lead inevitably to a blurring between senses. Stock points out that modern concordancing procedures, such as those available to COBUILD lexicographers, which provide a cotextual span on either side of the word (the node) under analysis can aid the process of disambiguation. Here different collocational and colligational patterns entered by the node word can aid differentiation. For example, the different senses of *post* can be distinguished according to whether it is count/non-count: for example, *There's a large post/some post for the headmaster today* = letters, etc.; *Forward your cheque by post* = postal service; *There are ten posts a day in central London* = collection or delivery of post. Similarly, *post* in the sense of 'position/appointment' can be differentiated from post ('wooden stake') or ('station, outpost') as a result of its collocational environments: for example, *He is soon to take up an exciting new post in Malaysia.* For further discussion, see Cowie (1982, pp. 53–7)[4] who discusses related patternings with the words *tour* and *crease*, and Stock (1984) who discusses the contextual and co-textual disambiguation of the nominal *bite.* Stock points out, however, that not all word senses can be divided up in this way. She cites the example of a word such as *culture* whose senses are not so divisible because the word is frequently used in a vague way with a sometimes convenient slippage for the user between its various senses (the exception is its technical meaning as in *blood cultures*):

(1) It's a case of culture shock.
(2) The development of pop culture owed much to Buddy Holly.
(3) The professor attended a conference on Javanese culture.
(4) She is a woman of great culture and breeding.
(5) Different cultures have to learn to co-exist.
(6) The metro is a part of modern urban culture.

(See Stock, 1984 for more extensive and authentic corpus-based citation.) The indeterminate boundaries between these different senses make it a hold-all kind of word available for distribution in related contexts without any too precise denotation. The problem for the lexicographer is that the senses are sufficiently related to discount separate numbered entries in a dictionary but sufficiently diverse to demand some kind of categorization. Stock proposes that a subdivided numbering system would enable the word to be split into its main senses (1, 2, 3, etc.) with subsenses entered as 1a, 1b, 1c, etc. This recognizes the clines of meaning which exist from monosemy to polysemy and, in the absence of clear guidance from within linguistic–lexicological description, constitutes the beginnings of a practical lexicographic solution.

Drawing a line from monosemy to polysemy remains one of a number of stubborn problems for lexicologists and lexicographers alike. Jeffries and Willis (1982b) propose a system for the diagnosis of polysemy and of lexical field membership by means of an analysis of case relations or what they term *participant roles*;[5] Cruse (1982) proposes a number of direct and indirect tests to measure lexical ambiguity with reference to notions of 'sense-cluster' and 'sense spectrum'; Cowie (1982) argues that there is no good reason for giving special weighting to any one disambiguating criterion largely because meaning relations are seen to hold between the different, distinguishable senses of lexemes and not between lexemes as such. It is clear that analysis of structural relations between these differentiable senses of a lexical item can be of value for describing words in dictionaries and especially in lexicons where semantic groupings form the organizational basis. For example, the separate senses of the verb *rise* can be differentiated simply by cross-reference to relations of antonymy. For example:

rise–set	(sun/moon)
rise–fall	(temperature)
rise–sink	(cakes, etc.)

In fact, the semantic organizations of words in lexicons do not always separate out senses in this way, a practice which may cause potential difficulties for the appropriate learning of polysemous words in an EFL context. (For reviews of published lexicons with reference to some of the above criteria and issues see Fox and Mahood, 1982; Jeffries and Willis, 1982a).

Other widely discussed issues in lexicography include the use of examples in the definition of lexical items; the appropriate ordering system for the words which make up an entry; the demarcation of style-values in learners' dictionaries (for discussion in this area see Chapter 9). In the case of use of examples the lexicographer needs to decide how far to define a word's meaning and thus not compromise on accuracy or to sacrifice such precision in the service of explaining clearly to the non-specialist general user (see Hanks, 1979); and in the process also to resolve exactly what are the main differences between the speech acts of defining and explaining. In the case of presentational ordering the difficult decision for the lexicographer is to resolve, again especially with polysemous words, which sense of the word to introduce first so that it serves to clarify the definition (or explanation) of subsequent items. With a word such as *literature*, for example, should the first reference be to it in its most frequent sense of imaginative, creative writing or might this context be better elucidated if the less frequent senses of the word as written material (e.g. 'Have you any *literature* on holidays in Spain?') appear as the leading category? It is clear that the lexicographer will benefit from theoretical refinement by linguists and also that lexicographic work can cross-fertilize such development (see Ilson, 1985a), but the decisions and intuitions of groups of professional lexicographers will not be easily supplanted.

6.6 Corpora, computers and lexicography

The most significant developments in lexicography in the past two decades have involved more extensive corpora of spoken and written language and the creation of sophisticated computer-based access tools to such corpora. The greatest innovations have been stimulated by the COBUILD project at the University of Birmingham, UK and the influence of such work can be measured by the fact that by the late 1990s all major English-language learner-dictionary projects have incorporated reference to extensive language corpora and developed computational techniques for extracting lexicographically significant information from such corpora. See the Bibliography of language corpora for details of corpora referred to in this book.

6.6.1 The COBUILD project

The COBUILD is one of the largest and most ambitious lexical research projects ever undertaken. COBUILD stands for *C*ollins *B*irmingham *U*niversity *I*nternational *L*anguage *D*atabase and is largely funded by the publisher William Collins (now HarperCollins). It is based in the School of English at the University of Birmingham under the direction of Professor John Sinclair who is, in addition to having major responsibility for lexical and lexico-grammatical research, editor-in-chief of the major lexicographic and other related publications of COBUILD, which began with the publication in 1987 of the ground-breaking *Collins COBUILD English Language Dictionary* (*CCELD*). The latest edition is the *Collins COBUILD English Dictionary* (*CCED*), published in 1995. The COBUILD corpus – previously termed the Birmingham Collection of English Text (BCOET) – was re-named The Bank of English in 1991 and at the time of writing (1997) stands at 320 million words.

The principal aim underlying COBUILD research is to investigate in as much detail as possible how the English language is actually used at a given moment in time in both speech and writing, and to allow such evidence to inform publications aimed at learners of the English language. As the project developed through the 1980s, it became clear that such evidence could only be made available by building a multi-million-word corpus and *CCELD* (1987) draws on a core database of 7.3 million words and makes supporting reference to a general corpus of 20 million words. For an account of early COBUILD corpus development see Renouf (1987).

Because most of the publications produced by COBUILD are for non-native users of English, there has been less interest in the kinds of specialized one-off uses of language which are often of major interest in dictionaries for native users of English. There has been greater interest in the most central and typical uses of the language. Evidence in COBUILD dictionaries is, therefore, usually given by illustrating meaning and usage by way of citations taken from the most typical, and sometimes even the most banal, examples of language. The examples cited are corpus-based and therefore include real uses of English attested in actual, naturally-occurring usage. They are not, therefore, the made-up examples and citations of lexicographers which had characterized foreign language lexicography before 1987. (For a discussion of lexicographic evidence, see Sinclair, 1985 and a range of papers in Sinclair (ed.), 1987a.) In pre-corpus days, evidence about the language used in some dictionaries relied on hand-collected data. This is evidence, of course, and is to be preferred to intuition and introspection but it cannot provide a picture of relative frequencies of usage. Computer-assisted word-searches are inevitably faster and can also provide data on the syntactic and collocational properties of words. This can be instrumental in differentiating different senses of a word or word unit.

The main innovations of this first COBUILD dictionary (*CCELD*, 1987) and its latest edition (*CCED*, 1995) can be summarized – with reference to sample entries – as follows:

1 Citations are examples of real English and do not involve made-up examples. The citations selected have been attested with reference to corpus evidence.
2 Linguistic and stylistic differences between spoken and written usage, and British-English and American-English usage can be separately stored and marked accordingly in dictionary entries. Pragmatic information concerning use in context, level of formality and related features is also provided, where appropriate.
3 Most crucially, relative frequencies of occurence are indicated and, most innovatively, in entries for individual lexical items, the order of senses in multi-sense words corresponds to their frequency order in the corpus. See the entry for *mug* in Figure 6.1.
4 Concordancing techniques (see the sample concordancing lines for *decline* in Figure 6.2) allow illustration of the main collocational and colligational properties of a word. Such properties can be made part of the explanation of a word's meaning (see also Chapter 3,

mug /mʌg/ **mugs, mugging, mugged** ◆◆◇◇◇

1 A **mug** is a large deep cup with straight sides and   N-COUNT
a handle, used for hot drinks. *He spooned instant
coffee into two of the mugs.* ▶ A **mug** of something   N-COUNT:
is the amount of it contained in a mug. *He had been*   usu N of n
drinking mugs of coffee to keep himself awake.

2 If someone **mugs** you, they attack you in order to   VERB
steal your money. *I was walking out to my car when*   V n
*this guy tried to mug me... He has been mugged
more than once.* ✦ **mugging, muggings** *Bank rob-*   N-VAR
*beries, burglaries and muggings are reported al-
most daily in the press... We usually think of a vic-
tim of mugging as being someone elderly.*

3 In informal British English, if you say that some-   N-COUNT
one is a **mug**, you mean that they are stupid and   [PRAGMATICS]
easily deceived or misled by other people. *He's a
mug as far as women are concerned... I feel such a
mug for signing the agreement.*

4 In informal British English, if you say that some-   PHRASE:
thing is **a mug's game**, you mean that it is an activ-   v-link PHR
ity that is not worth doing because it doesn't give
the person who is doing it any benefit or satisfaction. *I used to be a very heavy gambler, but not any
more. It's a mug's game... Dieting is a mug's game.*

5 Someone's **mug** is their face; an informal use. *He*   N-COUNT:
managed to get his ugly mug on the telly.   usu poss N

mug up. In British English, if you **mug up** a sub-   PHRASAL VERB
ject or **mug up** on it, you study it quickly, so that   =swot up
you can remember the main facts about it; an in-
formal expression. *...visitors who want to mug up*   V P n (not pron)
their knowledge in the shortest possible time... It is   V P on n
advisable to mug up on your Spanish, too, as few lo-   Also V P
cals speak English.

mugger /mʌgəʳ/ **muggers.** A **mugger** is a person   N-COUNT
who attacks someone violently in a street in or-
der to steal money from them.

muggy /mʌgi/. **Muggy** weather is unpleasantly   ADJ-GRADED:
warm and damp. *It was muggy and overcast.*   oft it v-link ADJ
   =humid

mug shot, mug shots. A **mug shot** is a photo-   N-COUNT
graph of someone, especially a photograph of a
criminal which has been taken by the police; an

Figure 6.1 A dictionary entry for *mug.*
Source: CCELD, 1987.

especially Sections 3.5 and 3.6). Significant lexical patterns and
grammatical behaviour are separately highlighted in *CCELD* and
CCED in a separate column which is positioned in parallel with the
relevant entry.

5   Explanations are written in complete sentences (not in abbreviated
phrases or codes), follow a strategy of clear, accessible language
(without recourse to a defining vocabulary), and involve a use of
natural syntactic formulae. For example, '*if*-clauses' are used for
purposes of explanation, just as they frequently are in everyday
discourse. Thus, lexical items are defined in context, often using
the most frequent patterns which surround them in actual use,
rather than as disembodied entities. A defining vocabulary is not
employed but a note in *CCED* (1995, p. xviii) states that 'most
words in our definitions [are] amongst the 2,500 commonest words
of English'.

1.	its contribution to national student politics has	declined.	Attempts to launch an Alternative left o
2.	ts, did they not, Clay Jones? Jones: They rapidly	declined.	Bill Sowerbutts. Often, they would disa
3.	spiral could get worse, as the level of activity	declined.	But, on Keynesian arguments, this could
4.	ntries—real (P 67) disposable spending power has	declined.	But for how long will the trade unions a
5.	licy towards the west, her active involvement has	declined.	But in the visits of British Maoists to
6.	know that the sort of lot of people generally has	declined.	((C)) Oh, it has. There are figures to p
7.	In 1966. But since 1971 the WPPE's influence has	declined.	Frequent changes of address, the failure
8.	ian Defence, the Muzio Gambit, the Queen's Gambit	declined.	Most of them are not only learned for t
9.	nt, and in that one Month, the crime rate sharply	declined.	Our Political Opponents and other Bodies
10.	attlefield, as distinct from the rear areas, soon	declined.	Refugees were posing an acute and growin
11.	izon became level and blue and clipped as the sun	declined.	That was another time of comparative coo
12.	t that our industrial performance has relatively	declined.	against that of other countries. If
13.	made her an importer. The value of her currency	declined.	along with the purchasing power of her
14.	he had not read the report. Slowly, the industry	declined.	and its members took up other activities
15.	5, pressure in the United States since prices have	declined	and costs have gone up," explained a GE
16.	he Second World War, modernist Fine Art in France	declined	and fell; in Britain it barely survived
17.	es also miners or railway workers, for so long in	declined	and troubled industries. Many varied moti
18.	psychology and so on, and they've certainly not	declined	as a whole. Our numbers of applications e
19.	workers in the total working population actually	declined	between 1911 and 1941. Class divisions w
20.	p's own interest in the physical side of marriage	declined	but he persuaded himself that this was o
21.	from 18 to 9 percent of the market; Lucky Strike	declined	even more sharply, from 14 to 6 per cent.
22.	d so far, and had been told so often that she had	declined	even further, that she had eagerly adopted th
23.	number of paddy holdings, and their average size	declined	from four-fifths to half an acre. Many
24.	he share of the rural areas in total population	declined	from an average of 84 percent in 1950 to
25.	in terms of seats; the number of Congress Members	declined	from 371 to 361; the CPI stayed steady at
26.	ain's share of world shipbuilding had as a result	declined	from 50% in 1914 to under 10% in 1964. In
27.	rship has stagnated and its electoral performance	declined	further, a whole range of new organisatio
28.	in March (and a revision discovered they had not	declined	in February after all). Wage settlement
29.	farms and farm families in New England has not	declined	in 1970, and the average age of farmers
30.	instead. Surprisingly, however, this tendency has	declined	in the mid-1970s, and savings have remain
31.	per head of population has, in some cases actually	declined	in the last ten years among the developin
32.	oded messages received by the ordinary person has	declined	in favour of coded messages. We may guess
33.	t, let alone against a Labour government. The RCP	declined	in spirit and in numbers and in 1949 diss
34.	—is this still the case, or have social sciences	declined	in undergraduate popularity? Well, first
35.	t the British Aircraft Industry is defunct; it's	declined	of course: the Americans are the leaders
36.	ited range fires. But the number of prairie fires	declined	sharply with the white man's arrival. As
37.	ehaves in imagination. It may be that Britain had	declined	so far, and had been told so often that s
38.	nization. With many thousands in jail, membership has	declined	to half a million by late 1936, and the a
39.	it is true that the authority of parliament has	declined	with the growth of the great producer in
40.	rate. "The average age of dwellings has steadily	declined,	writes E. F. Carter of the Stanford Res

Figure 6.2 Example from *BCOET* corpus: Extract from concordance for *declined*.
Source: *BCOET*, 1987.

employed but a note in *CCED* (1995, p. xviii) states that 'most words in our definitions [are] amongst the 2,500 commonest words of English'.

6   The COBUILD emphasis on the most frequent words in the language does not foreclose on the pragmatic or discourse functions of some of these frequent words. Thus, discourse markers (such as *now*, *well* and *right*) and 'content-less', propositionless words (see Section 4.5), which have been largely ignored in previous dictionaries of this type, are also accorded illustration and explanation.[6] A word such as *fine*, for example, is explained in a range of different senses, but its meaning and function in conversational replies and as a marker of conversational boundaries (as in: 'How are you? I'm *fine* thanks' or 'Is there anything anyone wants to add to this? OK, *fine*. Let's move on') are also indicated. Figures 6.3 and 6.4 illustrate in this respect differences in the treatment of *now* as a discourse marker in both CCELD and the *Longman Dictionary of Contemporary English* (*LDOCE*, 1987).

In the years following the publication of *CCELD*, great efforts were invested in further corpus development as it was realized that lexico-grammatical description could be even better using a corpus with more words and broader coverage from more varieties of the English language. For example, Clear *et al.* (1996) note that in the 7.3-million-word core corpus (1987) there is only evidence that the word *taciturn* is used predicatively, but the general 20-million-word corpus (as of 1987) reveals that it is also used as a premodifier and regularly with another negative adjective as in *taciturn and unfriendly*. Descriptions were modified in the light of this further evidence.

The COBUILD corpus has informed work on grammar (see Section 3.6) and on idioms, including the *Collins COBUILD Dictionary of Idioms* (1995). The latter gives unique guidance concerning both the frequency of different idioms and the different patterns which idioms form in varying degrees of fixedness. The corpus has also informed work on a dictionary of collocations – *Collins COBUILD English Words in Use* (1997) – which describes over 100,000 collocations in a range of lexical patterns. This is supported by attested examples from the corpus. Parallel publications include a series of concordance samplers for use in the classroom and CD-ROMs giving a wide variety of linguistic profiles of word usage. Simultaneously, the corpus is being continually updated to include a wider variety of spoken forms and data from other Englishes around the world.

now /naʊ/: 1 Now is used 1.1 to refer to a time in the present time, often in contrast to a time in the past or the future. You may be talking about what is actually happening at the moment or about the present stage of your life or about the present stage of history. EG *It is now just after one o'clock... What if a shark came along right now?... I'm going home now... Calculators are now owned by a high percentage of school children... She has three children now...... a now historic production of Under Milk Wood* ▶ use J as the subject of a verb, or after a preposition. EG *Now is the time to find out... Goodbye for now ... From now on, you are free to do what you like.* 1.2 to specify the length of time that something has lasted, from the time it started until the present time, EG *'How long have you been keeping bees?'–'For five years now'... It's two weeks now since I wrote to you... How long have you lived here now?*
— ADV — = at present — ADV WITH VB: AFTER NG/A

2 Now is also used with the past tense, especially in novels and stories, to refer to the particular time in the past that you are speaking or writing about, as opposed to any later or earlier time. EG *It was ten o'clock now... They were walking more slowly now... By now the country had changed dramatically.*
— ADV WITH VB: ALSO AFTER PREP

3 Just now means a very short time ago. EG *I apologize for my outburst just now... I was talking to him just now.*
— PER: USED AS AN A — I recently

4 If you say 'It's now or never', you mean that something must be done immediately, because if it is not done immediately there will not be another chance to do it.
— CONVENTION

5 You can say 'Now for...' when you are going to change the subject and talk about something different, EG *... and now for some more of your letters... Now for the question of your expenses.*
— PER + NG

6 If you say that something will happen any day now, any moment now, or any time now, you mean that it will happen very soon. EG *Any day now, the local authority is going to announce a major housing scheme... They should arrive any time now.*
— PER: USED AS AN A

7 If you say that something happens now and then or every now and then, you mean that it happens sometimes but not very often or regularly. EG *Now and again my method appears to work... Every now and then there is a confrontation.*
— PER: USED AS AN A — = occasionally

8 Now also means as a result of what has recently happened. EG *I was hoping to see you tomorrow. That won't be possible now... It's the most beautiful city I have ever seen. Now I understand why you come back so often.*
— ADV WITH VB

9 Now that or now is used when you want to say that the effect of something that has happened is that something else takes place. EG *Now that she's found him, she'll never let him go ... Now that I am old, I can read all the books I've always meant to read... I like him a lot now he's older.*
— CONJ SUBORD — I because

10 Now is also used 10.1 at the beginning of a sentence, to introduce information which is relevant to the part of the story or account that you have reached and which needs to be known before you can continue. EG *Daisy's only dangerous fault was her willingness to kick. Now, a camel can kick you in any direction, within a radius of six feet... Now this king had three daughters.* 10.2 in spoken English, to introduce a contrast, EG *I don't know anything about car engines. Now, if Richard was here, he'd be able to help you.* 10.3 in informal spoken English, as something to say while you think of what to say next. EG *Well now. I've got the following suggestions... Now, let's stop for a moment there... I've got her address somewhere. Now let me see.* 10.4 to give a slight friendly emphasis to a request or command. EG *I must get back to work. Run along, now... Be very careful now... Give me the gun. Quick now!* 10.5 in spoken English, as a friendly way of trying to calm or comfort someone. EG *There now, don't cry ... Now, come on. Be sensible.*
— ADV SEN — = well — ADV SEN — = however

11 Now, now is used in spoken English 11.1 as a friendly way of trying to comfort someone. EG *'Now, now,' the doctor said, taking her gently by the hand. 'You mustn't get so upset.'* 11.2 as a friendly way of introducing a warning to someone not to behave in a particular way. EG *Now, now, there's no need to be nasty.*
— CONVENTION — = there there

12 Now then is used in spoken English to attract people's attention when you want to say something to them. EG *Now then, sleepyhead! It's time to go to bed... Now then, who's for a cup of tea?*
— CONVENTION — = right

Figure 6.3 A dictionary entry for *now*.
Source: CCELD, 1987.

now¹ *nau. adv* **1 a** at this time: at present: *I had a headache this morning, but I'm all right now.* | *We used to live in Bristol but now we live in London.* | *A journey that used to take several weeks can now be made in a few hours.* **b** at the time just mentioned, e.g. in a story or an account of past events: *He opened the door. Now the noise was very loud.* **2** at the time just following the present: at once: *We've finished our dinner so now let's have some coffee.* | *Now for* (= now we will have) *the next question.* | *They'll be here any time now.* **3 a** (used to introduce a statement or question): *Now, I don't know if you'll agree with this, but I'd like to make a suggestion.* **b** (used to add force to a command, warning, etc.): *Now then, what's going on here?* | *Be careful now!* | *Now, now, stop crying!* —compare THERE³ **4** (used pafter an expression of time) calculating from or up to the present: *It hasn't been working properly for three weeks now.* | *It's now 27 years. It's 27 years now since he died.* **5 (every) now and then/now and again** at times: sometimes: *She meets her old boyfriend for a drink now and then.* | *I like to visit art galleries now and again.* **6 now . . . now** sometimes . . . and sometimes: *The market is very unstable, with prices now rising, now falling.*

now² *n* [U] the present time or moment: *Now is the time to tell him the truth.* | *The time for action is now!* | *Up to/Until now we've had no problems.* | *He should have finished by now.* | *As of now From now on* (= starting now) *the bank will close at 3.30 pm.* | *Goodbye for now.*

now³ also now that—cont because (something has happened): *Now (that) John's arrived, we can begin.*

Figure 6.4 A dictionary entry for *now*.
Source: LDOCE, 1987.

The most substantial insight to have been generated by COBUILD research is, as explored in Chapter 3, that grammatical and lexical patterns are co-selected and mutually interdependent. Clear *et al.* (1996) have expressed this as follows:

> Particular grammatical patterns tend to co-occur with particular lexical items, and – the other side of the coin – lexical items seem to occur in only a limited range of patterns. The interdependence of grammar and lexis is such that they are ultimately inseparable, working together in the making of meaning.
>
> (Clear *et al.*, 1996, p. 313)

It is likely that future developments in lexicography will follow such insights; in the meantime it is worth reflecting that the publication of the first COBUILD dictionary in 1987 was greeted as idiosyncratic and unproven but that in the ten years which have ensued corpus-based lexicography following COBUILD lines has been adopted as standard practice in research, linguistic description and publishing.

With such a database considerable potential exists for innovative diversification into areas such as: the construction of lexically graded syllabuses appropriate to textbooks for foreign-language learners; frequency counts for language learning purposes, especially for the design of more 'lexically authentic' materials;[7] dictionaries of collocations; lexicons with field-specific semantic groupings; fuller specification of style levels (see case study in Chapter 9). This is all-in-all a movement towards the kind of 'associative lexicon' advocated by Makkai (1980)[8] and all of which would contribute substantially to the teaching and learning of English.[9]

6.7 Further major innovations (1990 onwards)

Other major and influential contributions to EFL lexicography have continued with subsequent editions of the *Longman Dictionary of Contemporary English* (*LDOCE*, 2nd edn, 1987; 3rd edn 1995) and the *Oxford Advanced Learner's Dictionary* (*OALD*, 5th edn, 1995). Cambridge University Press have also published a learner's dictionary: the *Cambridge International Dictionary of English* (*CIDE*, 1995). Although influenced by COBUILD's computational methodology and in particular by the now established pre-requisite of a corpus of linguistic evidence, subsequent innovations and developments have uniquely evolved according to different presentational principles.

In terms of corpora, both *LDOCE* and *OALD* have benefited from the British National Corpus (BNC) – a corpus of 100 million words of written and 10 million words of spoken English – in the development of which both publishers (Longman and OUP; see Bibliography of language corpora for full details) have been partners. Additionally, Longman has further extensive corpora of American English which inform all dictionaries including the *Longman Dictionary of American English*, the *Longman Lancaster Corpus* (*LLC*) – a corpus of 30 million words of written English – developed with advice from Prof. Geoffrey Leech at Lancaster University and a 10-million-word learner corpus including written texts from students at all levels from over 70 different language backgrounds. The latter is designed to provide evidence of the kinds of lexical mistakes most frequently made by learners as well as guidance concerning the kinds of words most likely to be understood by learners of English in dictionary definitions and explanations. Evidence from spoken corpora, in particular, has informed *LDOCE* (1995) in that the top 3,000 most frequent words in speech (as opposed to writing) are marked out for special attention. See the diagram given near the entry for *mean* in *LDOCE* (1995) at Figure 6.5.

Other particularly characteristic features of *LDOCE* (1995) include:

1   a continuing adherence to a finite defining vocabulary and to varied definition styles. However, of the words referred to in Section 6.2, *bacteria, arch, conscience, determine* and *empire* have all been removed from the 1995 edition of the defining vocabulary which is being constantly revised in the light of research with users. Another avowed aim is, where possible, to define the unit of meaning rather than individual words; this means that there are regular entries for phrases as well as for words. Selection restrictions on particular word forms are also clearly indicated.

2   a newly introduced feature called 'signposts' to aid learners with the disambiguation of polysemous items. Signposts help the learner to make mental connections with the word in the context in which they encountered it.

3   corpus-based but not corpus-bound materials. Examples are given in an order which is most likely to help the learner rather than solely on the basis of the relative frequency of the exemplified sense. Authentic citations from the corpus are similarly not always helpful to the learner and in *LDOCE* it is an important principle that pedagogic mediation should precede the reality of the example.

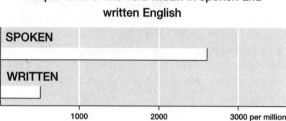

This graph shows that the verb **mean** is much more common in spoken English than in written English. This is because it is used in a lot of common spoken phrases.

Figure 6.5 Frequencies of the verb *mean* in spoken and written English. *Source: LDOCE*, 1995.

freak¹ /friːk/ *n* |C| **1 bike/fitness/film etc freak** *informal* someone who is so interested in bikes, fitness etc that other people think they are strange or unusual: *Carrot juice is a favourite with health-food freaks.* **2** someone who looks very strange or behaves in a very unusual way: *Women who were good at physics used to be considered freaks.* **3** something in nature, such as a strangely-shaped plant or animal, that is very unusual: *One of the lambs was a freak - it had two tails.* | **a freak of nature** (something physically strange or unusual) *By some freak of nature there was a snowstorm in June.* **4 control freak** someone who always wants to control situations and other people

Figure 6.6 A dictionary entry for *freak*. *Source: LDOCE*, 1995.

See the above example entry from *LDOCE* (1995) in Figure 6.6.

The fifth edition of *OALD* (1995) and the first edition of *CIDE* (1995) similarly contain numerous innvovations. *CIDE* draws on the 100-million-word Cambridge Language Survey (now the Cambridge International Corpus, or CIC), with an emphasis on different national variations in English use and containing practical yet inventive features such as lists of false friends in English in comparison with fourteen other languages. *CIDE* also contains guide words which in the case of polysemous words orient the reader to the main or core meaning of the words listed in a single entry.

OALD (1995) represents a marked extension of a number of key features and some innovations in other areas, with the 1995 edition offering a treatment of 2,800 new words and meanings when compared with earlier editions. Additional features include: 90,000 corpus-based examples (drawn from the 100-million-word British National Corpus and the 40-million-word Oxford American-English Corpus); notes and illustrated pages giving information on cultural differences between British and American English; extensive usage notes covering areas of grammar and meaning which cause difficulty; and a defining vocabulary (now expanded to 3,500 words) is retained for purposes of definition and explanation. Figure 6.7 illustrates these features in the form of a sample dictionary page.

6.7.1 Lexicography and English-language learning: Contrasts and comparisons

Table 6.1 summarizes some basic data about the four main learner's dictionaries (*CCED* [*COBUILD*], *CIDE*, *LDOCE* and *OALD*), versions of which were all published in 1995. Comparisons between these dictionaries depend, however, on the criteria adopted for comparison and the grounds can never therefore be entirely neutral, nor can any comparison be entirely valid without extensive empirical testing with users. However, among the evaluative frameworks to which reference needs to be made, at the very least according to the publishers' own criteria, are:

1   clarity of definition and explanation, and the extent to which defining vocabularies assist in this aim;
2   authenticity, naturalness and pedagogic mediation of examples;
3   ease of access to the most frequent uses and core meanings (which are, of course, not necessarily identical);
4   the extent to which words are shown in natural syntactic and collocational environments;
5   the extent to which polysemous words and words which have different meanings in different phrasal forms is appropriately explained; ease of access to them;

A detailed comparison of these dictionaries is given in a special feature of the *International Journal of Lexicography*; see in particular, Bogaards (1996) and Herbst (1996). See also Béjoint (1994). Cameron (1998) raises valuable issues concerning the absence of diachronic *here.* ,miss 'out (on sth) (*infml*) to lose an opportunity to benefit from sth or to enjoy oneself: *If I don't go to the party. I'll feel I'm missing out.*

► **missing** *adj* **1(a)** that cannot be found or that is not in the usual place; lost: *The book had two pages. missing/two missing pages.* ○ *The hammer is missing from my tool-box.* (**b**) not present: *He's always missing when there's work to be done.* **2(a)** (of a person or an animal) absent from home and impossible to find: *a police file on missing persons* ○ *They reported that their child had gone missing for a week.* ○ *Our cat's been missing for a week.* (**b**) not present after an accident, a battle, etc but not known to have been killed: *26 passengers on the liner were reported* (*as*) *missing.* **the missing** *n* [pl v]: *Captain Jones is among the missing.*

■ **,missing 'link** *n* (usu *sing*) a thing needed to complete a series.

miss³ /mɪs/ *n* a failure to hit, catch or reach sth that one has tried to hit, catch or reach: *score ten hits and one miss* ○ *The ball's gone right past him – that was a bad miss* (ie he ought to have stopped, caught, etc). See also NEAR MISS. **IDM** give sth/sb a 'miss (*Brit infml*) **1** to omit sb/sth: *I think I'll give the fish course a miss.* **2** to decide not to do sth one normally does: *I think I'll give badminton a miss* (ie not play it) *tonight.*

missal /'mɪsl/ *n* a book containing the prayers. etc used at Mass throughout the year in the Roman Catholic Church.

misshapen /ˌmɪs'ʃerpən/ *adj* (esp of the body or a limb) not having the normal shape: not formed normally.

missile /'mɪsaɪl; *US* 'mɪsl/ *n* **1** an object or weapon that is thrown at fired a: a target: *Missiles hurled at the police included stones and bottles.* ⇒ picture. **2** an explosive weapon directed at a target automatically or by means of an electronic device: *ballistic/nuclear missiles* ○ *missile bases/sites/launching pads.* ⇒ picture. See also GUIDED MISSILE.

mission /'mɪʃn/ *n* **1** a group of people sent, esp abroad, on political or commercial business: *a British trade mission to China* ○ *go/send sb on a fact-finding mission* **2(a)** a group of religious people sent esp to remote areas to teach others about Christianity: *a Catholic/Methodist mission in Africa.* (**b**) a building or group of buildings where the work of these people is done: *a mission station/school/hospital.* **3** a particular task done by a person or a group: *a top-secret mission* ○ *mission control/headquarters* ○ *The squadron flew a reconnaissance mission.* **4** a particular aim or duty that one wants to fulfil more than anything else: *Her mission in life is to help AIDS victims.*

missionary /'mɪʃənri; *US* -neri/ *n* a person sent to teach the Christian religion to people who are ignorant of it: *Catholic/Anglican missionaries* ○ *missionary work* ○ *speak with missionary zeal* (ie great enthusiasm and faith).

missis = MISSUS.

missive /'mɪsɪv/ *n* (*fml or joc*) a letter, esp a long or official one.

misspell /ˌmɪs'spel/ *v* (*pt, pp* misspelled or mispelt /-'spelt/) to spell sth wrongly: [Vn] *My name had been misspelt.* ► **misspelling** *n.*

misspend /ˌmɪs'spend/ *v* (*pt. pp* misspent/.'spent/) (esp passive) to spend or use one's money, time, etc foolishly or wrongly: [Vn]: *misspent 'energy* ○ *a ,misspent 'youth.*

missus (also **missis**) /'mɪsɪz/ *n* **1** (*infml or joc*) (used after *the, my, your, his*) a person's wife: *How's the missus* (ie your wife)? ○ *My missus hates me smoking indoors.* **2** (*sl*) (used as a form of address to a woman): *Are these your kids, missus?* Compare MISTER **2**.

mist /mɪst/ *n* **1** [U,C] a cloud of tiny drops of water hanging just above the ground. Mist is not so thick as FOG but is still difficult to see through: *hills hidden/shrouded in mist* ○ *Mist patches on the roads are making driving difficult.* ○ (*fig*) *The origins of the story are lost in the mists of time.* ○ *She looked at him through a mist of tears.* ⇒ note at FOG. **2** [sing] a fine spray of liquid, eg from an AEROSOL can: *A mist of perfume hung in the air.*

► **mist** *v* – (sth) (up) to cover sth or become covered with tiny drops of water: [Vn, Vnp] *Her breath misted* (*up*) *the window-pane.* [Vp] *The mirror has misted up.* [V, Vpr] *His eyes misted* (*with tears*). **PHRV** ,mist 'over to become covered with mist: *When I drink something hot, my glasses mist over.* ○ *His eyes misted over.*

misty /'mɪsti/ *adj* (-ier, -iest) full of or covered with mist: not bright or clear: *a misty morning* ○ *misty weather/hills* ○ *misty rain* ○ *misty eyes/colours.* **mistily** *adv.*

mistake¹ /mɪ'steɪk/ *n* **1** an action or opinion that is foolish or wrong: an error of judgement: *This isn't my bill – there must be some mistake.* ○ *I made a mistake about Julie – she's quite nice really.* ○ *It was a big mistake to send her to boarding-school.* ○ *A week after the wedding she realized she had made a terrible mistake.* **2** a word, figure, sum, etc that is not correct: *spelling mistakes* ○ *The waiter made a mistake in adding up the bill.* **IDM** and '**no mistake** (*infml*) without any doubt: *She's a strange woman and 'no mistake',* **by mi'stake** accidentally: in error: *I took your bag instead of mine by mistake.* **make no mi'stake (about sth)** (*infml*) do not be deceived into thinking otherwise: *Make no mistake (about it), we're facing a major financial crisis.*

NOTE Compare **mistake, error, blunder, fault** and **defect.** They all refer to something that has not been done correctly or properly. Mistake is the most general and used in most situations: *The letter had quite a few mistakes in it.* ○ *Going on a camping holiday with young children was definitely a mistake.* **Error** is used when talking about calculations, and in technical or formal contexts: *I think there are a few errors in your calculations.* A **blunder** is a stupid or careless and quite serious mistake made because of bad judgement: *A hospital blunder led to 500 cancer patients getting the wrong radiation treatmeat.*
   Fault emphasizes a person's responsibility for a mistake: *Tom broke the window, but it was my fault for letting him play football in the house.* A fault can also be an imperfection in a person or thing: *There was a design fault in the train doors.* ○ *I accepted my father's faults because I loved him.* A **defect** is a serious imperfection: *The causes of many birth defects have not yet been discovered.*

mistake² /mɪ'steɪk/ *v* (*pt* mistook /mɪ'stok/ *pp* mistaken / mɪ'steɪkən/) **1** to be wrong or to get a wrong idea about sb/sth: [Vn] *I must have mistaken your meaning/what you meant.* ○ *You can't mistake their house – it's painted bright green.* [Vn-adj] *She mistook his smile as indicating agreement.* [Vn to inf] *I mistook you to mean that you wanted to come.* **2** – sb/sth **for** sb/sth to suppose wrongly that sb/sth is sb/sth else: [Vnpr] *She is often mistaken for her twin.*

[Vn to inf] = verb + *to* infinitive   [Vn.inf (no *to*)] = verb + noun + infinitive without *to*   [V.*ing*] = verb + -*ing* form

Figure 6.7 A sample dictionary page.
Source: OALD, 1995.

Table 6.1 Some data about four learner's dictionaries of English

	LDOCE	OALD	COBUILD (CCELD, CCED)	CIDE
First edition (year)	1978	1948	1987	1995
editor(s)	P. Procter	A.S. Hornby	J. Sinclair P. Hanks	P. Procter
Latest edition/year	3/1995	5/1995	2/1995	1/1995
editor(s)	M. Rundell	J. Crowther	J. Sinclair G. Fox	P. Procter
No. of pages (a–z)	1,644	1,392	1,951	1,701
No. of other pages	64	78	38	91
No. of definitions claimed	> 80,000	65,000	> 75,000	100,000
No. of examples claimed	–	90,000	100,000	> 100,000
Corpora	LLC + BNC	BNC + OAEC	BE	CLS

After: Bogaards, 1996.

Abbreviations:
LLC – Longman Lancaster Corpus (30 million words)
BNC – British National Corpus (100 million words)
OAEC – Oxford American English Corpus (40 million words)
BE – Bank of English (200 million words; as of 1994)
CLS – Cambridge Language Survey (100 million words)

information in many modern dictionaries arguing that important cultural and ideological inflections become thereby deleted.

6.8 A dictionary for production

The *Longman Language Activator* (1994) is, uniquely, a production dictionary. It is aimed at intermediate to advanced learners of English and is designed around a conceptual map of the core words of English. These 1,052 key concepts include words such as *sad/unhappy* around which are grouped, in a kind of atlas of meaning, a further thirteen related words and phrases such as *be fed up with*, *be down in the dumps*, *depressed*, *miserable*, *downcast* and *glum*. These related words and their different levels of meaning and style are explained with reference to the core concept in such a way as to help students produce or generate a range of expressions.

This information about meaning helps learners who know what they want to say but are seeking for more precise expressions; the learner should feel confident about expressing his or her ideas because information about a range of related meanings is given clearly and in accessible definitions (using a defining vocabulary). One aim of a **production dictionary** is to generate greater learner autonomy by encouraging learners to check, prior to use, how a word is used and in what collocational patterns it is found. **Decoding dictionaries** involve, generally but not exclusively, less active modes of understanding. By contrast, the *Longman Language Activator* is essentially an **encoding dictionary**. The example in Figure 6.8 for the key concept of *borrow*, taken from the dictionary, illustrates the thesaurus-like nature of its entries.

6.9 Conclusions and prospects

English-language lexicography has undergone a phase of considerable invention and innovation in the last three decades of the twentieth century. A number of problems in the presentation of lexical information, particularly to language learners, have been solved and there have been considerable advances in the treatment of fixed and idiomatic expressions. Also, given the kind of corpora now available to lexicographers there is also considerable potential for a movement towards the kind of associative lexicon advocated by Adam Makkai in 1980 (Makkai, 1980) and, as a next step, more extensive treatment of style levels (see case study in Chapter 9).

It is paradoxical that the most significant advances in the description of lexico-grammatical patterns have coincided with a time when the interests of linguists have shifted towards patterns of lexis in discourse. This means that lexicography is probably on the verge of even more exciting developments, including a major issue to address, in both theory and practice, in demarcating where grammars stop and where dictionaries start.

Several questions remain, however, which require urgent solutions. Chief among them is: *how* will lexicographers take a more discourse-based approach which demands attention to words in context? Words in contexts tend to have variable, even negotiable meanings. But lexicographers tend to be concerned mainly with meaning as a property of words and expressions in abstraction from the contexts in which they are used. Does this mean that dictionaries will only record the most fixed and specialized meanings of the more fixed expressions? Or will a range of new, simple and economic conventions be developed to handle contextual associations? It is clear that computer-based lexicography with access to large corpora is in the forefront of such developments and that work on lexis in discourse as described in Chapter 4 will come to exercise greater influence on lexicographic practice. This book is not the

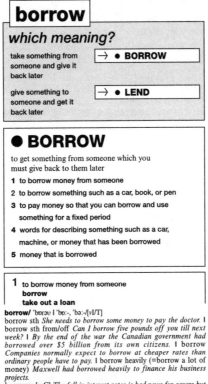

Figure 6.8 A dictionary entry for *borrow*.
Source: *Longman Language Activator*, 1994.

place to seek such answers, since it is mainly concerned to provide an overview of landmarks in a number of areas. However, one neglected area in lexical entry design which has received insufficient attention is that of stylistic associations or style-values. The problems created by such associations are contingent on those of describing words in discourse contexts, and the area will be seen to be of considerable importance to non-native language users. A preliminary discussion of this topic is undertaken in the case study which comprises the final chapter of this book.

Notes

1 Note in this connection the publication of books which 'accompany' dictionaries and which supply guidance on their use and suggest related teaching procedures, for example, Underhill (1980); Goodale (1995).

2 Weinreich (1980) notes that there will tend to be restricted collocability if the verb is used figuratively rather than literally (e.g. 'foot the bill'); the semi-metaphorical use of *fan* and *entertain* may conceivably account for the semi-restrictedness in collocation.

3 Note, for example, that *soft* and *tender* are often cited as synonyms: 'The skin felt *soft/tender*'; 'He touched her *softly/tenderly*'. But there are collocational restrictions: The snow was *soft/*tender*; The bruise was *tender/*soft*; The meat was *tender/*soft*. For useful teaching suggestions in this area see Keen (1978, p. 65).

4 Cowie's paper (Cowie, 1982) discusses a range of disambiguation procedures including determination of superordinate, antonymy tests, selection of synonyms etc. He concludes that the demarcation of polysemy is extremely difficult. He cites the following sense of *post* (meaning here 'letters', 'parcels', etc.) and points out that relations of dependency and contrast commonly hold between the meaning-divisions of lexemes; for example:

(1) The post is terribly slow in England ('conveyance of post').
(2) You can just catch the last post ('collection of post').

The sense of *post* here thus requires further subdivision and the identity of the lexeme owes as much to 'its own *internal* semantic breakdown and of the meaningful relations established by its sense divisions' than to its *external* structural semantic relations with other lexemes.

5 Participant roles are a test of the possible separation of meanings in terms of the various *entities* which *participate* in an *action*. The test is applied so far only to verbs denoting spatial movement, change of state, change of custody, contact and communication. The test forms part of work by the Oxford University Press Lexical Research Unit, under the direction of A.P. Cowie and based at the University of Leeds, which aims to explore how polysemy is patterned in particular semantic micro-fields. For example,

(1) Mary assembled the crew.
(2) Mary assembled the bookcase.

can be differentiated by reference to the different participant roles of crew ('actor') and bookcase ('product' or 'object of result'). For further discussion and analysis see Jeffries and Willis (1982b).

6 Examination of the corpus reveals, for example, a whole range of different pragmatic functions for a conjunction such as *if*. Traditional entry design might mark *if* as signalling the introduction of a conditional clause but the range of functions is very large indeed. The following are merely selections from the COBUILD database: 'the rates are good, *if* not better, than many term shares'; 'her voice was, *if* not perfect, at least nearly so'; 'He's very strong *if* rather small'; 'it's a great opportunity, a paid holiday *if* you like'; 'he's earning £20,000 a year, *if* not more'; '*if* it's an offence, it's an offence'; 'it's not as *if* he were a relative'; '*if* only we could make a radio'; '*if* you can just sign that for me, thank you'. For example, the function in the last

example is that of polite request in spoken contexts. In this example, the pragmatic function may be more accurately termed one of polite digression: '*if* I might just come in here for a moment and say a word in his defence'.

7 Willis and Willis (1987–8) is a beginner's course-book for foreign learners of English in active preparation using actual corpus-based citations and introducing lexical items with reference to frequency statistics drawn from COBUILD data.

8 Makkai uses the word 'associative' in its Saussurean sense in an article 'Theoretical and practical aspects of an associative lexicon for 20th century English' (Makkai, 1980). He is interested in trying to represent lexicographically a speaker's accumulated total knowledge of the structural associations of a lexical item(s):

> Dictionaries, by and large, have tended to ignore the associative groupings of lexemes as they form NATURAL SEMANTIC NESTS, around concretely observable and abstract (nonobservable) entities, and their traditional reliance on alphabetization endeavoured to present a totality of the available lexis while ignoring frequency of usage, exact range of dialectal habitat, the speaker's sociological status, etc.
>
> (Makkai, 1980, p. 127)

9 For further relevant surveys see Stein (1979), Hartmann (1981b) and Bogaards (1996).

7 Learning and teaching vocabulary

> Building up a vocabulary is a complicated process, and one that takes a long time. By $1\frac{1}{2}$ years or so, children may have around fifty words, and a couple of years later, many have several hundred. But the process does not stop there, at the age of 4 or 5. Children as old as 8 or 9 are still working out complicated word meanings, e.g. the meanings of terms like *promise, cousin* and *although*. And adults go on acquiring vocabulary over many years. Words like *inconcinnous* or *widdershins* send many of us to the dictionary.
>
> (Eve Clark)

7.0 Introduction: Some historical perspectives

For many years vocabulary was the poor relation of language teaching. Its neglect has been in part due to a specialization in linguistic research on syntax and phonology which may have fostered a climate in which vocabulary was felt to be a less important element in learning a second language. The following statement by Gleason, while strangely appearing to suggest that vocabulary does not have 'content' or 'expression', typifies attitudes held in the 1960s:

> In learning a second language, you will find that vocabulary is comparatively easy, in spite of the fact that it is vocabulary that students fear most. The harder part is mastering new structures in both content and expression.
>
> (Gleason, 1961, p. 7)

There may also have been an underlying perception that significant structural description and generalization is possible within syntax, where relations are finite, but less likely within lexis, where relations are theoretically infinite. Also, the syntactic structures to be learned can be more easily specified in a syllabus than can either the number, type or range of vocabulary items which may be required. Major works on EFL/ESL syllabus design such as Wilkins (1976) and Munby (1978) are, for example, unhelpful on the question of vocabulary. Yet lexical items are powerful indices of 'expression' and are regularly marked attitudinally. Mistakes in lexical selection may be less generously tolerated outside classrooms than mistakes in syntax. It is interesting, in fact, to test the kinds of responses we may have to the following statements if used to us and about us:

(1) You look fit and weedy these days.
(2) You can looked nice and fit this day.

We might speculate whether the negative attitudinal marking carried, even if unintentionally, by the item *weedy* in (1) can override any adverse judgements of competence in syntactic usage in (2).

Since the late 1970s, however, there has been a revival of interest in vocabulary teaching, especially in Great Britain where lexical research projects were in any case undertaken in the late 1960s (e.g. Sinclair *et al.*, 1970) and where deeper roots have always existed in the vocabulary-control movement and EFL lexicography (see, for example, McArthur, 1978). Explorations in lexical semantics (e.g. Lyons, 1968; 1977) were accompanied by developments in vocabulary teaching, though these did not necessarily run in parallel. Representative samples of interest in vocabulary teaching and its development in the 1970s and 1980s can be found in a number of articles (e.g. Judd, 1978; Twaddell, 1973; Lord, 1974; Richards, 1976; and in volumes such as Gavins and Redman, 1986; and Carter and McCarthy, 1988).

The focus of this chapter will be on issues in vocabulary teaching to 'beginners' in the early stages of learning a second or foreign language and on problems and prospects in advanced vocabulary teaching; it is thus a focus which is at either end of a formal classroom-oriented peda-gogical spectrum but one which should enable readers interested in vocabulary teaching and learning at intermediate levels to construct some appropriate frames of reference. The main, but not exclusive, emphasis within this focus will be on principles rather than on specific teaching procedures.

The second part of this chapter, which is explicitly devoted to teach-ing, necessarily develops insights into, and reports on, lexical acquisi-tion research relevant to specific teaching problems and procedures. Thus, a firm basis is supplied for considering the intricate inter-dependencies between vocabulary *teaching* and theories of vocabulary *learning*. Finally, the main principle enunciated throughout this chapter is that as vocabulary learning develops it should be a main aim of vocabulary teaching to put students in the position where they are capable of deriving and producing meanings from lexical items both *for themselves* and *out* of the classroom.

The first step in this examination of vocabulary teaching and learning will be in the direction of vocabulary-acquisition research. As Meara (1980) reports, the field here is, parallel to that of teaching vocabulary, 'a neglected aspect of language learning'. Recently, however, research has become more extensive even though numerous important questions remain largely unanswered, and some textbooks on second-language acquisition (e.g. Ellis, 1985) do not see vocabulary independently from acquisition of syntax. The first sections report on work on early vocabulary acquisition in a first language (L1) where there exists a longer tradition of research. Even though the focus in this chapter is on formal classroom-oriented second-language (L2) acquisition and teaching, where the main issues of early cognitive and conceptual development do not pertain, it will be argued that the more that is known about acquisition generally, the more teaching and learning generally may benefit. For reasons of space, distinctions made by Krashen (1981) between acquisition and learning are not debated and the two terms are used interchangeably.

7.1 Early words: Mother-tongue English

The 1970s and early 1980s witnessed an intensive scrutiny of the processes of mother-tongue language acquisition in English. There is space in this section to do no more than isolate some main trends in the research with specific reference to vocabulary development in the pre-school phase. The attempt to describe what is specifically semantic in that development should reveal that easy distinctions between syntactic, semantic and pragmatic features are not possible. Important questions concerning the relations between linguistic and cognitive development as well as arguments concerning the relative primacy of concept formation and linguistic identification can be found in relevant surveys and discussions in Fletcher and Garman (1979), Elliot (1981), Kates (1980, Ch. 3) and Lock and Fisher (1984). Three main bodies of research will be briefly reviewed: Clark's **semantic-feature acquisition hypothesis**; Nelson's **functional core concept**; and Bowerman's research into **semantic prototypes.**

Clark (1973) stresses the role of perceptual information in a child's semantic representation of words. Her view is that a word possesses a set of semantic features but that children initially assign meanings on the basis of what they encode to be a word's prominent perceptual characteristics. Thus, a *ball* may be primarily distinguished as being *round*, as opposed to *soft*, *yellow* or *squashy* or that it can *bounce* or *roll* – all less perceptually prominent features which may be, of course, subsequently acquired. The basis of Clark's semantic-feature acquisition hypothesis is thus one of perceptual primacy and it provides an explanation for the commonly observed characteristic of **overextension**. Overextensions result when the child uses a *semantic feature* to generalize to other objects. For example, a child might refer to an apple or a door-knob as a ball, or overextend the meaning of the utterance *ticktock* (meaning 'clock') to watches, the dials of a weighing machine, a cooker or a TV set. Table 7.1, adapted from Clark (1973), illustrates the hypothesis further. See Clark (1993) for more recent extensions of this work.

In contrast to Clark's assignment of primacy to perceptual features, Nelson (1974) proposes that the concept underlying the distinction made by the child may be formed according to the functions or actions associated with the object. In other words, in the case of *ball* the essential semantic core is not that it is perceived as round but that it functions in a particular way as a result of the way the child interacts, or engages in activity with the ball. What is important, therefore, is what an object does or what a child can do with or to it. Nelson puts it as follows:

> The child focusses his attention for the first time on a ball which his mother picks up and bounces across the living room carpet. He rolls it back to her. The particular actions he and his mother are engaged in change from time to time. (He may *throw* the ball, it may get lodged under the sofa or even knock over and break something.) The ball, however, is a constant factor and the child's concept of ball depends on his interaction with it, not upon verbal cues such as his mother saying 'This is a ball.'
>
> (Nelson, 1974, p. 277)

Nelson cites interesting supporting evidence for her view in that it is rare for children to have in their initial lexicon items which regularly surround the child, like items of furniture; more likely to be present will be items like *spoon*, *shoe* and *doll* with which he or she has regular action-based encounters. Nelson's functional core concept does not invalidate the property of overextension or underextension;[1] it simply approaches the semantic attributes of words from a different perspective.

Table 7.1 Examples of new terms and overextensions in L1 acquisition

Perceptual dimension	Language being learned	Child's form	First referent	Overextensions
shape	English	bird	sparrows	cows, dogs, cats, any animal moving
shape	English	kotibaiz	bars of cot	large toy abacus, toast-rack with parallel bars, picture of building with columns
sound	Russian	dany	sound of bell	clock, telephone, door-bells
taste	French	cola	chocolate	sugar, tarts, grapes, figs, peaches
touch	Russian	va	white plush dog	muffler, cat, father's fur coat

Source: Clark, 1973.

Although more research is required, it is reasonable to conclude that perceptual *and* functional criteria play an important part in early lexical acquisition, at least as far as reference to objects is concerned. We should, however, note in this respect work on semantic prototypes by Bowerman (1978) which challenges a basic assumption of Clark and Nelson. For Bowerman, no set of features nor any single semantic core determines the meaning acquisition of particular words. For example, Bowerman's daughter's use of *kick* first occurred when she propelled a ball forward with her foot. Subsequently, she used *kick* in the following situations: when she kicked an immovable floor fan, when she pushed her stomach against a mirror or a sink, at the sight of an object being propelled, as when she moved a ball with the wheel of a tricycle, at the movement of a moth fluttering on a table, and for the action of cartoon tortoises kicking their legs in the air. Bowerman argues that for her daughter *kick* involved waving limbs, sudden sharp contact with an object and an act of propulsion but that it was not possible to isolate similarities between features or to determine which particular feature(s) is critical or 'prototypical'.

Bowerman's research at least demonstrates clearly the kinds of combinations of features which have to be acquired by a child before they can be said to have appropriated the semantics of the adult use of a word but the investigations reported here raise further problems and questions. First, how appropriate is it to see the child's lexicon as simply an incomplete version of the adult's, and to what extent does such a pre-theoretical assumption condition the interpretations made by adults of the 'meanings' children produce? And can the possibility of metaphoric uses by children be discounted (e.g. Gardner *et al.*, 1975; see also Elliot, 1981, pp. 85–90; and Winner, 1988)? Secondly, is it feasible to analyse children's lexical acquisition in isolation from a parallel analysis of the situational and communicative contexts in which the words are used and, if so, then what kind of taxonomy of contexts would be necessary? Thirdly, what is the relationship between production and comprehension of the meanings of words, how might this affect processes of 'extension' and what explanatory potential might such a relationship have for examining the primacy of mental representation over linguistic representation of objects? Fourthly, how far is it realistic to isolate semantic development, as we are in fact doing here, from the acquisition of the syntactic and discoursal meanings of words? Is word-meaning based on semantic properties which are somehow intrinsic to the words, or do meanings emerge, as Halliday (1975) argues, as a result of a structuring by the child of words in relation to other words within an overall scheme of functions which are social, interpersonal and individual in their linguistic realization (see also Grieve and Hoogenraad, 1979)? And, finally, examination of the linguistic and communicative interrelations of meanings highlights the acquisition of non-referential items such as prepositions, grammatical words, comparatives, etc. – all of which are part of the acquisition of a lexicon. Interesting recent research into lexical acquisition in one-year-olds questions the relationship between the performance of an action and the naming of an object which is central to most theories in the 1970s (cf. Schwartz, 1983); and studies of mother–child interaction with one-year-old subjects conclude that the way mothers regulate and maintain interaction can systematically influence the development of personal–social words *before* that of object labels (see Tomasello and Todd, 1983).

7.2 The growth of word meaning: Children into adults

One of the most fundamental studies of vocabulary development in children and adults is by Jeremy Anglin. Anglin's work, summarized in *The Growth of Word Meaning* (Anglin, 1970), is characterized by an overt concern to chart development over a large span of years and to draw general conclusions concerning the main landmarks of that development. His work also makes use of informants from different age groups who are subjected directly to tests designed to measure the growth of what Anglin terms a 'subjective lexicon'. Anglin's main findings can be summarized as follows:

7.2.1 The syntagmatic–paradigmatic

This refers to the finding that in tests of free association young children will link words from different parts of speech, whereas older subjects respond by providing words which are predominantly of the same part of speech. Thus for children the concept 'eat' is associated with a stimulus word *table*. For adults the most common response to the word is *chair*. Other tests which involve asking informants to *cluster* a list of twenty words into semantically related sets reveal that younger subjects work on a **syntagmatic** principle of ordering according to thematic relations, whereas older subjects cluster words into fewer groupings. The groupings of the older subjects are reported to be less idiosyncratic, to contain words which are **paradigmatically** related (i.e. they can be substituted syntactically) – and this includes words which are antonyms – and/or which regularly belong to the same conceptual category (i.e. are hyponyms). One aspect of lexical development then, is the increasing perception of syntactic, semantic and conceptual *relations* between words.

7.2.2 Concrete–abstract progression

Related to the above, an important dimension is a growth in awareness of the more abstract relations which hold between words. The awareness of these relations manifests itself more in the way in which lexical items can be collocated than in a distinctly measurable set of hierarchically organized or nested features relating words. For example, adults show much wider tolerance of the possible predicates a noun might share than children who, for example, generally operate with tighter semantic categories. For example, according to Anglin, children up to a certain age would consider *the cauliflower sneezed* as not admissible within any context. Having appropriately demarcated such relations, adults can develop to greater degrees of abstraction in their use of lexical items and have a stronger basis, too, for the use of metaphoric expressions and for greater expressivity in general. For example, research by Asch and Nerlove (1969) confirms that a child at three years of age categorically denies that adjectives such as *bright*, *hard*, etc. can be used to describe people, whereas by the age of 12 increasing comprehension has led to exploitation of more extended meaning of these and similar terms (see also Gardner *et al.*, 1975).

7.2.3 Generalizations

Although this should not be taken as evidence for powers of abstraction, the growth of lexical meaning can also be measured on another level as the ability to distinguish broad classes to which words belong. Such development is from the ground up (Anglin, 1970, p. 59). In other words, the child might first see that roses and petunias are *flowers* and that ashes and oaks are *trees;* then that flowers and trees are *plants;* then that plants are *living things*, etc. This will greatly facilitate the increasing ability to relate categories of features reported above.

Anglin's study is one worth consulting by those interested in first- *and* second-language teaching and research. It provides a useful basis for considering lexical development over a broader age span than is normal in language-acquisition studies. His data is limited and the scale of the study a little overambitious, but the empirical nature of research works to substantiate hypotheses about lexical development grounded in a sharply linguistic awareness of the organization of words. Clark (1993) provides a thorough review of a range of related research.

7.3 L1 and L2

What conclusions can be drawn concerning the learning of words in a first language (L1) for studies of second-language (L2) acquisition? Are we talking about related or dissimilar processes? The following sections explore key issues such as: What is a difficult word for learners of a language? Are some words easier to learn than others? Are there distinct stages which are passed through on the way to acquiring a knowledge of what and how a word means? From even the very limited survey of some issues in first-language acquisition, is it possible to draw up the basis of an agenda? The following points might be noted:

1   Words exist in a kind of semantic space. Knowing a word in a language involves knowing what parts of the space it does and does not occupy. The first-language learner acquires this knowledge by experimenting with words in a large range of contexts. Are second-language learners given sufficient opportunities to over- and underextend words?
2   Knowing a word in a language means to know *both* its syntagmatic and paradigmatic relations. To know a word is also to know it in context. Syntactic and semantic knowledge must also include pragmatic knowledge.
3   Comprehending a word is not the same thing as producing a word.

Production is generally a more active process but could be regarded as more difficult.

4   Concrete words are generally learned first and are generally easier to retain and to recall. Abstract words may be more 'difficult'. It is interesting to ask here, too, whether grammatical or function words – which, since they are contentless and are not concrete as such – are more or less difficult to learn than abstract words. Also such grammatical words may be encountered more frequently. This issue has not been extensively researched, though it is touched on in Section 7.16.

5   Knowing words in 'generalized' groups of semantically related items might be encouraged as an important stage in L2 learning (see Section 7.12).

6   Are words known independently or are they only really *known* in context?

Limitations of space prevent more extensive examination of these issues here, although a number of them are taken up in subsequent sections of this chapter. In any more developed view of L1/L2 relations it is also important to examine further recent research into first-language lexical errors (slips of the tongue, malapropisms, children's misuses) and their implications for how the mental lexicon is organized and how words might be perceived (see Fay and Cutler, 1977; Cutler and Fay, 1982; Fromkin, 1980; Schreuder and Weltens, 1993; Aitchison, 1994). Channell (1988) reviews research and its relevance for second-language learning and teaching. Channell stresses the importance of learners first encountering words as independent units marked for stress and for phonological shape as an aid to retention. She points to the need for much more vocabulary to be taught and learned as a separate activity rather than, say, as part of a grammar or reading lesson. However, this poses once again the question of static (isolated words) as opposed to dynamic (words in discourse contexts) approaches to vocabulary learning and teaching (see Sections 7.11 and 7.13). A safe assumption here may be to ensure that both dimensions are attended to. Finally, as we proceed to examine second-language vocabulary learning, we have to remember that whatever the possible connections between L1 and L2 vocabulary learning, L2 studies do not generally draw on L1 research. See Meara (1997) on the consequences of different research traditions.

7.4 Memorization

This section considers some questions relating to the retention and recall of vocabulary items in the initial stages of language learning. At such a stage it is clear that words cannot effectively be learned in context and must therefore be assimilated as single (or paired) items. In particular, this raises questions concerning the appropriacy of mnemonic techniques.

Single words are conventionally learned in lists of paired words or 'paired associates'. The lists contain a word from the target language: either a synonym in that target language, or a translation in the mother tongue, and these are sometimes accompanied by a picture or some means of graphical representation. Relevant research (e.g. Kellogg and Howe, 1971) suggests that such procedures are usefully complementary. By such means, too, as Nation (1990, Ch.10) reports, large numbers of words are learned directly and, given sufficient repetition, retained. For example, research by Crothers and Suppes (1967) revealed that seven repetitions were sufficient for learners to master 108 new Russian–English word pairs and that 80 per cent of a further 216 word pairs were learned by most of the control group of learners after only six repetitions. The research raises generally unanswered questions about word 'difficulty' and translation, *types* of repetition, whether the learning leads primarily to active or passive knowledge, length of retention, and so on; but it does serve to underline that quantities of initial vocabulary can be learned both efficiently and quickly and by methods such as rote learning which are not always considered to be respectable. It may be dangerous to underestimate such a capacity.[2]

Further questions raised are whether translation and repetition are the *only* means by which words can be learned and whether the kind of 'picturing' of words which can accompany learning can or should be of a particular type. Research in this domain points quite conclusively to the value of what has been termed the ***keyword technique***. The technique, according to Atkinson and Raugh:

> divides the study of a vocabulary item into two stages. The first stage requires the subject to associate the spoken foreign word with an English word, the keyword, that sounds like some part of the foreign word; the second stage requires him to form a mental image of the keyword interacting with the English translation.
>
> (Atkinson and Raugh, 1975, p. 126)

Drawing on findings of psycholinguistic research studies, Nation (1983) has outlined and illustrated the main principles and procedures (see also Nation, 1980; 1982; 1990, Ch.10):

> One of the strangest and yet most effective techniques for associating a foreign word with its translation is the 'keyword' technique. Let us look at how this technique could be used by a learner of Malay to associate the Malay word *pintu* with its English translation *door*. First the learner thinks of an English word that sounds like *pintu* or like a part of it, for example, the word *pin*. This is the keyword. Second the learner imagines a pin stuck into a door, or a picture of a pin with a door in it! The more striking or unusual the image, the more effective it is.

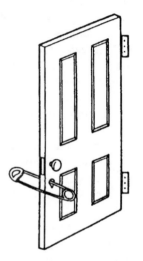

> This image then is the linking association between *pintu* and *door* because it contains a clue or key to the sound of the foreign word (*pin–pintu*) and it contains the key to the translation of the foreign word (a door).

(Nation, 1983, p. 101)

Too much should not, of course, be claimed for this technique and most writers on the topic stress that it should be deployed as only one among several possible learning techniques. It is clearly difficult to illustrate in this way words which are not readily representable by objects or to find picturable associations between words with no propositional content. As a technique, it is also time-consuming and research does not clearly specify whether the 'associations' should be created by a teacher for a class or left to the creativity of individual class members. There is also the possibility that spelling and pronunciation might be interfered with (though extensions can be made to assist with irregular spellings such as 'island = *is* land' etc.) However, the clear principle which emerges is that the more words are analysed or are enriched by imagistic and other associations, the more likely it is that they will be retained. Such a technique, linking – as it does – form, meaning and structure through cues which, in turn, facilitate a combination of productive and receptive senses, does appear to have advantages over an exclusive focus on straightforward translation and rote learning. In the *early* stages of learning foreign-language vocabulary, it is one example of an aid to memorization which teachers might explore further.[3]

7.5 What is a difficult word?

Learning vocabulary effectively is closely bound up with a teacher's understanding of, and a learner's perception of, the *difficulties* of words. The difficulty of a word may result, *inter alia,* from the relations it can be seen to contract with other words, either in the native or target language, whether it is learned productively or receptively; as well as from its polysemy, the associations it creates, its pronuncability, whether it lends itself to keyword teaching techniques and, in the case of advanced learners, from the nature of the contexts in which it is encountered (see Section 7.11). The kinds of interplay between these and other complex factors cannot be adequately explored here. Instead, there will be an emphasis on early learning and on the kinds of 'language-internal' difficulties resulting from the *forms* of words and how these might be best presented. The emphasis on word-form is given because much research has highlighted this as a significant factor in learnability. Matters of grading, sequencing of presentation and the relevance of definition of a core vocabulary for language learning will be discussed in Section 7.18 and the relative advantages of teaching vocabulary in both word lists and contextually in Sections 7.10 and 7.11.

Consideration of form here follows appropriately from the preceding section because one important element in learning new words is the degree of effective *formal* linking learners can establish between a word in the target language and a cognate word in the mother tongue. Indeed, according to research by Craik and Lockhart (1972), oral repetition is not necessarily an effective way of assimilating new words; recalling the *form* of a word is found to be more productive. As we saw in the previous section, the more opportunities that can be found for formal transfer between foreign and mother-tongue words, the better the chances of retention. But, concentration here on specifically *linguistic* form should not preclude the possibility or even necessity for other links and transfers to be made available to assist memorization.

Research reported in Nation (1982, pp. 18 ff) suggests that similarities in sound, morphology or etymology can assist word memorization. By such procedures the German word *Hund* (dog) may be more easily retained than the French *chien*, because of its etymological and sound similarity with the English *hound*. Another example would be the Malay word *buku* (book). More memorizable still would be words which are international loan words such as *telephone*, *radio* and *television*, which have many close cognate forms in other languages. Significant research here is that by Cohen and Aphek (1980). They found that students of Hebrew, who tried a range of interlingual and language-internal mnemonic associations, generally retained new words with greater efficacy. Students reported three main categories of association:

1   Semantic and phonological links between L1 and L2, e.g. Hebrew *benayatim* (meanwhile) connected with English *been a time*.
2   Phonological links in L2, e.g. *tsava* (army)/*tsena* (leave).
3   Semantic and phonological in L2, e.g. *lifney* (before) connected with *lifamin* (sometimes).

Of these, the third category, which makes use of two access networks to the L2 mental lexicon, was found to be the most efficient, though the first category was more advantageous at early stages of learning; also, levels of proficiency may well be significant. Further research is needed before the requisite 'translations' between lexicons or within a single L1/L2 lexicon can be more precisely defined and caution must be continually exercised to avoid the kinds of confusions and unlearning that can take place through misguided analysis of parts of words or through the establishment of false cognates. Examples of the former would be the German word *unbedingt* (definitely) which, if analysed morphologically, may misleadingly suggest from its prefix *un* that it is a negative. An example of the latter would be the word *Rezept* in German which means 'medical prescription' as well as 'recipe' . (See also Ilson, 1983, for an argument for teaching an ability to use *etymological* derivation analysis in L2.)

Reference to translation raises one further issue which should be dealt with at this stage: namely, the effect on the burden of learning of the *order* of presentation of equivalent word pairs. Here research is limited and this issue itself is closely connected with whether the word is learned for productive use or for purposes of comprehension only, but Nation (1982, p.20) concludes that if vocabulary is needed for writing in the target language then a learning sequence of mother-tongue word → foreign word would be appropriate; but a direction of foreign word → mother-tongue word may be more appropriate if only reading skills are required.

7.6 The Birkbeck Vocabulary Project

This section has to begin by recognizing the largely independent senses connected with the use of the word *association* in the literature on lexicology and on vocabulary learning and teaching. The first sense is the most widely used and refers to the store of words and the interrelations between them in a speaker's mental lexicon. Associations here will be mostly psycholinguistic in character. The second sense, which is used quite extensively in Chapters 8 and 9, refers to the additional meanings words can convey as a result of being associated with particular social, pragmatic or cultural contexts. The semantic space occupied by such associations will be generally more sociolinguistic in character. The emphasis in this section will be on the former with particular consideration given to the psycholinguistic research of the Birkbeck Vocabulary Project at the University of London.

It is the aim of most word-association studies to access the complex organizational store of information possessed by fluent speakers of a language. Research into vocabulary acquisition in a second or foreign language investigates the responses to words of groups of learners at different stages of competence in order to evaluate the nature of this store as a developing entity and to assess possible implications for the ways in which words might be studied in teaching contexts. Necessarily, such studies move beyond accounts of *formal* relations between words towards more complex semantic domains. The studies are important for understanding the processes of beginning to learn a foreign-language vocabulary.

In the 1980s, the Birkbeck Vocabulary Project was one of only a few into vocabulary acquisition in a second language. Its operation was small-scale but the research which it stimulated promises much. More detailed reports of the work of this project can be found in Meara (1980; 1982; 1984b).

The main question addressed by this research was 'What does a [second-language] learner's mental lexicon look like and how is it different from the mental lexicon of a monolingual native speaker?'

(Meara, 1982, p.29). Related closely are other questions. In posing these, the project team recognized the paucity of previous research although the work of Levenston, and questions concerning future research raised by him (see especially Levenston, 1979), is recognized as an important exception. Other related questions include:

1   Under what conditions does a learner's mental lexicon most effectively expand and grow?
2   How can we best understand the processes involved in integrating new L2 words into a learner's mental lexicon and are there differences between monolingual and second-language learners in the way lexical knowledge is stored?
3   Is it better to see L1 and L2 vocabulary as an undifferentiated whole?
4   In what way is vocabulary learning to be seen as different from learning at other linguistic levels (e.g. grammatical structures)?

The questions are, of course, closely interrelated but they can all be seen to have important implications for how vocabulary in a second language might be most effectively *taught*. The point to underline here is that unless satisfactory answers are obtained to the question of just what it *is* that learners *learn* when they acquire new words in another language, then teaching procedures will be to some extent a hit-and-miss affair. (It is regrettable, therefore, that books devoted to practical approaches to vocabulary teaching proceed without due recognition of issues in vocabulary *learning*: for example, Wallace (1982) contains little about issues in learning with the result that teaching strategies are proposed from a basis of, at best, untested assumptions.) Thus, as vocabulary acquisition in a second language develops several marked instabilities occur and it becomes clear that learning is not simply a matter of putting a word from the target language together with the L1 meaning. It is the nature of these 'instabilities' that Meara and his associates are interested in investigating. The basic research tool adopted in their work is a simple and widely known one of word-association tests. (For a useful introduction to the whole area of word associations see Campbell and Wales, 1970.)

   Word associations may be conventionally divided into two main classes of association: ***paradigmatic*** and ***syntagmatic***. Thus, given the word *dog* syntagmatic associations would be those which formed some sequential relationship with the stimulus word. These responses, such as *bark*, *bite* and *furry*, would allow the formation of a grammatical sequence to the left or right of the word. Paradigmatic responses involve words which are from the same grammatical class as the stimulus item. That is, supplied with the word *dog*, the associations of those tested would produce examples such as *cat, wolf, animal* and *pet*. As we have seen in Section 7.2 adults generally produce paradigmatic responses whereas children, until approximately the age of seven, have a tendency to produce responses which are syntagmatic. Additionally, they produce *clang associations*, that is, the response is motivated more by phonological than semantic resemblance, e.g. *dog* → *clog, frog*. The results of initial tests have been summarized by Meara (1982) as follows:

> The word associations produced by non-native speakers differ fairly systematically from those produced by native speakers. Surprisingly, learners' responses tend to be more varied and less homogeneous than the responses of a comparable group of native speakers. This is an odd finding because learners must have a smaller, more limited vocabulary than native speakers, and this might lead one to expect a more limited range of possible responses. Learner responses are not generally restricted to a subset of the more common responses made by native speakers, however. On the contrary, learners consistently produce responses which never appear among those made by native speakers, and in extreme cases, it is possible to find instances of stimulus words for which the list of native speaker and learner responses share practically no words in common. The reasons for this are not wholly clear, but one contributory factor is the fact that learners have a tendency to produce clang associations like young children. A second contributory factor is that learners very frequently misunderstand a stimulus word, mistaking it for a word that has a vague phonological resemblance to the stimulus. This clearly leads to maverick responses, but these cannot be dismissed out of hand. The frequency of the phenomenon suggests that actually identifying foreign language words reliably is a major problem for many learners, and this seems to be the case even when the words are simple, and when the learners themselves claim to know them.
>
> (Meara, 1982, pp. 30–1)

Table 7.2 illustrates the kinds of typical responses obtained from adult native-speaking English learners of French (for fuller description of the test, see Meara, 1984b). Meara makes no excessive claims for his research and recognizes the limited scale of its operation, but the table does demonstrate clearly the extent to which phonological associations

Table 7.2 Associations made by native English speakers to French stimulus words. All these associations illustrate some sort of phonological or orthographic confusion

Stimulus	Response	Source of confusion
béton	animal	bête
béton	stupide	bête
béton	conducteur	bâton
béton	orchestre	bâton
béton	téléphoner	jeton
béton	Normandie	breton
fendre	permettre	défendre
naguère	eau	nager
caque	poulet	cackle (?)
caque	rigoler	cackle
caque	gateaux	cake
semelle	dessert	semolina (?)
semelle	odeur	smell
traire	essayer	try
cruche	important	crucial
émail	lettre	mail
émail	chevalier	mail
dru	dessiner	drew
toupie	argent	2p (?)
toupie	cheveux	toupé
risible	lavable	rinsable (?)
risible	incre	rinsable (?)
jeter	hurler	hurl
mou	vache	!!! *etc.*

Source: Meara, 1984a.

may over-determine responses even when or perhaps because the control group has a limited vocabulary in the target language. It also shows that there is a degree of patterning in the responses in so far as consonants and consonant clusters remain relatively stable, while vowel segments are weaker and more variable. But, such patterning apart, Meara reports that these 'instabilities' in learners' responses are not notably homogeneous and some can change from one week's testing to the next. In addition to the more obvious but important conclusion that there are real differences in the lexical organization of L2 learners compared with native speakers, there appears to be no clearly established semantic network to the internalized lexicon which a learner has in the early stages of learning a second language. Interestingly, this supports the research reported in Section 7.3 which shows the primacy of phonological structure in L1 speech errors. Subsequent research, reported in Meara

(1984b), also reinforces general impressions of how different languages can produce different word handling, recognition and storage problems. For example, for Spanish-speaking learners of English syllables may play a more important role in lexical representation; whereas for Chinese-speaking learners of English, there are particular difficulties with long words:

> They seem to pay more attention to the ends of words than native English speakers do, which suggests that they have to construct words out of their parts, instead of using sequential redundancies to enable them to read words as wholes.
>
> (Meara, 1984b, p. 234)

The research undertaken by the Birkbeck Vocabulary Project is not without significance and the results of its psycholinguistically oriented work will continue to inform thinking about vocabulary learning and its relations to teaching. It is worth pointing, however, to some potential limitations of the work not always explicitly recognized by the researchers. The first is that working with single words and single-word translational equivalents, begs some key questions of definition. The use of discrete vocabulary items may tend to obscure or even mis-represent the nature of the map drawn between words by speakers of a language. Not only do greater complexities in translation occur when the stimulus words are increased beyond the common stock of easy one-for-one correspondences, but increasing a vocabulary necessarily involves knowing a word in more than its semantic sense. It involves knowledge of its inflections and derivations as well as its possible pragmatic functions (see especially, Martin, 1984) and can also involve increasing complexities in mapping its sociolinguistic and associative properties. Words are more than psycho-semantic in their relations. Secondly, as Cowie (1984) points out in a review of work by Meara and others, much also depends on our definition of a word and whether we believe acquisition of words involves a mental accumulation of discrete items, or whether we recognize (1) that from an early stage fixed expressions involving groups of words have an important part to play (see Yorio, 1980; Nattinger, 1980; 1988; Cowie, 1988, and Section 7.13), and (2) that, in part because they are often core words, the stimulus words in association tests are regularly polysemic. As the lexical store of learners grows, so a complex semantic structuring and restructuring evolves. A third limitation may be that learning words in a new language is not unconnected with such motivational factors as how important or useful a word may be perceived to be by learners themselves (see Richards, 1970).

To draw attention to potential limitations is not to discredit the achievements of the Birkbeck project; it is to underline the kinds of complexities attendant on work in this field. Indeed, Meara (1984b) admits to dealing with a static, decontextualized version of a lexicon (and one tested only under 'classroom' conditions), which in reality is in constant flux. Control of data in language necessarily involves idealization and the findings of Meara and others are valuable in relation to that control. However, greater use must be made of even the limited findings of lexicologists, sociolinguists and discourse analysts concerning lexical organization and moves need to be made beyond research strategies which are wholly psycholinguistic and thus from just one source discipline.

Since the beginning of the 1990s the formal work of the Birkbeck Vocabulary Project has not continued, largely due to the transfer of its research director, Paul Meara, from Birkbeck College, University of London to the University of Swansea. The work in vocabulary acquisition research inspired by that project continues in other forms of course (see Section 7.7); and a Swansea Vocabulary Project now embraces a wide range of research, such as several innovative developments of vocabulary tests, including checklist tests. Recent and related work is reviewed in Meara (1997) and all the early work on L2 vocabulary acquisition is reviewed in Meara (1992; 1996).

7.7 Recent developments: The explicit–implicit continuum

As we have seen so far in this chapter, we have not been explicitly taught the majority of words which we know. We must therefore conclude that beyond a certain level of proficiency in learning a language, and a second or foreign language in particular, vocabulary development is more likely to be mainly implicit or incidental. In vocabulary acquisition studies, key research questions are therefore to explore the points at which explicit vocabulary learning is more efficient when it becomes implicit vocabulary learning, to ask what are the most effective strategies of implicit learning, and to consider the implications of research results for classroom vocabulary teaching.

In the late 1980s and the 1990s, research in these fields has developed exponentially. At the same time researchers have continued to question what exactly is meant by terms such as efficient and effective in relation to short-term and long-term vocabulary learning. A definition of learning a word depends crucially on what we mean by a word, but it also depends crucially on how a word is remembered, over what period of time and in what circumstances it can be recalled, and whether learning a word also means that it can be retained. Also, recognition of the importance of implicit vocabulary learning does not preclude continuing exploration of the ways in which explicit vocabulary learning can be enhanced through teaching and of which aspects of vocabulary are amenable to instruction and study. We may not have been explicitly taught all the words we know but that does not automatically entail that we have not taught ourselves and certainly cannot account for the fact that some learners are more effective learners than others.

Ellis (1995) identifies four main points along a continuum from explicit to implicit vocabulary learning:

1   A strong implicit learning hypothesis holds that words are acquired largely by unconscious means.
2   A weak implicit learning hypothesis holds that words cannot be learned without at least some noticing or consciousness that it is a new word which is being learned.
3   A weak explicit learning hypothesis holds that learners are basically active processors of information and that a range of strategies are used to infer the meaning of a word, usually with reference to the context in which it appears.
4   A strong explicit learning hypothesis holds that a range of metacognitive strategies are necessary for vocabulary learning. In particular, the greater the depth of processing involved in the learning, the more secure and long term the learning is likely to be.

Hypothesis (1) has been most strongly advanced by Krashen (1981; 1989); Hypothesis (2) draws on observations found in several sources reporting research into language awareness and consciousness-raising: for example, Schmidt (1990); Hypothesis (3) draws in particular on work in Sternberg (1987) who reports that 'most vocabulary is learned from context' by means of strategies of inference, and on Hulstijn (1992) who also reports research in which learners retained better words learned by them in context rather than in marginal glosses; Hypothesis (4) draws most strongly on work on levels of processing by Craik and Lockhart (1972) (see also p. 195 above and survey in Nattinger, 1988).

Of these hypotheses Hypothesis (4) has been most actively pursued in recent years with conclusions reached in a number of studies (see, in particular, several papers in Coady and Huckin (eds), 1997, and Ellis (ed.), 1994). Craik and Lockhart's work has been particularly influential in its conclusion that the more processes that are involved in the learning of a word, the superior the retention and the recall. For example, their experiments asked learners learning a word to consider its formal shape, other words it rhymes with, the semantic field in which it belongs, synonyms for it, and the kinds of sentence patterns into which it fits.

Related and subsequent research (e.g. Crow and Quigley, 1985; Brown and Perry, 1991) involving keyword techniques (including mediation between L1 and L2), semantic fields and inference from context has further underlined what Ellis (1995) effectively summarizes:

> Metacognitively sophisticated language learners excel because they have cognitive strategies for inferring the meanings of words, for enmeshing them in the meaning networks of other words and concepts and imagery representations, and mapping the surface forms to these rich meaning representations. To the extent that vocabulary acquisition is about meaning, it is an explicit learning process.
>
> (Ellis, 1995, p. 16)

The importance of developing metacognitive strategies should not, however, suggest to teachers and learners that implicit vocabulary learning is to be discouraged. Given the complexities of word knowledge and the range of factors involved in knowing a word, most researchers have accepted that different types of word knowledge are learned in different ways, that different strategies entail different purposes for vocabulary use, and different kinds of storage of the word in the mind. For example, Stanovich and Cunningham (1992) assert that people who read more know more words, not least because reading affords the time to work out meanings from context in ways which are less likely to occur in speech, though their findings have not always been unequivocally accepted or agreed with. See also a range of papers on this and related issues in Huckin, Haynes and Coady (eds) (1993).

Thus, at more advanced levels reading can be essential for vocabulary development; at beginning levels, strategies of rote memorization, bilingual translation and glossing can be valuable in assisting learning of, for example, the phonetic and graphological shapes and patterns of words. In so far as surface forms of basic concrete words are concerned, then explicit learning may be more likely to help; in so far as the semantic, discoursal and structural properties of less frequent, more abstract words are concerned, then implicit learning may be more likely to help. Recent vocabulary-acquisition research suggests strongly, however, that it is preferable to think in terms of continua from explicit to implicit and from implicit to explicit, and to continue to direct research at points along such continua. (See also Schmitt and McCarthy (eds), 1997, especially Part 2.) There is further discussion of these issues, especially issues of vocabulary, reading and context, in Section 7.14 which is devoted to vocabulary development and teaching.

7.8 Transitions

The tentativeness and inconclusiveness of much of the research reported in the first part of this chapter indicates the extent to which vocabulary still remains a neglected aspect of language learning. It is clear that information about how words are learned is quite crucial to vocabulary teaching, and that adequate theories of word learning need to draw on L1 *and* L2 research findings. Similarities and differences between the mental lexicon structures of L1 and L2 require further investigation. Although evidence is not conclusive that an L1 and L2 lexicon is an undifferentiated whole, and although further analysis of word behaviour across the 'boundaries' is required, an L2 user's mental lexicon does *resemble* that of L1, and speakers make phonological, semantic and associational links between them. More extensive examination of both errors and associations might provide a useful basis for vocabulary development in L1 and L2.

In the second part of the chapter, some teaching approaches and strategies will be reviewed. The close relations between learning and teaching will be stressed (even if firm conclusions cannot always be drawn), and further research into acquisition reported. The second part of this chapter is approached, however, from the positive conviction that vocabulary teaching can and should be foregrounded as a more discrete feature of the study of languages than has been the case in the past.

7.9 Vocabulary and language teaching: Introduction

In view of what has been said in the previous section, it is somewhat paradoxical that vocabulary teaching was central to early developments in the profession of English language teaching (see Section 7.10). It is only in the last ten years or so, however, that there has been a reactivation of interest. In the critical review of some of these developments that follows word lists, and especially recent computer-based constructions, are treated quite extensively as they are of continuing importance to language teachers. And cloze procedures, which are continuously and widely used in language teaching, are also reviewed for their contribution to vocabulary development. The notion of core vocabulary is examined again here and arguments advanced for and against the usefulness of such a notion for language teaching. Some promising recent developments in the relationship between discourse analysis and vocabulary teaching are also reviewed. Both these sections draw on descriptions of lexis outlined in Chapters 2 to 4.

7.10 Word lists: Vocabulary for beginners

This short section reviews some of the main landmarks in what has come to be called the *vocabulary-control movement*. It does so by focusing on Michael West's *A General Service List of English Words* (GSL). Published in 1953, GSL is the outcome of almost three decades of major work in English lexicometrics. The main figures associated with this work are Michael West himself, whose work in English as a foreign language was concentrated in Bengal in India, and Harold Palmer – one of the founding fathers of English language teaching – who was Director of the Institute of English Language Teaching in Tokyo from 1923– 1936. The history of their association and academic collaboration on the development of vocabulary and other teaching materials has been lucidly charted by Howatt (1983, Ch. 17). West is also known for his *New Method Readers* and his *New Method Dictionary* which make use of controlled vocabulary for, respectively, graded reading in a second language and for a lexicographic definition vocabulary.

West's GSL grew organically from major studies in the 1930s on vocabulary selection for teaching purposes. These studies culminated in the Interim Report on Vocabulary Selection (1935) (known as the 'Carnegie Report') which in turn issued in the first GSL which was published in 1936. The revised GSL (1953) made particular use of word counts such as that of Thorndike and Lorge (1944), developed in the USA. It should also be noted that the GSL developed at the same time as and along not dissimilar lines to C.K. Ogden's Basic English (see Chapter 1) and that the two schemes ran in parallel and in competition for many years. West's GSL has had by far the most lasting influence and the 1953 word list is widely used today forming the basis of the principles underlying the *Longman Structural Readers*. West's notion of a limited defining vocabulary is one of the main informing design principles of the *Longman Dictionary of Contemporary English* (*LDOCE*, 1978) (see Section 6.2).

The main criteria of West, Palmer and others for the selection of vocabulary for learning in the early stages of acquisition are that:

1   The frequency of each word in written English should be indicated.
2   Information should be provided about the relative prominences of the various meanings and uses of a word form.

Both these criteria, which were more extensively developed in the 1953 edition than in previous versions, provide particularly useful guidance for teachers deciding which words and which meanings should be taught first. The list consists of 2,000 words with semantic and frequency information drawn from a corpus of 2 to 5 million words. It is claimed that knowing these words gives access to about 80 per cent of the words in any written text and thus stimulates motivation since the words acquired can be seen by learners to have a demonstrably quick return. Other criteria adopted in the selection of words include their universality (words useful in all countries), their utility (enabling discussion on as wide a subject range as possible), their usefulness in terms of definition value.[4] The list can be seen to result from a mixture of subjective and objective selection criteria.

A representative example of an entry for the GSL in Figure 7.2 is that of the word *head* (West, 1953, p. 228). In the case of this word, 2216e here indicates the estimated number of occurrences in 5 million words (the frequency of most items in GSL is calculated in relation to such a corpus; here the corpus was smaller and the figure has been scaled up).

The advantages for teachers of this kind of detailed break-down are considerable. But there are some disadvantages, too. One is that the list is to some extent outdated. It contains words from counts made in the 1930s and even earlier. A number of common 1980s words do not appear; for example, there are no entries for *pilot, helicopter, television* or *astronaut*. Another is that the corpus on which the lists are based is a written corpus. As a result not only do a number of the words appear distinctly 'literary' but data about spoken usage is not available for contrastive purposes. This does reflect one of West's main aims which was to provide a list for pre-reading or simplified reading materials. However, this main impulse to provide a practical research tool for basic literacy development conditions the 'usefulness' or 'utility' principles which, since they are mainly subjective, are in any case difficult to retrieve. Richards (1974, p. 71) has questioned the inclusion on this basis of certain items such as *mannerism, vessel, ornament, mere, stock, motion* and *urge*, which to him seem of limited utility, and has pointed to anomalies of exclusion from certain semantic fields. For example, *doctor, engineer, teacher* and *nurse* are included as occupations but *carpenter, plumber* and *mason* are excluded in favour of *footman*. Also, *trader, merchant* and *dealer* are all included when under the principles of definition value any one could effectively replace the others.

More serious, though understandable given available concordancing procedures at the time, is the absence of information on collocations and collocational frequencies. Also, the notion of defining words which have 'coverage' because they are common or central enough in the lexicon to stand in for other words is insufficiently developed. The notion is more rigorously and extensively applied by West in his *New*

HEAD   2216e

head, n.	(1) (*part of body*)
	A hat on my head
	Head and heart (= *intelligence and*
	feeling) (5%)
	Will cost him his head (= life) (2%)
	Wiser heads; count heads
	(= *persons*) (1%)
	Phrase: over head (= *above*) 63%
	(2) (*top*)
	Head of a bone, plant, page,
	procession 13%
	(3) (*idea of leadership*)
	Head of the school
	Head clerk
	At the head of the whole business 14%
head-/	Head-rest, head-hunter, *etc.* 1%
	Phrases:
	Head to foot 0.2%
	Head or tail 0.3%
	Keep, lose one's head (= *control*) 0.4%
	[On your head be it, 0.4%;
	off his head = *mad*, 0%]
head, v.	Headed the list
	All came in headed by Mr. X
	Gold headed stick 5%
	[Heading for = *going towards*, 0.4%]
heading, n	Newspaper heading, *etc.* 2%

----

headache, n., 16e; **head-dress**, n., 8e; ? [**headland**, n., 14e; **headline**, n., 40e] [**headlong**, adv., 36e; **headway**, n., 10e]

Figure 7.2 General Service List: Entry for *head*.

Method Dictionary (1935) and *Minimum Adequate Vocabulary* (1960) which define the meanings of 24,000 entries within a vocabulary of 1,490 words, but the relationship between these words and the GSL words is not particularly clear. Finally, as we shall see in Sections 7.12 and 7.18, West can be criticized for not giving adequate consideration to the notions of the 'availability' and 'familiarity' of words though no current research was available to him at that time.[5] The GSL is not without its disadvantages, but it was a considerable advance on any previous word lists and remains one of the most innovative examples of foreign-language pedagogy and lexicometric research this century.

We shall return to the matter of word lists in Sections 7.16 and 7.18. The next section considers issues which relate to the encounter by learners of new words in more diverse contexts. Necessarily, this takes us squarely into the learning and teaching of vocabulary at more advanced levels.

7.11 Words in context

The previous section has discussed direct means of vocabulary learning. This section concentrates on strategies which learners can use to decode for themselves the meanings of words. Its focus is on indirect means.

Vocabulary control has considerable benefits. Learning the most frequent 2–3,000 words in a language provides a firm basis of about 80 per cent of the words likely to be encountered. But, as Honeyfield (1977) points out:

> even a very diligent student who graduated from a course after learning all the 3,000 selected words would find, on encountering an unsimplified text, that somewhere between 10 and 20 per cent of the words are unknown to him. And these words are by definition the more infrequent words in the language. They may be crucial to the meaning of a passage but may occur only once in a chapter or book.

Indirect means are therefore necessary for learning these words since, whatever the virtues of keywords and other memorization techniques, it is hardly practical to continue with direct methods. A law of diminishing returns sets in. This does, of course, beg questions concerning the relationship between direct and indirect learning of vocabulary and of productive and receptive approaches. But it is clear that the more advanced the learner becomes, the more 'inferential' or 'implicit' and learner-centred vocabulary learning strategies will have to become.

If words are not to be learned as discrete items then they will be learned *in context*. The first question to ask, therefore, is what exactly is understood by *context*. Is it a simple matter of learners encountering the new word in a stretch of naturally occurring text? What part might be played by translation? What is the appropriate linguistic environment for a *context*? Is the upper limit a sentence, a clause, a phrase or a collocation? How can sufficient variation in context be introduced in order to ensure that learners grasp the more delicate meanings of a word?

One method, with particular reference to reading, has been proposed by Nation (1983, p. 89; see also Nation, 1980; Clarke and Nation, 1980, and numerous textbook illustrations in Long and Nation, 1980). It involves the learner in seeking clues to meaning by following a number of defined steps which lead from the form of the word itself, to its immediate context, and then to its operation in the surrounding context. According to Nation (1990; p. 162) 'the strategy is just a means of acquiring the unconscious skill that an efficient reader already has'. He assembles the 'steps' as follows:

Step 1   Look at the unknown word and decide its part of speech. Is it a noun, a verb, an adjective, or an adverb?

Step 2   Look at the clause or sentence containing the unknown word.
If the unknown word is a noun, what adjectives describe it?
What verb is it near?
That is, what does this noun do, or what is done to it?
If the unknown word is a verb, what nouns does it go with?
Is it modified by an adverb?
If it is an adjective, what noun does it go with?
If it is an adverb, what verb is it modifying?

Step 3   Look at the relationship between the clause or sentence containing the unknown word and other sentences or paragraphs. Sometimes this relationship will be signalled by a conjunction like *but*, *because*, *if*, *when*, or by an adverb like *however*, *as a result*. Often there will be no signal. The possible types of relationship include cause and effect, contrast, inclusion, time, exemplification, and summary.

Step 4   Use the knowledge you have gained from steps 1 to 3 to guess the meaning of the word.

Step 5   Check that your guess is correct.

    1   See that the part of speech of your guess is the same as the part of speech of the unknown word. If it is not the same, then something is wrong with your guess.

    2   Replace the unknown word with your guess. If the sentence makes sense, your guess is probably correct.

    3   Break the unknown word into its prefix, root and suffix, if possible. If the meanings of the prefix and root correspond to your guess, good. If not, look at your

guess again, but do not change anything if you feel reasonably certain about your guess using the context.

Experience has shown that using affixes and roots alone as a means of guessing meanings is not very reliable. Also, once a word has been analyzed according to its parts, this guess at its meaning is more likely to result in twisting the interpretation of the context than allowing interpretation of the context to modify the guess of the meaning. So, by leaving the use of affixes and root until the last step in the strategy, the learner is more likely to approach interpretation of the context with an open mind.

(Nation, 1990, pp. 162–3)

Similar strategies to those described here, and again with reference to reading, are proposed in Honeyfield (1977) and Kruse (1979). The direction proposed by Kruse is parallel to Nation in terms of progression from 'word building' to 'definition clues' and then to 'inference clues' which require higher levels of analytic skills.[6] Likewise, Honeyfield illustrates a range of exercises for developing the skills of inferring from context. These include cloze exercises (See Section 7.15), words-in-context exercises and context-enrichment exercises. The latter is illustrated as follows:

INSTRUCTIONS: This exercise will help to direct your attention to the kind of information that a context may give you. In the exercise there are three sentences, each one adding a little more information. Each sentence has three possible definitions of the italicized word. On the basis of information in the sentence, decide if the definition is improbable, possible or probable. Write one of these words on the line for each definition.

1   We had a whoosis.
      a tropical fish   _____
      an egg beater   _____
      a leather suitcase   _____
2   We had a whoosis, but the handle broke.
      a tropical fish   _____
      an egg beater   _____
      a leather suitcase   _____
3   We had a whoosis, but the handle broke, so we had to beat the eggs with a fork.

a tropical fish   _____

an egg beater   _____

a leather suitcase   _____

(Nation, 1983, p. 40)

In context (1) the word cannot be guessed since all definitions are possible; in (2) the information supplied should enable students to rule out tropical fish; in (3) the only probable definition is that it is an egg beater. For further commentary on cloze procedures and on the use of nonsense words see Section 7.15.

The inevitability of learners encountering words in context (and increasingly so as the learner becomes more advanced), and inferential strategies which might put this increased learning load on a systematic basis have been examined above. To conclude this section on context and vocabulary teaching it is necessary briefly to review research which addresses a fundamental question connected with processes. Is learning words in context more *effective* than other available means? It can certainly be efficient and can put the learner much more in control of his own learning but what might be the advantages and disadvantages to encountering and processing words in this way?

In an experiment conducted with Finnish learners of English Pickering (1982) examined findings reported in Seibert (1930) (see also Seibert, 1945) that learning foreign language words in context was inferior (that is, fewer words were learned) to learning words in pairs with native-language translations of the items concerned. Although most language teachers prefer to present words for more advanced learners in context, it has not been convincingly demonstrated that the information learners obtain from meeting words in a variety of contexts is more beneficial, either in terms of knowledge of forms or meanings of lexical items, than either translation or simply looking up the word in a dictionary. This may be especially the case when they have to recall a lexical item productively as opposed to decoding it receptively. Pickering's experiment enables him to conclude that the context condition is slightly more conducive to learning than paired associates but his conclusions are heavily qualified and he points to the need for further research. The same general conclusions were reached by Cohen and Aphek in their work on the role of mnemonic associations in foreign language word learning with reference to Hebrew and English (Cohen and Aphek, 1980; see Section 7.5). They concluded additionally that the recall of words in context is positively related to the proficiency level of the informants (measured by pre-tested knowledge of words in context and by reading comprehension). Thus, the more advanced the learner, the more likely they are to benefit from learning words in context. As yet, however, it is difficult to draw precise lines to suggest when a move from keyword techniques or translation in pairs or from using a monolingual or bilingual dictionary/word list to context-based inferential strategies is best instituted. The most realistic approach is probably to recognize that learning occurs along a cline or continuum with no clearly marked stages of transition, and that a mixture of approaches should be adopted.

Subsequent research as well as current teaching practice should, however, face some key issues in this area. The central questions involve consideration of exactly what kind of output is expected from the learning of the target vocabulary. Crucial here is the fact that a learner's active/productive vocabulary is always smaller than his or her passive/receptive vocabulary.[7] That is, learners might be able to recognize a given lexical item when it is presented to them or they may be able to infer its meaning, but this is not at all the same thing as recalling items for use. There are important differences here, too, between recognition and recall in spoken and written contexts and the teacher has an important role to play in differentiating the respective dimensions (see Sections 7.13 and 4.6). Also relevant here might be a pre-teaching of lexical items as a means to aiding either recall or recognition. Existing research has focused on learners learning new words, but anyone who has learned a foreign language knows that memorization is an ebbing and flowing process and often involves words which are already 'known'. What then are the most effective means of reinforcing an *existing* lexical stock? Lastly, there is the issue of the circumlocutory strategies adopted by native speakers when faced with recall failure. The use of hold-all frozen lexical items such as 'whatsisname', 'thingummy', 'stuff', and 'vague' language such as 'and things', 'sort of', 'or so', etc. facilitates on-going discourse. At what point, if at all, might such terms be taught? (see Brown, 1979). A number of these questions and others connected with the issues of word pairs versus context are raised in Nation (1983, pp. 107–8), Bruton (1983) and Meara (1984a, p. 186). The last two sources are in reviews of Wallace (1982).

7.12 Word sets and grids: Vocabulary for advanced learners

Not only are there few textbooks specifically devoted to vocabulary enlargement but of those that do exist few are derived from linguistically principled descriptions of the lexicon. This is not to say that there can be automatic transpositions between linguistic methods of analysis and applications to language teaching; it is rather to point to a disparity between emphasis on grammar and a paucity of what teachers consider appropriate models for vocabulary teaching. Generally, vocabulary teaching is viewed as necessary but tends to be taught by means of item selection from reading passages or as a cumulative by-product of a syllabus dominated by the structures and communicative functions of sentences.

A recent and interesting exception is *The Words You Need* (Rudska *et al.*, 1982; see also *More Words You Need,* Rudska *et al.,* 1985). The organizing principle is that of Adrienne Lehrer's work on semantic structure of words in conceptually related domains (Lehrer, 1974b) (see also Section 3.2). Psycholinguistic support for the books' method is also provided by research reported in Cornu (1979) which indicates that individuals tend to recall words according to the categories or semantic fields in which they are conceptually mapped.

The learners envisaged for the book will have an existing basic vocabulary of approximately 2,500 words and the 10 thematically based units of *The Words You Need* aim to increase this by a further 700. However, instead of the words being introduced singly or in paired associates, the enlargement takes place by means of 'grids' in which words from the same semantic field are subjected to a modified componential analysis and/or to an analysis which reveals the common collocates of the target items (for further discussion of grids and suggested teaching procedures see Harvey, 1983; Stieglitz, 1983; Sökman, 1997). Lexical items are learned in groups and not as single items. Occasionally, but not systematically, further dimensions to the semantic space occupied by the particular words are described by means of scales which indicate the formality or intensity of the items. Some words are taught as synonymous pairs and there is also an accompanying range of well-tried vocabulary teaching exercises such as gap filling, providing derivatives, etc. The diagrams in Figure 7.2 give some indication of the procedures adopted by Rudska *et al.* Figures 7.3a and 7.3d show the way in which the semantic components of the words are analysed in relation to each other; Figure 7.3b is a scale which marks degrees of intensity attaching to items and Figure 7.3c indicates the more predictable collocational partnerships. (For further analysis of the principle see Channell, 1981.)

Some criticisms have been levelled at these methods (see particularly Porter and Williams, 1983). First, the grid approach can easily be made to suggest a static model of word meanings which learners learn and the grids can thus come to assume a degree of prescriptiveness for teacher and learners. There is a further problem, too, in that a natural order of acquisition for learners may be to learn more core meanings first and

	affect with wonder	because unexpected	because difficult to believe	so as to cause confusion	so as to leave one helpless to act or think
surprise	+	+			
astonish	+		+		
amaze	+			+	
astound	+				+
flabbergast	+				+

Figure 7.3a A semantic grid for components of words meaning 'being surprised'.
Source: Rudska *et al.*, 1982.

least ←――――――――――――――――――――――――――――→ greatest

surprise   astonish   amaze   astound flabbergast *surprise*

Figure 7.3b A scale marking degrees of intensity for words meaning 'being surprised'.
Source: Rudska *et al.*, 1982.

	woman	man	child	dog	bird	flower	weather	landscape	view	house	furniture	bed	picture	dress	present	voice
handsome		+									+				+	
pretty	+		+	+	+	+		+	+	+		+	+	+		
charming	+		+							+				+		+
lovely	+		+	+	+	+	+	+	+	+	+	+	+	+	+	+

Figure 7.3c A semantic grid of typical collocational patterns of words meaning 'attractive'.
Source: Rudska *et al.*, 1982.

then gradually acquire extended senses and related meanings. In this connection, Porter and Williams question the 'psycholinguistic validity' and 'naturalness' of simultaneously analysing *sets* of words (although see discussion in Section 7.3). Secondly, it is sometimes difficult to control the metalanguage or explanatory terms used. Definitions can be more complex semantically than the word being defined. For example, 'affect with wonder', 'having well-proportioned features' or 'suggests feminity or delicacy' in the grid in Figure 7.3d. Thirdly Porter and

	making a pleasant impression on the senses	close to an ideal	worthy of being loved	suggests relative smallness	suggests femininity or delicacy	arousing interest	causing pleasure	suggests lightness and grace	may suggest having good manners	may suggest sexual attraction	having well-proportioned features	well made or of good quality	often suggests strength	often suggests dignity	or	result of great generosity
beautiful	+	+														
lovely	+		+													
pretty	+		+	+												
charming	+				+	+	+	+								
attractive	+				+					+						
good-looking	+								+							
handsome	+										+	+	+	+		+

	woman	man	child	dog	bird	flower	weather	landscape	view	day	village	house	furniture	bed	picture	dress	present	voice	proposal
beautiful	+		+	+	+	+	+	+	+	+	+	+	+	+	+	+	+	+	
lovely	+		+	(+)		+	+		+	+	+	+	+	(+)	+	+	+	+	
pretty	+		+		+	+			+		+	+		+	+	+			
charming	+	+	+								+	+					+		
attractive	+	+									+	+				+		+	+
good-looking	+	+	+	+															
handsome	+	+														+			

Figure 7.3d Semantic grids for words meaning 'attractive'.
Source: Rudska *et al.*, 1982.

Williams charge that, in spite of the accompanying thematically organized reading passages, learners do not encounter the words in sufficiently varied contexts for there to be any real sense of a dynamic appropriation of semantic features. And Nation (1990, p. 47) points to problems of 'cross-association' in which learners confused words with similar meanings. (See also Laufer, 1997.) Nevertheless, such criticisms are valid only in relation to how the book is used. Teachers sensitive to teaching vocabulary in context will not present the grids as immutable,

---

——— 1 ———

a Here is a 'vocabulary network'. Can you complete it with words from the box? (Then add *one more* object for each room.)

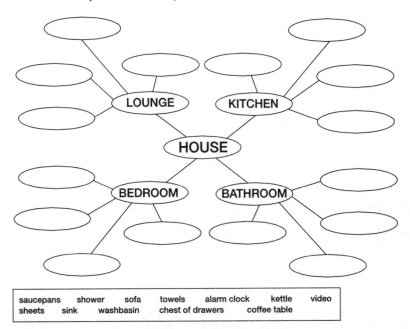

| saucepans | shower | sofa | towels | alarm clock | kettle | video |
| sheets | sink | washbasin | chest of drawers | coffee table | | |

b In which room do you normally:
listen to music?   waste time?
daydream?   think about your problems?
have arguments?   feel most relaxed?

Now compare your answers with a partner.

c Why do you have certain things in certain rooms? For example, why not put the television in the bathroom? Why not put the sofa in the kitchen? Think of some more examples and ask your partner to explain them.

Figure 7.4 A game-like task for vocabulary learning.
Source: Redman and Ellis, 1989.

The following adjectives can all describe hair. Fill in the circles and box and notice the progressions (e.g. longer–shorter).

  frizzy   black   auburn   dark brown   long   blond   shoulder-length   curly
  mousy   red   light brown   wavy   cropped   ginger   jet-black   mid-brown

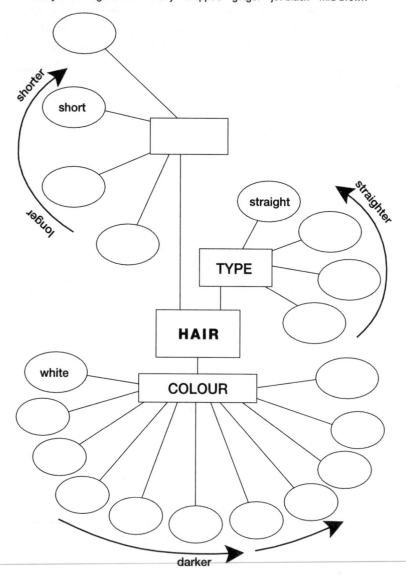

Figure 7.5 A game-like task for vocabulary learning.
Source: Gairns and Redman, 1986. © Cambridge University Press.

but rather as hypotheses which learners can test against further data; the analytical techniques can thus be seen to further creative and dynamic ends. Such access to word-meanings may also be much more productive than looking up words in a dictionary since words are best defined in relation to each other, so that fine gradations and differences of meaning can begin to be measured in as efficient and economic a manner as possible. It is also likely that the associations generated by and across words in this kind of semantic network aid both the retention and recall of words by learners (see Section 7.3 and note 11 at the end of this chapter). In this connection we might also note a proposal by Nattinger (1988) for teaching *metaphor sets*, which supports the organizational principles of *The Words You Need* and *More Words You Need*. Nattinger follows work by Lakoff and Johnson (1980) (see Section 5.7) and argues that the lexical items in a metaphor set such as ARGUMENT IS WAR (e g 'His criticisms were *on target*' 'He *attacked* his argument using a subtle *strategy*') should be taught in terms of their *associative bonding*. In the 1980s and 1990s this interest has expanded considerably by means of books and edited collections devoted to the topic: for example, Carter and McCarthy, 1988; Carter and Nation, 1989; Nation, 1990; McCarthy, 1990; Hatch and Brown, 1995; Schmitt and McCarthy (eds), 1997.

It should also be remembered that these books presuppose an existing lexical stock and are concerned with vocabulary *development*; it is at upper-intermediate to advanced stages that semantic and stylistic errors are frequent and it is in this latter respect that the collocational descriptions may prove especially valuable (see also Brown, 1974). Even though the status of the *word* may not appear particularly problematic to the authors, the books have innumerable uses and, in conjunction with Morrow's *Skills for Reading* (Morrow, 1980) and, more recently, McCarthy *et al.* (1985), were probably the only textbooks in the 1980s which approached vocabulary teaching both in a linguistically principled way and as something more than an adjunct to other areas of language development.

Grids, sets and networks of various kinds offer a systematic basis for vocabulary development and since the publication of *The Words You Need* there have been a number of related attempts to develop them at different levels and for different purposes, including for beginning students. Recently too, an emphasis has fallen on visual representation as a means to stimulating links between words and sets of words. Figure 7.4 from Redman and Ellis (1989), and Figure 7.5 (both tasks extracted from Gairns and Redman, 1986) indicate how game-like tasks can be both visually stimulating (with possible benefits to memorization) and meaning related. Unlike many other grids, there are clear possibilities for representing vocabulary in different ways for groups of learners other than advanced students. Recently, Lazar (1996) has also suggested an explicit teaching of underlying metaphoric sets as a way of extending vocabulary. For a recent and helpful review of trends in teaching second-language vocabulary with particular reference to semantic orderings and classifications of various kinds see Sökman (1997). Other recently developed and widely used vocabulary-teaching materials at intermediate to advanced levels include: Wellman, 1992; Harmer and Rossner, 1991; and McCarthy and O'Dell, 1994, the latter of which implements a number of McCarthy's proposals outlined above.

7.13 Vocabulary in discourse: Fixed expressions and lexis in use

The Words You Need by Ruska *et al.*, (1982) concentrates on vocabulary development mainly with reference to written text. The vocabulary enrichment takes place in the context of what are mainly reading activities. The meanings of words will form part of a learner's more receptive vocabulary since few of these activities explicitly encourage productive use. In spite of obvious difficulties and a lack of research in this domain, possibilities are being explored for widening the scope of vocabulary teaching. A basis to this widening is a clear assumption that knowing a word involves knowing how to *use* the word syntactically, semantically *and* pragmatically (i.e. discoursally).

McCarthy (1984a) illustrates a range of approaches to vocabulary teaching which draw on work on the functions of lexical patterning above the level of the sentence. McCarthy is concerned above all to show that using lexis in discourse is not an abstract static exercise in classification into sets or normal collocations, but a dynamic *process* of continuous reclassification. As he puts it:

> The belief that vocabulary skill is clearly more than understanding the componential features of words and recognising their typical collocations, more than the ability to define a word or slot it into a sentence, leads me to propose that the key to a new approach to vocabulary teaching lies in an examination of . . . relations between lexical items.

(a) above sentence level
(b) across conversational turn boundaries

(c) within the broad framework of discourse organisation.

(McCarthy, 1984a, pp. 14–15)

As an example relevant to (a) and (c) McCarthy proposes the following kind of task. Random sentences lacking in overt discourse markers are presented for combining into two short texts:

(1) The sofa is covered in leather.
(2) Lilac is very nice.
(3) The footstool is too.
(4) Cloth is not half as nice.
(5) There's one in bloom just over the porch.
(6) The scent is heavenly.
(7) The suite is very plush.

(McCarthy, 1984a, p. 17)

Here lexico-semantic partnerships such as *lilac–scent–bloom* have to be activated in order for a text to be formed. (See also Swales, 1983 for further related examples.) Exploration of the role of lexis in written discourse, particularly in the creation of cohesive textual relations, has also included re-assembly exercises from jumbled sentences and paragraphs (see especially research and examples reported in Rixon, 1984, and, with reference to English for special purposes, Swales, 1983; see also Section 7.15 for discussion of discourse cloze). Of further relevance to the teaching of lexis in discourse is the work on lexical cohesion and on lexical signalling reported in Sections 4.2–4.4. Crombie (1985) points out that this should not simply mean that more attention should be given to conjunctions in vocabulary teaching; it means that the learner should be creatively involved in a recognition of the role of lexical items in the realization of semantic relations:

> Clearly these signalling lexical items are as significant in the creation and interpretation of discourse as are conjunctions, and it is important that we should incorporate them into a language learner's vocabulary as early as possible . . . It is equally important that learners should be encouraged to develop a sensitivity to the ways in which the various relationships between lexical items may themselves contribute to semantic relational identification.
>
> (Carter, 1986, p. 91)

Encouragement to working with lexis in spoken discourse for purposes of (b) 'across conversational turn boundaries' above reveals 'the potential of lexical relations for the realization of important functions such as concurrence, divergence, topic-change, transaction-closing etc.' (McCarthy, 1984a, p. 15; see also McCarthy, 1988). McCarthy suggests that learners be encouraged to exploit the discourse potential of synonyms, hyponyms or antonyms across speaking turns. It is more usual in coursebooks for such relations to be realized by straight repetition or by the use of grammatical proforms (e.g. *yes, it is*; *you are, aren't you*, etc.) One of McCarthy's exercises for practising production involves the use of the following:

(A)   Agree, with synonym
        (a) He was very strange
        (b) Yes, very odd
(B)   Agree, with antonym
        (a) Joe didn't stick to the subject
        (b) He wandered off too much

. . .

(F)   Agree, with a less specific word (a superordinate)
        (a) The cat is great company
        (b) All pets are
(G)   Agree, with a more specific word (a subordinate)
        (a) Books are badly printed nowadays
        (b) Especially paperbacks

(McCarthy, 1984a, p. 19)

Another exercise can involve the use of core and non-core items (see Chapters 2 and 4) across boundaries. Thus:

(a) Were you cross?
(b) I was furious.

(a) Were you furious?
(b) I was cross.

The main purpose of such exercises is to assist learners to encode and negotiate the ways in which lexical items can be scaled in relation to each other for different communicative functions. McCarthy argues that this is quite different from but as equally important as viewing lexical items as isolated and decontextualized 'meanings' to be resolved by recourse to a dictionary or by exclusive reference to more static structural semantic definitions.

In the development of lexical discourse competence one more area is important. This concerns the role in discourse of fixed expressions (see Chapter 3, especially Sections 3.5 ff). Fixed expressions are both creative of discourse relations and are crucial to the maintenance of that discourse. They serve, for certain communicative purposes, to provide a relatively stereotyped, stable and prosaic response to events perceived as recurring and formulaic. There are potential difficulties such as the kind of cultural opacity embedded in some idioms (e.g. *my Sunday best*); but the utility of such prefabricated discourse-sensitive units is that interlocutors are saved the trouble of inventing new lexical meanings and can use expressions which are predictable because they are formally and, often, contextually 'fixed'. Vocabulary use does not always require users constantly to make creative interpersonal negotiations and renegotiations; it also requires the acquisition of specific fixed expressions which help simply to maintain discourse relations. Such relations are thus at the opposite end of a spectrum from those described by McCarthy (see above). Examples range from what Nattinger (1980) terms 'polywords' and defines as 'short phrases with extremely low variability whose meaning exists apart from syntax (e.g. *my old man, at my place*) to 'deictic locutions' which are more patterned routines. 'Deictic locutions' are still relatively frozen patterns but they function 'to direct the flow of the conversations by marking attitudes' (e.g. *as far as I know, if I were you, further to my letter of*). Nattinger also has a category of 'situational utterances' which serve less to mark attitudes than to encode an appropriate social or interpersonal response (e.g. *nice to meet you, cold enough for you?, are you sure?*). The whole topic of 'vague language' and 'fixed expressions' is treated more extensively in Chapters 3 and 4 (see Sections 3.7 and 4.5), and in Nattinger (1988), and Nattinger and DeCarrico (1992), who propose a lexical syllabus based on such patterns and outline a range of teaching procedures. The point to underline here is that such features of the lexicon are not normally taught, whether directly or indirectly, yet they are essential items of lexis in discourse.

7.13.1 Fixed expressions and learnability

Writing of first language acquisition, Bolinger (1976) challenges the more widespread view that children learn words as individual items:

> In the beginning stages a child apprehends holistically: the situation is not broken down, and neither is the verbal expression that accompanies it. That is why the first learning is holophrastic: each

word is an utterance, each utterance is an individual word, as far as the child is concerned. It is only later that words are differentiated out of larger wholes . . . The whole chunks that we learn also persist as coded units even after the chemical analysis into words has partially split them up. An extreme example is 'How do you do?' That it is functionally a single piece is proved by its condensation to 'Howdy?'

(Bolinger, 1976, p. 100)

Again caution needs to be exercised against too ready a transfer from L1 assumptions to L2, particularly when lexical acquisition research of this kind is limited. But consideration of lexis in discourse raises a central question of when in second-language teaching the learning of fixed expressions is best encouraged, and at what point some clearly holistic tendencies in language are best developed. The relation between fixed expressions and their memorability, and thus their storage and production as complete units, is also illustrated by the primarily phonological patterns on which large numbers of routinized collocations are based (e.g. *wine and dine*; *spick and span*; *to all intents and purposes*; *an apple a day keeps the doctor away*; *long time, no see*). (For further examples and discussion, see Alexander, 1978, 1984b; Pawley and Syder, 1983; Ellis, 1984, Ch. 4.) Recently, major syllabus re-orientation has been proposed along such lines with recommendations that language teaching should be more explicitly based on lexical foundations.

7.14 Lexical foundations for language teaching

The rapid growth of computerized corpora of English during the past few decades and especially in the 1990s has provided language teachers and syllabus designers with hitherto unavailable information about word frequency and word patterns, and about how words are deployed in a diverse range of both spoken and written contexts of use. These tendencies have led to an increased specification of the type of lexis on which teachers and learners should focus.

Sinclair and Renouf (1988), basing their arguments on evidence from the COBUILD corpus (see Section 6.6.1), argue for what they call a *lexical syllabus* – a syllabus which should take pedagogic precedence over both grammar and communicative notions and functions. The lexical syllabus ensures that essential grammatical (and other) structures and functions will be learned automatically because the most frequent words and word combinations are chosen for teaching, and because of their insight that core grammatical words such as *the*, *of*, *I*, *that*, *was*, *a* and *and* make up nearly 20 per cent of a typical English text, and that in a lexical syllabus based on frequency the main grammatical forms should automatically occur in the correct proportions.

> Almost paradoxically, the lexical syllabus does not encourage the piecemeal acquisition of a large vocabulary, especially initially. Instead it concentrates on making full use of the words the learner already has, at any particular stage. It teaches that there is far more general utility in the recombination of known elements than in the addition of less easily usable items.
>
> (Sinclair and Renouf, 1988, pp. 142–3)

Sinclair and Renouf's ideas are developed further by Willis (1990) who also explains the rationale underlying *The COBUILD English Course* (Willis and Willis 1987–88).

Lewis (1993), in a ground-breaking book entitled *The Lexical Approach*, draws inspiration from the work of COBUILD and earlier work on lexical syllabi but prefers instead to concentrate for a teaching foundation on what he terms **lexical chunks**. Lewis stresses the importance of learners learning chunks of language made up of lexico-grammatical patterns, a large number of which are pre-patterned in some way and may therefore be used in the kind of formulaic, rehearsed way which, while increasing learning of key structures, can also reduce communicative stress on the part of the user. Following on from work by Nattinger (1980) and Nattinger and DeCarrico (1989; 1992) Lewis argues *inter alia* for the following main characteristics of a 'lexical approach':

1 Students should be taught more base verbs rather than spending time on tense formation.
2 Content nouns should be taught in appropriate chunks which include frequent adjectival and verbal collocations.
3 Sentence heads such as *Do you mind if*, *Would you like to* should be focused on.
4 Suprasentential linking should be explicitly taught.
5 Prepositions, modal verbs and delexical verbs (such as *take a swim* and *have a rest*) should be treated as if they were lexical items.
6 Metaphors and metaphor sets should be taught on account of their centrality to a language.

Like Sinclair and Renouf and Willis, Lewis stresses the importance of word and lexico-grammatical frequency but places greater emphasis on usefulness to the learner so that frequency does not become an overriding criterion. In *Implementing The Lexical Approach* (1997) Lewis goes several steps further in elucidating the approach, offering a range of classroom-based studies and a wide variety of suggested teaching procedures. Figure 7.6 offers some ways in which a relatively neglected word such as *just* – which is one of the most frequent words in English – can be taught via a range of contexts, including institutionalized contexts of use, and contexts in which it is embedded in formulaic structures.

In parallel with the work of Lewis and Willis in Britain, Nattinger and DeCarrico in the USA were furthering their studies of repertoires of fixed expressions in a publication entitled *Lexical Phrases and Language Teaching* (Nattinger and DeCarrico, 1992). They take a particular descriptive interest in institutionalized expressions which may be regularly used to perform social or 'pragmatic' functions and thus provide an easily retrievable frame for written or spoken communication. For example, Nattinger and DeCarrico point to the sigificance of macro- and micro-organizers in the interactional management of language and underline how these 'lexical phrases' can be learned and then used and re-used. The increased effort involved in producing new words can be to some extent mitigated by the reduced processing effort of recycled lexical phrases. In their book several examples are given of how potentially useful are such signals to the effective management of academic spoken and written discourse.

7.15 Cloze and its uses

7.15.1 Procedures

Cloze procedure was introduced over 40 years ago and its applications have been numerous. It has been used for measuring the readability of textbooks, a reader's degree of comprehension of a text, both aural and written, and as a means of teaching and testing linguistic proficiency in a second or foreign language. It is a widely used and apparently simple technique and is examined here within a framework of vocabulary teaching because the most immediate focus of the procedure involves deletion of lexical items, and because the technique is frequently used as a means to advance vocabulary development and assessment.

It is also widely recognized that more research is required before problems and extensions associated with the procedure can be effectively analysed. A summary of some basic presuppositions of the cloze procedure might be made as follows:

Keyword: just

Match these remarks and responses:

1. Would you like a cup of coffee?
2. Are you ready? It's time we were off.
3. It looks as if the train is going to be late.
4. Were you late last night?
5. Everybody is worried about the situation.
6. They've changed their mind again.
7. It's almost 9 o'clock. It's time we got started
8. Have you got Helen's phone number there

a. That's just what we don't need.
b. Oh, it's not just me, then.
c. No, we got there just in time.
d. I think so. Just a moment – I'll have a look.
e. Not just now, thanks.
f. Don't worry. I think everything is just about ready.
g. That's just what I expected.
h. Right, I'll just get my coat.

Notice all the responses include the word *just*. It is very difficult to translate *just*, but it is used in a lot of fixed expressions. Can you think of a similar word in your own language? Learn the responses so you can use them yourself. Make sure you know the equivalents in your language.

Sometimes *just* is used to make a problem or mistake seem less important or serious:

It just slipped my mind.
I just couldn't get there any earlier.
I'm just not going to get upset about it.

Pres. Perfect:	*I've just passed my exam.*	(*just* = very recently)
Pres Cont.:	*I'm just making some tea.*	(*just* = emphasising exactly now)
was going to:	*I was just going to ring you.*	(*just* = very soon after now)
Can I just ask/tell you/say that . . .		(If you know an interruption will be quick)
I was talking to her just now.		(*just now* = a short time ago)
I couldn't tell you just then.		(*just then* = at that particular time)

Figure 7.6 Suggestions for ways of teaching awkward and frequently occuring words such as *just*.

Source: Lewis, 1997. © Language Teaching Publications.

1   Cloze procedure is a measure of the similarity between the patterns that a decoder is anticipating and those than an encoder has used. Words are blanked out (deleted) from a passage and a decoder has to restore them. The redundancy of the message in most normal naturally occurring texts should be such as to allow accurate insertions into the blanks. The theory underlying this 'redundancy' is also referred to as the 'grammar expectancy theory' (see Oller, 1979).

2   *Grammar expectancy* is best interpreted as involving syntactic, semantic and contextual uses. It presupposes the process of reading to be what Goodman (1967) has termed a 'psycholinguistic guessing game' and has described in the following terms:

> Reading is a selective process. It involves partial use of available minimal language cues selected from perceptual input on the basis of the reader's expectations. As this partial information is processed, tentative decisions are made to be confirmed, rejected or redefined as reading progresses.
>
> (Goodman, 1967, p. 148)

Not only does this assume the reader to be involved in a process which is genuinely interactive (as opposed to a merely reactive one) but it also means that decoding entails a sensitivity to both the immediate linguistic expectations and the longer-range contextual constraints created by a text. A reader will thus use co-textual as well as contextual clues and deletion needs to be designed in such a way as to preserve this.

3   Research has demonstrated that, for purposes of testing language proficiency, deletion is best conducted within a range from every fifth word to every twelfth word. If the deletion rate exceeds this margin then it is likely that there will be too much redundancy in the text for prediction to be an effective test; conversely, if, say, every third or fourth word is deleted then there will be insufficient redundancy for a reasonable measure of language competence to be assessed. The most common deletion rate is taken to be every seventh word but debate has taken place concerning the effect on distribution of context and function words if the rate is increased or decreased beyond or below every seventh word.[8]

4   For teaching purposes task-related variations in procedure can be instituted. These can involve wider fluctuations in deletion rate, experiment with prediction of lexical items or even fixed expressions as opposed to single orthographic words, substitution of a stretch of spoken discourse for the more usual paragraphs of

written text, the use of clues, use of nonsense words or an item such as *targetword*, in place of gaps and so on. In the case of the latter, Alderson and Alvarez (1978) argue that the use of a 'real' word as opposed to blanks preserves a more natural flow to the text provoking the same sort of reaction as to an unknown word and facilitates a clearer focus on techniques of inference.

7.15.2 Discourse cloze

An interesting extension of typical cloze activities is made in a study by Deyes (1984). The study raises questions about our understanding of the operation of lexical items in discourse, which, as we have seen in Chapter 4, is at only very preliminary stages of investigation. However, Deyes argues for an extension from random deletion to what he terms a *discourse cloze*:

> If a truly discourse cloze is to reflect the reader's ability to follow information through the text and use contextual clues as well as co-textual ones then, it is argued, theme and rheme, as units of information, provide criteria for item deletion.
>
> (Deyes, 1984, p.128)

His central thesis is:

> that interpretation can be tested by requiring students to replace not single words but communicative units: Such units may be textually recoverable but there should also be some whose replacement shows an interpretation of the wider context.
>
> (Deyes, 1984, p.129)

Deyes's research, which involved over 700 Brazilian students' responses to a range of tests, concludes that care needs to be exercised in the selection for deletion of information-carrying propositions. Thus, deletions from topic sentences would necessarily be rare but could be made from certain clauses and sentences consequent to these topic sentences.

Communicative units which place excessive demands on students' world knowledge or which are irrecoverable because their importance to the information structure is either peripheral or too central should also be avoided. It is also necessary to ensure a spread of theme, transition and rheme deletions. Deyes illustrates these principles with the following text and appended commentary:

Brisbane, which is the capital of the Australian state of Queensland, has a more relaxed atmosphere than Sydney, perhaps because of its pleasant sub-tropical climate. Its situation is not as impressive as Sydney's, but (1) ____ which runs through the city centre, is full of ocean-going boats, ferries – and small boats as well.

The way of life is probably the most pleasant and relaxed that you will find anywhere in a big city. People usually have large and beautiful gardens so that they can spend (2) ____ outside.

No one (3) ____ too much about clothes – it is most comfortable to go around in shorts and without shoes. While I was in Queensland I often used to relax (4) ____ with friends on Brisbane's fantastic beaches – and during the week too.

As in traditional cloze tests, the first sentence is left complete, because it includes a number of superordinate propositions relevant to the understanding of the frames of reference of the subsequent discourse.

(1)   is a theme deletion recoverable from collocational clues in the rest of its clause. Acceptable answers should contain the notion of 'river', though they would not be expected to include the name of the river, as this would probably be outside students' frames of reference.
(2)   requires replacement of a rheme in a proposition representing a 'normal consequence' of facts that are denoted in the superordinate topic sentence of the same paragraph. Acceptable answers would contain some time concept.
(3)   is in a sense the reverse of (2) in terms of propositional relations. Here an item (transitional/rheme) is deleted from a superordinate proposition, since content can be inferred from the explicit consequence which follows.
(4)   requires an adverbial element whose replacement depends on understanding the contrast made by the subsequent time adverbial.

It is worth noting that the deletions represent a variety of communicative values, as well as the full range of syntactic units (S, O, P, and A respectively). Initial piloting has shown encouraging results in terms of informal correlations with reading assessments. Answers were allowed in the students' first language to avoid the productive element.

(Deyes, 1984, pp. 133–4)

Deyes's proposals are valuable ones and appear to come to close to the notion of reading as a 'psycholinguistic guessing game' (cf. Goodman above) in that students engaged in this discourse cloze would have to read back and forth across a *developing* discourse drawing information from it as a whole and interpreting it; they could not complete it successfully by relying only on syntactic or semantic clues. There has to be comprehension in context; whereas in some cloze tests some gaps can be filled even if they appeared in isolated sentences. Also, the deleted items in Deyes's example are not limited to the cohesive system where mutually exclusive and closed grammatical items have to be substituted. In terms of Widdowson's (1978, p.23) distinction between *text* and *discourse*, such a procedure as this would be a *text cloze* but not a genuinely *discourse cloze*. In a discourse cloze students are required to demonstrate their understanding not just of the language system but of 'the communication as a whole'.

This is not to say that Deyes's proposals do not need to be refined. For example, as Deyes himself points out, how is deletion frequency to be determined, what is an acceptable response (particularly where relatively large numbers of open-class alternatives may be available and how is an even distribution ensured between theme, transition and rheme? Conversely, should it indeed be even? Also, certain text-types such as descriptions or narratives which often do not assume knowledge on the decoder's part and which, therefore, carry a high and often easily retrievable information load, may be more suitable than passages from textbooks or newspapers or expository writing which may assume previous knowledge. There are also potential problems in students using more than one 'orthographic' word substitution (particularly if they are accustomed to single-word cloze) and with the sequencing of discourse cloze in relation to the kinds of cloze tests more appropriate for less advanced learners. Much depends here on whether discourse cloze is seen primarily as a teaching or testing device, a distinction which is not sharply drawn by Deyes. But the proposals and procedures outlined do capture the dynamic nature of lexis in discourse and are worthy of serious further investigation by teachers and researchers.[9] In particular, this section might be read in conjunction with the analysis of lexis in discourse undertaken by Hasan (1980; 1984) and others. See above Chapter 4 (especially Section 4.8). Weston (1996) is a recent exploration with particular reference to problems in prose fiction.

7.16 Computer corpora and word lists once more

As W.N. Francis, co-compiler with H. Kuchera of a word corpus *Computational Analysis of Present-Day American English* (Kuchera and Francis, 1967), has put it, the important thing computers can do for developing materials is 'to count things, to compare things, to sort things and find things'. This section reviews, briefly, some implications for vocabulary teaching and materials development of some of the extensive and refined information about words made available by computer corpora. In essence, a corpus is a massively detailed word list which can only be effectively used for pedagogical purposes when a synthesis is made of those linguistic and other components relevant to vocabulary learning and teaching.

In Chapter 3 the general conclusion reached was that knowing a word involves knowing how to use the word *syntactically, semantically* and *pragmatically*. Martin (1984), we will recall (see Section 3.10), classified 'four dissonances' which characterize problems of vocabulary use of advanced learners: *stylistic* (**dunk* the chicken pieces in the beaten egg mixture), *syntactic* (*the author *purports* that tobacco is harmful), *collocational* (*I used to be a *large* smoker) and *semantic* (*I was badly *damaged* in the accident). (For Martin, there will be a further subdivision of pragmatic knowledge into stylistic and collocational.) Although there is obvious categorical overlap, computers can supply helpful information at all these levels. The most fundamental 'information' to be obtained from a multi-million-word corpus concerns *frequency* of use. It is of obvious utility to learners of a language to know the most frequent words and, in the case of pragmatic uses, where there are preferred patterns rather than absolute rules, to know the most frequent collocational and stylistic patterns. Assuming that a corpus is itself not stylistically restricted and is appropriately programmed, then information concerning the *range* of a word across texts should also be available.

In the case of a verb such as *add*, for example, it is possible to calculate:

1   a type-token frequency ratio of the item; that is, the number of occurrences of a verb such as *add* in relation to the number of words in the whole corpus or to particular genres or text-types in the corpus;

2   the range of distribution of the item (including, where relevant, differences between spoken and written text);

3   its typical collocates (e.g. *add* typically takes objects which are

ingredients – *salt, sugar, milk,* etc. – or qualities – *interest, colour, beauty,* etc. – or direct quotation – here the past tense more frequently ensues);

4   its preferred syntactic patterning relative to genre, e.g. in texts about hobbies or skills, and much more concentratedly in technical texts, it is regularly used in conjunction with the passive voice;

5   the frozen collocates or 'prefabs' (Bolinger, 1976, p.1) of which it is a part, e.g. *added attraction, add one more, add up to,* etc.;

6   its grammatical dependencies and distributional frequencies when in phrasal verb form, e.g. in the case of *add up to* two of every four instances are followed by reference to quantity.

(Analysis based on McKay, 1980a)

Concordances from the COBUILD corpus (the Bank of English) reveals information along not dissimilar lines and principles. (See Sinclair, 1985, for a corpus-based analysis of the item *decline* which relates interestingly to that of *add* above.) We might note at this point, too, the advantages of working from more specialized and homogeneous corpora. In a forerunner to COBUILD one separate but specific count was made of lexical items in the discourse of textbooks for foreign students of English. Such data can allow attestable inferences to be drawn concerning the degree of artificiality or constructedness of such language compared with the naturally occurring text which is the basis of the main corpus. See also proposals by Lyne (1983) for obtaining rank listings of items characteristic of a particular register by using a 'general' corpus as a control, as well as Phillips (1986) for computational analysis of 'lexical macrostructures' in text using a statistical technique of 'cluster analysis'.

Computer corpora allow access to detailed and quantifiable syntactic, semantic and pragmatic information about the behaviour of lexical items. There is little doubt that such corpora offer invaluable data for vocabulary materials development. But there are obvious dangers in using such data without carefully interpreting it *as data* and without careful assessment of the kinds of pedagogic criteria which might inform its use. Pedagogic issues will be examined in the next section; to conclude this section, some questions concerning the nature of the information supplied by a computer-based corpus will be discussed:

1   The relationship between the raw frequency of a word and its usefulness is not a direct one and is by itself not necessarily a sufficient condition for vocabulary selection. Richards (1974, p. 72) points out that:

Statistical studies of word distribution show that in normal discourse a high percentage of words occur only once. These account for over 50% of the word types (different words). A small percentage of the words in normal discourse is repeated often accounting for as much as 80% of the word tokens (total occurrences of words in the sample).

Bongers (1947, p. 143) and others have likewise claimed that the 2,000 most frequent words in a language will account for 80 per cent of any text. But it is also the case that many high-frequency words are low in information content; that is, the low-frequency words will often be crucial to an understanding of the discourse.

2   In a related sense, infrequent words are likely to have a narrow *range* (measured as the number of contexts or text-types in which an item occurs). There will be a correlation between decrease in frequency of occurrence and narrowness of range. Also, a significant proportion of words have very limited occurrences. In one word count (Carroll *et al.*, 1971), 35,079 types (40.4 per cent) occurred only once. But words with low frequency may be significant for a particular domain of use and may be frequent within that context (see also Hofland and Johannson, 1982).

3   Teaching materials and vocabulary teaching strategies will need to take particular account of (1) and (2) above. It should also be pointed out in this connection that the high-frequency words in English have more homonyms, inflected and derived forms than low-frequency words. In addition to teaching implications, this means that word frequency counts need to be checked carefully for lemmatization. That is, if *fly* is a frequent word, which particular meanings of the form *fly* are frequent and in what proportions? If the word *see* is frequent then the degree of frequency attached to its meanings which have *understand* and *look* as synonyms must be checked.

4   Corpora need to be examined carefully for the definition of *word* which is used as a basis of the collection. This returns us to issues raised regularly in the course of this book: that is, what does the corpus and its concordances tell us about *lexical items* as opposed to *orthographic words*? Can the frequency and range of fixed expressions or multi-word idioms or phrasal verbs be measured? Again, it can be pointed out that the most frequent or core words (see above Chapter 2) are most likely to have the property of extension which involves contracting partnerships with other grammatical and lexical words some of which may not, on their own, be particularly frequent. This makes the style of presentation of a

concordance one of some importance and makes the need for a span of items on either side of the keyword a quite crucial one (see also Section 6.6).

5 It is important for a corpus to be representative of different genres or text-types so that range is a genuine range and items are not statistically frequent because of an idiosyncratic database. Differences between spoken and written text also have to be clearly acknowledged for lexical items have different distributions according to their occurrence in either spoken or written contexts. (See Renouf, 1983, 1987, for principles of construction for the Birmingham Collection of English Text corpus, now COBUILD, as well as Carter and McCarthy, 1997, on CANCODE.) It must also be noted that spoken and written contexts can affect materially the grammatical distribution of items in relation to criteria of frequency. For example, nouns are more frequent in spoken than in written discourse (see Ochs, 1979; Brown 1982; and on adverbials in spoken English, Crystal, 1980a).

6 The storage of words in the mental lexicon may not necessarily conform to significant patterns of distribution according to any of the criteria outlined above. This has lead some researchers to propose that the 'availability' or 'familiarity' of a word may be a more significant criterion of importance. According to Richards (1974, pp. 76–7) 'available words are known in the sense that they come to mind rapidly when the situation calls for them'. Thus, psychologically, a frequent word *come* and an infrequent word *pencil* may be known or available in different ways. Research by Michea (1953) has suggested that concrete nouns are recalled from one context to another with greater facility than abstract nouns or grammatical/ function words. This has led Richards to propose a related notion of the 'familiarity' of a word which he defines as 'a factor of the frequency of experiencing words, their meaningfulness and their concreteness'. Richards measured word familiarity by asking informants to assess how often they would anticipate seeing, hearing or using certain words, and on this basis in Richards (1974) produced his own word list. There are numerous interesting correlations between such a list and other frequency indices such as Kuchera and Francis (1967).

7.17 Words and limits: Which words and how many words?

As we have seen, a major question which continues to be actively investigated by vocabulary researchers is the optimal size of the learner lexicon for differing communicative purposes. And a related question is how such size can be measured and, where appropriate, assessed in classroom-related vocabulary tests.

It is generally accepted that second-language learners need to increase their vocabulary size by about 1,000 words a year, in addition to making up a 2–3,000 word shortfall, in order to match the growth of a native speaker's vocabulary. However, if it is accepted that knowing the most frequent 2,000 words in English delivers understanding of between 80–90 per cent of words likely to be encountered, the question still remains of how knowledge of the remaining words, which are often quite crucial in understanding a text, can be effectively measured, how they might be graded in significance for learners, and how such knowledge can be assessed. And, as a further reminder of issues of size and scale, Simpson (1988) estimates (though without any hard evidence) that an average native speaker may encounter a million words of spoken and written language per day; and Nation and Waring (1997) estimate that an average native-speaking adult has a vocabulary size of 15–20,000 word families.

Until there are agreed definitions of what a word is, of seminal processes of L2 acquisition, and of what to include in a 'lexical syllabus', then the question of what can be revealed by a vocabulary test is bound to be relative. In the meantime the kinds of developmental work being undertaken by cloze-based measures, as reported in Section 7.15, remain the most likely to yield significant advances; and the increasingly sophisticated questions generated concerning word knowledge (see Section 7.7) remain an equally significant framework within which questions concerning vocabulary learning, vocabulary size and vocabulary testing can be posed. More detailed surveys and explorations of issues of vocabulary size are given in Nation (1990, Chs 2 and 5), Nation and Waring (1997) and, on testing issues, Read (1997).

7.18 Core vocabulary and language study: Back to the core

In Chapter 2 a number of specific linguistic tests were proposed in order to determine more precise and systematic grounds for the identification of a core vocabulary within the lexicon of a language. It was also recorded that the notion of a core vocabulary could be one with considerable potential for application to language teaching. At the same time it was cautioned that there need be no necessary relationship between linguistically principled specification and pedagogical contexts. This is an appropriate point, therefore, to review the issue of core vocabulary and language study; such a review will also serve to summarize some key points made in the course of both the last section and this chapter as a whole.

From a pedagogic point of view it is obvious that a purely linguistic determination of coreness in vocabulary, however systematic and detailed, will be insufficient for some purposes. As we have seen, one central problem is that of the relationship between core vocabulary items and their learnability and teachability. The most frequent, 'simple' or 'neutrals' words are also those which can be among the most problematic when it comes to syntactic derivations or the often multiple senses they carry. In the case of the more polysemous words this necessitates decisions as to which *meanings* to teach first. It also brings with it problems associated with memorization and lexical recall. That is, more research is needed to test whether the formal features of words may cause more difficulties for learners than their semantic features and whether therefore extending word meanings of polysemous but formally stable lexical items may provide an easier burden than that of learning new forms. For example, a word such as *light* may, in spite of its obvious polysemy, be more assimilable than *go*, which has many different inflected forms according to its verbal function (going, went, gone).

There are also important subjective measures of coreness of which the more 'objective' tests necessarily fail to take sufficient account. A good example of this would be Richards's investigation of notions of availability and familiarity reported in Section 7.16. In this, too, the complex relationship between lexis and syntax in processes of simplification cannot be discounted. Also highly relevant is a more obvious point that different subjects or domains in the curriculum have their own lexical cores (see Swales, 1990 and discussion in Section 4.9). Much depends, therefore, once again on a specification of useful or core vocabulary in relation to learning purpose and, in this respect, frequency, range and distribution of occurrence may be of especial significance. Praninkas (1972) and, on a more limited scale, Ghadessy (1979) offer interesting studies of frequency within a specific range of university-level textbooks (particularly relevant to teaching English for subject-specific purposes). Also significant are Perera's analysis of vocabulary in school textbooks (Perera, 1982) and Carson's (1985) study of classical influences on formality in lexis. Finally, a potentially serious limitation to the more language-internal of the tests for core vocabulary might be that they result in a static model of only the particular mental lexicon of particular informants. These informants in turn are reacting passively to decontextualized lexical items and the results obtained may thus be of limited value for teaching lexis in discourse or for laying any foundations for the kind of 'dynamic' vocabulary teaching advocated by McCarthy (Section 7.13).

These theoretical problems can have practical outcomes in the compilation of pedagogic word lists. For example, should *start* (a regular verb) be taught before *begin* (irregular, but more frequent)? Should words such as *just*, *really*, *even* be included? They have high frequency in spoken corpora but a word like *just*, for example, does not appear with the same frequency in corpora of written texts.[10] There is also the problem of teaching such items in contexts which are sufficiently authentic for their crucial role in discourse relations to be revealed. Further, should items which are more 'useful' for context-based language teaching such as *spend money* appear before related collocations which are more frequent (e.g. *spend/waste time*)? And what about general words which are not especially frequent or core according to most tests but which can supply useful descriptive terms in the classroom? Examples here would be: *means*, *ways*, *feeling*, *action* and *problem*. More obviously still, 'familiar' words which are non-core according to linguistic tests such as *television*, *radio* and *telephone* (that is, words which are often easily translatable) or 'classroom words' such as *chalk*, *blackboard* and *desk*, cannot be easily excluded from pedagogical core lists. It will be apparent, too, that notions of core vocabulary have greater relevance to teaching vocabulary in the initial rather than more advanced stages of language learning. But, in spite of these kinds of limitations, the notion of core vocabulary is an attractive one and the tests proposed in Chapter 2 do provide a general systematic account of 'coreness' in vocabulary. Core vocabulary is not a simple yes/no category but if the most basic and central words in the lexicon of a language are able to be specified with some rigour then the advantages for language teaching in particular should not really need to be rehearsed. As we saw in Section 7.16 frequency alone is not an adequate measure of coreness, but a synthesis of corpus-based frequency analysis, linguistic specification of coreness by principled testing and a blend of insights of the kind which produced the *General Service List* (West, 1953) could, in spite of the cautions exercised here, result in sound, up-to-date and widely usable pedagogical word lists. The present stage of research into core vocabulary is a preliminary one, but it is a notion which requires and deserves fuller investigation.

7.19 Conclusions: Knowing and teaching vocabulary

On the basis of general conclusions reached by the review in this chapter, *knowing a word* in a second or foreign language might be said to have the following main characteristics:

1 It means knowing how to *use* it productively and having the ability to *recall* it for active use, although for some purposes only passive knowledge is necessary and some words for some users are only ever known passively.
2 It means knowing the likelihood of encountering the word in either spoken or written contexts or in both.
3 It means knowing the syntactic frames into which the word can be slotted and the underlying forms and derivations which can be made from it.
4 It means knowing the relations it contracts with other words in the language and with related words in an L1 as well.
5 It means perceiving the relative coreness of the word as well as its more marked pragmatic and discoursal functions and its style-levels.
6 It means knowing the different meanings associated with it and, often in a connected way, the range of its collocational patterns.
7 It means knowing words as part of or wholly as fixed expressions conveniently memorized to repeat – and adapt – as the occasion arises.

Progress in the development of vocabulary-teaching materials is impressive but will continue to be limited to some extent by the scope of vocabulary-acquisition research. The following observations are offered in parallel to conclusions above concerning 'knowing a word' but with the knowledge that they are preliminary in a number of senses:

1 For most learning purposes, vocabulary needs to be taught for comprehension and for production. Comprehension relies on strategies which help learners to understand lexical items and to store them in memory. Production relies on strategies which help learners to activate their lexical store, retrieve items from memory and use them in contextually appropriate ways. Some teaching techniques are better suited for comprehension than for production, and vice versa. For example, as a teaching technique cloze procedure (see Section 7.15) encourages skills of lexical comprehension, especially in reading.

2   In the early stages of learning a language a range of techniques to aid memorization is necessary. In particular, teaching techniques which foster imagistic and picturable associations across L1 and L2 can be valuable. Particular attention should be given to phonological patterns to aid retention in the lexical store (see Sections 7.3 and 7.4). There is a need for a psycholinguistic perception of words as individual 'entities' to be reconciled with more pragmatic, social encounters with words in discourse contexts of actual use.

3   Teaching vocabulary in early language learning requires constant reference to the notion of certain words being more core than others. Word lists should be scrutinized in the light of theories of core vocabulary (see Sections 7.10 and 7.18).

4   The more advanced the learner becomes and the more emphasis is placed on production then the more teaching of words in a network of semantic associations should be activated. The teaching of words in semantic sets or grids can be beneficial here (see Section 7.12).

5   The skills of guessing and of using contextual clues to make inferences is important, especially in reading in a foreign language and especially if the learner is to become more self-reliant (see Section 7.15).

6   Teaching fixed expressions can be valuable at all levels and is especially important to allow learners access to more routinized aspects of production and to the essential skills of maintaining discoursal relations through language use. 'Fixed expressions' also include here collocations, idioms, etc. (see Sections 7.13).

7   Teaching words in discourse fosters the development of advanced skills of production but encourages appreciation of the syntactic, semantic and pragmatic functions of lexical items at all levels. The fuller activation of these skills is dependent on the kinds of knowledge of lexical patterning which only extensive computer databases can reveal; but, in particular, skills of negotiating, meaning and marking attitudes can be extended if attention is given to lexical items in texts and discourse contexts (see Section 7.13). Too great a focus on learning vocabulary as individual decontextualized items may lead to neglect of these skills.[11]

Of course, much depends on learning context and purposes and the above descriptions beg a number of key questions about learning vocabulary of the kind raised in Sections 7.5–7.7 and Section 7.11 in particular. And, as Richards (1976, p. 83) very valuably points out, relating words and meanings 'is always an active process of reconstruction

. . . (and) . . . much of the way a particular meaning is formed cannot be recorded in a dictionary'. That is, a word's meaning is rarely static and users must continually construct representations of what they are reading, hearing or saying before meanings can be fully activated. But the review here does indicate numerous possibilities for vocabulary development in language learning. Above all, it constitutes an indirect argument for a more extensive reinstatement of *vocabulary* as a justifiably separate domain in language teaching.[12]

Notes

1 An example of 'underextension' would be where a general word was restricted to only one subset of a possible range of referents, e.g. *furniture* for *chair*, or *vehicle* for *bus*.

2 For further relevant research along these lines see especially Saragi *et al.* (1978).

3 See Craik and Tulving (1975, p. 270): 'It is abundantly clear that what determines the level of recall or recognition of a word event is not intention to learn, the amount of effort involved, the difficulty of the orienting task, the amount of time spent making judgements, or even the amount of rehearsal the items receive; rather it is the qualitative nature of the task, the kind of operations carried out on the items, that determines retention.' It is necessary to ask, however, how many or how few words are learned by such means and for how long they might be retained.

4 Definition value is, of course, closely related to utility. In the terms discussed in Section 2.1, core words will have definition value if they pass the substitutability test. That is. core words can stand in for other words for purposes of definition. Thus, *thin* is used to define 'skinny' or 'slim' and *give* is used to define 'denote' or 'award', but the reverse does not normally apply. Another important aspect of West's work is that of the 'lexical distribution principle'. This applies particularly to West's *New Method Readers* and involves an even distribution of new words across a text so that learners do not become frustrated by insufficient practice and consolidation of what has been already learned.

5 In his introduction to *GSL* West (1953) has the following to say about *cover*:

> This is the converse of Point 2 above (*Necessity*). An item may be frequent but unnecessary. Thus 'for the time being' is not uncommon but is adequately covered by 'for the present'. 'For the time being' is costly, since the word 'being' here is remote in meaning from To be, whereas 'present' is used in its normal root sense. Tricky idioms are often of less value than an extra word as cover for an idea.
>
> (West, 1953, p. ix)

In other words and in necessarily impressionistic terms, West recognizes the need for selecting words for the list which are useful because users will recognize them in their primary or 'core' or 'root' senses.

6 Kruse does, however, offer a detailed proposed subdivision of each of her categories and supplies a sequence of linguistically marked examples of the

kinds of progression which might be developed. For example, with 'inference clues' she marks 'example', 'summary' and 'experience' as different indices of the kinds of inference allowed by different texts. Thus, in 'experience' the reader must decide from his own experiences what is the probable meaning in:

The dog snuffled and *moped* as he walked from the room.

Whereas in 'summary' information is supplied which facilitates decoding:

The *forsythia* was covered with the golden flowers that bloom in early spring.

Kruse's article is recommended strongly to teachers wishing, for example, to provide lexically based graded comprehension exercises.

7 For extensive discussion and review of research in the area of active versus productive learning in relation to vocabulary items, see Nation (1983, pp. 105–13). One area not generally covered in the research is whether grammatical words are learned in the same kind of way to lexical words. Or does the *frequency* of grammatical words mean that they (or a subset of them) do not need to be explicitly taught?

8 Alderson (1979) argues that the balance is disturbed with increases and decreases in the deletion rate; his claims are disputed, however, by Foley (1983) who also draws attention to the importance of specifying the purposes or goals envisaged for cloze procedure. Foley argues that cloze deletions are a blunt instrument which cannot, as Alderson (1979) and Johnson (1981) claim, be subjected to statistical analysis 'in a way which suggests that one item is essentially separate from and independent of any other'. Foley demonstrates that the same proportion of 6:4 in the relation of content to function words is present whatever the deletion rate within a span of every eighth to every twelfth word.

9 Clarke and Nation (1980) ask the following questions about guessing words from context. Their list is especially relevant for supplementing discussion here concerning lexical cloze procedures:

Does the skill (of guessing words from context) transfer from one language to another. . .? Will practice in guessing in the mother-tongue automatically result in improvement in guessing in the foreign language and vice-versa? . . . Is a score on a cloze test a reliable measure of how well a learner can guess word meanings? How much does practice with cloze tests develop the skill of guessing word meanings? . . . Certain parts of speech are easier to guess than others. Is there an optimum density of new words to known words which will help guessing?

(Clark and Nation, 1980, p. 217)

Additionally, a particular problem is that cloze makes it almost impossible to reproduce the conditions of *spoken* discourse. It presents us with *product* rather than *process*; that is, the recipient can see what comes *after* as well as before the deleted item. This means that, although some foreign listeners might need to be encouraged to use *post-* as well as *pre-item* clues, lexical prediction is generally under-utilized. However, for specific techniques which encourage such prediction, see the oral 'Guided response vocabulary tests' in McCarthy *et al.* (1985).

10 Citations of relative frequency made here are supported by reference to the COBUILD Project word-frequency lists held at Birmingham University and updated as of May 1984. The project has listings from spoken and written corpora (see Renouf, 1983). In the case of *just*, for example, it can also be noted that it is ranked fifty-second in the Lund corpus (based on spoken data) but that it does not appear in the top 100 most frequent words in either the LOB (Lancaster, Oslo, Bergen), or Brown corpora (based on written text). See also 4.6 above and McCarthy and Carter (1997).

11 See also Crombie (1985):

> The fact that systematic relationships between lexical items control the way in which they function in semantic relational realization provides support for the commonly held view that lexical items should be presented to language learners as far as possible in sets . . . and in other ways which highlight the relationships between them.

> (Crombie, 1985, p. 91)

12 It is regrettable that lack of space has not allowed fuller treatment of the role of lexicons in vocabulary teaching, especially the innovative *Longman Lexicon of Contemporary English* (1981) edited by Tom McArthur. But for reviews see Fox and Mahood (1982) and Jeffries and Willis (1982a).

Part III

Case studies

8 Case study: Lexis, tones and ironies

8.0 Introduction

The final part of this book comprises two case studies in informant-based lexical analysis: one is devoted to an exploration of associations in some examples of modern literary texts and the other is devoted to a discussion of style-marking of lexical items in monolingual dictionaries of English for second- and foreign-language learners. In both studies methodologies are proposed which involve making more extensive use of native-speaking informants. In Chapter 8 specific tests which incorporate informants' responses to lexical items are reported; in Chapter 9 the procedure is more informal but the argument is still a strong one and is rooted in proposals for employing more informant tests in the lexicographic construction and presentation of particular lexical entries. As we have seen from Chapters 5 and 6, it is in the area of stylistic marking that lexical studies of literature and lexicographic treatment are in some ways deficient. It is hoped that the following case studies may be seen as a small step towards remedying those deficiencies and in answering, in part at least, Uriel Weinreich's call:

> The most urgent need in semantics is for fresh empirical evidence obtained by painstaking study of concrete lexical data.
>
> (Weinreich, 1966, p. 473)

In the case study in this chapter I want to argue for an approach to the linguistic study of literary irony based on lexical analysis. Previous studies have tended to discern the presence of irony in a text chiefly by reference to the levels of syntax and the semantics of speech-act analysis.[1] Although such approaches are valuable, greater descriptive adequacy might be achieved if fuller reference were made to *lexis* and, more particularly, to the interpenetration of linguistic levels. I also argue that measuring lexical patterns and effects in a literary text requires reference to readers who are alert to the existence of specific literary genres and that in these cases a layer of literary 'text convention' needs to be built into the analytical model. I shall show that an *empirical* investigation of readers' responses to lexical organization can usefully complement, and to some degree refine, existing procedures for the description of literary irony. A basic presupposition in the study is that it is **verbal irony** which a linguistic approach can most usefully illumine and that the use of the term by literary critics tends to lack theoretical motivation and thus rarely has much explanatory power. The study here draws in particular on preparatory discussion of analyses of lexis and its role in literary text study in Chapter 5 (especially Sections 5.3 and 5.4). The primary aim is not to build up an interpretation but to examine the role of lexis in the creation of conventional 'literary' tropes (see here especially discussion in Sections 5.6 and 5.7).

8.1 General framework

First some general observations about irony are made which it is hoped will provide a framework for subsequent discussion. At its most basic, irony involves some kind of semantic opposition. However, meaning something ironically is not meaning two things (ambiguity) but meaning one thing in a certain way. For example, making a statement ironically:

(1) Charlie works hard!
(2) Brilliant! (on breaking an expensive vase)

involves saying something which is not true and which your hearer(s) can recognize to be false either as a result of their encyclopaedic knowledge or by recalling some previous pronouncement or prediction.[2] (Sometimes the knowledge can be signalled by the speaker's use of particular intonational or paralinguistic effects.) As Grice has observed, therefore, irony breaks a fundamental conversational maxim. To be precise, it is the second set of Grice's maxims, the Maxim of Quality, which has been regarded as central to any analysis of irony (Grice, 1975; 1978):

2 *Maxim of Quality*
   Supermaxim: 'Make your contribution one that is true'
   Maxims:

(a) 'Do not say what you believe to be false.'

(b) 'Do not say that for which you lack adequate evidence.'

Grice argues that the most logical 'implicature' to a flouting of Maxim (2a) is one of taking the opposite meaning. Thus, if we know Charlie is lazy and know that the speaker does not want vases broken, then we infer a semantically opposite meaning for examples (1) and (2) above. I shall return to Grice's conversational maxim in order to argue for a fuller explanation of irony by reference to other maxims in his model in addition to the Maxim of Quality.

Irony thus comes close to deception and telling lies but in a way which is intended to be seen through. This intentional aspect can be simply demonstrated by the fact that an ironic utterance cannot be interpreted by chance. Alternatively, if you say *I was being ironic*, your irony has failed to achieve the proper effect. There is no such verb phrase as *I ironize* or phrase like *speaking ironically* (to set alongside acceptable utterances such as *figuratively speaking* or *I was speaking metaphorically*). In the following example:

(3) It's ironic that Bill is such a good goalkeeper.

we would not be implying the opposite of the proposition that Bill is a good goalkeeper but commenting, in fact, on the inherent situational irony in some specific event surrounding Bill's good goal-keeping. It may be safely concluded, then, even on this brief examination, that verbal irony is essentially an ***indirect speech act***. That is, it functions as an utterance which communicates covertly rather than explicitly between a speaker and hearer.

The reference made in the above comments to speakers and hearers, propositional truth, speech acts, etc. explains to some extent why linguistic investigators have pursued the topic of irony from within a framework of what is generally called pragmatics. Analysis in this pragmatic domain is a fruitful line of inquiry. However, it may be dangerous to pursue this line exclusively.

8.2 Gricean analysis of irony: Lexical perspectives

One of the problems of confining analysis to the terms of speech-act theory can be illustrated by examination of the following much-quoted sentence:

> (4) It is a truth universally acknowledged that a single man in pos-
> session of a fortune must be in want of a wife.
>
> (Jane Austen, *Pride and Prejudice*)

Here it can be demonstrated that the primary speech act performed is
that of an assertion of truth rather than an assertion concerning the
propositions in the dependent clause. Pratt (1977) has argued as follows:

> The speaker of this sentence is making a claim about a hypothetical
> assertion regarding the interests of moneyed bachelors. Further-
> more, the assertion about which the claim is made is one with which
> the reader is likely to disagree, that is, one he is likely to regard as
> failing to fulfil one or other of the maxims of Quality.
>
> (Pratt, 1977, p. 167)

If no such assertion has been made or is likely to be made (the
economic circumstances and conventions of early nineteenth-century
England would have made it more likely for the unmarried woman to be
'in want of' the moneyed bachelor), then the implication is that someone might make such an assertion. If the reader discerns a speaker or
narrator as that 'someone' making the assertion then the author can be
interpreted as dissociating herself from this 'truth' and thus, in accordance with Gricean implicatures, suggesting the opposite to be the case
and intending the whole sentence to be an ironic one.

But there are other, simpler ways of demonstrating the same point
without the need for any kind of explicit pragmatic analysis. Irony is
also communicated here by a process of lexico-syntactic 'overloading'.
First, if a truth is a truth it does not need to be 'universally acknowledged'. Therefore, the post-modifying phrase draws attention to itself
and casts some doubt on the same 'truth'. Secondly, and in a related
way, the fact that it is *universally* acknowledged does not necessarily
mean the author need acknowledge it. Here the suppression of agency
(by whom?) adds to her potential distance from the assertions made and
leaves room for contrary and ironic effects to be signalled. Jane Austen's
'deception' is a little more opaque than in examples (1)–(3) because the
reader has to imaginatively reconstruct a context for the utterance but
the point is that ironic effects are produced by pragmatic, syntactic *and*
lexico-semantic means. Indeed, recognition of the 'semantic densities'
produced by such means may, in part at least, be constitutive of the
'literariness' of this text (see Section 5.5).

Another problem, this time brought about by restricting an account
of irony to too limited an area of pragmatic analysis, can be illustrated

by an attempt to specify how an ironic tone is communicated in other texts. In Carter (1982a) initial discussion is undertaken of a poem by W.H. Auden entitled 'The unknown citizen' (the poem is reprinted in the article but is also widely anthologized and appears in numerous collections of Auden's poetry).

As with example (4), in 'The unknown citizen' the presence of irony can be detected but again the speaker seems to intend what he says to be taken as literal and truthful. The irony must therefore subsist somewhere in the relations between the poet, the reader and what has been discernably created as his speaker in the poem. If the speaker does not reveal conditions for us to take his meaning in some other way then Auden must make him do it as part of his (Auden's) communication with the reader.[3]

One prominent intuition I have experienced in reading 'The unknown citizen' is that the speaker simply goes on too long. The speaker might therefore be breaking another of Grice's maxims, the Maxim of Quantity. This is the first of Grice's maxims:

1 *Maxims of Quantity*
   (a) 'Make your contribution as informative as is required (for the current purposes of the exchange).'
   (b) 'Do not make your contribution more informative than is required.'

I tested this intuition with reference to forty-two informants,[4] 66 per cent of whom marked a span in the text from 'frigidaire' to 'education' where they felt the text began to become 'more informative than is required' and where they felt the speaker could effectively have stopped without detriment to his assertion that all was well with the citizen.

One main implicature from overinformative discourse is that the speaker is not entirely sincere, that is, we may suspect him to be attempting to hide something or oversell something to us ('Methinks the lady doth protest too much'). This is even more notable here in that the speaker is not being merely boring, because he packs in so much *new* information which in turn is supported by evidence. Auden thus manages to question *how* and *why* it is one man knows so much about another, reinforcing this doubt by titling the poem 'The *unknown* citizen'. It is infringement of the Maxim of Quantity which first draws our attention to this. Syntax is not additionally utilized in as prominent a way as in example (4) but a different maxim in the Gricean model is. The result is still to get us to doubt the truth of the speaker's statement and to make us infer a contrary meaning. In this context, though, there is a stronger 'satiric' overtone in that the content of the poem forces us to ask what kind of social or political situation makes such knowledge of the citizen possible.

Ironic effects are produced in a number of ways and an exclusive concentration on a single linguistic level, a single mode of analysis, or, in the case of the Gricean model, a single set of maxims, can lead to analysis which is generally inadequate and lacking in subtlety. The analyst needs to be alert to different kinds of ironic effect and to how these can be brought about by manipulation of different features of the language system. Winner (1988) is an exploratory study of children's reactions to such features.

8.3 Irony, lexis and genre

In the poem by Auden below I perceive that Auden is being ironic about 'the greatest figure of the day'. But whatever the kind of irony involved it does not appear to lend itself readily, in the same way as the previous texts at least, to analysis in terms of Gricean maxims, or other kinds of analysis, whether largely lexico-syntactic or pragmatic.

> *Who's Who*
>
> A shilling life will give you all the facts:
> How Father beat him, how he ran away,
> What were the struggles of his youth, what acts
> Made him the greatest figure of his day:
> Of how he fought, fished, hunted, worked all night,
> Though giddy, climbed new mountains; named a sea:
> Some of the last researchers even write
> Love made him weep his pints like you and me.
>
> With all his honours on, he sighed for one
> Who, say astonished critics, lived at home;
> Did little jobs about the house with skill
> And nothing else; could whistle; would sit still
> Or potter round the garden; answered some
> Of his long marvellous letters but kept none.

I claim here that a main part of the irony lies in the fact that the 'life' is related in a rather trite, predictable, off-hand and unpoetic manner. This is made even more noticeable by the text being in the form of a sonnet, a literary mode which my literary 'competence' informs me is more usually associated with stylistically elevated proclamations of love. But the above comments are unduly impressionistic. Some tests were therefore devised which set out to explore and to attempt to measure the intersubjective validity of these impressions (see Appendix I in Section 8.5). As in the example of 'The unknown citizen' these were informant tests, to which eighty respondents produced workable results.

Tests 1 and 4 confirmed that informants shared an impression that the language was 'unpoetic' and would not be the kind of norm adhered to by, say, nineteenth-century sonneteers. Tests 2 and 3 involved informants being asked to predict words to fill gaps which had been blanked out in the text of the poem and in prose versions of the same text.[5] The results recorded indicate a higher level of accurate prediction in the prose versions that in collocations of lexical items in the context of the poem thus adding further confirmation to intuitions concerning the ordinariness of the language. Test 5 produced consistently only two phrases which were felt to be at all unusual in the context of the poem. It is interesting to note that a lexical item such as 'potter' was singled out as being unusual in a poem but was quite regularly predicted in the context of the prose version of the same sentence. Finally, test 6 used a formality cline in which informants were asked to mark six sentences made up from the text of the poem along a scale 1 (formal) to 5 (informal).

One overall conclusion which can be drawn here is that there is a distinct lack of fit between the genre (a poem), the kind of poem within that genre (a sonnet) and the kind of lexis conventionally expected to belong in such a poem. The reversal of expectation brought about by analysis of lexical patterns and the generally semiotic (rather than distinctly linguistic) properties of the genre style work as it were to bring about a reversal of the literal meanings of that text. We do not now take the statements about 'the greatest figure of his day' quite so literally and we perhaps begin to regard the 'love' referred to in the sestet in a rather more questioning and ironic light. Much more work and attestation will need to be done in this area before firm conclusions can be drawn but it can be said that as a linguistic level in literary text lexis can bring out its own kind of effects.

The next two examples are brief and exploratory. The first is taken from the opening two stanzas of another poem by W.H. Auden.

Mundus et Infans

Kicking his mother until she let go of his soul
Has given him a healthy appetite: clearly, her role
    In the New Order must be
To supply and deliver his raw materials free;
    Should there be any shortage,

She will be held responsible; she also promises
To show him all such attentions as befit his age.
   Having dictated peace.

With one fist clenched behind his head, heel drawn up to thigh
The cocky little ogre dozes off, ready,
   Though, to take on the rest
Of the world at the drop of a hat or the mildest
   Nudge of the impossible,
Resolved, cost what it may, to seize supreme power and
Sworn to resist tyranny to the death with all
   Forces at his command.

The text is particularly interesting in that it is far from homogeneous
and unitary as far as lexical choice is concerned. Using informants to
assess the predictability of collocations by gap-filling (see Appendix II
in Section 8.5) also reveals that certain items are regularly predicted,
although a significant proportion of informants (62 per cent) eschew
the same choices in blanked-out versions of the poem (again confirming
that in a poem we do not expect to find what are effectively clichés such
as *supply and demand raw materials, to be held responsible, all such
attentions as befit, with all forces at his command*, etc.) Again, a basis is
laid here for an interpretation of the text in terms of reversal of expectations and meanings – at the very least our view of the first months of a
baby's life is prevented (ironically by some predictable, clichéd lexis)
from being sentimental and clichéd. Testing informants' responses to
the lexical patterns of this text by use of a formality cline also confirms
impressions that another prominent feature is the constant switches
from informal to formal levels and vice versa. It is interesting to explore
the inherent possibilities of what may be loosely termed 'register mixing' (see also Section 5.2) for the creation of other layers of irony.[6] One
hypothesis which might be explored is that a shift from formal to
informal items along a cline can produce an ironic tone of criticism of
the subject or the way of seeing the subject (e.g. *all such attentions as
befit his age* → *cocky little ogre*). Whereas, in the reverse cases, which
involve a shift from informal to formal, informants report that an
altogether more humorously ironic effect is produced. Ezra Pound was
one of the first to draw attention to the ironies created in poetry by
switches in the usual 'concomitants' and 'acceptances' of words (see
particularly Section 5.3):

LOGOPOEIA, 'the dance of the intellect among words', that is to say, it employs words not only for their direct meaning, but it takes count in a special way of habits of usage, of the context we *expect* to find with the word, its usual concomitants, of its known acceptances, and of *ironical play*. [Italics added]

(Pound, 1927, p. 25)

Another related example of register switching and one closely related to Passage C in Section 5.6 (p. 136) is an extract from Muriel Spark's *The Prime of Miss Jean Brodie*.

Miss Lockhart in the science room was to Sandy something apart surrounded by three lanes of long benches set out with jars half-full of coloured crystals and powders and liquids, ochre and bronze and metal grey and cobalt blue, glass vessels of curious shapes, bulbous, or with pipe-like stems. Only once when Sandy went to the science room was there a lesson in progress. The older girls, big girls, some with bulging chests, were standing in couples at the benches, with gas jets burning before them. They held a glass tube full of green stuff in their hands and were dancing the tube in the flame, dozens of dancing green tubes and flames, all along the benches. The bare winter top branches of the trees brushed the windows of this long room, and beyond that was the cold winter sky with a huge red sun. Sandy, on that occasion, had the presence of mind to remember that her schooldays were supposed to be the happiest days of her life and she took the compelling news back to Jenny that the Senior school was going to be marvellous and Miss Lockhart was beautiful.

The text is a rich and subtle one containing a number of complex linguistic–aesthetic effects. But attention should be given to the final sentence. I perceive this to be a prominent instance of a subtly pervasive irony in the text. Its effect depends, of course, in part on what has preceded it but the ironic tone is produced first by the creation of a 'dual voice' (see Pascal, 1977; McHale, 1978) and the ensuing transition from one to the other in the course of the sentence and secondly by a process of lexico-syntactic overloading not dissimilar to that discussed in relation to example (4) from Jane Austen.

This is most apparent in the structure 'Sandy . . . had the presence of mind to remember' where the author reports that Sandy feels some kind of conscious obligation to undergo the essentially involuntary act of 'remembering' (this is reinforced semantically by the 'supposed to be' in the reported clause). The effect is almost one of remembering to remember and as a result Sandy is presented to us as perhaps preferring to forget or as conceiving of her schooldays as being something contrary to happy. The duality or ambivalence of her response is reinforced by opposing lexical patterns: on the one hand, the distinctly authorial reporting voice, and on the other hand, the existence of items such as *compelling, marvellous, beautiful* which (though this would need to be tested) may be perceived to belong to the schoolgirl register of Sandy and her friends. The lexical contrasts mirror across the whole passage the dislocation of Sandy's view of things and thus prevent us from taking what she says at face value. The switching of register is instrumental in the creation of ironic effects although we also have another example here of how the subtlety of many ironic tones sometimes requires multi-levelled points of reference in the course of its analysis. In any case, the notion of irony by register switching is one which merits closer attention (see also Sperber and Wilson, 1981, pp. 311–14; and Wilson and Sperber, 1992).

8.4 Conclusions

The preceding discussion can be represented by Figure 8.1. That is, irony is communicated when there is knowledge of a pragmatic falsehood (e.g. a violation of Gricean maxims – Quality and Quantity, in particular – and/or a violation of text conventions, genre, etc.). Ironic speech acts crucially depend on the hearer/reader's access to encyclopaedic knowledge, with this encyclopaedic knowledge leading to reinterpretation of the direct core meaning of the lexical items used. An interface between direct and indirect meaning produces what is often a semantically contrary meaning. If, for some reason, the hearer/reader

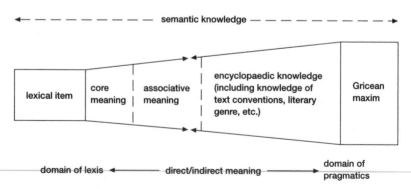

Figure 8.1 Knowing the meaning of words.

does not realize from his pragmatic knowledge that there is a clash between circumstances and the speaker/writer's assertion, then the assertion will be accepted as true. In other words there will be *no* interface established between direct and indirect meaning, between semantic and encyclopaedic knowledge and hence *no* irony will result.

Finally, this case study should be seen as a contribution to literary stylistics in which the main focus is on the specific operation of lexis in a number of poetic and prose texts. I hope that the suggestions made here – and in the next chapter – particularly with reference to some uses of informant analysis, may provide a basis for further developments in both methodology and description in what is, as we have pointed out, a neglected area of stylistic investigation.

8.5 Appendices: Informant tests

Appendix I: W.H. Auden's 'Who's who': Informant analysis of lexis

Results of Tests 1–6 (details of tests below)

Test 1: The following items were maximally underlined by informants (80 in total) to have not been usable by a poet of the previous century:

l.2	'beat him'	22%	l.11	'Little jobs'	46%
l.6	'giddy'	38%	l.13	'potter'	68%
l.8	'weep his pints'	6%	l.9	'astonished	
l.8	'like you and me'	22%		critics'	28%

Test 2a: The following words were predicted:

l.4	'greatest'	12%	l.8	'me'	2%
l.6	'giddy'	0%	l.11	'little'	0%
l.8	'pints'	0%	l.13	'potter'	12%
			l.14	'marvellous'	0%

Test 2b: The following words were predicted:

l.4	'greatest'	20%	l.8	'me'	28%
l.6	'giddy'	0%	l.11	'little'	18%
l.8	'pints'	0%	l.13	'potter'	42%
			l.14	'marvellous'	0%

Test 3a: The following words were predicted:

1.4	'figure'	20%	1.11	'jobs'	12%
1.8	'weep'	0%	1.14	'long'	8%
1.8	'you'	80%			

Test 3b: The following words were predicted:

1.4	'figure'	32%	1.11	'jobs'	56%
1.8	'weep'	0%	1.14	'long'	8%
1.8	'you'	88%			

Test 4:   The following items were marked as belonging to an expected level of 'poetic diction':

NIL

Test 5:   The following items were marked as unusual collocations given the context of the poem:

   1.8 'weep his pints', 1.13 'potter round the garden'

Test 6:   The six sentences were marked on the formality cline 1–5 as follows:

   Sentence 1 – mostly 3
   Sentence 2 – mostly 3 or 4
   Sentence 3 – mostly 5
   Sentence 4 – mostly 4
   Sentence 5 – mostly 5
   Sentence 6 – mostly 3 or 4

Tests 1, 4 and 5

This poem was written by W.H. Auden in 1934. Underline any words, phrases or constructions which, as far as you know, would not have been used by a poet of the previous century. Also circle any words which seem to you to belong to what might be termed 'poetic diction'. Finally, please indicate by a cross any groups of words which you would not normally expect to find together. You are, of course, at liberty both to underline *and* to circle words or, indeed, not to mark any words at all. It is quite possible that, for you, the words employed by Auden do not fit into any of the above categories.

   A shilling life will give you all the facts:
   How Father beat him, how he ran away,
   What were the struggles of his youth, what acts
   Made him the greatest figure of his day:

Of how he fought, fished, hunted, worked all night,
Though giddy, climbed new mountains; named a sea:
Some of the last researchers even write
Love made him weep his pints like you and me.

With all his honours on, he sighed for one
Who, say astonished critics, lived at home;
Did little jobs about the house with skill
And nothing else; could whistle, would sit still
Or potter round the garden; answered some
Of his long marvellous letters but kept none.

Test 2a

Please fill in the gaps left in the poem below with what you consider to
be an appropriate word.

A shilling life will give you all the facts:
How Father beat him, how he ran away,
What were the struggles of his youth, what acts
Made him the . . . . figure of his day:
Of how he fought, fished, hunted, worked all night,
Though . . . . climbed new mountains; named a sea:
Some of the last researchers even write
Love made him weep his . . . . like you and . . . .

With all his honours on, he sighed for one
Who, say astonished critics, lived at home;
Did . . . . jobs about the house with skill
And nothing else; could whistle, would sit still
Or . . . . round the garden; answered some
Of his long . . . . letters but kept none.

Test 2b

Please fill in the gaps left in the following sentences with what you
consider to be an appropriate word.

(1) His acts made him the . . . . figure of his day.

(2) Though . . . ., he climbed new mountains.

(3) Love made him weep . . . . like you and . . . .

(4) She did . . . . jobs about the house with skill.

(5) She would sit still or . . . . round the garden.

(6) She answered some of his long . . . . letters but kept none.

Test 3a

Please fill in the gaps left in the poem below with what you consider to be an appropriate word.

A shilling life will give you all the facts:
How Father beat him, how he ran away,
What were the struggles of his youth, what acts
Made him the greatest . . . . of his day:
Of how he fought, fished, hunted, worked all night,
Though giddy, climbed new mountains; named a sea:
Some of the last researchers even write
Love made him . . . . his pints like . . . . and me.

With all his honours on, he sighed for one
Who, say astonished critics, lived at home;
Did little . . . . about the house with skill
And nothing else; could whistle, would sit still
Or potter round the garden; answered some
Of his . . . . marvellous letters but kept none.

Test 3b

Please fill in the gaps left in the following sentences with what you consider to be an appropriate word.

(1) His acts made him the greatest . . . . of his day.

(2) Love made him . . . . his pints like . . . . and me.

(3) She did little . . . . about the house with skill.

(4) She answered some of his . . . . marvellous letters but kept none.

Test 6

Please mark the following sentences on a scale 1–5 according to how formal you consider the sentences to be. Underline any words which seem to you to be particularly formal, i.e. a long way from casual conversation. Mark with a cross any words which seem to you to be particularly informal, i.e. very close to casual conversation.

Please place the number in the space provided after each sentence.

1 = very formal; 3 = quite formal; 5 = informal and approximate to casual conversation.

(1) These acts made him the greatest figure of his day._____

(2) Though giddy, he climbed new mountains and
named a sea.   _____

(3) Love made him weep his pints like you and me._____

(4) With all his honours on, he sighed for one who
lived at home and did little jobs about the house. _____

(5) She would sit still or potter about the house. _____

(6) She answered some of his long marvellous
letters but kept none.   _____

Appendix II: W.H. Auden's 'Mundus et infans': Informant analysis of lexis

Reasons of space permit only one example of the tests used in connection with W.H. Auden's 'Mundus et infans'. Here informants are asked to fill in appropriate gaps in Test A before proceeding to Test B. The basic purpose is to explore whether informants fill in the same words or have different assumptions about lexical collocations in poetry.

Test A

(1) Kicking his mother until she let go of his . . . . has given
him a . . . . appetite.

(2) Their role in the New Order must be to . . . . and deliver
the raw . . . . free.

(3) Should there be any shortage, you will be held . . . .

(4) She promised to show him all such attentions as . . . . his
age.

(5) With one fist clenched behind his head, the . . . . little ogre
dozes off.

(6) He resolved to .... supreme power and was sworn to
.... tyranny with all the .... at his command.

Test B

Kicking his mother until she let go of his ....
Has given him a .... appetite: clearly, her role
In the New Order must be
To .... and deliver his raw .... free:
Should there be any shortage,
She will be held ....: she also promises
To show him all such attentions as .... his age.
Having dictated peace,

With one fist clenched behind his head, heel drawn up to thigh
The .... little ogre dozes off, ready
Though, to take on the rest
Of the world at the drop of a hat or the mildest
Nudge of the impossible.
Resolved, cost what it may, to .... supreme power and
Sworn to .... tyranny to the death with all
.... at his command.

Notes

1 See, for example, articles by Muecke (1973); Tanaka (1973); Werth (1977); Amante (1980); and Leech (1983a; 1983b).
2 The notion of irony as 'echoic mention' is developed in articles by Sperber and Wilson (1981), and Wilson and Sperber (1992).
3 For fuller details of a basic theory of literary communication see Widdowson (1972; 1975).
4 Informants in each of the following tests were undergraduate students of English Language and Literature and may therefore be deemed by certain recognizable measures to have some degree of literary competence. Interesting extensions to the tests could also be developed using native-speakers with no definable literary competence. There are, of course, drawbacks to empirical investigation of lexis in literature. Chief among these can be its ahistoricism. For fuller discussion see Carter (1979, especially Ch. 4) as well as discussion in Section 5.4.
5 The choice of which lexical items to blank out is with the analyst who works from his own intuitions and impressions. In testing for collocability relations it was seen as essential for adjacent items to be tested simultaneously.
6 The term 'register' is used here only as a useful hold-all term to embrace switches in lexical association in relation to different contexts of situation and not in any precise technical sense.

9 Case study: Style, lexis and the dictionary

9.0 Introduction

The discussion in Chapter 6 reviewed progressive attempts to design learner dictionaries for productive use. As we saw, there has been an emphasis on appropriate presentation of syntactic and lexico-semantic information both of single words and fixed expressions. Fuller definition or explanation of the *use* of words has to focus on the sociolinguistics' of words, that is, their use in contexts of communication. As Ayto (1983, p. 95) has put it there is often more to the complex set of semantic relationships between similar lexical items than strict lexical differentiation, and any dictionary worth its salt ought to do its best to reflect this.' Putting across the required lexico-semantic information necessitates greater attention to both the pragmatic functions and communicative properties of words. In particular, the *associations* carried by lexical items need to be defined in as systematic and accessible a manner as possible. The case study presented in this chapter explores such a direction; in part at least the study is one in lexical stylistics and thus bears some comparison with the methodological and descriptive aims of the case study undertaken on lexis and literature in Chapter 8.

A further connection is that in both studies it is argued that informant tests are necessary prerequisites for a more refined discrimination of the associations of words.

9.1 Semantics, associations and definitions

This section reviews some basic positions concerning word meaning and its definition and thus offers some theoretical preliminaries to subsequent analysis in which much is theoretically implicit. No discussion of lexical associations can operate independently of a theoretical position and the points listed here should enable basic presuppositions to be seen and challenged.

Attempting to describe lexical associations brings us up against questions concerning the appropriate limits of semantics. As we have seen from previous chapters (see Sections 1.9 and 1.11.1), there is a recognized division between *conceptual meaning* and what is variously termed expressive, stylistic or *associative meaning*.[1] Other terms would be *denotation* versus *connotation*. In the case of the former, that is, conceptual or denotative meaning, analytic definitions are sought by reference to conceptual–referential properties of the word and this usually involves eliminating what is inessential by listing in what are contrastive and mutually exclusive categories basic semantic components of the word. Thus a word is human or non-human (+ or −HUMAN), inanimate or animate, male or female, child or adult, concrete or abstract, dynamic or static, and so on (see Goodenough, 1956; Katz and Fodor, 1963). The ideal theoretical' dictionary (cf. Leech, 1981, Ch. 11) would thus set up a hierarchy of progressively narrower categories until the word is sufficiently disambiguated from other lexical items. The position articulated here is that such precise and systematic definition seeks the constant and stable meaning of a word; by contrast, associative meaning is less fixed and measurable and is dependent on essentially relative and variable contextual factors. If semantic definitions of the connotative–associative functions of words are to be provided then it must be by similar analytic means. However, a problem with this kind of atomization is that some words require ever finer sets of gradations and that the inherent indeterminacy of certain words cannot be adequately described by such means (see Lakoff, 1973). Such procedures, as Bolinger (1965) points out, do not adequately allow for the ranges' of meaning carried by words. A good example of the opposition between conceptual–denotative and associative–connotative analysis is provided by Ayto (1983) who gives the example of the word *man* in the following citations: Be a man, my son'; a real man'; a typical man'; not much of a man' and asks pertinently:

> Where does the lexicographer step into this welter of evidence and say here we have a denotative meaning that I can formulate purely descriptively, there a range of connotations which are not lexicographically significant and for which I must refer the user to his knowledge of the real world'?

(Ayto, 1983, p. 97)

The meanings' of *man* here include adult male, possessing courage and resolution, demonstrating insensitivity. Should they all be recorded in a dictionary entry for *man*?

One extreme theoretical position would be to argue that there is lexicographically no such thing as connotation and that to qualify for entry a connotation must in effect have become a denotation in its own right – that is, according to Ayto (1983, p. 96) there exists no linguistically ascertainable trace of a connotational link with the original denotative sense'. By such a criterion man' in the sense of courageous and resolute would qualify but the sense of man as insensitive' or exploitive' is too contextually, even ideologically constructed to be established without reference to knowledge of the world, or at least of a particular world. (The issue of ideology is taken up below.) It is not a denotation in its own right. However, what is acceptable according to linguistic theory is not necessarily an automatic determinant of lexicographic practice, as Ayto readily admits. It is also difficult with less clear-cut cases than *man* to draw any definite line between what is denotation and connotation and, as argued below, the lexicographer's own exclusive experience is not necessarily the most reliable source. Description of associative meaning needs to take account of the *use* of words in contexts and such meaning can be studied and presented systematically if greater reference is made to *users*.

There are two relevant contexts for determining the associative properties of words: a socially situated context and a linguistic context of other words and structures at different linguistic levels. The *social* context requires definition of lexical items in terms of a model of communication which, as far as possible and practicable, will encompass an account of *who* uses the word to *whom*, *when*, *where*, for *what* purpose and in connection with *what* topic. Any such model will be a dynamic one and will be subject to variation in the nature relative prominence of its features and will allow not so much for an *a priori* established meaning as for the emergence or negotiation of meaning.[2] However, such attempts to locate specific words or specific senses of words within a sociolinguistic context should not be taken to imply any abrogation of responsibility for specifying denotative features. The determination of associative meaning should not relieve lexicographic practice of the necessity, where relevant, for componential analytic definition. For example, it should be clear that only limited access is given to the meanings of a lexical set such as *impudent*, *rude*, *cheeky* or *saucy* if only *either* denotative *or* connotative properties are defined. If genuine lexical communicativity and greater refinement in both dictionary entries and vocabulary teaching materials is to be encouraged, then greater synthesis than at present of *both* dimensions is required. For a related argument for description of what he terms style values' see Hartmann (1981a; 1981b; 1983b).

The second relevant context in assessing lexical association is one of the other surrounding words. Such relationships are primarily collocational as described in Section 3.2. The basic premise here is that words are known by the company they keep and, as discussed in Chapter 6 (Section 6.6), advances in lexical computing are beginning to provide attestable data on such partnerships. Entries for words thus need to include information which takes account of relations of words which are intrinsically semantic, provides indices of frequency and habitualness of use and which reveals something of their sociolinguistic character. Restricting definition to only one aspect or plane of meaning', whatever the practical difficulties involved, may not make for a well-motivated lexicography. As Waldron (1967, p. 102) puts it: If words are so different in the kind of criteria involved in their use, the pattern of meaning made by their interrelation must be immensely more complex than a one-plane analogy can suggest.'

Words contain and conceal ideology. When we talk about the use of words *in context* it should not be forgotten that contexts are socially, sexually and politically constituted. For example, the word *democratic* means different things within different ideological frameworks. (For a good discussion of ideological problems in the writing of dictionary entries see Doroszewski (1974) – especially his analysis of the way items such as *strike-breakers* can mean very different things according to the political position taken; for discussion in relation to translation and foreign-language teaching see Brumfit, 1978.) Compilers of dictionaries need to be alert to such issues in the construction of examples as well as to the essentially conservative and dominant-ideology-preserving role of dictionaries in society (for initial discussion of this see Quirk, 1977). Additionally, it is important to bear in mind that English is an international language and that there are several cultures which use English as a second language or as an institutionalized variety. The kinds of associations described and the meanings defined in monolingual dictionaries for non-native speakers reflect usage in British English (though variants for American English are plentiful in *OALD*, 1995 and especially *LDOCE*, 1995). Thus, in important respects British culture will be lexicalized. The consequences of this are partly ideological and Kachru (1980) has pointed out the need for dictionaries, or at least dictionary supplements, of regional varieties of English. Kachru recognizes the complex issues of norms' and image' in connection with such varieties, but he also warns of inherent dangers of cultural hegemony in a world-wide use of dictionaries of British or American English. And there is extensive discussion of historical, etymological, cultural and ideological factors in the production of national variants of an English Dictionary' in Delbridge (1983).

The basic theoretical position adopted in this case study might be summarized as follows. The user of a dictionary needs to have information about the operation of words at different levels and about the interaction of words in and across levels. Thus definitions will include reference to phonology, grammar, componential semantics, lexical collocation, associations with communicative contexts and with cultural and ideological codes. Only by such means will an appropriate semantic profile be made available. The first part of this chapter has sought to describe recent advances at a number of such levels. The plane of associative meaning, is, as we have seen, particularly complex; but it is one which is relatively neglected in pedagogical lexicography and merits further examination.

9.2 Semantic space

The term **semantic space** is borrowed from Osgood *et al.* (1957). Their study is one – among very few – which explicitly tackles measurement of the associations or connotations of words (see Section 2.1.8). This was done in a series of essentially psycholinguistic experiments in which subjects are asked to rate words on a number of bipolar scales. The scales are marked at either end by antonyms (e.g. *weak–strong, rough–smooth, tense–relaxed*) but are graduated in a kind of cline to allow various degrees of intermediate choice between these extremes. When the points on all the various scales are linked up and averaged out across the number of subjects tested there emerges a semantic profile for the word in question: that is, we come to see, at least for the individuals concerned in the experiments, what kind of semantic space the word occupies. The most interesting conclusions from this study concern the three independent scales of meaning which are reported to have the greatest psychological reality. By far the most prominent of these is a scale of *evaluation* (exemplified most unequivocally by the extremes good'–bad'). The next most significant were found to be potency' (strong'–weak') and activity' (active'–passive'). Most of the words tested by Osgood *et al.* are words for concepts (e.g. *lady, sin, congress*, etc.) but the operation of the main scales can be exemplified in outline as follows:

1   *Evaluation*: Take the word *mean* and some of its main synonyms such as *parsimonious, thrifty, stingy, tight, ungenerous*. Without undertaking any tests it can probably be recognized that the words carry different degrees of evaluation. *Thrifty*, for example, would probably be more positively evaluated than, say, *stingy*, while *parsimonious* might occupy a place somewhere towards the neutral part of the positive'–negative' scale. Different words allow different judgemental attitudes to be recorded.

2   *Potency*: This scale allows for different degrees of intensity to be maintained in the way different words describe actions, events, conditions, etc. The following words would probably be differently marked according to the criterion of potency': *rude, impudent, cheeky, petulant, shameless, saucy, insulting*. For example, to call someone or some action *cheeky* is to attribute to it greater weakness (or seriousness) than to describe it as *insolent*. *Saucy* might be marked as even weaker and may – since there is overlap between scales – carry positive associations in certain contexts. (In fact, as far as words and ideology are concerned it would be interesting to test a hypothesis that *saucy* is usually attributed to women – by men – or to actions by women – and children?)

3   *Activity*: Whereas the potency scale is more connected with space, the activity scale has to do with the rapidity of movement expected of a stimulus-object. It is more of a temporal matter. For example, over a period of time business can *grow, develop, expand, stagnate, decline, prosper, progress*. Each of the words carries its own associations of activity/passivity.

Osgood *et al.* (1957) are quick to point out the obvious factor of overlap. For example, their research found that in general the scales representing the factor of activity were not as independent of other factors as (1) and (2) above; that is, items marked as active' overlapped regularly with positive' evaluation and strong' in potency. They stress, too, that these three scales are not the only independent dimensions, although repeated studies in a variety of cultures and with different sets of scales have consistently pointed to these three main dimensions as the ones that apply most generally and most saliently (Osgood, 1962). For purposes of summary and clarification a scalar map for the semantic scope of *rude* and related words is given in Figure 9.1a and a diagrammatic representation on the axes of evaluation and potency for *cheeky* in Figure 9.1b.

But one important scale or dimension in the semantic space of a word missing from Osgood's study is that of a cline for formality

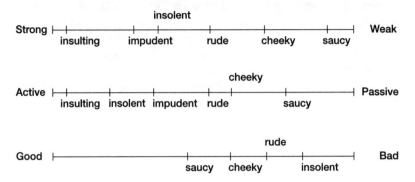

Figure 9.1a Representing semantic space: Using scales for words with the meaning rude'.

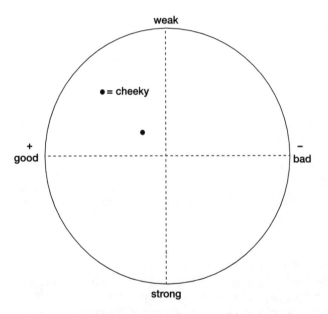

Figure 9.1b Representing semantic space: Diagrammatic presentation of the meaning of *cheeky*.

(informal–formal). This scale is distinctly sociolinguistic. The scales below embrace words in an attitudinal framework of a speaker's reactions and responses but a scale of formality would more directly reflect social practice in the use of words in communicative discourse between participants. The problems caused for foreign speakers of English in appropriately selecting from the many words for friend' (e.g. *mate*, *associate, colleague, pal, chum, buddy*, etc.) indicates the need for some greater precision and clarity in the presentation in the classroom, text-book and dictionary of what is essentially information concerning the degree of formality in the lexical relations contracted by the different words and generated in different contexts. If we return to the words for rude' (Figure 9.1) then the sociolinguistic account of the same words given by a formality cline (Figure 9.1c) adds a necessary and significant dimension. As in Figures 9.1a and b the model here is an idealized one and works only according to my own intuitive assessment. Actual inter-subjective tests may give very different results. Some useful words and word groupings for preliminary testing/scaling might include *bolshy, aggressive, contentious, quarrelsome, narky*, or *friendly, matey, amicable, fraternal, cordial, comradely*.

9.3 Informants and the measurement of meanings'

How is informant testing for lexical associations actually done? What kind of information does it provide? How subjective or objective is it? What are the advantages and disadvantages for lexicography and/or vocabulary teaching materials?

Informant testing is as fraught with difficulties as any attempt at assessment involving human judgement but some relatively large-scale studies using informants have been undertaken and information on par-ticular techniques developed is fairly accessible (Quirk and Greenbaum, 1970; Sinclair *et al.* 1970; Zgusta, 1971, pp. 235–9; Sinclair and Jones, 1974; Miller, 1971; Lehrer, 1974a; Carter, 1979, especially Ch. 4). Such studies demonstrate that the following are probably the main questions/problems to be resolved by researchers.

1   *How many informants to use:*
    There are a number of extrinsic factors here such as the size of the corpus of words to be tested, the availability of informants, costs incurred and so on. But a constant number needs to be fixed on to facilitate a regular statistical calculation of results. The number would need to be large enough to provide sufficiently representative

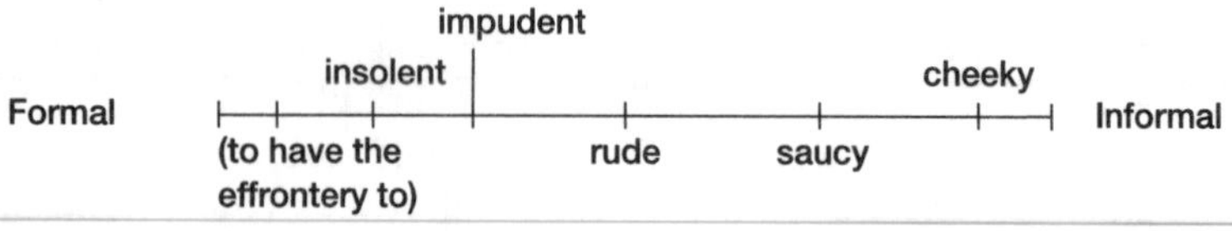

Figure 9.1c Representing semantic space: An informal–formal scale for words with the meaning rude'.

subdivision according to the kind of sociolinguistic criteria outlined in (2). By informants here is meant not the panel of experts in particular areas of usage to which lexicographers can refer, but non-specialists who will not necessarily be conscious of their native expertise in the language.

2   *How informants are to be selected:*
A range of criteria should be considered here in the light of the studies cited above but, for me, the most important are age, sex, social class and educational attainment. A range in the age of informants is important because it is in the nature of lexical associations to be subject to diachronic shifts in intensity, formality, etc. and thus in meaning. For example, *fab* or *gear* or *freak out* or *turn on* probably do not now have the expressive force once carried in the 1960s and could either not be recognized or simply not used by certain informants. In a related way, certain expressions may not be in general currency but may continue to be used by members of a particular generation (e.g. *we stayed at a hotel* may become *we put up at an hotel* in the usage of older informants). Sex and social-class related differences operate similarly (see Trudgill, 1974 for a host of examples); differences in educational attainment can produce different responses to words, especially along the formality cline – see (4) below. One final problem here is the very large numbers of informants needed to give adequately representative samples of responses to regionalisms or fully to mark differences in lexical associations for informants according to their geographical distribution. Recent studies (e.g. several articles collected in Trudgill, 1978) present refined techniques for measurement according to clear sociolinguistic criteria, but decisions about the numbers of informants required will affect whether such information is recorded in a standard' or a dialect' dictionary.

3   *In what kind of linguistic contexts are the target words to be presented:*
Labov (1972) reports results of informant tests which are obtained without the knowledge of the informant. These were face-to-face exchanges between the interviewer (using hidden microphones) and the informant, and in which the target word was elicited by a question which necessitated its use in reply. But Labov was testing for sociophonological variables rather than for lexical associations. Face-to-face spoken exchanges are the most natural and spontaneous means of elicitation. But it is both extremely time-consuming for the interviewer and difficult not only consistently and uniformly to elicit the required lexical items without

unnaturally forcing the conversation but also to allow for those inevitably shifting sociopersonal relationships between informant and interviewer which can condition which words are used. Under such circumstances considerable variations in language occur along the axis of encoder → decoder however constant the topic or setting or stated purpose of the discourse.

The most practicable procedure, therefore, may be to present the target words by means of written questionnaire. This is both economic and ensures a certain consistency of presentation. But problems must still be acknowledged. First, there is the nature of the linguistic context in which the word is situated. Is the word to be introduced in isolation or in the context of a phrase, clause, sentence or a higher level of organization? The argument for locating a target word in specific linguistic context is that measurement of its affective properties depends on responses to its actual use in connection with words and levels of language structure.

Secondly, the problem of a spoken/written continuum is never entirely eliminable when the test involves a written context. Given that one considerable advantage of informant analysis of this kind is that access is provided to less public, more intimate and colloquial lexical associations, there is a basic anomaly in eliciting such associations when the context is the rather more formal one of written text. That is, informants may respond differently to the same words when they hear them and in another way when they read them. For certain informants written contexts may be more or less of a norm. One factor here may be a different attitude to and value placed on the written word and literacy generally (see Milroy, 1980).

A basic tactic in the design of informant tests which takes account of the possible dangers and problems outlined here would be, as was the case with the literary tests in Chapter 8, to present the test words in the context of a questionnaire and to elicit responses to single words but to show the span of words to be in unambiguous relation to one another. This limits the lexical items to a syntagmatic axis only but it can serve to free them from *too* direct a correlation with written discourse. A further instruction could be given to informants that they are to imagine in their assessment of a word's associations that it is being employed in casual conversation'. (For further discussion of casual conversation' as a norm in sociolinguistic work on language variation see Crystal and Davy, 1969; Chan, 1974; Milroy, 1980.)

4 *How to cope with the observer's paradox:*

The paradox is that unselfconscious responses to language cannot easily be elicited because the observer's or informant's participation in an event changes the nature of the event; for example, a particular problem here is one of how to prevent the inherent formality of any test or questionnaire from conditioning responses to formality. That is, the nature of the exercise may result in words being assessed rather more formally (or weakly' or positively') than would be the response to them in the dynamism of actual discourse production. There is also the further problem that in a test' some informants may mark a word according to what they feel is expected of them. This can have important implications in the case of the more slang' or colloquial' items. What results may be the informant's *attitude* to a word rather than an accurate assessment of its communicative value. Such information would be in itself of interest to students of language but the nature of the information is difficult to isolate in the absence of follow-up interviewing. (For a related discussion of these problems see Béjoint, 1979.) Psycholinguists try to get round the observer's paradox by running experiments ostensibly about a completely different issue from the one being investigated, so that participants are not influenced by reflecting on what is expected of them.

5 *Which lexical items to select:*

From the point of view of recording results in dictionary entries or vocabulary teaching materials the criteria for selecting words for testing and for defining a core word around which results can be grouped needs to be explicitly worked out and stated. It is clear that in the initial stages of such work only a limited number of groups of words can carry assessment of their associative meaning. (Suggestions and procedures for this are developed in Section 9.4)

6 *How to account for collocability and associations:*

Associations can be changed slightly according to which words the tested item collocates with. My intuitions tell me that *cocky* collocates regularly with *little* (as in *cocky little devil*) or that *rough* collocates with *old* (as in *rough old pub, isn't it?*) Or, that *nice and* collocates regularly with many items especially on the positive side of an evaluation cline.[3] In eliciting lexical associations it should be remembered that tests need to be devised to allow adequate access to lexical collocations, particularly in informal discourse. However, much can depend on the nature of the texts used in the corpus.

There seem to be two main advantages to be derived from using informants. The first is that the facts' ascertained do have some **inter-subjective validity**. The results do not pretend to be completely objective (even if there is such a thing) but they do move us beyond the purely subjective whim of the lexicographer. The following statement in a paper by a well-known lexicographer to a seminar of the British Association of Applied Linguistics represents a rather random impressionism:

> Any attempt to write a completely analytical definition of any common word in natural language is absurd. Experience is too diverse for that. What a good dictionary offers instead is a typification. The dictionary definition summarises what the lexicographer finds to be the most typical common features, in his experience, of the use, context, and collocations of the word.
>
> (Hanks, 1979, p. 38)

(For a related argument see introduction to Hindmarsh, 1980.) Although the first two claims are fairly unexceptional, what is suggested by the claims for his experience' may be more dangerous. It abrogates to the experience of the sensitive individual lexicographer a double-edged authority'. First, the claim denies the need for the kind of empirical validation or substantiation which might be provided by the experience of others. Secondly, and a little more insidiously, the typification' imposes its own authority. People consult a dictionary as a source of authority. It does not interact with its readers. Its role can be to settle arguments about word meaning or use or spelling. What is typical about a word's meaning, collocational range or associations may perhaps be no more than the typical' experience of one individual or a small group of individuals. To some degree informant testing prevents a potential source of experience sensitivity and authority from becoming authoritarianism.[4]

The second main advantage is that such procedures allow some evidence to be available to support decisions concerning lexical associations and to enable a more precise and differentiated account to be given of terms like slang', colloquial', archaic', etc. For example, the *OED* entry for *slap* lists *slap down* as colloq.' (colloquial) while *slap-happy* and *slap-up* is cited as sl.' (slang). But there seem to be no clear operational criteria for the different terms. See also discussion of the lexeme *hang-up* in Hartmann (1981b).

Above all, and particularly where clines and scales are utilized, the use of informants' responses demonstrates an intrinsic principle of word meaning: that meaning is often gradable or negotiable rather than fixed. As far as social' meaning is concerned, there *emerges* a range of available meanings open to participants in discourse. Informant testing can help demarcate some limits and constraints on these patterns and ranges, and underline that the classification of a word as slang' or colloquial' can be potentially limiting as well as confusing, especially for the non-native speaker seeking to determine acceptability. Therefore the results of the tests are best viewed in the form of reasonable hypotheses which should be verified or adjusted in the light of linguistic findings.

9.4 Core vocabulary and the dictionary: A sample entry

In this section I discuss the crucial point of how the findings of informant research in lexical associations might be presented in a clear and accessible way. The example given is that of a dictionary entry but there is no reason why similar principles cannot be adopted for language teaching purposes. The case study outlined here is limited in the number and range of informants used (mostly family, friends and university students of English) and is described here only for purposes of illustration. The word concerned is *thin* and a range of its paradigmatic variants. The range affects uses of words meaning thin' applied to animate entities. In this instance the informant tests are restricted to two main scales: *formality* and *evaluation* (and it should be recognized that very different profiles might emerge from analysis from different scales). The results obtained here are interesting though perhaps not wholly unexpected. Conflating these results along a 1–10 formality cline (with informants asked to rate words according to a measure of 1 = informal : 10 = formal – see Chan, 1974 for discussion of acceptability to informants of the terms formal' and informal') the words are marked along the scale as shown in Figure 9.2a. The results on an evaluation scale are shown in Figure 9.2b.

Here the fact that two or three words belong in the positive dimension of the scale clearly demonstrates that semantically related words or words from a lexical set can be used and are regarded with different degrees of emotional or attitudinal attachment. To be *slim* is to be *thin*, but it is also to attract rather more approbation than to be *skinny*. See Waldron (1967, p. 89) for further discussion of what he terms the inherent emotive or evaluative attachments words carry. Good related examples he gives include *mutilate, cram, gloat* and *carp*. Also of significance is the instance of thin' being recorded in the middle of both scales (see the notion of a *core word* in Chapter 2). But the relative distance between words is more obvious, throwing into considerable doubt

a. *Formality scale*

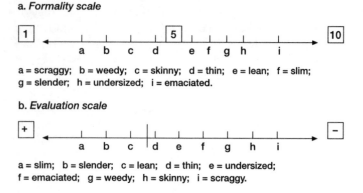

a = scraggy;   b = weedy;   c = skinny;   d = thin;   e = lean;   f = slim;
g = slender;   h = undersized;   i = emaciated.

b. *Evaluation scale*

a = slim;   b = slender;   c = lean;   d = thin;   e = undersized;
f = emaciated;   g = weedy;   h = skinny;   i = scraggy.

Figure 9.2 Two scales, to measure formality and evaluation, for words with the meaning thin'.

any supposition that *scraggy* is a proper synonym for *emaciated* or *slim*.

I have not discussed questions of activity' or potency' (it would be interesting to test what kind of associations are carried by *weedy* in this latter respect), or concealed ideological assumptions such as the fact that *slim* and *slender* may be more regularly connected with the female' figure (hence the fairly widespread use of *slender* in slimming advertisements). Neither has due consideration been given to possibilities for informants of associative overlap in the case of some words. *Lean*, for example, collocates with *meat* – its antonym might be *fatty* – and thus it is hard to know to what extent the positive evaluation may stem from this context. It must also be recognized that thin' has other paradigmatic variants: for example, thin' = fragile' as in *The defence looks a bit thin*. So must the regular use of thin' in idioms (see Figure 9.3). And, of course, not all the scales would be appropriate for all the words.

The multi-planed or multi-dimensional analysis of lexical information needs to be accessibly presented. Preferably the information needs to be stored under one entry in a dictionary and by the focus of one word for most teaching purposes. As most dictionary entries stand at present, the duplication of information relating to a lexical set seems unnecessarily uneconomic. Take, for example, two entries for slender' and slim' within one page of each other in the *OED*.

> *Slender*, a. Of small girth or breadth, slim not stout, (stem, waist, pillar, girl, hand); . . .

> *Slim*, a., + v.i. (-mm-) 1, Of small girth or thickness, slenderly built, of slight shape; . . .

THIN (c)

> (I) (a) Quality of size of people, animate objects. Lacking weight. Fat (ant.)
> *Thin* (C) (5+/–); *skinny* (3–); *weedy* (2–); *scraggy* (0/2–); *lean* (5/6+); *slim* (6+); *slender* (7/8+) (as *slim* especially of *woman's* figure); *undersized* (8–); *emaciated* (8/9 –).

(I)   (b) Relating to the narrow dimensions of the object e.g. a *thin* slice of bread; a *thin* strip of metal, etc.

(II) (a) = (i) fragile, flimsy, delicate, scanty, slight. Thick (ant.) (The defence looks very *thin*; This material is too *thin*). (ii) shallow, inauthentic (*thin* excuse, evidence, disguise). (iii) LEAN (a) not fatty (*lean* meat); (b) scarce, unprofitable (*lean* years, *lean* crops). (iv) SLIM etc.

(III) *Thin* (chance, hopes); slender (chance, opportunity, income, means, acquaintance); slim (chance) etc.

(IV) Through thick and *thin*; the *thin* end of the wedge; disappear into *thin* air; *thin*-skinned; all skin and bones, etc.

N.B. Entries for lexical items listed under (I) could simply be referred to the entry under the core word. e.g. Skinny – see THIN (C)

Figure 9.3 A dictionary entry for *thin*.

Similar repetitiveness can be found in entries for most of the other words distributed across our cline for thinness. It seems incongruous and wasteful to have an entry for skinny' citing emaciated' and an entry for emaciated' citing skinny' irrespective of any consideration of their synonymity.

The information about related words needs to be channelled through one entry focused on a core word. The core word may be defined in outline as that word from a related set which either:

1 contracts the most collocations with other words; or
2 has the greatest orientation towards the middle or neutral point in the range of scales/clines used for informant analysis; or
3 has the most other meanings; e.g. thin' = fragile', though there will be overlap with (1) here; or
4 usually has an accepted antonym; e.g. *thin–fat*. It is more difficult to find a precise antonym for more associative, less neutral items; e.g. *weedy, corpulent, obese*; or
5 cannot easily be defined in terms of the other words. For example,

in a set: *smile, grin, grimace* and *smirk* the last three words can be defined in terms of the first with a modifying adverb or adverbial phrase. To define smile requires a more basic conceptual–componential description. (For empirical tests along these lines see Carter, 1982c, and Section 2.2.); or

6   some combination of these factors. Relative coreness' can be defined in terms of the number of different criteria met by the core word.

To decide upon a core word is no easy task since it would seem to involve verification from a computer corpus (especially in the case of (1)), successful employment by informant testers of intuitions in the formation of an appropriate hypothesis (especially in the case of (2)) and (especially for (3)) extensive drawing on a team of experienced lexicographers.

But if this seems a complicated procedure then the saving in space plus the much more useful, pragmatic and interrelated information seems a considerable bonus. A good case could also be made for a dictionary or vocabulary-teaching materials to be organized around a limited number of core words as long as the criteria for their selection were explicitly worked out.

An entry for the thinness continuum – thin' taken as the core word – might run along lines as in Figure 9.3. The numbers 1–10 indicate the rating given to individual words along the formality cline. Here it should be noted that a vital ingredient in lexical associations – that of gradation and variability – can be preserved by not limiting words to one point in the scale. In fact, the more informants used the greater the likelihood of fuzziness in the rating of some words. Thus users can work with the notations in the form of hypotheses. The plus or minus marks (+, −) indicate which side of the evaluative line the word has been estimated. The results, it should be remembered, are based on *two* scales only. One principle of the notation system is to be as simple as possible but, if it were deemed necessary, notation for finer gradation along the evaluation scale can be devised as well as further scales introduced (see Figure 9.4). Roman numerals might demarcate the entry for a core word as follows:

Ia   – Scalar analysis of thin' (C = core word) and related items within a sense (here thinness relating to human and animate entities).

Ib   – Other neutral' uses of thin' and related words.

II   – Other meanings of thin' and related words with different parts of speech (IIi), (ii), (iii), etc.

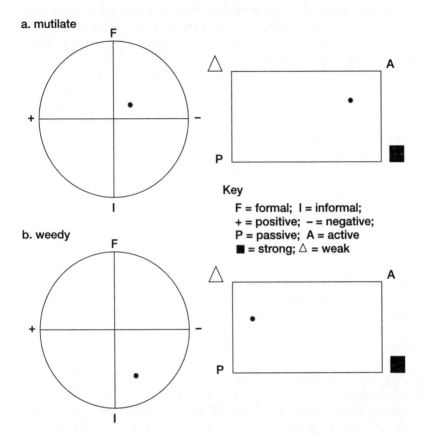

Figure 9.4 Diagrammatic representation of semantic space for two words.

III   – Indication of prominent collocability range of items listed under (I).

(IV) – Idioms; metaphoric and figurative range; tone.

Other important considerations apart, the conflation of eight or nine separate entries under one heading constitutes a tremendous saving in space.

9.5 Conclusion

A number of points remain unanswered and undeveloped. The first one is that the final example, *mutilate* (Figure 9.4), should serve as a reminder that a description of lexical associations, however delicate, will not necessarily deliver a comprehensive definition of a word's meaning. In this case a componential description is required to explain the semantic feature ± PARTS-OF-THE-HUMAN-BODY (as direct object) which differentiates *mutilate* from a supposed synonym such as *annihilate*. (See Sections 3.10 and 7.16, and Jain, 1979; 1981, for criticism of glossing techniques which set up false equivalences between lexical items.) Conversely, a componential description could not by itself capture essential differences in the way such words are used. Neither can it be forgotten that, however useful, the description of associations is *relative* both to the nature and limitations of the informant tests and to the particular scales and clines used.

Another question concerns the appropriate notation of a range of different types of lexical association. Useful discussions of the issues exist (e.g. Hartmann, 1981a; 1983b) and models have been developed which can be utilized in addition to those proposed in this chapter (see McDavid, 1979, and particularly the scalar analyses of Cassidy, 1972). In this connection, should potentially confusing descriptive terms such as colloquial' or slang' be dispensed with when it is possible for such notions to be appropriately graded on the formality cline?

Further interesting challenges accompany attempts to define the tone' of a word, something which in dictionaries is variously indicated by stylistic labels such as derogatory (derog.) or ironic (iron.).[5] How do we distinguish between lexical items which are intrinsically ironic'/sarcastic' (e.g. That's a bit *thick*'), occur in a set phrase (You're a *fine* one, you are!') or in longer stretches of text? What are the criteria for determining an archaic' tone for a word – an important element since such words can be used to produce distinct, usually humorous effects; for example, I like the look of your *steed*' or So this is your *abode*'. Furthermore, what in the nature of collocability relations would allow us to refer confidently to cliché' or stereotype' in the description of lexical items? And how can we incorporate acknowledgement of the ideological reinforcement carried not only by individual words but by some of our most common metaphoric expressions? (See Lakoff and Johnson, 1980, Lakoff and Turner, 1989, for a range of examples.)

Finally, such developments in the description of associations must not be allowed to outpace a constant evaluation of the needs of the user. As Béjoint (1981; 1994) and others have pointed out (see Section 6.2), innovations in lexicography cannot ignore the fact that many foreign-language learners use a dictionary primarily for reference, rather than for collocational information, or an assessment of the associative values of words. Innovations in this kind of area can easily result in notations which are either too complex or too finely differentiated for the usually conservative needs of the user; dictionaries and vocabulary-teaching materials dealing with the area of lexis and associative meaning need to provide clear encouragement and education as to their appropriate use.

But if pedagogical dictionaries are to encourage greater competence in the production of language, then greater refinement in the description of associative meaning does need to be introduced. It is in the light of the obvious need for a more communicative' approach to vocabulary study and teaching that this case study should be seen and judged.

9.5.1 *Further conclusion (1997)*

The arguments advanced in this chapter have been taken further and practically applied in a number of lexicographic contexts. For example, the *Longman Language Activator* (1994) (see Section 6.8) shows considerable potential for demarcating different levels of style and meaning in groups of synonymically arranged words. Also all recent editions of dictionaries produced for learners of English (see Section 6.7) have attempted to give more information concerning usage and to increase learners' understanding of pragmatic meaning of keywords; keywords which in some cases form a focal point around which other words are semantically grouped. And as advocated by Carter and Bool (1989), fuller attention has been accorded to the ways in which words encode cultural meanings, and how entries need to explain such meanings – a task often necessitated by lexicographic and related materials drawing on naturally occurring data which, by definition, has not been pedagogically mediated. For example, the *Longman Dictionary of English Language and Culture* (1992) is based on real examples from newspapers, films and television programmes which are used to explain the connotations, allusions and associations which many words carry, though the problem still remains, as argued in this chapter, of both finding an adequate notation for such meanings or any fully adequate means of representing such meanings for language learners.

What can help research to build on this chapter is fuller consideration of naturally occurring data together with fuller attention to the most pre-eminent pragmatic meanings which concordances reveal. Very often, as shown in the examples given in Section 3.6, words which appear to be neutral, and are often described in dictionaries in such terms, are revealed by corpus study to carry distinctively negative or positive meanings. See the pragmatic meanings which attach to verbs such as *set in* (see again Section 3.6), negative meanings carried by the verb *cause* (as in *cause trouble/accident/damage/concern*), or the correspondingly positive associative meanings carried by the verb *provide* (as in *provide comfort/relief/services/training*). Stubbs (1996, pp. 173ff) gives a range of further examples. Failure to observe naturally occurring data in the form of multi-million-word corpora can mean a failure to notice such features.

9.6 Coda

> Even when poetry has a meaning, as it usually has, it may be inadvisable to draw it out. Perfect understanding will sometimes almost extinguish pleasure.
>
> (A.E. Housman)

The tone of the conclusion to this final chapter of the book is typical of that adopted in a number of places in this book. This tone is characterized by a number of hedges, qualifications and notes of caution such as: *a number of questions remain unanswered*; *more research is needed*; *it is hoped that*; *greater refinement of description is required*.

In view of so much caution, and in the absence of answers to so many questions, it is a wonder the book has got written at all. Clearly much does need to be done both in the development of descriptive frameworks of the kind outlined in Chapters 1–4, in the domain of applications (covered in Chapters 5–7, though there are of course numerous other applications and potential applications), and in the extension of case studies both similar to and different from those undertaken in Chapters 8 and 9. Although there are undoubtedly many questions posed in this book, and although answers are not by any means readily available to all of them, it is clear that an increasing number of applied linguists are beginning to address such questions. Vocabulary is now on the agenda in several domains of applied language study.

One conclusion which can be drawn here is particularly apparent from the discussion in this final chapter . It is that, however detailed and systematic accounts of vocabulary will become, and however much more refined applications will develop, vocabulary will always be resistant to too great a degree of systematization. Fuzziness is an inherent characteristic of most words when located in contexts of use. One does not have to be a poet to realize that analysis can be destructive (though that is not a reason to suspend analysis) or to be A.E. Housman to believe that there is a sense in which words will always have the final word.

This book has set out to do little more than provide an overview of some selected perspectives on developments in vocabulary studies and to provide some starting points for further beginnings in the study of vocabulary and its uses. All perspectives are necessarily partial but this book will have been of some service if the biases of the guide are recognized at the same time as landmarks have been pointed out.

Notes

1 The term here is not used in the Saussurean sense of associative' which includes etymological, phonological and morphological interrelatedness between words. For helpful discussion, see Waldron (1967, pp. 96–8). For an interesting proposal for a lexicon designed along Saussurean associative lines, though with particular attention to computer-based measures of collocational frequency, see Makkai (1980).

2 Examples of lexical items with intrinsically negotiable meanings might be *politician, diligent, official*. Thus, *he's a good politician* can be construed positively or negatively depending on context; *diligent* can be used in a testimonial to damn or to praise. Negotiability is also directly related to prominence in speech; for example an *official* is likely to be interpreted with negative connotations. (See also McCarthy, 1984b; see also Section 4.3.)

3 It is interesting to compare the following:

These trousers are awfully tight	(–)
These trousers are tight	(±)
These trousers are nice and tight	(+)

4 For discussion along these lines see Wells (1973) and Barnhart (1980). The issue revolves around whether authority is interpreted as power to influence action, opinion or belief' or power to enforce obedience'. It is another example of the socio-ideological role of dictionaries.

5 Tones' in lexis is the subject of extensive discussion and an attempt at categorization in Empson (1951). But he ignores the *socio*linguistic' differentiation in tones (however difficult they may be to measure) carried by oppositions such as *patio/terrace, snaps/photos, restaurant/canteen, car/jalopy*, and their respective associations.

Bibliography

Adams, V. (1973) *An Introduction to Modern English Word-Formation* (London: Longman).

Aisenstadt, E. (1979) Collocability restrictions in dictionaries', in Hartmann, R.R.K. (ed.) (1979), pp. 71–4.

Aisenstadt, E. (1981) Restricted collocations in English lexicology and lexicography', *ITL (Institut voor Taege paste Linguistiek)*, vol. 53, pp. 53–61.

Aitchison, J. (1994) *Words in the Mind*, 2nd edn (Oxford: Blackwell).

Alatis, J.E. (ed.) (1972) *Studies in Honor of A.H. Marckwardt* (Washington, DC: TESOL).

Alderson, C. (1979) The cloze procedure and proficiency in English as a foreign language', *TESOL Quarterly*, vol. 13, no. 2, pp. 219–27.

Alderson, C. and Alvarez, C. (1978) The development of strategies for the assignment of semantic information to unknown lexemes in text', *Mextesol Journal*, vol. 2, no. 4, pp. 46–55.

Alexander, R.J. (1978) Fixed expressions in English: A linguistic, psycho-linguistic and didactic study', *Anglistik und Englischunterricht*, vol. 6, pp. 171–88.

Alexander, R.J. (1984a) Fixed expressions in English: Reference books and the teacher', *English Language Teaching Journal*, vol. 38, no. 2, pp. 127–34.

Alexander, R.J. (1984b) Idiomaticity and other related problems', manuscript, English Language Research, University of Birmingham.

Amante, D.J. (1980) Ironic language: A structuralist approach', *Language and Style*, vol. 13, no. 1, pp. 15–26.

Anderson, E.C. (1975) Cups and glasses: Learning that boundaries are vague', *Journal of Child Language*, vol. 2, pp. 79–103.

Anglin, T. (1970) *The Growth of Word Meaning* (Cambridge, Mass.: MIT Press).

Apresyan, Y.D., Mel'čuk, I.A and Žolkovsky, A.K. (1969) Semantics and Lexicography: Towards a new type of unilingual dictionary', in Kiefer, F. (ed.) (1969) pp. 1–33.

Arnaud, P. and Béjoint, H. (eds) (1992) *Vocabulary and Applied Linguistics* (Basingstoke: Macmillan).

Asch, S.E. and Nerlove, H. (1969) The development of double-function terms in children: An exploratory investigation' in de Cecco, J.P. (ed.) (1969) pp. 283–90.

Atkinson, R.C. and Raugh, M.R. (1975) An application of the mnemonic keyword method to the acquisition of a Russian vocabulary', *Journal of Experimental Psychology*, vol. 96, pp. 124–9.

Ayto, J. (1983) On specifying meaning', in Hartmann, R.R.K. (ed.) (1983a) pp. 89–98.

Barnhart, C. (1980) What makes a dictionary authoritative?', in Zgusta, L. (ed.) (1980) pp. 33–42.

Bauer, L. (1980) *Longman Dictionary of Contemporary English:* Review article', *RELC Journal*, vol. 11, no. 1, pp. 104–9.

Bauer, L. (1983) *English Word-Formation* (Cambridge: Cambridge University Press).

Baxter, J. (1980) The dictionary and vocabulary behaviour: A single word or a handful?', *TESOL Quarterly*, vol. 14, no. 3, pp. 325–36.

Bazell, C. (1954) The sememe' in Hamp, E. *et al.* (eds) (1954), pp. 329–41.

Bazell, C., Catford, J.C., Halliday, M.A.K. and Robins, R.H. (eds) (1966) *In Memory of J.R. Firth* (London: Longman).

Becker, J.D. (1975) The phrasal lexicon', in Nash-Webber, B. and Schank, R. (eds) (1975), pp. 70–3.

Béjoint, H. (1979) The use of informants in dictionary making', in Hartmann, R.R.K. (ed.) (1979) pp. 25–30.

Béjoint, H. (1981) The foreign student's use of monolingual dictionaries. A study of language needs and reference skills', *Applied Linguistics*, vol. 2, no. 3, pp. 207–22.

Béjoint, H. (1994) *Tradition and Innovation in Modern English Dictionaries* (Oxford: Clarendon Press).

Belsey, C. (1980) *Critical Practice* (London: Methuen).

Bennett, T. (1979) *Formalism and Marxism* (London: Methuen).

Benson, M. (1985) Collocations and idioms', in Ilson, R. (ed.) (1985b) pp. 61–8.

Benson, M., Benson, E. and Ilson, R. (1997) *The BBI Dictionary of English Word Combinations* (Amsterdam: John Benjamin).

Berlin, B. and Kay, P. (1969) *Basic Color Terms* (Berkeley, CA: University of California Press).

Berry, H.M. (1977) *Introduction to Systemic Linguistics*, vol. 2: *Levels and Links* (London: Batsford).

Bhaba, H. (1994) *The Location of Culture* (London: Routledge).

Biber, D. and Finegan, E. (1989) Styles of stance in English: Lexical and grammatical marking of evidentiality and affect', *Text*, vol. 9, no. 1, pp. 93–124.

Biggs, C. (1982) In a word, meaning', in Crystal, D. (ed.), pp. 108–21.

Bloomfield, L. (1933) *Language* (London: Allen & Unwin).

Blum, S. and Levenston, E.A. (1978) Universals of lexical simplification', *Language Learning*, vol. 18, no. 2, pp. 399–415.

Blum, S. and Levenston, E.A. (1979) Lexical simplification in second language acquisition', *Studies in Second Language Acquisition*, vol. 2, no. 2, pp. 57–76.

Bogaards, P. (1996) Dictionaries for learners of English', *International Journal of Lexicography*, vol. 9, no. 4, 277–320.

Bolinger, D. (1965) The atomization of meaning', *Language*, vol. 41, no. 4, pp. 555–73.

Bolinger, D. (1976) Meaning and memory', *Forum Linguisticum*, vol. 1, no. 1, pp. 1–14.

Bolinger, D. (1980) *Language: The Loaded Weapon* (London: Longman).

Bolinger, D. (1985) Defining the indefinable', in Ilson, R. (ed.) (1985b), pp. 69–73.

Bongers, H. (1947) *The History and Principles of Vocabulary Control* (Woerden: Wocopi).

Bowerman, M. (1978) The acquisition of word meanings: An investigation of some current conflicts', in Waterson, N. and Snow, C. (eds) (1978), pp. 263–85.

Bronzwaer, T. (1970) *Tense in the Novel: An Investigation of Some Potentialities of Linguistic Criticism* (Groningen: Wolters-Noordhof).

Brown, D. (1974) Advanced vocabulary teaching: The problem of collocation', *RELC Journal*, vol. 5, no. 2, pp. 1–11.

Brown, G. (1982) The spoken language', in Carter, R.A. (ed.) (1982b), pp. 75–87.

Brown, G. and Yule, G. (1983) *Discourse Analysis* (Cambridge: Cambridge University Press).

Brown, J. (1979) Vocabulary: Learning to be imprecise', *Modern English Teacher*, vol. 7, no. 1, pp. 25–8.

Brown, T.S. and Perry, F.L. Jnr (1991) A comparison of three learning strategies for ESL vocabulary acquisition', *TESOL Quarterly*, vol. 25, pp. 655–70.

Brumfit, C. (1978) The English language, ideology and international communication: Some issues arising out of English teaching for Chinese students', *ELT Documents: English as an International Language*, ETIC, The British Council, pp. 15–24.

Brumfit, C.J. (1981) Being interdisciplinary: Some problems facing applied linguistics', *Applied Linguistics*, vol. 2, no. 2, pp. 158–64.

Bruton, A. (1984) Review of Wallace, M., *Teaching Vocabulary*', *English Language Teaching Journal*, vol. 38, no. 1, pp. 58–60.

Bublitz, W. (1989) Repetition in spoken discourse', in Mullenbrock, H.J. and Noll-Wieman, R. (eds) *Anglistentag 1988 Göttingen: Vorträge* (Tübingen: Niemeyer), pp. 352–68.

Burgmeier, A., Eldred, G. and Boyd Zimmerman, C. (1991) *Lexis: Academic Vocabulary Study* (Englewood Cliffs, NJ: Prentice Hall).

Butler, C. (1984) *Interpretation, Deconstruction and Ideology* (Oxford: Clarendon Press).

Cameron, D. (1998) Dreaming the dictionary: *Keywords* and corpus linguistics', *Keywords: A journal of cultural materialism*, vol. 1, pp. 35–46.

Campbell, R. and Wales, R. (1970) The study of language acquisition', in Lyons, J. (ed.) (1970), pp. 242–60.

Carroll, J.B., Davies, P. and Richman, B. (1971) *The American Heritage Word Frequency Book* (New York, NY: American Heritage Pub. Co.).

Carter, R. (1978) Register, style and teaching some aspects of the language of literature', *Educational Review*, vol. 30, no. 3, pp. 227–36.

Carter, R. (1979) Towards a Theory of Discourse Stylistics', unpublished PhD dissertation, University of Birmingham.

Carter, R. (1981) Studying language: An integrated approach to lexis in literature', *English in Education*, vol. 15, no. 3, pp. 404–8.

Carter, R. (1982a) Responses to language in poetry', in Carter, R.A. and Burton, D. (eds) (1982), pp. 28–55.

Carter, R. (ed.) (1982b) *Linguistics and the Teacher* (London: Routledge and Kegan Paul).

Carter, R. (1982c) A note on core vocabulary', *Nottingham Linguistic Circular*, vol. 11, no. 2, pp. 39–51.

Carter, R. (1982d) Language, literacy and the assessment of language', *British Educational Research Journal*, vol. 8, no. 1, pp. 85–90.

Carter, R. (1983) You look nice and weedy these days: Lexical associations, lexicography and the foreign language learner', *Journal of Applied Language Study*, vol. 1, no. 2, pp. 172–89.

Carter, R. (1985a) Core vocabulary and discourse in the curriculum: A question of the subject', *XXth SEAMEO Regional Conference* (Conference Proceedings, RELC, Singapore).

Carter, R. (1985b) Stylistics', in *Annual Review of Applied Linguistics*, vol. 5, ed. Kaplan, R.B. (New York, NY: Cambridge University Press), pp. 92–100.

Carter, R. (1986) Good word!: Vocabulary, style and coherence in children's writing', in Harris, J. and Wilkinson, J. (eds) (1986) pp. 91–120.

Carter, R. (1988) Vocabulary, cloze and discourse', in Carter, R.A. and McCarthy, M.J. *Vocabulary and Language Teaching* (London: Longman), pp. 161–80.

Carter, R. (1997) *Investigating English Discourse: Language, literacy and literature* (London: Routledge).

Carter, R. and Bool, H. (1989) Vocabulary, culture and the dictionary', in Tickoo, M. (ed) *Learners' Dictionaries: State of the Art*, RELC Anthology Series 23 (Singapore: SEAMEO), pp. 172–82.

Carter, R. and Burton, D. (eds) (1982) *Literary Text and Language Study* (London: Edward Arnold).

Carter, R. and Long, M.N. (1987) *The Web of Words: Language-Based Approaches to Literature, Students' and Teachers' Books* (Cambridge: Cambridge University Press).

Carter, R. and Long, M.N. (1991) *Teaching Literature* (London: Longman).

Carter, R. and McCarthy, M. (1988) *Vocabulary and Language Teaching.* (London: Longman).

Carter, R. and McCarthy, M. (1997) *Exploring Spoken English* (Cambridge: Cambridge University Press).

Carter, R. and McCree, J. (eds) *Language, Literature and the Learner: Creative Classroom Practice* (Harlow: Longman).

Carter, R. and Nash, W. (1983) Language and literariness', *Prose Studies,* vol. 6, no. 2, pp. 124–41.

Carter, R. and Nash, W. (1990) *Seeing Through Language: A guide to styles of English writing* (Oxford: Blackwell).

Carter, R. and Nation, I.S.P. (eds) (1989) *Vocabulary Acquisition,* AILA Review, vol. 6.

Cassells, J.R.T. (1980) Language and learning – a chemist's view', *Teaching English,* vol. 14, no. 1, pp. 24–7.

Cassidy, F.G. (1972) Toward more objective labeling in dictionaries', in Alatis, J.E. (ed.) (1972), pp. 49–56.

Catford, J.C. (1983) Insects are free: Reflections on meaning in linguistics', *Language Learning,* vol. 33, no. 5, pp. 13–32.

Cecco, J.P. (ed.) (1969) *The Psychology of Language: Thought and Instruction* (New York: Holt, Rinehart and Winston).

Chan, R.K. (1974) A Methodology for the Analysis of Formality in English', unpublished PhD dissertation, University of Reading.

Channell, J. (1981) Applying semantic theory to vocabulary teaching', *English Language Teaching Journal,* vol. 35, no. 2, pp. 115–22.

Channell, J. (1988) Psycholinguistic considerations in the study of L2 vocabulary acquisition', in Carter, R. and McCarthy, M. (1988), pp. 83–96.

Channell, J. (1993) *Vague Language* (Oxford: Oxford University Press).

Chapin, P. (1971) What's in a word: Some considerations in lexicological theory', *Papers in Linguistics,* vol. 4, pp. 259–77.

Chatman, S. (ed.) (1971) *Literary Style: A Symposium* (Oxford: Oxford University Press).

Chilton, P. (1983) Autonomy and paradox in literary theory', *Journal of Literary Semantics,* vol. 12, no. 1, pp. 73–91.

Ching, M.K.L., Haley, M.C. and Lunsford, R.F. (eds) (1980) *Linguistic Perspectives on Literature* (London: Routledge & Kegan Paul).

Clark, E. (1973) What's in a word?', in Moore, T.E. (ed.) (1973), pp. 65–110.

Clark, E. (1993) *The Lexicon in Acquisition* (Cambridge: Cambridge University Press).

Clarke, D.F. and Nation, I.S.P. (1980) Guessing the meanings of words from context: Strategy and techniques', *System,* vol. 8, no. 3, pp. 211–20.

Clear, J., Fox, G., Francis, G., Krishnamurty, R. and Moon, R. (1996) COBUILD: The state of the art', *International Journal of Corpus Linguistics,* vol. 1, no. 2, pp. 305–16.

Cluysenaar, A. (1976) *Introduction to Literary Stylistics: A Discussion of Dominant Structures in Verse and Prose* (London: Batsford).

Coady, J. and Huckin, T. (eds) (1997) *Second Language Vocabulary Acquisition* (Cambridge, Cambridge University Press).

COBUILD (1996) *Grammar Patterns: 1. Verbs* (Glasgow and London: Harper Collins).

Cohen, A. and Aphek, E. (1980) Retention of second language vocabulary over time: Investigating the role of mnemonic associations', *System*, vol. 8, no. 3, pp. 221–35.

Cohen, J. (1979) The semantics of metaphor', in Ortony, A. (ed.) (1979), pp. 65–77.

Cole, P. (ed.) (1978) *Syntax and Semantics*: Vol. 9, *Pragmatics* (New York: Academic Press).

Cole, P. and Morgan, J.L. (eds) (1975) *Syntax and Semantics*: Vol. 3, *Speech Aids* (New York: Academic Press).

Congleton, J.E., Gates, Edward J. and Hobar, Donald (eds) (1979) *Paper in Lexicography in Honour of W.N. Cordell*, Dictionary Society of North America (Terre Haute, IN: Indiana State University).

Cook, G. (1990) *Discourse* (Oxford: Oxford University Press).

Cook, G. (1992) *The Discourse of Advertising* (Oxford: Oxford University Press).

Cornu, A.M. (1979) The first step in vocabulary teaching', *Modern Languages Journal*, vol. 63, pp. 262–72.

Corson, D. (1985) *The Lexical Bar* (Oxford: Pergammon).

Coulmas, F. (1979) On the sociolinguistic relevance of routine formulae', *Journal of Pragmatics*, vol. 3, pp. 238–66.

Cowie, A.P. (1978) The place of illustrative material and collocations in the design of a learner's dictionary', in Strevens, P. (ed.) (1978), pp. 127–39.

Cowie, A.P. (1981) The treatment of collocations and idioms in learner dictionaries', *Applied Linguistics*, vol. 2, no. 3, pp. 223–35.

Cowie, A.P. (1982) Polysemy and the structure of lexical fields', *Nottingham Linguistic Circular*, vol. 11, no. 2, pp. 51–64.

Cowie, A.P. (1983a) On specifying grammar', in Hartmann, R.R.K. (ed.) (1983), pp. 99–108.

Cowie, A.P. (1983b) English dictionaries for the foreign learner', in Hartmann, R.R.K. (ed.) (1983), pp. 135–43.

Cowie, A.P. (1984) Review of Meara, P., *Vocabulary in a Second Language*', *Reading in a Second Language*, vol. 1, no. 2, pp. 198–204.

Cowie, A.P. (1988) Stable and creative aspects of vocabulary use', in Carter, R. and McCarthy, M. (1988), pp. 126–39.

Craik, F.I.M. and Lockhart, R.S. (1972) Levels of processing: A framework for memory record', *Journal of Verbal Learning and Verbal Behaviour*, vol. 11, pp. 671–84.

Craik, F.I.M. and Tulving, E. (1975) Depth of processing and the retention of words in episodic memory', *Journal of Experimental Psychology*, vol. 104, pp. 268–84.

Crismore, A. (1990) Metadiscourse and discourse processes', *Discourse Processes*, vol. 13, pp. 191–205.

Crombie, W. (1985) *Process and Relation in Discourse and Language Learning* (Oxford: Oxford University Press).

Crothers, E. and Suppes, P. (1967) *Experiments in Second Language Learning* (New York: Academic Press).

Crow, J.T. and Quigley, J.R. (1985) A semantic field approach to passive vocabulary acquisition for reading comprehension', *TESOL Quarterly*, vol. 19, pp. 497–513.

Cruse, D.A. (1977) The pragmatics of lexical specificity', *Journal of Linguistics*, vol. 13, pp. 153–64.

Cruse, D.A. (1982) On lexical ambiguity', *Nottingham Linguistic Circular*, vol. 11, no. 2, pp. 65–80.

Cruse, D.A. (1986) *Lexical Semantics* (Cambridge: Cambridge University Press).

Crystal, D. (1972) Objective and subjective in stylistic analysis', in Kachru, B. and Stahlke, H. (eds) (1972), pp. 103–14.

Crystal, D. (1980a) Neglected grammatical factors in conversational English', in Greenbaum, S. *et al.* (eds) (1980), pp. 153–66.

Crystal, D. (1980b) *A Dictionary of Linguistics and Phonetics* (London: Deutsch).

Crystal, D. (1981) *Directions in Applied Linguistics* (London: Academic Press).

Crystal, D. (ed.) (1982) *Linguistic Controversies* (London: Edward Arnold).

Crystal, D. and Davie, D. (1969) *Investigating English Style* (London: Longman).

Cummins, J. and Simmons, R. (1983) *The Language of Literature* (London: Pergamon).

Cutler, A. and Fay, D. (1982) One mental lexicon, phonologically arranged', *Linguistic Inquiry*, vol. 13, no. 1, pp. 107–13.

Davie, D. (1967) *The Purity of Diction in English Verse*, rev. edn (London: Chatto & Windus).

Davies, A., Howart, A. and Criper, C. (eds) (1984) *Interlanguage* (Edinburgh: Edinburgh University Press).

Deese, J. (1965) *The Structure of Associations in Language and Thought* (Baltimore: Johns Hopkins Press).

Delbridge, A. (1983) On national variants of the English dictionary', in Hartmann, R.R.K. (ed.) (1983a), pp. 23–40.

Deyes, A. (1984) Towards an authentic discourse cloze', *Applied Linguistics*, vol. 5, no. 2, pp. 128–37.

Dillon, G.L. (1981) *Constructing Texts* (Bloomington, IN: Indiana University Press).

Dixon, R.M.W. (1971) A method of semantic description', in Steinberg, D. and Jakobovits, L.A. (eds) (1971), pp. 436–70.

Doroszewski, W. (1974) *Elements of Lexicology and Semiotics* (The Hague: Mouton).

Dressler, W. (1970) Towards a semantic deep structure of discourse grammar', in *Papers from the 6th Regional Meeting of the Chicago Linguistic Society*, (Urbana, IL: University of Illinois Press).

Eagleton, T. (1983) *Literary Theory* (Oxford: Blackwell).

Eaton, T. (1972) *Theoretical Semics* (The Hague: Mouton).

Eaton, T. (1978) Literary semantics: Modality and "style"', *Journal of Literary Semantics*, vol. 7, pp. 5–28.

Eliot, T.S. (ed) (1954) *Literary Essays of Ezra Pound* (London: Faber).

Elliot, A. (1981) *Child Language* (Cambridge: Cambridge University Press).

Ellis, N. (ed.) (1994) *Implicit and Explicit Learning of Languages* (London: Academic Press).

Ellis, N. (1995) Vocabulary acquisition: Psychological perspectives and pedagogical implications', *The Language Teacher*, vol. 19, no. 2, pp. 12–16.

Ellis, R. (1984) *Classroom Second Language Development* (Oxford: Pergamon).

Ellis, R. (1985) *Understanding Second Language Acquisition* (Oxford: Oxford University Press).

Empson, W. (1951) *The Structure of Complex Words* (London: Chatto & Windus).

Engels, L. (1988) The effect of spoken and written-to-be-spoken English on word frequency counts of written English', in Klegraf, J. and Nehls, D. (eds) (1988) *Essays on the English Language and Applied Linguistics on the Occasion of Gerhard Nickel's 60th Birthday* (Heidelberg: Julius Groos), pp. 407–25.

Fairclough, N. (1995) *Critical Discourse Analysis* (London: Longman).

Fay, D. and Cutler, A. (1977) Malapropisms and the structure of the mental lexicon', *Linguistic Inquiry*, vol. 8, no. 3, pp. 505–20.

Fernando, C. (1996) *Idioms and Idiomaticity* (Oxford: Oxford University Press).

Fernando, C. and Flavell, R. (1981) *On Idiom: Critical Views and Perspectives* (published by Exeter Linguistic Studies: University of Exeter).

Firth, J.R. (1957) The technique of semantics', in *Papers in Linguistics 1934–51* (Oxford: Oxford University Press).

Fish, S. (1970) Literature in the reader: Affective stylistics', *New Literary History*, vol. 2, pp. 123–61.

Fish, S. (1980) *Is There a Text in This Class?: The Authority of Interpretive Communities* (Cambridge, MA: Harvard University Press).

Fletcher, P. and Garman, M. (eds) (1979) *Language Acquisition* (Cambridge: Cambridge University Press).

Foley, J. (1983) More questions on assumptions about cloze testing', *RELC Journal*, vol. 14, no. 1, pp. 57–69.

Foley, J. (ed.) (1996) *J.M. Sinclair on Lexis and Lexicography* (Singapore: Unipress).

Fowler, R. (1982a) *Literature as Social Discourse: The Practice of Linguistic Criticism* (London: Batsford).

Fowler, R. (1982b) Anti-language in fiction', in Fowler, R. (1982a), pp. 142–61.

Fowler, R. (1991) *Language in the News: Discourse and ideology in the press* (London: Routledge).

Fowler, R., Kress, G., Hodge, R. and Trew, T. (1979) *Language and Control* (London: Routledge & Kegan Paul).

Fox, J. and Mahood, J. (1982) Lexicons and the ELT materials writer', *English Language Teaching Journal*, vol. 36, no. 2, pp. 125–9.

Francis, G. (1985) *Anaphoric Nouns*, Discourse Analysis Monographs, 11 (English Language Research, University of Birmingham).

Francis, G. (1994) Labelling Discourse: An aspect of nominal-group lexical cohesion', in Coulthard, M. (ed.) *Advances in Written Text Analysis* (London: Routledge).

Fromkin, V. (1980) *Errors in Linguistic Performance* (New York: Academic Press).

Gairns, R, and Redman, S. (1986) *Working with Words* (Cambridge: Cambridge University Press).

Gardner, H., Kircher, M., Winner, E. and Perkins, D. (1975) Children's metaphoric productions and preferences', *Journal of Child Language*, vol. 2, pp. 125–41.

Gass, S. and Selinker, L. (eds) (1983) *Language Transfer in Language Learning* (Rowley, MA: Newbury House).

Ghadessy, M. (1979) Frequency counts, word lists and materials preparation: A new approach', *Forum*, vol. 17, no. 1, pp. 24–7.

Gibbs, R. (1994) *The Poetics of Mind* (Cambridge: Cambridge University Press).

Giles, S. R. (1983) Delimited by discourse: Some problems with the new critical practice', *Renaissance and Modern Studies*, vol. 27, pp. 139–50.

Gimson, A.C. (1981) Pronunciation in EFL dictionaries', *Applied Linguistics*, vol. 2, no. 3, pp. 250–62.

Givon, T. (ed.) (1979) *Syntax and Semantics 12: Discourse and Syntax* (London: Academic Press).

Gleason, H.A. (1961) *An Introduction to Descriptive Linguistics* (New York: Holt & Rinehart).

Goatly, A. (1997) *The Language of Metaphors* (London: Routledge).

Goodale, M. (1995) *English Dictionary Workbook* (London: HarperCollins).

Goodenough, W.H. (1956) Componential analysis and the study of meaning', *Language*, vol. 32, pp. 195–216.

Goodman, K.S. (1967) Reading: A psycholinguistic guessing game', *Journal of the Reading Specialist*, College Reading Association, vol. 6, pp. 259–64 and 266–71.

Greenbaum, S. (1970) *Verb-Intensifier Collocations in English* (The Hague: Mouton).

Greenbaum, S., Leech, G.N. and Svartvik, J. (eds) (1980) *Studies in English Linguistics for Randolph Quirk* (London: Longman).

Greenberg, J.H., Ferguson, C.A. and Moravesik, E. (eds) (1978) *Universals of Human Language*: Vol. 3, *Word Structure* (Stanford: Stanford University Press).

Grice, P. (1975) Logic and conversation', in Cole, P. and Morgan, J.L. (eds) (1975), pp. 51–8.

Grice, P. (1978) Further notes on logic and conversation', in Cole, P. (ed.) (1978), pp. 113–27.

Grieve, R. and Hoogenraad, R. (1979) First words', in Fletcher, P. and Garman, M. (eds) (1979), pp. 93–104.

Guiraud, P. (1971) Immanence and transitivity of stylistic criteria', in Chatman, S. (ed.) (1971), pp. 16–23

Gutwinski, W. (1976) *Cohesion in Literary Texts* (The Hague: Mouton).

Hale, K. (1971) A note on a Walbiri tradition of antonymy', in Steinberg, D. and Jakobovits, L.A. (eds) (1971), pp. 472–83.

Halliday, M.A.K. (1964) Descriptive linguistics in literary studies', in Halliday, M.A.K. and McIntosh, A. (eds) (1966), *Patterns of Language: Papers in General, Descriptive and Applied Linguistics* (London: Longman), pp. 56–69.

Halliday, M.A.K. (1966) Lexis as a linguistic level', in Bazell, C. *et al.* (eds) (1966), pp. 148–62.

Halliday, M.A.K. (1975) *Learning How to Mean* (London: Arnold).

Halliday, M.A.K. (1978) Antilanguages', in *Language as Social Semiotic* (London: Edward Arnold), pp. 164–82.

Halliday, M.A.K. (1989) *Spoken and Written Language* (Oxford: Oxford University Press).

Halliday, M.A.K. and Fawcett, R.P. (eds) (1987) *New Developments in Systemic Linguistics, Vol. 1: Theory and Description* (London: Francis Pinter).

Halliday, M.A.K. and Hasan, R. (1976) *Cohesion in English* (London: Longman).

Hamp, E., Householder, F. and Austerlitz, R. (eds) (1954) *Readings in Linguistics*, vol. 2 (Chicago, IL: University of Chicago Press).

Hanks, P. (1979) To what extent does a dictionary definition define?' in Hartmann, R.R.K. (ed.) (1979), pp. 32–8.

Harmer, J. and Rossner, R. (1991) *More Than Words* (London: Longman).

Harpin, W. (1976) *The Second R': Writing Development in the Junior School* (London: Allen & Unwin).

Harris, J. and Wilkinson, J. (1986) *Reading Children's Writing: A Linguistic View* (London: Allen & Unwin).

Hartmann, R.R.K. (ed.) (1979) *Dictionaries and Their Users*, Papers from the 1978 BAAL Seminar on Lexicography, *Exeter Linguistic Studies*, vol. 1, no. 4.

Hartmann, R.R.K. (1981a) Style values: Linguistic approaches and lexicographical practice', *Applied Linguistics*, vol. 2, no. 3, pp. 263–73.

Hartmann, R.R.K. (1981b) Dictionaries, learners, users: Some issues in lexicography. Review Article', *Applied Linguistics*, vol. 2, no. 3, pp. 297–303.

Hartmann, R.R.K. (ed.) (1983a) *Lexicography: Principles and Practice* (London: Academic Press).

Hartmann, R.R.K. (1983b) On specifying context', in Hartmann, R.R.K. (ed.) (1983a), pp. 109–19.

Hartmann, R.R.K. (ed.) (1984) *LEXeter '83 Proceedings* (Tübingen: Max Niemeyer).

Harvey, P.D. (1983) Vocabulary learning: The use of grids', *English Language Teaching Journal*, vol. 37, no. 3, pp. 243–6.

Hasan, R. (1971) Rime and reason in literature', in Chatman, S. (ed.) (1971), pp. 299–329.

Hasan, R. (1980) The texture of a text', in Halliday, M.A.K. and Hasan, R., *Text and Context: Aspects of Language in a Social Semiotic Perspective* (Tokyo: Sophia University).

Hasan, R. (1984) Coherence and cohesive harmony', in Flood, J. (ed.) *Understanding Reading Comprehension* (Newark, Del.: International Reading Association), pp. 181–219.

Hasan, R. (1987) The grammarian's dream: Lexis as most delicate grammar', in Halliday, M.A.K. and Fawcett, R.P. (eds).

Hatch, E. and Brown, C. (1995) *Vocabulary, Semantics and Language Education* (Cambridge: Cambridge University Press).

Herbst, T. (1996) On the way to the perfect learners' dictionary: a first comparison of OALD5, LDOCE3, COBUILD2 and CIDE', *International Journal of Lexicography*, vol. 9, no. 4, 321–57.

Herrnstein-Smith, B. (1978) *On the Margins of Discourse: The Relation of Literature to Language* (London & Chicago, IL: University of Chicago Press).

Hindmarsh, R. (1980) *Cambridge English Lexicon* (Cambridge: Cambridge University Press).

Hoey, M. (1983) *On the Surface of Discourse* (London: Allen & Unwin).

Hoey, M. (1991) *Lexis in Text* (Oxford: Oxford University Press).

Hofland, K. and Johannson, S. (1982) *Word Frequencies in British and American English* (Bergen: Norwegian Computing Centre for the Humanities).

Holub, R. (1984) *Reception Theory* (London: Methuen).

Honeyfield, J. (1977) Word frequency and the importance of context in vocabulary learning', *RELC Journal*, vol. 8, no. 2, pp. 35–42.

Hornby, A.S. (1948) *A Learner's Dictionary of Current English* (London: Oxford University Press).

Howatt, A.R.P. (1983) *A History of English Language Teaching* (London: Oxford University Press).

Huckin, T., Haynes, M. and Coady, J. (eds) (1993) *Second Language Reading and Vocabulary Learning* (Norwood, NJ: Lawrence Erlbaum Associates).

Hudson, R.A. (1980) *Sociolinguistics* (Cambridge: Cambridge University Press).

Hulstijn, J. (1992) Retention of inferred and given word meanings: Experiments in incidental vocabulary learning', in Arnaud, P. and Béjoint, H. (eds) *Vocabulary and Applied Linguistics* (Basingstoke: Macmillan), pp. 113–25.

Hunston, S., Francis, G. and Manning, E. (1997) Grammar and vocabulary: showing the connections', *English Language Teaching Journal*, vol. 51, no. 3, pp. 208–16.

Hutchinson, T. and Waters, A. (1981), Performance and competence in ESP', *Applied Linguistics*, vol. 2, no. 1, pp. 46–59.

Ilson, R. (1983) Etymological information: Can it help our students?', *English Language Teaching Journal*, vol. 37, no. 1, pp. 76–82.

Ilson, R. (1985a) The linguistic significance of some lexicographic conventions', *Applied Linguistics*, vol. 6, no. 2, pp. 162–72.

Ilson, R. (ed.) (1985b), *Dictionaries, Lexicography and Language Learning* (Oxford: Pergamon/The British Council).

Jain, M.P. (1979) *Longman Dictionary of Contemporary English*: Review Article', *Indian Journal of Applied Linguistics*, vol. 4, no. 1, pp. 86–104.

Jain, M.P. (1981) On meaning in the foreign learner's dictionary', *Applied Linguistics*, vol. 2, no. 3, pp. 276–86.

Jeffries, L. and Willis, P. (1982a) Review of McArthur, T., *Longman Lexicon of Contemporary English*', *English Language Teaching Journal*, vol. 36, no. 4, pp. 277–8.

Jeffries, L. and Willis, P. (1982b) Participant (case) roles and lexical analysis', *Nottingham Linguistic Circular*, vol. 11, no. 2, pp. 1–19.

Johnson, R.K. (1981) Questioning some assumptions about cloze testing', in Read, J.A.S. (ed.) (1981), pp. 177–206.

Jordens, P. and Kellerman, E. (1981) Investigations into "transfer strategy" in second language learning', in Savard, J. and Laforge, L. (eds) (1981), pp. 195–215.

Judd, E.L. (1978) Vocabulary teaching and TESOL: A need for re-evaluation of existing assumptions', *TESOL Quarterly*, vol. 12, no. 1, pp. 71–6.

Kachru, B. (1980) The new English and old dictionaries: Directions in lexico-graphical research on non-native varieties of English', in Zgusta, L. (ed.) (1980), pp. 71–104.

Kachru, B. and Stahlke, H. (eds) (1972) *Current Trends in Stylistics* (Edmonton: Linguistic Research Inc.)

Kaplan, R. (ed.) (1980) *On the Scope of Applied Linguistics* (New York, NY: Newbury House).

Kates, C.A. (1980) *Pragmatics and Semantics* (Ithaca, NY: Cornell University Press).

Katz, J.J. and Fodor, J.A. (1963) The structure of a semantic theory', *Language*, vol. 39, pp. 170–210.

Keen, J. (1978) *Teaching English: A Linguistic Approach* (London: Methuen).

Keller, E. and Warner, S.T. (1976) *Gambits*: Vols I–II (Ottawa, Canada: Public Service Commission, Supply and Services).

Kellerman, E. (1977) Towards a characterisation of the strategy of transfer in second language learning', *Interlanguage Studies Bulletin*, vol. 2, no. 1, pp. 58–145.

Kellerman, E. (1983) Now you see it, now you don't', in Gass, S. and Selinker, L. (eds) (1983), pp. 112–34.

Kellogg, G.S. and Howe, M.J.A. (1971) Using words and pictures in foreign language learning', *Alberta Journal of Educational Research*, vol. 17, pp. 89–94.

Kiefer, F. (ed.) (1969) *Studies in Syntax and Semantics* (Dordrecht: Reidel).

Kintgen, E.R. (1984) *The Perception of Poetry* (Bloomington, IN: Indiana University Press).

Krashen, S.O. (1981) *Second Language Acquisition and Learning* (Oxford: Pergamon).

Krashen, S.O. (1989) We acquire vocabulary and spelling by reading:

Additional evidence for the input hypothesis', *Modern Languages Journal*, vol. 73, pp. 445–64.

Kress, G. and Hodge, R. (1993) *Language as Ideology*, 2nd edn (London: Routledge).

Kruse, A.F. (1979) Vocabulary in context', *English Language Teaching Journal*, vol. 33, no. 3, pp. 207–13.

Kuchera, H. and Francis, W.N. (1967) *A Computational Analysis of Present-Day American English* (Providence, RI: Brown University Press).

Kuhns, R. (1972) Semantics for literary languages', *New Literary History*, vol. 4, no. 1, pp. 91–106.

Labov, W. (1972) *Sociolinguistic Patterns* (UK edition, 1978, Oxford: Blackwell).

Lakoff, G. (1973) Hedges and meaning criteria', in McDavid, R. and Duckert, A.R. (eds) (1973), pp. 144–53.

Lakoff, G. and Johnson, M. (1980) *Metaphors We Live By* (Chicago, IL: University of Chicago Press).

Lakoff, G. and Turner, M. (1989) *More than Cool Reason: A Field Guide to Poetic Metaphor* (Chicago: University of Chicago Press).

Lam, A. (1984) The relative importance of content words and function words in the reading comprehension of English as a second language learners', Ann Arbor, MI: University Microfilms.

Laufer, B. (1997) What's in a word that makes it hard or easy: some intralexical factors that affect the learning of words', in Schmitt, N. and McCarthy, M. (eds).

Lazar, G. (1996) Using figurative language to expand students' vocabulary', *English Language Teaching Journal*, vol. 50, no. 1, pp. 43–50.

Leech, G.N. (1969) *A Linguistic Guide to English Poetry* (London: Longman).

Leech, G.N. (1981) *Semantics*, 2nd edn (Harmondsworth: Penguin).

Leech, G.N. (1983a) Pragmatics, discourse analysis, stylistics and "The Celebrated Letter"', *Prose Studies*, vol. 6, no. 2, pp. 142–57.

Leech, G.N. (1983b) *Principles of Pragmatics* (London: Longman).

Leech, G.N. and Short, M.H. (1981) *Style in Fiction* (London: Longman).

Lehrer, A. (1974a) Homonymy and polysemy: Measuring similarity in meaning', *Language Sciences*, 3, pp. 33–9.

Lehrer, A. (1974b) *Semantic Fields and Lexical Structure* (London: Elsevier).

Levenston, E.A. (1976) The contextualisation of lyric poetry', *Journal of Literary Semantics*, vol. 5, no. 2, pp. 61–77.

Levenston, E.A. (1979) Second language acquisition: Issues and problems', *Interlanguage Studies Bulletin*, vol. 4, no. 2, pp. 147–60.

Levinson, S. (1983) *Pragmatics* (Cambridge: Cambridge University Press).

Lewis, M. (1993) *The Lexical Approach: The state of ELT and a way forward* (Hove: Language Teaching Publications).

Lewis, M. (1997) *Implementing The Lexical Approach* (Hove: Language Teaching Publications).

Lipski, J.M. (1976) On the metastructures of literary discourse', *Journal of Literary Semantics*, vol. 5, no. 2, pp. 53–61.

Lock, A. and Fisher, E. (eds) (1984) *Language Development* (London: Croom Helm).

Lodge, D. (1977) *The Modes of Modern Writing: Metaphor, Metonymy and the Typology of Modern Literature* (London: Edward Arnold).

Long, M.N. and Nation, I.S.P. (1980) *Readthru* (Singapore: Longmans).

Lord, R. (1974) Learning vocabulary', *International Review of Applied Linguistics*, vol. 12, no. 3, pp. 239–47.

Louw, W. (1993) Irony in the text or insincerity in the writer?: The diagnostic potential of semantic prosodies', in M. Baker *et al.* (eds) *Text and Technology* (Amsterdam: John Benjamin), pp. 157–76.

Low, G. (1988) On teaching metaphor', Applied Linguistics, vol. 9, no. 2, pp. 125–47.

Lyne, A.A. (1983) Word frequency counts: Their particular reference to the description of languages for special purposes and a technique for enhancing their usefulness', *Nottingham Linguistic Circular*, vol. 12, no. 2, pp. 130–40.

Lyons, J. (1968) *An Introduction to Theoretical Linguistics* (Cambridge: Cambridge University Press).

Lyons, J. (ed.) (1970) *New Horizons in Linguistics* (Harmondsworth: Penguin).

Lyons, J. (1977) *Semantics*, 2 vols (Cambridge: Cambridge University Press).

Lyons, J. (1981) *Language, Meaning and Context* (London: Fontana).

McArthur, T. (1978) The vocabulary control movement in the English language, 1844–1953', *Indian Journal of Applied Linguistics*, vol. 4, no. 1, pp. 47–68.

McCarthy, M. (1984a) A new look at vocabulary in EFL', *Applied Linguistics*, vol. 5, no. 1, pp. 12–21.

McCarthy, M. (1984b) Some pragmatic features of written text', manuscript, English Language Research, University of Birmingham.

McCarthy, M. (1988) Some vocabulary patterns to conversation in Carter, R. and McCarthy, M. (1988), pp. 181–200.

McCarthy, M. (1990) *Vocabulary* (Oxford: Oxford University Press).

McCarthy, M. and Carter, R.A. (1994) *Language as Discourse: Perspectives for language teaching* (London: Longman).

McCarthy, M. and Carter, R. (1997) Written and Spoken Vocabulary', in Schmitt, N. and McCarthy, M. (eds) (1997), pp. 20–39.

McCarthy, M. and O'Dell, F. (1994) *English Vocabulary in Use* (Cambridge: Cambridge University Press).

McCarthy, M., MacLean, A. and O'Malley P. (1985) *Proficiency Plus: Grammar, Lexis, Discourse* (Oxford: Blackwell).

McDavid, R. and Duckert, A.R. (eds) (1973) *Lexicography in English* (New York, NY: Academy of Sciences).

McDavid, V. (1979) Dictionary labels for usage levels and dialects', in Congleton, J.E. *et al.* (eds) (1979), pp. 21–36.

MacFarquhar, P.D. and Richards, J.C. (1983) On dictionaries and definitions', *RELC Journal*, vol. 14, no. 1, pp. 111–24.

McHale, B. (1978) Free indirect discourse: A survey of recent accounts', *Poetics and the Theory of Literature*, vol. 1, no. 3, pp. 235–87.

McIntosh, A. (1966), Patterns and ranges', in McIntosh, A. and Halliday, M.A.K., *Patterns of Language: Papers in General, Descriptive and Applied Linguistics* (London: Longman), pp. 182–99.

McKay, S.L. (1980a) Developing vocabulary materials with a computer corpus', *RELC Journal*, vol. 11, no. 2, pp. 77–87.

McKay, S.L. (1980b), Teaching the syntactic, semantic and pragmatic dimensions of verbs', *TESOL Quarterly*, vol. 14, no. 1, pp. 17–26.

Mackey, W.F. and Savard, J.-G. (1967) The indices of coverage', *International Review of Applied Linguistics*, vol. 5, nos 2–3, pp. 71–121.

Mackin, R. (1978) On collocations: "Words shall be known by the company they keep"', in Strevens, P. (ed.) (1978), pp. 149–65.

Makkai, A. (1972) *Idiom Structure in English* (The Hague: Mouton).

Makkai, A. (1978) Idiomaticity as a language universal', in Greenberg, J.H. *et al.* (eds) (1978), pp. 401–48.

Makkai, A. (1980) Theoretical and practical aspects of an associative lexicon for twentieth century English', in Zgusta, L. (ed.) (1980), pp. 125–46.

Martin, J.R. (1992) *English Text: System and Structure* (Amsterdam: John Benjamins).

Martin, J.R. and Rotherey, J. (1981) Writing project reports: 1980 and 1981', *Working Papers in Linguistics*, vols 1–2 (Sydney: University of Sydney Press).

Martin, M. (1984) Advanced vocabulary teaching: The problem of synonyms', *The Modern Language Journal*, vol. 68, no. 2, pp. 130–7.

Meara, P. (1980) Vocabulary acquisition: A neglected aspect of language learning', *Language Teaching and Linguistics: Abstracts*, vol. 15, no. 4, pp. 221–46.

Meara, P. (1982) Word associations in a foreign language: A report on the Birkbeck Vocabulary Project', *Nottingham Linguistic Circular*, vol. 11, no. 2, pp. 29–37.

Meara, P. (1983) *Vocabulary in a Second Language*, Specialised Bibliography, 3 (London: CILT).

Meara, P. (1984a) Review of Wallace, M., *Teaching Vocabulary' System*, vol. 12, no. 2, pp. 185–6.

Meara, P. (1984b) The study of lexis in interlanguage', in Davies, A., *et al.* (eds) (1984), pp. 225–35.

Meara, P. (1992) *Vocabulary in a Second Language*. Vol. 3. Reading in a foreign language. 9.

Meara, P. (1996) The dimensions of lexical competence', in Brown, G., Malmkjaer, K. and Williams, J. (eds) *Performance and Competence in Second Language Acquisition* (Cambridge: Cambridge University Press), pp. 35–53.

Meara, P. (1997) Towards a new approach to modelling vocabulary acquisition', in Schmitt, N. and McCarthy, M. (eds) 1997, pp. 109–21.

Mel'čuk, I. (1981) Meaning-text models: A recent trend in Soviet linguistics', *Annual Review of Anthropology*, vol. 10, pp. 27–62.

Michea, R. (1953) Mots frequents et mots disponibles', *Les Langues Modernes*, vol. 47, pp. 338–44.

Miller, G. (1971) Empirical methods in the study of semantics', in Steinberg D. and Jakobovits (eds) (1971), pp. 569–85.

Milroy, J. (1977) *The Language of Gerard Manley Hopkins* (London: Deutsch).

Milroy, L. (1980) *Language and Social Networks* (Oxford: Blackwell).

Mitchell, T.F. (1971) Linguistic "goings-on": Collocations and other lexical matters on the syntagmatic record', *Archivum Linguisticum*, vol. 2, (N.S.) pp. 35–69.

Montgomery, M. (1986) *An Introduction to Language and Society* (London: Methuen).

Moon, R. (1984) Monosemous words and the dictionary', manuscript, English Language Research, University of Birmingham.

Moon, R. (1997) Vocabulary connections: Multi-word items in English', in Schmitt, N. and McCarthy, M. (eds) (1997), pp. 40–63.

Moon, R. (1998) *Fixed Expressions and Idioms in English: A corpus-based approach* (Oxford: Oxford University Press).

Moore, T.E. (ed.) (1973) *Cognitive Development and the Acquisition of Language* (New York, NY: Academic Press).

Morgan, J.L. and Seliner, M.B. (1980) Discourse and linguistic theory', in Spiro, R.J. *et al.* (eds) (1980), pp. 165–200.

Morrow, K. (1980) *Skills for Reading* (Oxford: Oxford University Press).

Mountford, A. (1976) The notion of simplification and its relevance to materials preparation for English for science and technology', in Richards, J.C. (ed.) (1976), pp. 143–62.

Muecke, D. C. (1973) The communication of verbal irony', *Journal of Literary Semantics*, vol. 2, pp. 35–42.

Munby, J. (1978) *Communicative Syllabus Design* (Cambridge: Cambridge University Press).

Nash-Webber, B. and Schank, R. (eds) (1975) *Theoretical Issues in Natural Language Processing* (Cambridge, MA: Bolt, Baranck & Newman).

Nation, I.S.P. (1980) Strategies for receptive vocabulary learning', *Guidelines: RELC Supplement*, vol. 3, pp. 171–5.

Nation, I.S.P. (1982) Beginning to learn foreign language vocabulary: A review of the research', *RELC Journal*, vol. 13, no. 1, pp. 14–36.

Nation, I.S.P. (1983) *Teaching and Learning Vocabulary* (English Language Institute: University of Wellington).

Nation, I.S.P. (1990) *Teaching and Learning Vocabulary* (Boston, MA: Heinle and Heinle).

Nation, I.S.P. and Waring, R. (1997) Vocabulary size, text coverage and word lists', in Schmitt, N. and McCarthy, M. (eds) (1997), pp. 6–19.

Nattinger, J. (1980) A lexical phrase-grammar for ESL', *TESOL Quarterly*, vol. 14, no. 3, pp. 337–44.

Nattinger, J. (1988) Current trends in vocabulary teaching', in Carter, R. and McCarthy, M. (1988), pp. 62–82.

Nattinger, J. and DeCarrico, J. (1992) *Lexical Phrases and Language Teaching* (Oxford: Oxford University Press).

Nelson, K. (1974) Concept, word and sentence', *Psychological Review*, vol. 8, no. 4, pp. 267–85.

Nida, E. A. (1975) Analysis of meaning and dictionary making', in *Exploring Semantic Structure* (Munich: Wilhelm Fink), pp. 117–35

Norris, C. (1982) *Deconstruction: Theory and Practice* (London: Methuen).

Nunan, D. (1994) *Introducing Discourse Analysis* (Harmondsworth: Penguin).

Ochs, E. (1979) Planned and unplanned discourse', in Givon, T. (ed.) (1979), pp. 51–80.

Ogden, C.K. (1930) *Basic English: A General Introduction* (London: Kegan Paul, Trench & Trubner).

Ogden, C.K. (1968) *Basic English: International Second Language*, revised edn (New York, NY: Harcourt Brace).

Oller, J. (1979) *Language Tests at School* (London: Longman).

Ortony, A. (ed.) (1979) *Metaphor and Thought* (Cambridge: Cambridge University Press).

Ortony, A. (ed.) (1993) *Metaphor and Thought*, 2nd edn (Cambridge: Cambridge University Press).

Osgood, C.E. (1962) Studies on the generality of affective meaning systems', *American Psychologist*, vol. 17, pp. 10–28.

Osgood, C.E. (1976) *Focus on Meaning*, Vol. 2, *Explorations in Semantic Space* (The Hague: Mouton).

Osgood, C.E., Suci, G.J. and Tannenbaum, R.H. (1957) *The Measurement of Meaning* (Urbana, IL: University of Illinois Press).

Owen, C. (1993) Corpus-based grammar and the Heineken effect: Lexico-grammatical description for language learners', *Applied Linguistics*, vol. 14, no. 2, pp. 167–87.

Owen, C. (1996) Do concordances require to be consulted?', *English Language Teaching Journal*, vol. 50, no. 3, pp. 219–24.

Owen, M. (1981) Conversational units and the use of *well*', in Werth, P. (ed.) *Conversation and Discourse* (London: Croom Helm), pp. 99–116.

Owen, M. (1985) The conversational functions of *anyway*', *Nottingham Linguistic Circular*, vol. 14, pp. 72–90.

Pascal, R. (1977) *The Dual Voice: Free Indirect Speech and its Functioning in the Nineteenth Century European Novel* (Manchester: University of Manchester Press).

Pawley, A. and Syder, F.H. (1983) Two puzzles for linguistic theory: Nativelike selection and nativelike fluency', in Richards, J.C. and Schmidt, R.W. (eds) (1983), pp. 191–227.

Pearce, R. (1977) *Literary Texts: The Application of Linguistic Theory to Literary Discourse*, Discourse Analysis Monographs, 3, English Language Research (Birmingham: University of Birmingham).

Perera, K. (1982) The language demands of school learning', in Carter, R.A. (ed.) (1982b), pp. 114–36.

Perren, G. and Trim, J.L. (1971) (eds) *Applications of Linguistics: Papers From the 2nd AILA Congress* (Cambridge: Cambridge University Press).

Persson, G. (1994) *Repetition in English: Part 1, Sequential Repetition* (Uppsala: Acta Universitatis Upsaliensi).

Petöfi, Janos (1985) Lexicon', in Van Dijk, T.A. (ed.) (1985b), pp. 87–102.

Phillips, M. (1985) *Lexical Structure of Text*, Discourse Analysis Monographs, 12, English Language Research (Birmingham: University of Birmingham).

Pickering, M. (1982) Context free and context dependent vocabulary learning', *System*, vol. 10, no. 1, pp. 79–83.

Porter, E. and Williams, D. (1983) Review of *The Words You Need'*, *Reading in a Foreign Language*, vol. 1, no. 1, pp. 68–71.

Pound, E. (1927) How to read', repr. in Eliot, T.S. (ed.) (1954), pp. 15–40.

Powell, M.J. (1992) Semantic/pragmatic regularities in informal lexis: British speakers in spontaneous conversational settings', *Text*, vol. 12, no. 1, pp. 19–58.

Praninkas, J. (1972) *American University Word List* (London: Longman).

Pratt, M.L. (1977) *Towards A Speech Act Theory of Literary Discourse* (Bloomington, IN: Indiana University Press).

Procter, P. (ed.) (1978) *Longman Dictionary of Contemporary English* (London: Longman).

Quirk, R. (1973) The social impact of dictionaries', *UK Annals of the New York Academy of Sciences*, vol. 211, pp. 76–88.

Quirk, R. (1977) Setting new word records', *Visible Language*, vol. 9, no. 1, pp. 63–74.

Quirk, R. (1982) International communication and the concept of nuclear English', in *Style and Communication in the English Language* (London: Arnold), pp. 37–53.

Quirk, R. and Greenbaum, S. (1970) *Elicitation Experiments in English: Linguistic Studies in Use and Attitude* (London: Longman).

Quirk, R., Greenbaum, S., Leech, G.N. and Svartvik, J. (1972) *A Grammar of Contemporary English* (London: Longman).

Read, J.A.S. (ed.) (1981) *Directions in Language Testing* (Singapore: Singapore University Press).

Read, J. (1997) Vocabulary and testing', in Schmitt, N. and McCarthy, M.J. (eds) (1997), pp. 303–20.

Redman, S. and Ellis, R. (1989) *A Way With Words* (Cambridge: Cambridge University Press).

Renouf, A. (1983) Corpus development at Birmingham University', manuscript, English Language Research, University of Birmingham.

Renouf, A. (1987) Corpus development', in Sinclair, J.M. (ed.) (1987a).

Richards, I.A. (1943) *Basic English and Its Uses* (London: Kegan Paul).

Richards, J.C. (1970) A psycholinguistic measure of vocabulary selection', *IRAL*, vol. 8, no. 2, pp. 87–102.

Richards, J.C. (1974) Word lists: Problems and prospects', *RELC Journal*, vol. 5, no. 2, pp. 69–84.

Richards, J.C. (1976) The role of vocabulary teaching', *TESOL Quarterly*, vol. 10, no. 1, pp. 77–89.

Richards, J.C. (ed.) (1976) *Teaching English for Science and Technology* (Singapore: Singapore University Press).

Richards, J.C. and Schmidt, R. (eds) (1983) *Language and Communication* (London: Longman).

Riffaterre, M. (1959) Criteria for stylistic analysis', *Word*, vol. 15, pp. 154–74.

Riffaterre, M. (1960) Stylistic context', *Word*, vol. 16, pp. 207–18.

Riffaterre, M. (1973) Interpretation and descriptive poetry: A reading of Wordworth's "Yew Trees"', *New Literary History*, vol. 6, no. 2, pp. 229–56.

Rixon, S. (1984) Italian readers' use of sequencing clues to solve a discourse puzzle: The importance of lexis', *Papers on Work in Progress, 12.*

Rosch, E. (1973) On the internal structure of perceptual and semantic categories', in Moore, T.E. (ed.) (1973), pp. 111–44.

Rossner, R. (1985) The learner as lexicographer: Using dictionaries in second language learning', in Ilson, R. (ed.) (1985b), pp. 95–102.

Rudska, B., Channell, J., Ostyn, P. and Putseys, T. (1982) *The Words You Need* (London: Macmillan).

Rudska, B., Channell, J., Ostyn, P. and Putseys, T. (1985) *More Words You Need* (London: Macmillan).

Ruhl, C. (1979) Alleged idioms with HIT', in Wölck, W. and Garvin, P.L. (eds) (1979), pp. 93–107.

Rundell, M. (1995) The BNC: A spoken corpus', *Modern English Teacher*, vol. 4, no. 2, pp. 13–15.

Saragi, T., Nation, I.S.P. and Meister, G.F. (1978) Vocabulary learning and reading', *System*, vol. 6, no. 2, pp. 72–8

Saussure, F. de (1974) *Course in General Linguistics* (London: Fontana).

Savard, J. and Laforge, L. (eds) (1981) *Actes du 5e Congress de l'AILA* (Quebec: Les Presses de l'Université de Laval).

Schiff, H. (ed.) (1977) *Contemporary Approaches to English Studies* (London: Heinemann).

Schiffrin, D. (1988) *Discourse Markers* (Cambridge: Cambridge University Press).

Schmidt, R. (1990) The role of consciousness in second language learning', *Applied Linguistics*, vol. 11, no. 2, pp. 129–58.

Schmitt, N. and McCarthy, M.J. (eds) (1997) *Vocabulary: Description, Acquisition and Pedagogy* (Cambridge: Cambridge University Press).

Scholfield, P. (1982) Using the English dictionary for comprehension', *TESOL Quarterly*, vol. 16, pp. 185–94.

Scholfield, P. (1997) Vocabulary reference works in foreign language learning', in Schmitt, N. and McCarthy, M. (eds) (1997), pp. 279–302.

Schonell, F. *et al.* (eds) (1956) *A Study of the Oral Vocabulary of Adults* (Brisbane and London: University of Queensland Press/University of London Press).

Schreuder, R. and Weltens, B. (eds) (1993) *The Bilingual Lexicon* (Amsterdam: John Benjamin).

Schuman, J.H. (1974) The implication of interlanguage, pidginization and creolization for the study of adult language acquisition', *TESOL Quarterly*, vol. 8, pp. 145–52.

Schwartz, R. (1983) Action in early lexical acquisition', *First Language*, vol. 4, no. 1, pp. 5–20.

Searle, J. (1979) Metaphor', in Ortony, A. (ed.) (1979), pp. 92–103.

Sebeok, T. (ed.) (1966) *Current Trends in Linguistics*, vol. 3 (The Hague: Mouton).

Seibert, L.C. (1930) An experiment on the relative efficiency of studying French vocabulary in associated pair versus studying French vocabulary in context', *Journal of Educational Psychology*, vol. 21, pp. 297–314.

Seibert, L.C. (1945) A study of the practice of guessing word meanings from a context', *Modern Languages Journal*, vol. 29, pp. 296–323

Seidl, J. (1978) *English Idioms and How to Use Them* (Oxford: Oxford University Press).

Simpson, J. (1988) The New Vocabulary of English', in Stanley, E.G. and Hood, T.F. (eds) *Words* (Cambridge: D.S. Brewer), pp. 143–52.

Sinclair, J.M. (1966) Beginning the study of lexis', in Bazell, C. *et al.* (eds) (1966), pp. 410–30.

Sinclair, J.M. (1981) Grammar in dictionaries', manuscript, English Language Research, COBUILD Project, University of Birmingham.

Sinclair, J.M. (1985) Lexicographic evidence', in Ilson, R. (ed.) (1985b), pp. 81–94.

Sinclair, J.M. (ed.) (1987a) *Looking Up: An Account of the COBUILD project in lexical computing* (London: Collins).

Sinclair, J.M. (1987b) Collocation: a progress report', in Steele, R. and Thread-gold, T. (eds) *Language Topics: Essays in Honour of Michael Halliday* (Amsterdam: John Benjamin), pp. 319–32.

Sinclair, J.M. (1991) *Corpus, Concordance, Collocation* (Oxford: Oxford University Press).

Sinclair, J.M. (1996) Units of Meaning', *Textus*, vol. 9, pp. 75-106.

Sinclair, J.M. and Coulthard, R.M. (1975) *Towards an Analysis of Discourse: The English Used by Teachers and Pupils* (Oxford: Oxford University Press).

Sinclair, J. M. and Renouf, A. (1988) A lexical syllabus for language learning', in Carter, R. and McCarthy, M. (1988), pp. 140–60.

Sinclair, J.M., Daley, R. and Jones, S. (1970) *English Lexical Studies*, Report no. 5060 (London: OSTI).

Sinclair, J.M. and Jones, S. (1974) English lexical collocations', *Cahiers de Lexicologie*, vol. 24, pp. 15–61.

Slobin, D. (1971) *Psycholinguistics* (Glenview, IL: Scott Foresman).

Sökman, A.J. (1997) Current trends in teaching second language vocabulary', in Schmitt, N. and McCarthy, M. (eds) (1977), pp. 237–57.

Sperber, D. and Wilson, D. (1981) Irony and the use-mention distinction', in Cole, P. (ed.), *Radical Pragmatics* (London: Academic Press), pp. 295–318.

Spiro, R.J., Bertram, B.C. and Brewer, W.F. (eds) (1980) *Theoretical Issues in Reading Comprehension* (Hillsdale, NY: Lawrence Erlbaum Associates).

Stainton, C. (1997) *Metadiscourse: The rhetorical plane of text*, Nottingham Working Papers, 2, Department of English Studies, University of Nottingham.

Stanovich, K.E. and Cunningham, A.E. (1992) Studying the consequences of literacy within a literate society: The cognitive correlates of print exposure', *Memory and Cognition*, vol. 20, pp. 51–68.

Steen, G. (1994) *Understanding Metaphor in Literature* (Harlow: Longman).

Stein, G. (1979) Nuclear English: Reflections on the structure of its vocabulary', *Poetica*, vol. 10, pp. 27–52.

Steinberg, D. and Jakobovitz, L. (eds) (1971) *Semantics: An Inter-disciplinary Reader* (Cambridge: Cambridge University Press).

Stenström, A.-B. (1990) Lexical items peculiar to spoken discourse', in Svartvik, J. (ed.) (1990) *The London–Lund Corpus of Spoken English* (Lund: Lund University Press), pp. 137–75.

Sternberg, R.J. (1987) Most vocabulary is learned from context', in McKeown, M.G. and Curtis, M.E. (eds) (1987) *The Nature of Vocabulary Acquisition* (Hillsdale, NJ: Lawrence Erlbaum), pp. 89–105.

Stieglitz, E. (1983) A practical approach to vocabulary reinforcement', *English Language Teaching Journal*, vol. 37, no. 1, pp. 71–6

Stock, P. (1984) Polysemy', in Hartmann, R.R.K. (ed) (1984), pp. 131–40.

Strevens, P. (ed.) (1978) *In Memory of A.S. Hornby* (Oxford: Oxford University Press).

Stubbs, M. (1980) *Language and Literacy* (London: Routledge & Kegan Paul).

Stubbs, M. (1982) Stir until the plot thickens', in Carter, R.A. and Burton, D. (eds) (1982), pp. 56–85.

Stubbs, M. (1983) *Discourse Analysis* (Oxford: Blackwell).

Stubbs, M. (1986a) Language development, lexical competence and nuclear vocabulary', in *Educational Linguistics* (Oxford: Blackwell) pp. 98–115.

Stubbs, M. (1986b) "A matter of prolonged fieldwork": Notes towards a modal grammar of English', *Applied Linguistics*, vol. 7, no. 1, pp. 1–25.

Stubbs, M. (1996) *Text and Corpus Analysis* (Oxford: Blackwell).

Svartvik, J. (1980) *Well* in conversation', in Greenbaum, S. *et al.* (eds), pp. 167–77.

Swales, J. (1983) Vocabulary work in LSP – a case of neglect?', *Bulletin CILA*, vol. 37, pp. 21–33.

Swales, J. (1990) *Genre Analysis* (Cambridge: Cambridge University Press).

Sweetser, E. (1990) *From Etymology to Pragmatics: Metaphorical and Cultural Aspects of Semantic Structure* (Cambridge: Cambridge University Press).

Tanaka, R. (1973) The concept of irony: Theory and practice', *Journal of Literary Semantics*, vol. 2, pp. 43–56.

Tannen, D. (1989) *Talking Voices* (Cambridge: Cambridge University Press).

Thorndike, E.L. and Lorge, I. (1944) *The Teacher's Word Book of 30,000 Words* (Columbia, SC: Columbia University Press).

Tickoo, M. (ed.) *Learners' Dictionaries: State of the Art*, RELC Anthology Series, vol. 23, (Singapore: RELC).

Tomasello, M. and Todd, J. (1983) Joint attention and lexical acquisition style', *First Language*, vol. 4, no. 3, pp. 197–212.

Tomaszczyk, J. (1981) Issues and development in bilingual pedagogical lexicography', *Applied Linguistics*, vol. 11, no. 3, pp. 287–96.

Toolan, M. (1984) Stanley Fish and the interpretive community of responding readers', *Dutch Quarterly Review*, vol. 14, no. 1, pp. 61–73.

Traugott, E. and Pratt, M.L. (1980) *Linguistics for Students of Literature* (New York, NY: Harcourt Brace).

Trudgill, P. (1974) *Sociolinguistics* (Harmondsworth: Penguin).

Trudgill, P. (ed.) (1978) *Sociolinguistic Patterns in British English* (London: Edward Arnold).

Twaddell, F. (1973) Vocabulary expansion in the TESOL classroom', *TESOL Quarterly*, vol. 7, no. 1 pp. 61–78.

Underhill, A. (1980) *Use Your Dictionary* (London: Oxford University Press).

Ure, J. (1971) Lexical density and variety differentiation', in Perren, G. and Trim, J. (eds) (1971), pp. 443–52.

Van Dijk, T.A. (1985a) Semantic discourse analysis', in Van Dijk, T.A. (ed.) (1985b), pp. 103–36.

Van Dijk, T.A. (ed.) (1985b) *Handbook of Discourse Analysis*, vol. 2, (London: Academic Press).

Van Peer, W. (1986) *Stylistics and Psychology: The Theory of Foregrounding Investigated* (London: Croom Helm).

Waldron, R.A. (1967) *Sense and Sense Development* (London: Deutsch).

Wallace, M. (1982) *Teaching Vocabulary* (London: Heinemann).

Waterson, W. and Snow, C. (eds) (1978) *The Development of Communication* (Chichester: Wiley).

Weinreich, U. (1966) Explorations in semantic theory', in Sebeok, T. (ed.) (1966), pp. 395–477.

Weinreich, U. (1980) Problems in the analysis of idioms', in Weinreich, U., *On Semantics*, eds Labov, W. and Weinreich, B.S. (Philadelphia, PA: University of Pennsylvania Press), pp. 208–64.

Wellman, G. (1992) *The Heinemann English Word Builder* (London: Heinemann).

Wells, R.A. (1973) *Dictionaries and the Authoritarian Tradition* (The Hague: Mouton).

Werth, P. (1977) The linguistics of double vision', *Journal of Literary Semantics*, vol. 6, no. 1, pp. 3–28.

West, M. (1935a) *Definition Vocabulary*, Department of Educational Research Bulletin, no. 4 (Toronto: University of Toronto).

West, M. (1935b) *Net Method Dictionary* (London: Longman).

West, M. (1953) *A General Service List of English Words* (London: Longman).

West, M. (1960) *Minimum Adequate Vocabulary* (London: Longman).

Weston, A. (1996) Picking holes: cloze procedures in prose' in Carter, R. and McCrae, J. (eds) *Language, Literature and the Learner: Creative Classroom Practice* (Harlow: Longman).

Widdowson, H.G. (1972) On the deviance of literary discourse', *Style*, vol. 6, no. 3, pp. 294–306.

Widdowson, H.G. (1975) *Stylistics and the Teaching of Literature* (London: Longman).

Widdowson, H.G. (1978) *Teaching Language as Communication* (Oxford: Oxford University Press).

Widdowson, H.G. (1981) Models and fictions', *Applied Linguistics*, vol. 2, no. 2, pp. 165–70.

Widdowson, H.G. (1983) *Learning Purpose and Language Use* (Oxford: Oxford University Press).

Widdowson, H.G. (1985) *Explorations in Applied Linguistics*, vol. 2 (Oxford: Oxford University Press).

Wierzbicka, A. (1984) Cups and mugs: Lexicography and conceptual analysis', *Australian Journal of Linguistics*, 4, pp. 205–55.

Wilkins, D.A. (1976) *Notional Syllabuses* (Oxford: Oxford University Press).

Willis, D. (1990) *The Lexical Approach: A new approach to language teaching* (London: HarperCollins).

Willis, D. and Willis, J. (1987–88) *The COBUILD English Course* (Glasgow: Collins).

Wilson, D. and Sperber, D. (1992) On verbal irony', *Lingua* 87 (1/2), pp. 53–76.

Winner, E. (1988) *The Point of Words: Children's Understanding of Metaphor and Irony* (Cambridge, MA: University of Harvard Press).

Winter, E. (1977) A clause-relational approach to English texts: A study of some predictive lexical items in written discourse', *Instructional Science*, vol. 6, pp. 1–92.

Winter, E. (1982) *Towards a Contextual Grammar of English* (London: Allen & Unwin).

Wittgenstein, L. (1953) *Philosophical Investigations*, translation G.E.M. Anscombe (London: Blackwell).

Wölck, W. and Garvin, P.L. (eds) (1979) *The Fifth LACUS Forum (1978)* (Columbia, SC: Hornbeam Press).

Yorio, C. (1980) Conventionalized language forms and the development of communicative competence', *TESOL Quarterly*, vol. 14, no. 4, pp. 433–42.

Zgusta, L. (ed.) (1971) *Manual of Lexicography* (The Hague: Mouton).

Zgusta, L. (ed.) (1980) *Theory and Method in Lexicography* (Columbia, SC: Hornbeam Press).

Zumthor, P. (1971) Style and expressive register in medieval poetry', in Chatman, S. (ed.) (1971), 263–81.

Bibliography of dictionaries

CCED (1995) *Collins COBUILD English Dictionary* (Glasgow and London: HarperCollins).

CCELD (1987) *Collins COBUILD English Language Dictionary* (Glasgow: Collins).

CED (1986) *Collins English Dictionary*, 2nd edn; 1st edn 1979 (Glasgow: Collins).

CED (1991) *Collins English Dictionary*, 3rd edn; updated 1994 (Glasgow and London: HarperCollins).

CIDE (1995) *Cambridge International Dictionary of English* (Cambridge: Cambridge University Press).

COD (1996) *Concise Oxford Dictionary*, 9th edn (Oxford: Oxford University Press).

Collins COBUILD Dictionary of Idioms (1995) (Glasgow and London: HarperCollins).

Collins COBUILD English Words in Use (1997) (Glasgow and London: HarperCollins).

Johnson, S. (ed.) (1755) *A Dictionary of the English Language* (London: W. Strachan).

LDOCE (1995) *Longman Dictionary of Contemporary English*, 3rd edn; 1st edn 1978, 2nd edn 1987 (London: Longman).

Longman Dictionary of American English, 2nd edn (1997) (London: Longman).

Longman Dictionary of English Language and Culture (1992) (London: Longman).

Longman Language Activator (1994) (London: Longman).

OALD (1995) *Oxford Advanced Learner's Dictionary*, 5th edn; 1st edn 1948, 3rd edn 1974 (Oxford: Oxford University Press).

ODCIE (1975) *Oxford Dictionary of Current Idiomatic English: Vol. 1* (eds A.P. Cowie and R. Mackin) (Oxford: Oxford University Press).

ODCIE (1983) *Oxford Dictionary of Current Idiomatic English: Vol. 2* (eds A.P. Cowie, R. Mackin, I.R. McCaig) (Oxford: Oxford University Press).

Oxford English Dictionary: A New Dictionary on Historical Principles (1928, 1933) (ed. J. Murray) (Oxford: Clarendon Press).

Oxford English Dictionary, 2nd edn (1986) (Oxford University Press).
Webster's Third New International Dictionary (1961) (ed. P. Gove) (Springfield, MA: Merriam). Now in its 10th edition.

Bibliography of language corpora

BCOET (1987) *Birmingham Collection of English Text*, now part of the Bank of English (Birmingham: University of Birmingham). 20 million words; written and spoken language.

BNC (1995) *British National Corpus* (available from The British Library and Longman, London; developed by Oxford University Press, Longman, Chambers Harrap, Lancaster University, The British Library, Oxford University Computing Service). 90 million words of written and 10 million words of spoken language.

Brown Corpus (1961) (developed at Brown University, Providence, RI). 1 million words of American English; written language.

CIC (1996) *Cambridge International Corpus*, formerly the *Cambridge Language Survey* (Cambridge: Cambridge University Press). 100 million words of mainly written language. Spoken part of *CIC*: *Cambridge and Nottingham Corpus of Discourse in English (CANCODE)* comprising 5 million words of spoken language.

COBUILD/Bank of English (1997) (developed by Collins, Glasgow and University of Birmingham, Birmingham). 320-million-word written and spoken corpus.

Corpus used for the *General Service List of English Words*. Word counts from written sources in 1930s; 2–5 million words.

London–Lund Corpus (1987). 500,000 words of spoken British English.

London, Oslo, Bergen (LOB) Corpus (1961/81). 1 million words of written British English; a parallel corpus to the Brown Corpus.

Longman–Lancaster Corpus (LLC) (1996). 30 million words of written and spoken British and American English.

Oxford American-English Corpus (OAEC). 40 million words.

Index

Adams, V. 13
affective stylistics 129–30
affix (prefix-suffix) 11–12, 31,
Aisenstadt, E. 70
Aitchison, J. 192
Alderson, C. 242
Alderson, C. and Alvarez, C. 229
Alexander, R.J. 66, 67, 161, 224
Amante, E.J. 262
anaphoric nouns 88–91
Anglin, T. 33, 47, 189–91
anti-language 110
antonymy 12, 19–21, 33, 38, 96–7,
   166, 182, 190, 222, 276–7
Apresyan, Y.D. 60, 78, 161
arbitrariness 146–7
Asch, S.E. and Nerlove, H. 190
associates (paired) 193, 212, 214
associations 22, 28–9, 31, 42–3, 49, 86,
   127–8, 135, 161,181, 183, 190,
   193–9, 219, 239, 263ff.; clang
   199–201; mnemonic 195–6, 212
Atkinson, R.C. and Raugh, M.R.
   193
attitudinal words 92, 94, 111, 185,
   273
Atwood, M. 145
Auden, W.H. 123, 127, 130, 251,
   252–4, 257–62
Austen, J. 250, 255
Ayto, J. 263, 264, 265

Bank of English (BE) 46, 167, 179,
   233
Barnhart, C. 283
Basic English 23–9, 31, 35, 206

Bauer, L. 13, 153
Baxter, J. 151
Bazell, C.E. 30
Becker, J.D. 66
Béjoint, H. 154, 177, 273, 280
Belsey, C. 147
Bennett, T. 147
Benson, M. 60, 78, 135, 161
Berlin, B. and Kay, P. 22, 35
Berry, H.M. 51
Bhaba, H. 147
Biber, D. and Finegan, E. 88
Biggs, C. 33
Birkbeck Vocabulary Project 197–202
Birmingham Collection of English
   Text (BCOET) 167, 170
Blair, Tony 109
Bloomfield, L. 5
Blum, S. and Levenston, E.A. 47
Bogaards, P. 177, 179, 182
Bolinger, D. 12, 32, 66, 109, 223–4,
   233, 264
Bongers, H. 234
Bowerman, M. 186, 188
Bridges, R. 120
British National Corpus (BNC) 175,
   177, 179
Bronzwaer, T. 123, 124
Brown, D. 219, 242
Brown, G. 93, 235
Brown, G. and Yule, G. 43, 79
Brown, J. 213, 219
Brown, T.S. and Perry, F.L. 204
Brumfit, C.J. xiv, 266
Bruton, A. 213
Bublitz, W. 98

Burgess, A. 110
Butler, C. 131, 139, 140, 141

Cain, J. M. 135
Cambridge and Nottingham Corpus
   of Discourse in English
   (CANCODE) 100
Cambridge International Corpus
   (CIC) 98–103, 176
*Cambridge International Dictionary of
   English* (*CIDE*) 174, 176–7
Cambridge Language Survey (CLS)
   176, 179
Cameron, D. 177
Campbell, R. and Wales, R. 198
Carroll, J.B. 46, 234
Carter, R. 37, 42, 88, 91, 104, 107,
   120, 123, 127, 128, 130, 131,
   149, 221, 251, 262, 270, 278; and
   Bool, H. 281; and Long, M.N.
   109, 123, 128, 147; and McCarthy,
   M. 103, 185, 219, 235; and
   Nash, W. 114, 132; and Nation, P.
   219
Cassells, J.R.T. 108
Cassidy, F.G. 280
Catford, J.C. 31, 163–4
Chan, R.K. 272, 275
Channell, J. 93, 192, 214
Chapin, P. 18
Chaucer, G. 139
Chilton, P. 131
Ching, M.K.L. 149
Clark, E. 47, 184, 186–8, 191
Clarke, D.F. and Nation, I.S.P. 209,
   242
clause-relations 75, 83, 155–6
Clear, J. 171, 174
cliché 54, 67–8, 254, 280
cline 14–15, 43, 68–9, 71–2, 76, 127,
   159, 160, 163, 267, 274–5; formality
   253, 268–71, 275–7
cloze 211–12, 226–9, 231, 242;
   discourse 221, 229–31
cluster 52, 233
Cluysenaar, A. 123
Coady, J. and Huckin, T. 203
COBUILD (Collins Birmingham
   University International Language
   Database) 46, 63–4, 81, 114, 144,

164, 167–71, 174, 182, 183, 224–5,
   233, 235, 243
COBUILD English Course, The 225
Cohen, A. and Aphek, E. 196, 212
Cohen, J. 141
coherence (and lexis) 75–6, 103–7,
   108
cohesion: lexical 75–6, 80–3, 103–7,
   113–14, 221
colligation 59–61, 62, 73, 164–5, 168
*Collins COBUILD Dictionary of
   Idioms* 171
Collins COBUILD English Dictionary
   (*CCED*) 168–71,177
*Collins COBUILD English Language
   Dictionary* (*CCELD*) 168–71, 172
Collins COBUILD Words in Use 171
Collins English Dictionary (*CED*) 40,
   154
collocation (collocability) 38–9, 51ff.,
   81–2, 87, 128, 148,159, 160–1,
   163–5, 168, 182, 215, 220–1, 253,
   273, 280; significant 124–6
competence: literary 129–31, 252–3
complementarity 17–19, 20, 134–5
componential analysis 17–19, 81, 103,
   143, 265
Computational Analysis of Present-
   Day American English 231–2
computer corpora 46, 62–4, 98–103,
   167–77, 224–5, 231–5
computing (and lexis) 45–6, 53, 98,
   103, 168, 174
Concise Oxford Dictionary (*COD*)
   11, 152
connotation 22, 161, 264–6
context 101, 137, 164, 195, 209–13,
   266
converseness 20
Cook, G. 79
core vocabulary 34–47, 68–9, 84–91,
   97, 98–103, 108–9, 236–9, 275–9
Cornu, A.M. 214
Corson, D. 108
Coulmas, F. 66
Cowie, A.P. 77, 154, 156, 157, 158,
   161, 163, 165, 166, 182, 201
Cowie, A.P. and Mackin, R. 77
Craik, F.I.M. and Lockhart, R.S.
   47, 195, 203

Craik, F.I.M. and Tulving, E. 241
Crismore, A. 85
Crombie, W. 84, 221, 242–3
Crothers, E. and Suppes, P. 193
Crow, J.T. and Quigley, J.R. 204
Crowe, J. 125–6
Cruse, D.A. 40, 48, 95, 163, 165
Crystal, D. xiv, 33, 92–3, 123, 235;
     and Davy, D. 272
culture-free 41–2
Culler, J. 137
Cummins, J. and Simmons, R.
     120,121
Cutler, A. and Fay, D. 192

Daily Mail 112
Daily Telegraph, The 34
Daneš 106
Davie, D. 122
Deese, J. 19, 33
definition(s) 152–4, 166, 175, 177,
     180, 201, 216, 241, 263–7
Delbridge, A. 267
denotation 33, 264–6
derivations 10–11, 43, 131–2, 157–8,
     201, 214
Deyes, A. 229–31
dictionaries 29–30, 150–67, 174–81,
     183, 266–7, 274, 275–82, 283
Dictionary of the English Language
     164
Dillon, G.L. 106
discourse, lexis in 79–91, 220–1;
     markers 93, 221
discourse, field of 43, 53ff.; mode of
     44–6; tenor of 44, 139
Dixon, R.M.W. 37, 45, 47–8
Doroszewski, W. 266
Dressler, W. 80

Eagleton, T. 131, 137, 147
Eaton, T. 130
Eliot, T.S. 123
Elliot, A. 47, 186, 189
Ellis, R. 186, 203, 204, 224
Empson, W. 283
Engels, L. 101
evaluation 42, 85–8, 109–10; scale
     267–8, 275–9
explanation 38, 108

explicit–implicit continuum 202–4
extension 39–40

Fairclough, N. 114
Fay, D. and Cutler, A. 192
Fernando, C. 159; and Flavell, R. 66
figuration 142–5
Firth, J.R. 38, 62
Fish, S. 129, 137
fixed expressions 65–70, 76,
     88, 158–62, 171, 220–4, 240
Fletcher, P. and Garman, M. 186
Foley, J. 242
formality (and lexis) 42–4, 127–8,
     195–6, 197, 214–15, 275–9
Fowler, R. 92–3, 109, 110
Fox, J. and Mahood, J. 166, 243
Francis, G. 63, 64, 89–90; with
     Hunston, G. and Manning, E. 63
frequency (word) 45–6, 89, 90, 91,
     98–103, 154, 157, 168, 176, 183–6,
     190, 192, 224–5, 232–5, 237–8,
     242
Fromkin, V. 192
functional core concept 187

Gairns, R. and Redman, S. 185, 218,
     219
Gardner, H. 189, 190
General Service List of English
     Words, A (GSL) 152, 206–9, 238,
     241
genre (and lexis) 91–4, 104, 107–8,
     235, 253
Ghadessy, M. 237
Gibbs, R.S. 142–5
Giles, S. 147
Gimson, A.C. 152
Gleason, H. 184
Goatly, A. 141, 145
Goodale, M. 182
Goodenough, W.H. 264
Goodman, K.S. 228, 231
Gove, P. 151
Gray, T. 122–3
Greenbaum, S. 59
Grice, P. 248–52, 256
Grieve, R. and Hoogenraad, R. 189
Guiraud, P. 129
Gutwinski, W. 80

Hale, K. 48
Halliday, M.A.K. 51, 58, 62, 77, 93, 110, 124, 148, 189; and Hasan, R. 81, 82, 88–9, 107
Hanks, P. 153, 166, 274
Harmer, J. and Rossner, R. 220
Harpin, W. 106
Harris, J. and Wilkinson, J. 106
Hartmann, R.R.K. 183, 266, 274, 280
Harvey, P.D. 214
Hasan, R. 21, 51, 105, 106, 107, 148, 231
Hatch, E. and Brown, C. 219
Herbst, T. 177
Herrnstein-Smith, B. 137
Hindmarsh, R. 274
Hoey, M. 84, 85
Hofland, K. and Johannson, S. 183, 234
Holub, R. 129, 131
Honeyfield, J. 209, 211
Hopkins, G.M. 123
Hornby, A.S. 152, 156
Housman, A.E. 282
Howatt, A.R.P. 28, 163, 206
Huckin, T., Haynes M. and Coady J. 204
Hudson, R. 33, 41
Hulstijn, J. 203
Hunston, S. 64, 222; and Thompson 88
Hutchinson, T. and Waters, A. 48
hyponymy: hyperonym 21, 40, 74, 81, 96–7, 222

ideology 108–14, 117, 131, 122–3, 146–7, 179, 211, 266–7, 280
idiom 5–7, 32, 54–5, 64–5, 65–8, 69, 76–7, 134–6, 145, 161, 171
Ilson, R. 32, 150, 163, 166, 196
Implementing the Lexical Approach 226
incompatibility 20–1
inflections 10–11, 24, 45, 100–1, 201
informants 33, 35–6, 119, 128ff., 189, 212–13, 247ff., 270–5; tests 127, 131, 190, 253–62
irony 248–56

Jain, M.P. 74, 153, 280

Jeffries, L. and Willis, P. 165–6, 182, 243
Johnson, R.K. 242
Johnson, S. 150, 164
Jordens, P. and Kellerman, E. 48
Judd, E.L. 185

Kachru, B. 266
Kaplan, R. xiv
Kates, C.A. 149, 186
Katz, J.J. and Fodor, J.A. 18, 264
Keen, J. 182
Keller, E. and Warner, S.T. 66
Kellerman, E. 48
Kellogg, G.S. and Howe, M.J.A. 193
keyword technique 193–5, 234
Kinnock, N. 111–13
Kintgen, E.R. 131
Krashen, S.O. 186, 203
Kress, G. and Hodge, R. 109
Kruse, A.F. 211, 241–2
Kuchera, H. and Francis, W.N. 231–2, 235
Kuhns, R. 130

Labov, W. 271
Lakoff, G. 264; and Johnson, M. 138, 142, 219, 280
Lakoff G. and Turner, M. 142
Lancaster, Oslo, Berlin (LOB) 242
Lam A. 106
Laufer B. 219
Lazar, G. 220
Leech, G.N. 18, 79, 122, 139, 175, 262, 264; and Short, M.H. 120
Lehrer, A. 21, 47, 55, 214, 270
lemmatization 46, 183, 234
Lewis, M. 225, 226, 227
Levenston, E.A. 122, 198
Levinson, S. 79, 139
Lexical Approach, The 225
lexicalization 80, 86, 108–14; over-110–11; re- 110
lexeme 7–9, 32
lexical: chunks 162, 225–6; density 91–4, 136–7; errors 72–6, 161, 185, 200; item 7–8, 14, 35, 38, 46, 53, 61, 83, 88, 93, 94–5, 106, 132–4, 148, 168, 183, 186, 190–1, 213, 214, 220–4, 233–4, 240, 273, 280, 283;

patterns 50ff., 88, 94, 106, 120–2, 124–8, 130–1, 134, 136, 155, 168, 220–4; set 37–8, 47, 52ff., 95–6, 113–14, 120–2, 124, 265; specificity 95–6, 110
lexical marking (marked/unmarked) 35, 43–4, 84–7, 95, 97–9, 105–6, 111; rendering 106–7
Lexical Phrases and Language Teaching 226
lexicality 13–14, 70–1
lexicography 150ff., 165
lexicons 87, 111, 132, 159ff., 166, 183, 188–9, 192, 196–7, 200, 235, 243
lexis (as a level) 50–3, 58–9, 247–8
Lipski, J.M. 123
literariness 132–8, 141, 142–5, 242
Lock, A. and Fisher, E. 186
Lodge, D. 139
logopoeia 123–4, 126–7, 254–5
London-Lund Corpus 45, 242
Long, M.N. and Nation, I.S.P. 166, 206, 210, 243
Longman Dictionary of American English 175
Longman Dictionary of Contemporary English (*LDOCE*) 36, 151–3, 155, 171, 173, 174, 175–6, 177, 206, 266
Longman Dictionary of English Language and Culture 281
Longman Lancaster Corpus 175, 179
Longman Language Activator 179–81, 281
Longman Lexicon of Contemporary English 243
Longman Structural Readers 206
Lord, R. 185
Louw, W. 63
Low, G. 220
Lucas, J.R. 89
Lyne, A.A. 233
Lyons, J. 3, 10, 20, 21, 35, 185

McArthur, T. 185, 243
McCarthy, M. 48–9, 59, 85–7, 90, 97, 102, 173, 175, 219, 220–3, 237, 242, 283; and Carter, R. 79, 92, 100, 242; and O'Dell, F. 220
McDavid, V. 280

MacFarquhar, P.D. and Richards, J.C. 153
McHale, B. 255
McIntosh, A. 56, 57–8
McKay, S.L. 75, 233
Mackey, W.F. and Savard, J-G. 46
Mackin, R. 59, 161
Makkai, A. 32, 162, 174, 180, 183, 283
Manning 63
Martin, J.R. 81
Martin, M. 73–4, 75, 201, 232
Meara, P. 47, 186, 192, 197–9, 200–2, 213
Melčuk, I. 3
memorization 25, 193–7, 219, 223–4, 237, 239
meronymy 21–2
metadiscourse 85, 89
metaphor 84–5, 124, 132, 138–41, 143–5, 147–8, 190, 219, 225
Michea, R. 235
Miller, G. 270
Milroy, J. 123, 272
Minimum Adequate Vocabulary 208
Mitchell, T.F. 56, 59
monosemy 134–5, 137, 163–7
Montgomery, M. 111
Moon, R. 163, 164
More Words You Need 214, 219
Morgan, J. and Seliner, M. 105, 106
morpheme 9–10, 32
Morrow, K. 173, 219
motivation 86–7, 143, 201
Mountford, A. 48
Muecke, D.C. 262
Munby, J. 185
Murray, J.A.H. 151, 164

Nation, I.S.P. 25, 32, 46, 193, 194, 196, 197, 209, 210–12, 213, 217, 219, 223, 236, 242; and Waring, R. 236
Nattinger, J. 66, 69, 162, 201, 203, 219, 223, 225; and DeCarrico, J. 66, 159, 223, 225, 226
Nelson, K. 186–8
New Method Dictionary 206–8
New Method Readers 206, 241
neutral words 95

Nida, E.A. 163
node 82, 164
Norris, C. 147

Ochs, E. 93, 184, 235
Ogden, G.K. 23–5, 28, 31, 35, 206
Oller, J. 228
open-choice principle 64–5
Ortony, A. 141
Osgood, C.E. 42, 267–8
Owen, C. 64
Owen, M. 93
*Oxford Advanced Learner's
    Dictionary* (*OALD*) 151–3, 155–7,
    174, 176–7, 178, 183, 266
Oxford American-English Corpus
    177, 179
*Oxford Dictionary of Current
    Idiomatic English* (*ODCIE*) 77, 160,
    161
Oxford English Dictionary (*OED*)
    15–17, 64, 151, 164, 274, 276
overextension 187–8
ownerless nouns 114

Palmer, H. 206
paradigmatic 190, 191, 198–9
participant roles 165–6, 182
particles 83
Pascal, R. 255
Pawley, A. and Syder, F.H. 66,
    224
Pearce, R. 122, 124, 130
Perera, K. 108, 237
Persson, G. 98
Pefőfi, J. 115
Phillips, M. 233
Pickering, M. 212
poetics 142–5
polysemy 7, 12–14, 30–1, 116, 135–6,
    142–3, 161, 163–7, 176–7, 182, 195,
    237
Porter, E. and Williams, D. 214,
    216–17
Pound, E. 123, 126, 254–5
Powell, M.J. 98
Praninkas, J. 237
Pratt, M.L. 250
Proctor, P. 152–3
proverbs 67–8

Quirk, R. 23, 35, 44, 151, 154,
    266; and Greenbaum, S. 270

range 56–8, 162, 171, 234, 264
Ranson, J.C. 125–6
Read, J. 236
Redman, S. and Ellis, R. 217, 219
reference, referent 15–17, 147
register 135, 262; register-mixing
    122–4, 136, 254
Reinhart 149
Renouf, A. 168, 225, 235, 242
reporting 108, 111–13
re-registration 135–6
Richards, I.A. 23–8, 31
Richards, J.C. 46, 72, 185, 201, 207,
    233, 235, 237, 240
Riffaterre, M. 130, 146, 149
Rixon, S. 221
root 10–11, 31
Rosch, E. 46
Rossner, R. 12
Rudska, B. 214–16, 220
Ruhl, C. 161, 164
Rundell, M. 100

salience 36–8, 44–6, 47–8
Saragi, T. 241
Saussure, F. de 146–7, 183, 283
Schiff, H. 137
Schiffrin, D. 93, 114
Schmidt, R. 203
Schmitt, N. and McCarthy, M. 204,
    219
Schonell, F. 101
Schreuder, R. and Weltens, B. 192
Schwartz, R. 189
Searle, J. 141
Seibert, L.C. 212
Seidl, J. 159
selection restriction 56–7, 74, 159–60,
    175
semantic feature hypothesis 186–7
semantic prosodies 62–5
semantic space 191, 214, 267–70,
    278–9
Shakespeare, W. 79
signalling (lexical) 42, 83–5, 86,
    88–91, 130, 221–2
Simpson, J. 236

Sinclair, J.M. 51, 53, 62–3, 64, 77, 81, 82, 155, 167, 168, 185, 225, 233, 270; and Coulthard, M. 93; and Jones, S. 49, 51, 270; and Renouf, A. 224, 225
Skills for Reading 219
Slobin, D. 19
Sökman, A.J. 220
span 49
Spark, M. 255
speech-act theory 249–50
Sperber, D. and Wilson, D. 256, 262
Stainton, C. 85
Stanovich, K.E. and Cunningham, A. E. 204
Steen, G. 141
Stein, G. 23, 29, 33, 35, 183
Stenström, A.-B. 99
Sternberg, R.J. 203
Stieglitz, E. 214
Stock, P. 164, 165
structural semantics 19–23, 139
Stubbs, M. 28, 39, 41, 44, 45, 48, 79, 81, 93, 94, 97, 114, 282
summary 42, 44, 48
superordinateness 20, 40–1, 74, 81, 135–6, 175, 182
Svartvik, J. 91, 93
Swales, J. 221, 237
Swansea Vocabulary Project 202
Sweetser, E. 144
synonymy 19–20, 33, 57, 73, 80–1, 96–7, 114–15, 124, 135, 161, 182, 222, 277
syntagmatic 58–61, 190, 191, 198–9

Tanaka, R. 262
Tannen, D. 98
Thomas, D. 120–1
Thorndike, E.L. and Lorge, I. 206
tokens (relevant, central and peripheral) 105–6, 107
Tomasello, M. and Todd, J. 189
Tomaszczyk, J. 161
Toolan, M. 131
transferability 48
Traugott, E. and Pratt, M.L. 120

Trudgill, P. 271
Twaddell, F. 185

Udall, J. 31
underextension 187, 241
Underhill, A. 182
Ure, J. 92

vague language 93–4
Van Dijk, T.A. 115
Van Peer, W. 112, 128, 130, 131
vocabulary: control movement 206–9; core see core vocabulary; teaching 46–7, 64, 205–43, 239–40; Vocabulary 1, 2 and 3 83–8; learning 184–205

Waldron, R.A. 266, 275, 283
Wallace, M. 198, 213
Webster's Third New International Dictionary 151
Weinreich, U. 32, 77, 159, 182, 247
Wellman, G. 220
Wells, R.A. 283
Werth, P. 262
West, M. 35, 152, 153, 206–8, 238, 241
Weston, A. 231
Wilson, D. and Sperber, D. 256
Widdowson, H. G. xiv, 46, 231, 262
Wierzbicka, A. 19
Wilkins, D.A. 185
Willis, D. 225, 226; and Willis, J. 225
Winner, E. 141, 189, 252
Winter, E. 83, 84–6
Wittgenstein, L. 149
word definition 4–7; formation 10–12, 195–7; general 13–15, 102–3; grammatical 8–9; lexical 7–8; orthographic 4–6; stress 6
Words You Need, The 214–16, 219, 220

Yeats, W.B. 145
Yorio, C. 66, 77, 162, 201

Zgusta, L. 270
Zumthor, P. 123